The Mandrakes

By Zachariah Jack

Copyright © 2017 by Zachariah Jack

License Notes This book is licensed for your personal enjoyment only. This book may not be re-sold or otherwise reproduced. If you would like to share this book with another person, please purchase an additional copy for each recipient. If you're reading this book and did not purchase it, or it was not purchased for your use only, then please return to your favorite book retailer and purchase your own copy. Thank you for respecting the hard work of this author.

This book is available in print at most online and other retailers.

Forward
The Mandrakes

Four men of alternative lifestyle. Introduced first in 'A High Country Tale', the four volume set marks down the early days of development of each of these unusual and exemplary human beings, relating how each eventually arrives in one another's lives.

Synopsis
The Teardrop, Volume 1

Lucas Laughlin Cevennes. Odd boy out. Had he been born a sheep, he would have been the black one. If he had been born into money, at the age of majority, he would have become the exiled trust fund baby. As it was, Luke fought proverbial currents, took roads less traveled, stuck to his guns, set high standards and learned from mistakes. He was a survivor. Oh, and he knew he was gay. From the ripe age of four, though no comprehension existed for the concept then. Born into the sinful state of Man, as constantly reminded by the evangelism enveloping him, a young boy learns of the difficulties involved in growing up different. He pictured himself as 'bent'. Through tribulative trial and error--- emphasis on error--- Luke finds that standing tall, in confidence of his own abilities, can be gaged differently by different people. It was all in the perspective. And bent looked pretty attractive to him...

One Clear Day, Volume 2

Rome, Georgia. USA. The center of the universe for Calumet Alfrederic Broadhearst. Not to be confused with the Eternal city or the steppes of western Asia, the home place nestled into a bend of the meandering Coosa River. The stately manse provided haven, safety, benevolence, family... grounding. All in the poignant setting of a former cotton plantation supported by slave labor. Innately aware of natural talents and fortes, to which he gravitates, Cal presses forward in unassuming, self-deprecating fashion. The favor of the gods and exemplary role models along with the blessing of excellent genes prove to be an exceedingly suitable combination for carving a mark in the world. As well as grasping the most from life. He comes to grips with obstacles, problems and aberrations in a more adult manner than most adults. Clear knowledge that his future holds one other in reserve with whom to share the path he travels provides emotional sustenance in good times and bad. The most difficult aspect is harnessing the slippery trait named patience through the frustratingly long wait for their appearance.

Call of the Loon, Volume 3

Prodigy. The last word young Jacob Winslow Marshall would conjure were he to apply description of himself. Prescience. Now, that was a concept which he understood, though he couldn't have picked the alien word out of a perp lineup. Until he could. Elkin Pond epitomized the beauty that was southern Vermont but in Jake's case the body of water provided separation between divergent worlds the boy inhabited. Finding succor in the warmth of an elderly couple's sphere on one side enabled ultimate divestiture from the ignorance, negativism and narrow-mindedness rampant at the boy's birthplace on the opposite edge of the pond. Though integrally important to him, the reasons for the tie to the hand-hewn home had dissolved the day his real Daddy left. From earliest years of Jake's life, he recognized a destiny of dramatic import in the dimness of a Texas horizon yet to be explored. The state remained as nameless as the intrinsic attribute --- prescience--- by which he drew the certainty. Until he learned it. He knew it to be where he must make way in order to fulfill purposes. Emphasis on the plural. There was a promise to be kept… and… Someone awaited.

Fallsworth, Volume 4

If only goats had evolved differently, developing the specific vocal folds and larynx, think what a story they might tell. Jeremy Fallsworth Kell. One of the Blue Mountain Kell clan--- Hagley Gap to be specific. The big family spat out children like a cut-rate combine. On the downhill slope of thirteen babies in fifteen years, Jeremy hardly raised a ripple upon his arrival. Though parents loved their children, so many in the brood left precious little time for individual experience. So, when the iconic Koromantyn up the mountain provided chance outlet for the young man, goat husbandry became an apprenticeship. The man himself rose to the role of parent, mentor, groomer, trainer and... well, family. Maybe not by blood, but by every other measure. And then some. Banishment to the capitol city after a calamitous sundering split the trip of goats from the young herder. Luckily, Kingston goats apparently communicated by the greater Jamaica goat pipeline. The boy saw them everywhere as he adapted to city life. The beasts watched. Becoming a father at barely eighteen changed the entire equation. Challenging the goatherd-cum-student to scale more than mountains in the metamorphosis to principled philosopher as foretold by the stars. Yes, the Jamaica goats in Ambergai Gee's herd most certainly had stories to tell. If perchance they were to grant audience to such a forum, the storytelling would be undoubtedly raveled in Lyaric: lilting dialect of the Rastafari. To a calypso beat. Claro que si...

Table of Contents

Forward—The Mandrakes..3
Synopsis—The Teardrop, Volume 1..5
One Clear Day, Volume 2..6
Call of the Loon, Volume 3...7
Fallsworth, Volume 4..8
The Mandrakes Volume I, The Teardrop..11
    Late Spring, 1995..13
    Summer, 1979..18
    Summer, 1988..23
    October, 1991..38
    April, 1992...43
    May, 1992...50
    January, 1993...59
    March, 1994...66
    October, 1995..69
    June, 1996..88
Volume II: One Clear Day...95
    1992..97
    July, 1997...114
    April, 2000...140
    March, 2004...168
    January, 2006...176
Volume III: Call of the Loon...185
    June, 1991..187
    May, 1994...195
    July, 1998...217
    November, 1998..230
    May, 1999...244
    December, 2002...246
    April, 2004...253
    January, 2006...265
Volume IV: Fallsworth..275
    January, 1991...277
    April, 1982...280
    July, 1982...284
    May, 1984...294
    July, 1989...301

April, 1990...318
July, 1990..328
April, 1991...334
October, 1992..341
April, 1993...344
June, 1996...362
Afterward—A High Country Tale.....................................371
Biography..373

The Mandrakes
Volume I, The Teardrop

Late Spring, 1995

The raindrop smack-dabbed me in the left eye. Splat. I winced involuntarily, blinking to diffuse the intruding loner, speculating from where the wetness had come. A cerulean sky was cloudless and the meadow around us treeless.

Upon clearing to focus again, I trained my sight back on the opposite horizon meeting the far edge of the grassy tree-edged athletic complex. To the spot I had been previously studying before the drop's trespass. Only myself and the pointer, Magda, were on the series of far flung soccer and rugby fields this late spring dawn, or so I had thought. A figure across the way dispelled that notion.

In curiosity, I gaged compact features of the distant person, watching as it stretched, arms up and over, legs spread, feet planted. The swarthy impressionist profile was blurred by three hundred yards of separation yet I could discern the presence as a person of color. It drew me.

Looking back on it, I should have read body language more astutely. And would have been better served to have paid attention to Magda's low, throaty growl as she also appraised the single distant being. But, I didn't. Instead, I admonished the big girl to hush, disliking an other-than-friendly reaction. In the moment, we regarded the man—I could now tell it was indeed a male by body movements—continue with limbering techniques commonly employed in commencing and finishing aerobics.

After brief assessment, we went on with our fetch game, picked up on realization Magda Lena's ropy drool wasn't a result of exertion. She had run across an orphan rubber ball somewhere earlier during our pre-dawn run and latched on to it, per her wont, then patiently awaited my notice. Various modes for invitation to play were common—Magda was a play demon, demanding multiple periods of such interaction daily. And, sometimes nightly.

Absorbing into familiar companionship, we disregarded the man, returning to ourselves. That is, until Magda pulled up short, swinging around in an athletic midair 180 twist, landing lithely on all fours to face a suddenly closer figure now loping our direction. Brief rumble of a growl again arose from her throat but cut short as she remembered my previous remonstrance. The handsome canine glanced back over her shoulder in a questioning look, ball in mouth. Inquiry as to my own feelings on the person's approach was plain by her face. Hair over her withers bristled involuntarily and the reaction set a small ripple of wariness through my own body. I paid attention to the dog, having come to trust her instincts in most situations.

Unfortunately, I was male. Blessed and cursed with two heads.

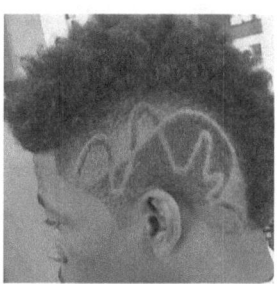

"Wassup?" The darkly complexioned short man intoned the greeting through a toothy grin. Deepness to the voice registered different than what I would have guessed by his frame and movements. Smoothly baritone, it rolled musically around my ears, conveying conviviality and friendliness, even in its brevity. Slowing to a walk, the clearly athletic individual sashayed closer. In a fluid movement, he whisked the light tank top up and over a sculpted curly head, the sides of which were carved in serpentine designs. A longer topnotch imbued the shorty with a bit of added height and the edginess of a newly re-popularized mohawk effect. He set to deliberately wiping down first his head, then his arms, pits and torso in rapscallion sensuosity. I was enthralled. Black men's versatility factor in haircut options had captivated me since high school days. This man's look and body language tugged my eyes like a puppeteer.

As the shirt cleared the artwork topping him, my eyes slid southward taking in the cut form, from nice pectorals down over slightly rounded abdominals covered by finely curled black hair disappearing under low-hanging gray gym shorts. Hugging sexy hips, the workout shorts complemented a starkly white jockstrap underlapping them. I was envious of the strap's proximity to the mounded mystery cradled inside. My tongue inadvertently licked encircling lips as they shaped into an inadvertent 'O' of praise for the hirsute physique now exposed before me.

"Gettin' hot out here already, ain't it?" The sheen of sweat coating him betokened truth to the comment. Still, I detected intent other than a need to cool off by the action. Not that I was complaining. The view was delectable. And the darkly colored player absolutely knew this.

The look on my face must be a total giveaway. Rarely had I ever been mistaken for a poker face, I thought, attempting to rein in growing interest. "Hot is a g-g-good word…y-yup," I stuttered stupidly, compounding the discomfiture pitiful in its evidence at a failed double entendre.

The man was glad for the less-than-confident reaction, I quickly grasped, confirming the fact by lightly cupping his right palm over the mass inside, coverage adeptly framing exactly what the well-built stud intended. Pulsed kneading of the mound set into motion several levels of reactions shared between the two of us, not least of which was perceptible swelling of the lump from which my offending eyeballs could not divorce themselves. Again, as intended. The man was in his element, toying with me.

My own junk lurched into action mode without consent, much to my chagrin. The effect tented the front of my running shorts in mere seconds. It proved the cue for which he was looking. His grin said it all, though my focus only tangentially reported this to a silly brain, vision tunneled toward the man's rising corpus, such as it was.

No more words passed between us just then, lust bespeaking a language of universal inference. The knowing lecher closed the remaining distance, cupping palm now replacing his own bulk with my traitorous organ.

'Wrong-headed' took an alternate meaning as the aroused male turned me by the rapidly engorging thing presently disavowing any cranial hegemony, leading us both back toward the tree cover twenty feet to my rear. What little remaining autonomy I commanded deserted me there.

Waist-high underbrush tickled my bare legs, waist and lower torso during a bridled walk into the shadows beneath spreading oaks. Upon reaching the huge flared trunk of one, I was lightly but firmly pushed back against rough bark. My running shorts descended in congruence with the experienced palmer directing me. Without any more than a soft, repetitive clucking sound, he squatted, bottoming them at my ankles while simultaneously facing into the prodigiously prideful, bouncing boner poking from my crotch. The idiot of a dickhead wrested complete control from my useless brain, and contrastingly, surrendered in total thrall to the crouching man. Two-faced thing. It possessed understanding of what was occurring. My addled brain, not so much.

Wiping a three-day stubble back and forth across my hyper-sensitive mess of a cock, the man's pair of full lips abruptly engulfed it as I dumbly watched. Squeezing against the sponginess encountered, they slid masterfully down over the beggar. An excess of saliva slathered the shaft in slow descent to the cul-de-sac that was my smooth groin. The nose following those fat lips nuzzled and rolled over and around the pubes basing my other head while this unnamed master proceeded to show a talent for which I was unready. And unaccustomed to accommodating. His mouth was supremely talented.

My locked knees buckled. Shudders of pleasurable waves enveloped me. Experienced hands and forearms lightly scraped me up and down in nappy friction. I surrendered to the plethora of stimuli unexpectedly kidnapping my senses.

At a calculated point of ascent toward ecstasy, the lips backed off. Through the haze of hormones, I heard a husky voice whisper, "Damn, boii, this be 'da bomb dick…I be gonna do this again…now hang on, runner boii man." With that, the lips resumed their truest calling. Over a precious few minutes, the tandem of the muscly tongue sharing the deep throat with my throbbing piece combined to methodically pump me to rapturous peak. Warm velvetiness of the toothed cavity remained married to the thickness of the shaft it was working, not separating again.

Upon sensing imminent success in its mission, that throat harvested the crop it had cultivated, climactically glugging down my proving jism in contented fashion. Like a cow chewing its cud. The man's hands roamed my body's zooming paroxysms as I delivered the goods by repetitive thrusts. Synchronous rhythm persisted between us for more minutes as the rolling waves smoothed gradually to a lolling lollop of a spasming piece. He was a kid on an all-day sucker.

Jarringly bamboozled in my perceptions, I felt strangely freed yet shackled. Rolled back eyes gradually righted themselves above my arched neck and I flexed it, gazing down satedly upon the diminutive squatter borrowing my midsection. His squelched grin attempted revival even amidst its glutted state as our eyes met. His expressed more gratification than would have been guessed… I was the recipient here, after all.

The service-oriented man backed slowly off my emptied shaft and smirked. "That be a all-time 'top two' listin' dick, runner boii. Stay tuned," was all he said through smeared lips. Arising, the cocksucker playfully slapped my dribbling sponginess and exited the leafy hideaway.

That was the entirety of my introduction to the Devil Incarnate.

Summer, 1979

Growing up, I had always proven to be an early budding late bloomer. At two and a half years of age, I had mimicked my older siblings' alphabet wherewithal. Without even singing it. I was writing names and words in puerile script by three. Using my left hand, I mirrored the expert penmanship taught to my older sister and brother. Proffering a first masterpiece one day at lunchtime for parental perusal, I awaited the expected adulation for the work, having seen such heaped on elder brethren for similar feats.

"My goodness, Lukie, look at what you've done," cooed my surprised Mama. The others were less blown away—I had stolen somebody else's thunder by the doing, it seemed, and there was a necessary price to be paid. Envy, I found out then, was a deadly sin.

"Mama, he copied from my schoolwork, and traced the letters. He din't write 'em hisself," tattled the ad lib liar, 'Beccah. I had not traced them, I thought. Noting the lack of attention to the earthshattering information, she added, "and he wrote it with the wrong hand."

The immediate change to a look of castigation from dear Mama brought a satisfied smugness to my idolized big sister's face. She sat back and complacently watched the sharp smack on the pale knuckles topping my dominant left hand, bringing stinging insult to a moldable young psyche. The dreaded anti-thumb-sucking glove was dug out within seconds, fastened into place by over-tight rubber bands which dug into my tender flesh. Told to leave the torture device in place until Daddy came home, both of my older and wiser sibs covered snickers of delight at the fall from grace. "He will want to hear all about such evil malfeasance," I was assured. The Devil had gotten into me.

Three hours passed before my Daddy, the hero, arrived. By then I was a trembling mass of sobbing nerves with a frightfully throbbing left hand. It pulsed and stung from lack of circulation. Mama informed me it was the retribution of the Lord for breaking His Word. I was well aware, she reminded me, that using my left hand for anything other than cleaning myself after pottying was expressly forbidden by The Book. Leaving me to wonder what should be done might that need arise in the present fix.

Within half an hour, though, neither were relevant factors. My creamy little buttcheeks had been leather belt whipped by then. Additive effects of multiple sites exuding painful manifestations left whacked knuckles and numbed hand forgotten. I wanted to suck that thumb bad as I cried to sleep in the dark of a supperless evening.

Next morning, the offensive appendage was unwrapped. The purplish extremity took three days to regain feeling and in several ways, that was worse. I didn't attempt writing for months after that.

The church pastor recommended entrance into kindergarten on my fourth birthday which coincided with the opening of the fall term. "Lukie is a prodigy in catechism and outstrips all the six-year-olds in Sunday school. Even some of the seven and eight-year-olds aren't a match for his memory. He knows his letters, all his colors and is able to count to one thousand without help. Enroll him in school." Antioch Christian School sat at the top of the hill overlooking our house. I was registered within the week and waited through the intervening weeks in wonderment of what may be coming.

Arriving the first day as the bell rang, my brother and sister abandoned me to my own devices at the front doors of the school. Sculpted cherubic hosts hovered protectively in perpetual admonition at the upper corners, offering precious little support.

The protective left glove had been securely rubber banded in place as a hedge against untoward behavior. I was hoping against hope that nobody wore leather belts inside those doors, gazing wistfully at the lane descending the hill as I contemplated my predicament.

A few stragglers scurried inside the doors without noticing my lost boy self. From behind came a softly feminine voice. Soothing uncomfortable bewilderment, it purred at me, "Honey, are you lost? What's happened to your hand? Is it hurt, sweetie?" Peering fearfully around, I found the comforting face of a brown-haired angel worriedly studying me. She came forward, leaned down, and scooped me into her warm bosom. I melted into the arms of my savior, Miss Wilson.

Two hours later, after a trip to the school nurse, gentle treatment to my alienated hand, and a visit to the principal's office, I was brought to Room 202 in the kindergarten wing and deposited amongst Miss Wilson and her twenty charges. Just in time for nap hour. A glass of warm milk, a chocolate chip cookie and multiple hugs later, I lay ensconced on a nap rug between two dreaming six-year-olds.

My eyes never left Miss Wilson that first day. Through catechism, visual arts, and right-handed finger-painting, I wasn't about to let the beautiful lady out of my sight. I even followed her when she left for the ladies' room, only to be—gently—rebuffed into remaining with the teacher's assistant until Miss Wilson's promised return.

At recess, another check-up by the nurse kept me inside. The white-haired woman seemed mystified by the gloving incident. Murmured voices from an adjoining room concluded with certainty that I had had a childish prank played on me but thankfully not suffered any ill-effects from the tight wrap.

I overheard further discussion about how to best inform my parents and just knew I would suffer further fall-out after that conversation. Not involving anyone else who might worsen my adversity at home was the reasoning employed for refusal to address their questions in the first place. Home was suddenly not high on my list of desired destinations that afternoon.

The fear apparently showed in my features. Miss Wilson took it upon herself to escort me home, much to my consternation, thinking my brother or sister may have done the mean deed. She knocked on our front door at the bottom of the hill and waited. I listened to the babbling creek down from the house and the lowing of cows on the far side there, wishing to hide amongst them rather than face dear Mama.

Miss Wilson introduced herself almost apologetically as Mama opened the door. Mama's wary look set off pangs of dismay in my frazzled brain, even as Miss Wilson hurried to assure her that I had behaved admirably though my first day, adding that there was a bit of worrisome news to tell her and my Daddy.

A look of incomprehension followed by barely disguised shock and disgust flashed over the young teacher's compassionate features as

Mama straight-forwardly imparted the lesson of 'the glove'. I shrank under the dining room table as the explanation proceeded, not understanding anything that was occurring. Only fathoming that something was not right. That irascible left thumb edged closer and closer to my mouth. I steeled a nascent four-year-old will to halt the sinful progression.

"She's not a true Christian," Mama told Daddy over a tense supper a few hours later. "She was judging me the whole time. I could see it in the woman's eyes. She is not devout." The two Christians that were my parents sat at the dining room table softly counseling one another over the imbroglio suddenly confronting them. I peeked from around the darkened doorway, attempting to decipher incomprehensibly complex issues integrally tied to me, missing another denied supper. The bad son. And, getting badder, I deduced.

"When I described the disciplinary method we use to teach the children" she went on, "the young lady had the nerve to inform me that it was not an acceptable form of intervention. She acted in an ungodly self-righteous way, saying that rubber bands could cause irreversible damage to Lukie. I told her that our Faith and Belief in our Lord would see to the proper methods and that we knew our pure road to stifling sin arising in youngsters, thank you very much. She pretty much huffed her way out the door and hinted we would be hearing from Pastor Stevens and the principal. Do you think she can do such a thing, dear?"

My Daddy answered in his monotone voice. The one auguring quiet, smoldering anger—we kids always knew to listen closer when his voice dropped—and the loss of volume not only kept me from hearing what he said, it chased ripples of goose pimples over me.

Sure enough in the next days, not only the pastor and principal Wilkins, but also the school nurse showed up at the front door in evening hours to pow-wow with my doting parents. To instill some parenting advice for them to 'think on'. It was not taken well and my name-in-mud was bandied about surreptitiously, much more to my dismay.

Thankfully, Old Testament cautions concerning left-handedness and its association with Beel-Zebub were put into perspective by New Testament teachings through the pastor. Medical necessity to stop stricturing techniques for teaching disciplinary methodology was stressed. I sustained no further primitive torture.

Unthankfully and notwithstanding, the haranguing on all sides from Daddy and Mama to siblings elevated to mental torture. I was tainted.

Miss Wilson's classroom became my port-in-the-storm. A place where left-handedness was not only accepted, it was a point of honor which Miss Wilson made certain to champion before my classmates. I was exonerated in the schoolroom sphere. My schoolwork subsequently excelled. Purposely pursuing finger-painting with the right hand, for ostensibly religious purposes, I became class scribe using the left, inwardly basking in the changed tone. Actions of politic necessity birth themselves early on in the evangelist community... I was proving a quick study.

The year of kindergarten neared its close with talk of the legendary school carnival ushering in summer break. Having been informed of the excitement and frivolity to be experienced on that final day, wariness of leaving my bastion of Antioch-embodied sanctuary was blunted by mental visions of fun promised for then.

During nights before the extravaganza, I can remember even now the strange exhibitions taking shape in my mind, gamboling through dreamscapes. Four-year-old mental machinations imagined all sorts of mirthful goings-on, one leading to the next, from night to night. All carried a common theme which, even then, I somehow knew to keep to myself.

Varying scenarios of the carnival enlivened nightly prophecies, strolling amongst lines of gaily decorated booths boasting games, prizes and goodies in the hallways and byways of a spectral Antioch. Laughter and fun pervaded all. Hours and hours of great merriment grew my infantile anticipation as grab bags, fishing booths, balloon popping, coin tossing, acrobatic feats by teachers, colorful costumes and delicious smells all came together to whet a kindergarten appetite for frivolity.

The concept instinctively relegated to the realm of sequestration, even in my age of innocence, was one perplexingly recurrent motif. It provided inexplicable titillation for a childish brain. With sole exception of the sainted Miss Wilson, no one but males of our species attended the fair in those dreams. Schoolmates, teachers, brothers, daddies, uncles, cousins, strangers. All were gender specific. What could that mean, I pondered? And was left to muddle through that conundrum for years to come.

Summer, 1988

"Here, Lukie, let me show you how to check," Sexy Rexy instructed, mentor that he was. The rhyming moniker meant little to the twelve-year-old virgin inhabiting my adolescent-cusping body. I had been warned earlier to keep watch for lake slugs---leeches--- common to Lake Cutaway. But the admonition had meant little to my greenhorn self. This esteemed older cousin meant to teach.

So, I watched, initially intrigued, as the carrot-topped worldly cousin of exceeding teenage beauty—all the girl cousins agreed--- brazenly pulled my swim trunks down from the perch just above my hips, baring the paleness of the smooth pubic surface underneath.

A newly tanned, sunburnt demarcation between exposure and coverage registered in my head while a pubescent peter sproinged attentively, and uncalled on, from its nest there. A dark gray slimy blob above and to the side of the suddenly awakened organ shared multi-level focus in an unforeseen flood of sheer terror. What was happening? The mind shrieked on seeing these split planes of obscene effects abruptly bared without forewarning above my shucked shorts.

Angst only compounded by powers of ten upon seeing and feeling Sexy Rexy's fingers grasp the sucking parasite around its edges, then unceremoniously yank the thing from virgin white abdominal skin there. A sharp 'schhlop-pop' gave audible character to my silent scream. I wilted away from the grossness and the invading hand in mortification.

Pete, my private pet, only recently discovered for his duality of functions, bounced repeatedly off Rex's wrist and palm in withdrawal, dribbling something gooey across his fingers. Unaware whether the leech, the goo, the contact, or the combination of occurrences engendered it, my cousin evoked a throaty 'Yukkk' as he hurled the bi-ended sucking annelid into the lake and reached down to wipe the offending stuff on a mossy carpet edging the water. All in one motion.

Standing erect, he gazed again at the double lesions of the worm's attachment sites, unable to miss the rigid and embarrassingly arched worm-named-Pete. My secret trouser cohort seemed to search for the vacated hand just divesting from it, bobbing in hovering arcs like a cobra on the prowl.

"Damn, Lukie, where'd you get all THAT?" The vehemence in his sixteen-year-old voice quavered from base to treble and then back, proclaiming his still volatile manliness. It left me fearful that I had irreversibly insulted the golden boy of my maternal family branch while simultaneously wacking out at the awareness that the sanctity of my crotch had been unknowingly invaded by a slimy lake demon. Not certain how to address any of the turn of events now unfolding, I simply stood paralyzed, ogling the guiltscape I had somehow managed to cause.

Over ensuing seconds, we both sized-up the situation, gradually regaining quasi-abilities for cogency and sensate cognition. My cousin's eyes receded into their sockets and the whites of my own diminished in their owlish proportions as we both watched in mesmerized states while my proxy, Pete, continued his waggling propensity. He was 'sniffing' rare air for the first time in close eyeshot of another than myself.

The wiped fingers twitched in knowledge that they had been brushed and oiled by verboten action. But I noticed they also inched closer. "Those buggers are real tricky, now, Lukie," warbled Sexy Rexy, attempting composure, yet failing audibly. He reached out, tentatively, pinpointing the duo of tiny punctures, "See those? Uncle Sparky told me they have poison up inside of 'em. He said you should suck the crud out so's not to get sick. Or die."

He made eye contact at the moment the forefinger lightly poked the left puncture. His eyes flickered as Pete grossly overestimated himself, jumping upward and doing a measure of poking of his own. Mortification rebounded. This time, however, the hand didn't act like it had been singed. The light poking persisted. By both finger and Pete. "You should do that, Lukie."

"Do what?" I squeaked, very close to adolescent apoplexy by way too much sensory overload.

"Suck the poison out," he repeated. The multi-pointed contact persisted and while the finger lightly palpated the tummy wounds, the cobra waggled brazenly up and down the exposed wrist and forearm. Still no retraction. But gobs more goo.

"How do I reach it?" came my overly logical reply, now beginning to sense an overpowering wave of a poison-induced rush toward certain death.

"Well, Hell, cousin mine, I'm just sayin'," both of our minds jumping to the next option at the same time. Eyes back locked, finger and Pete completing the circle, we stood studying the problem, my will weakening by the second with the numbness of the toxic brew invading my life force. I began trembling and quivering in the quandary of impossibility that confronted me.

The next option couldn't be actuated any more than the first one could, I quickly deduced.

My cousin's gallant action ousted that point. Descending to a squat, placing a hand on either side of my waist, Sexy Rexy proceeded to shyly pucker two teenage lips, closing over the offending skin punctures at once. Lightly at first, then with more vehemence, they began sucking that dastardly poison right back out from where it had been injected. My light-headed rush toward death improved appreciably within seconds.

Pete, still waggling autonomously, rasped up and over and back, from the side of my cousin's neck, over the protruding ear and into the fine silkiness of the reddish-auburn topnotch crowning him. Interested as heck and without any idea of what to say. But apparently familiar with Braille.

Turning his head to the side, Rex spat a copious load of blood-tinged expectorate onto the moss below, rotated back, abutted Pete again, and continued sucking, harder, at the sites. Four or five repetitions of this action proved too much for Pete. The abomination suddenly spewed its own copious mixture of pearlescent poison, repeatedly jetting over and down my cousin's bare shoulder and back, leaving a viscous string of toxic sludge tight-roping from there over to his adjacent ear and silken locks.

Slowly glancing upward at my face, I observed a smirk of resignation perfuse his tanned features as one final insulting dribble strung itself from hair to eyebrow. Turning to spit a final time, my newly sworn enemy—how could the truth of the matter be anything else---abruptly arose. Expecting revulsion or fisted onslaught, I felt my body wince.

Much to my surprise, neither materialized. We both watched as the toxic smear tangoed downward over his cheek, muscled neck and pectoral. Then, wordlessly, he strode into the lakeside eddies. At waist depth, Prince Valiant dove forward into the chill clearness, lissome form submerging in cleansing immersion.

I forced myself to action, countering rather than thinking. Losing the ankled trunks and following his dive. Coldness shriveled the atrociousness of Pete's engorgement in the doing. The two of us emerged opposite one another twenty feet out, treading the greenness, in apprize of the harrowing scenario just obviated.

Expectations of condemning hatefulness never developed. Sexy Rexy stared into my eyes and smiled with a twinkle as he expounded on a crisis just solved by quick thinking. "Welp, Lukie... that's how ya' do the deed. Now, I don't be supposin' that all the details needs bein' talked on, so's how 'bout we two agree that I tell the tale back at camp...'K?"

Relief abounded. Prince Valiant, indeed.

Evening descended over the pristine lake occupying acreage to the far northern border of Minnesota, near Lake of the Woods. Two dozen members of my dear Mama's side of the family sat strewn around a growing bonfire, variably on the ground, flat rocks, or logs gathered in semicircle. A final sliver of sun flared out on the far horizon across Lake Cutaway. Dusk fell.

The men—serious fisherman--- all compared notes on the day's catch. Among three different boats and the banksiders, it seemed that the richest take of coveted Northern Pike had been hooked and strung by little Claire, my cousin by Mama's second sister. The aunts were not letting them overlook the fact.

Claire had been delivered breach nine years before this very night, umbilical cord strangulating her tiny legs at the knees. The result was a withering of neonatal calves and feet. Necessitating crutches and braces, the wisp of a girl had shown strong will by learning to swim over the ensuing developmental years. She was an eel in the water. Her safe haven. The camp at Cutaway Lake had been procured with Claire distinctly in mind; the rest of the cousins had become adepts in the domain, too. All manner of water sports busied the clan in available warm months. Winter sports were excelled at, as well.

Dear Mama and my hero Daddy had separated themselves from this unorthodox family branch early on. First moving out-of-state, allegedly for job opportunities, then widening the breach by evangelizing themselves, my brother and sister, and by extension, myself. These blood kin were virtual strangers in my eyes until the past two weeks.

Mama had suffered a debilitating fall in the springtime of the current year. Fracturing multiple vertebrae, she had been faced with hospitalization, long-term therapy, and seclusion. God was speaking mysteriously, it was rationalized. Daddy's family was caring for my two older siblings. 'Bekkah plus Elijah, the good children, had been placed in the care of Daddy's Daddy's coven. Religion subsumed them all. All the time.

My aunt, Ella, had been helping Mama through recent months, having temporarily moved into the household. Since her marriage was a childless one and her husband away for long periods, she wanted to help her sister. Observing the difficulties unintentionally brought down on myself during that time--- I was constantly in hot water through infractions of the strict living code by merit of being the 'curious' child---she noticed, then acted.

Through subtly persistent lobbying, agreement was reached allowing my accompaniment of the Laughlin branch to the family lake retreat for these summer months. Promises of adherence to strict rules for religious indoctrination were initialed in blood. Luckily for me, Aunt Ella's memory proved sorely lacking on that score. All brainwashing techniques were conveniently forgotten on the road out of town.

Since kindergarten, I hadn't been challenged regularly, bouncing from year to year between devotees of fundamentalism and more progressive teachers pursuing true educational curricula. The mercurial nature of my school experience made me wary and cautious. New people and new teachers were intensely evaluated for their proclivities, weighing signs of erudition versus indoctrination. I learned to roll with the changes required, but only at the stunting of creativity and scholarship. Too much effort had to be expended attempting to cover a natural thirst for knowledge. And regurgitate verses. Thus, my future held a narrowness of opportunity.

Arriving with Aunt Ella during the summer eve kick off at Camp Cutaway, my life transformed. Popcorn and Pepsi amid a boisterous game of Liverpool Rummy in the airy lodge wowed my senses. The simplicity was consuming. Non-judgmental camaraderie with blood relatives heretofore unknown won me over immediately. Innately recognizing the missing links for finding myself, I merged with aunts and uncles and cousins, reveling in the freedoms proffered.

In the manner of kindergarten at Antioch, the lake setting provided an epiphany for a stifled young brain and body. Along with an adeptness for water sports, enlightenment to widely ranging intellectual disciplines was encountered. The lodge's well-stocked library unsealed a smothered mind amidst benevolence of encouraging kinfolk. Its atmosphere afforded wide latitude for learning. Anything desired. Much came clear in that summer. Delving every subject that intersected inquisitive eyes, I was overwhelmed. Heaven was discovered there on earth. In the far northern reaches of Lake Country.

The blooming of the arrested early bud began then and there.

This sunset, with the conversation centering on a coming fish fry, compliments of cousin Claire and the supporting catch by the uncles, Aunt Ella queried me on inauguration to leech-bait status achieved earlier in the day. "How's the wounded veteran, Luke?" She was the only one reading my distaste for the condescending 'Lukie', another reason for my burgeoning loyalty and love of the woman.

"It's a little sore, but it's good, Aunt Ella," I assured her. She had nursed my stomach wounds upon Rex and my return from the far side cove, proclaiming it innocuous. Thankfully, Pete had behaved. To my immense relief. Rexy confided the story in the stark terms of a sixteen-year-old: search, yank, wash. No mention of the life-threatening travail expertly avoided by his swift, heroic actions. I was fine with that, not liking attention to an awkward subject, but did wonder silently about the lack of kudos my handsome cousin required. His stock with me increased in value by the act. We smiled at each other knowingly across the fire. No one seemed to notice. Perfect.

"Well, it is a rite of passage here in the North Woods," Uncle Sparky's gravelly voice broke in, "everyone has to experience the insult sooner or later. Best to know about how to mess with the buggers. It's good the things aren't deadly, or we'd all be toast, wouldn't we?" He chortled at the comment, with everyone else, missing the look of surprise flitting across my confused face by the revealing fact. Things that make you go, 'Hmmmmm'.

Stockard, fourteen-year-old cousin, piped up, redirecting my acute perplexity as we all prepped and roasted my first s'mores. "Who's gonna be up for a sunrise slalom tomorrow?" The change of subject brought a collective groan. All but a few around the fire wallowed in the sleep-in luxury summer vacation afforded. Apart from uncles, Claire, myself and Stockard, a sunrise skiing jaunt with a pre-dawn wake-up call enticed few.

Pre-dawn was my personally preferred time due to the chance for solitude; an apprehended respite from immediate family back home. By stirring at that part of the day, the world was my oyster. And would remain so for a lifetime, meditative as I was. So, yes, a ski jaunt sounded great, loving the newly discovered favorite sport.

The artful sport of slalom skiing had captivated me on the first attempt. By flawed teenage sophistry, the cousins--- all older by at least two years--- had thought to inaugurate-by-fire on that first Cutaway morning. Informing me dawn was the best time for such a sport, their initial miscalculation induced a distaste for dawn like their own. Second was failure to inform of any alternative besides the single ski method, which defined advanced water slalom. All guffawed behind my back in planning the most difficult introduction possible to keep my pre-teen self humble. As if that were an issue…

…The first night calmly pondered surrender to daybreak as Aunt Ella sleepily rolled over to peer out an open screened window. Registering the throb of the inboard-outboard motor thrumming to life focused her downward into the darkness that was lakeside. Dimly, she visualized an undersized ward and nephew awkwardly positioning a single long adult ski. Twice the optimal length for his size. Both feet were slackly bound into over-large bindings. The boy tread water while handling the more challenging mono-handled ski rope.

Having been fit with a belly belt float, actually preferred by experienced older skiers due to its brevity and minimal constriction, she figured the device had been chosen for the novice skier precisely to increase drag. The large size didn't cinch around his waist snugly, being intended for waists multiple inches larger than her nephew's 22-inch one. The thing was large enough for an easy slide to ankle level, or even over his head, with little impediment, rendering it more encumbrance than life-preserver.

Ella nearly jumped to the boy's defense, then checked herself, confident in the good-naturedness of all the older nephews and trusting their good sense. Besides, she had noted Luke's tenacity in the face of challenges. The boy's passive-aggressive response to hindrance was significant. It occurred to her that this might not turn out the way practical jokers were plainly devising.

Pulling the rope taut for take-off, Ella could almost hear the twelve-year-old's chattering teeth. He was wearing only a borrowed speedo swimsuit at the urging of his cousins: the suit favored by all experienced water athletes. Like the 'safety device', it tracted little support by virtue of a rookie's tiny hips.

Gunning the big Evinrude motor without a traditional hand signal warning, the boat accelerated with enough force to raise an eight-hundred-pound gorilla. She watched as the ski rope jerked from Luke's unprepared hands, whisking personless over the surface of the lake as the powerful boat, full of delighted cousins, quickly circled to offer a second chance. Ella observed the immense satisfaction the unfair move provided puerile senses of humor, rolling her eyes while they came around to line up the craft for continuation of their newly met cousin's morning of futility. First moments were not boding well for the twelve-year-old.

A second aligning of boat to skier proceeded with more useless instructions thrown at the freezing newbie, all levity lost on the diminutive boy as he focused on implementing every detail of their valued advice. Ella noticed that all relevant guidance was absent. The ski tip was not visible above the water, an essential element of which the cousins clearly overlooked informing the first-timer. His curly head bobbed up and down in the water, obscuring sightlines and flooding nostrils. The rope was angled in relation to the boat instead of straightly aligned; the handle much too large for allowance of small hands to gain secure purchase.

Again, the motor revved without warning to top speed by maxing the throttle. Roiling liquid enveloped the small boy's body and his head plunged underwater, surely 'waterboarding' his mouth and nose, Ella worried. The over-sized speedo and waist belt were indeed combining to suck him further under by the second.

Considering the balance factor obligatory for success at slaloming, and the imbalance imparted by the single-handled rope's uneven pull to the side of the ski, Aunt Ella waited for another snap of the rope indicating separation from the skier. Seconds passed. Concern the boy had been caught by the rope in some fashion provoked her anxiety level. Again, she tensed to jump to her nephew's defense, worrying over bad consequences. What were those boys thinking?

Then, out of crystal green water, a small crouching missile launched upward, emerging from the turgidity boiling around Luke. The ski pointed slightly above vertical and straight ahead, ski rope meticulously taut. Sudden absence of drag thrust the boy airborne, skeg clearing the surface: a typically lethal event for most old-handers. The effect normally caused loss of rudder and therefore control. Flips, twists and catastrophic somersaults commonly resulted; wipeout almost inevitable. Hopefully without injury, Ella's mind flashed.

As she and the boys witnessed, the skeg descended in deliberately controlled fashion, catching the agitated surface water underneath. A tiny rooster tail arose neatly behind it like a synchronized water feature. The adult ski settled, featherlike, onto the churning overlay. A little boy straightened up, arching his spine to a proper bend back over now rigidly straight legs. He stabilized on the surface of the pristine lake in the center of a turbid chevron behind the big boat, exhibiting uncommon poise. Clearly in his element.

On a slow arcing turn around the glassy mere over the next ten minutes, the new slalom ski-baby gained feel for the water, maneuvering in various small ways, experimenting. He challenged untried ski leg muscles and investigated torque and traction of water geometry. Baby turns and curves, trial scoots, angling of body leans were serially tested.

Then, without notice or hesitation, a sudden zag outward widened to a venture up and over the turbulent treachery of one wake. Navigating it successfully, he then caught an edge, leaning gracefully into sheer smoothness of the tranquil façade peripheral to roughness behind the boat. An s-shaping curve propelled a smooth kick back in toward a re-crossing of that wake.

Whether purposely or by accident, Luke plowed forward at an angle, shooting up and over the rise. Once again airborne, he cleared the second wake's opposing crest. An adept move seldom attempted and often missed. A square landing was stuck as if practiced for years.

Ella didn't smile. She ear-to-eared at the sheer temerity evident in the pre-teen's body language. Watchful eyes of older cousins had collectively sagged to serial gapes, disbelieving of what they just beheld. Not only had little Lukie overcome an obstacle-course meant to demoralize him, he did it with style, aplomb, and athleticism rarely achieved by seasoned skiers. And, by Ella's estimation, any of the practical jokers.

When the boat finally completed a second full circle, it arrived back at the boat dock. Ground zero for the prickly beginning and shot-like emergence that had initiated Luke's virgin ride. He stuck another jump over both wakes once more and dug in a ski edge, picking up speed on the curve. Slingshotting loose off the rope, the boy surfed into a frictioned slide, collapsing backward at lake's edge. Sinking into a shimmer of wavelets, only a head of dripping ringlets framing a mouth full of gleeful teeth remained visible.

The haunting twitter of a loon to its mate and low rumble of an idling motor were the only sounds piercing morning quiet. No one spoke… no one made a sound at all.

It was only as he was coasting in after the rope release that shocked onlookers realized three things. Firstly, the boy possessed a natural talent for this balance-heavy sport. None of the cousins had begun skiing slalom. Like all beginners, they had started out on two skis. A fact of which Luke had been left ignorant. Second, he was first skier of the morning on first day at Cutaway. Luke had never seen anyone demonstrate any of this for him before accomplishing what he had just done.

And, thirdly, as he sank in slow-motion through the water surface, all hearkened on the fact that both speedo and waist float were nowhere to be seen. Lost in the tumult of take-off. His boy junk wobbled freely, side-to-side. It seemed over-large for a pre-teen and appeared to be inflating.

His maiden trip had been done completely free of all cover… or modesty.

Little Lukie hadn't broken any lake records. He had set the standard. The cousins were chastened. Every single one took the curly-headed youngster under their wing from that moment forward. Ella mused on such a quirky life lesson as this in quiet awe…

…After the campfire marking two weeks at Cutaway, with s'mores and fishtale-telling, under a full Strawberry Moon, two ski-junkie cousins, Lukie and Stockard, opted to bed down on the dock, eager for the coming break of day and a next ski adventure. Making pallets supplied by their aunts, the boys skinny-dipped and sniggled for an hour as moonbeams strafed them, silvery tongs bathing features in spectral array. The camp house up above fell into quietude, lights flicking off one-by-one until only spirits of the darkle persevered.

Perhaps it was the full moon. More likely, it was the nascent stirring of endocrine undertones providing provocation. Regardless, dreamscaping to a repositioned lunar globe led by an arching Artemis, Luke luxuriated in the sublime serenity of a soft nocturnal lake breeze. Bed coverings had long before been kicked clear by activity peculiar to restless writhings. The wafting zephyr deliciously caressed Luke's torso and legs. He reveled in night's song.

It was inevitable that such contentment exact a toll. Blood coursing through him under such illusioned conditions pooled subconsciously and before his brain had even registered the effect, he felt the pulsing bounce of his previously noted---by others; Luke had no basis for comparison---over-ample Pete, snaking at an angle over a tiny waist, and resting, between bobbles, over the edge.

A phantasmal palm reached tentatively towards it, then halted, considering the magnificently arching smoothness, a moonshadow wavering under it on skin and dock. Heat of an adjacent cousinly shoulder rasped Luke's in alien contact, making Luke jump. He exclaimed in surprise.

"Relax, Lukie, I'm just checking him out," Stockard's almost husky voice reassured. The eidolon delusion soothed a somnolent mind. With that, Luke did try easing the sudden tension his subconscious imbued. But, this illusory, unintentional contact was far too pleasurable for the perceived mortal sin that must be going down. Had to be: Lukie had absorbed the admonishing verses drilled into his memory through years of repetition. The only other relatable event had happened just the day before, he recollected. But Rexy's efforts had been necessitated by the menacing toxicant from the leech…then he recalled words alluding to the subject by his uncle. Maybe so, but maybe not. What was happening around here?

Conflicting emotions were warring in his ripening body and mind. Fear of Divine thunderbolts grew inside the storm cloud that was his conjuring mind. Yet, how in the big wide world, dreaming brain posited to askew thought processes, could anyone or anything make such delicious sensations a bad thing?

Something wasn't adding up. So, while he turned the problem over, instructions were followed. Luke lay still, except for uncontrollable quivering, absorbing the luscious effect in closed-eye ecstasy. After all, Stock was surely no devil…

He nearly jumped out of his skin when a sudden lightning strike of heat, manifested by exhaled breath, next shattered his misapprehending senses. Sitting bolt upright, he choked back a declaration of wonder as he now found Stockard leaning toward him, peering in curiosity. The almost concomitant arrival of a mirage gusher of whole cream, globular in its consistency, accompanied the sweetest feeling ever experienced. The rich milky stuff gave substance to a permanent mental image, ripe for reconjure in future fantasy settings of hormonally-induced pipe dreams.

His hands came up by reflex, grasping the glossy tresses covering the noggin sizing things up. Luke flashed on an epileptic classmate back home in the throes of 'a spell' and convinced himself that he was suffering one of those. Dang, he was ready to turn epileptic if this was the firsthand buzz!

Unable to control anything at all under the circumstances, his hands insentiently pressed and pushed. If he were indeed seizing or about to bring down deific reprisal, then it wasn't as bad as it was cracked up to be. That was the only other lucid thought taking form in his dreaming mind. Everything else constituted rainbows and butterflies.

Stockard backed away in a flash after Luke's hands let up, retching over dock's edge into black waters of the lake. "What ya' doin' Lukie? Ya' nearly smothered me!" The garbled words brought both the boys back to 'reality' in the delusional flight of fancy.

"Sorry, Stock... but what'd you do that for?" So frenzied by the fuzzy feelings still ricocheting inside him, he wasn't particularly coherent. "Did ya' do that on purpose?" He sank back down now, head and neck tense on the makeshift head roll. The throbbing that was Pete gave him abrupt cause for concern.

While he had produced such messes before, this was the first time not to awaken to the sticky smelliness. When it got him in trouble at home. Oh, or resultant to an accident. Like the day before. Either way, it had never lasted so long nor felt so good. Even amidst the roving physical cacophony which he grasped must be an illusion of fantasy, his ears were still ringing and the goosebumps roving his body were plastering subconscious senses even as he spoke.

"Well," Stock replied, red-faced, "no... I don't think so. It's just that your thing is ginormous. We all saw it the first day you were here. When I saw it again, now, I decided to get a close up...and...well...you kinda went-off..." The cousin stammered that last part out, like he had just then thought of it.

While Luke had sure enough pushed, he hadn't meant to any more than Stock claimed he had. If neither of them had intended their uninhibited dream actions, Luke deduced that Pete had been down there needing help; hands only answering the call. And then it had exploded. Intuiting no reasonable meaning whatever, the boys talked about it while Stockard spritzed his face with lake water.

"Do you do that every time?" Connoting an allusion to the gusher of a gully washer, Luke shook his head, then nodded it, then shook it again. His head ended up traveling in circles.

"I dunno, Stock, that was the first time for that to happen that way...I usually just kinda' wake up to it... or something," not wanting to let on about the day before with Rexy. He wasn't a tattler, like 'Bekkah, after all. Despite awareness this episode was only a figment of his imagination, he wasn't shattering the effect brooking the contrasting realms by admitting it in this subliminal state of mind.

"Sure did think I was done-in, Cuz. You nearly freaked me out." His words didn't match the tone. Luke was pretty sure that his cousin was not hating what happened. But, allowing him to save face, Luke kept quiet.

Finally settling back down side by side on their pallets, gazing at the silver orb upstairs, the two made more and diminishing small talk until drifting off, night sounds rhapsodizing around them, dreamscape colluding to mesh two worlds.

The haunting cascade of hoots called out as if inside Luke's ear. The eerie mantra reverberated off somewhere a short way away and boomeranged back in rounds. Two slumbering boys scrambled upright out of a sound sleep at the unnerving resonance, tangling clumsily in each other's legs. The result vaulted them both over the edge of the dock.

A strike of cold envelopment caused a shock of physical pain. Surfacing, the duo sputtered at each other in confusion, catching the thrashing of great wings out of the corner of their eyes. Drawing attention, they watched as the splendid outline of a great horned owl rose effortlessly from the dock, not five feet from where the sleepers had just reposed.

Butt naked as they both were--- Luke groggily puzzled at reasons for that--- chill of the morning stimulated them the more as they hoisted up and out, back onto the dock. He remembered a mutual decision the two had tacitly made upon climbing out from a bedtime swim the night before, engrossed in talk of silly and profound things, comfortable in the state of freeness under cover of shadows.

Immediately after that memory, Luke hit on the dreamt nocturnal event. The two grinned in mutual awkwardness at their gawky awakening, simultaneously wondering about what the other was grinning.

No shame, no remorse. Luke felt newly wrought. Where were all those constantly ratcheted-up guilt pangs that wracked his conscience and stalked his existence back home in Texas? In that other world. The twelve-year-old felt freshly hatched here in this spot. Remorse eluded him. This world was entirely different in its mood. Luke felt like he belonged.

The boys rolled up the pallets, air drying, then donned swim trunks as they anticipated the ski spree soon to come, taking pleasure in the nip of pre-dawn against skin. Needing to await at least one older cousin or adult, the two sat and talked, feet dangling in the water.

Before long, they heard faint shuffling movements from inside a still-darkened camp house. Muffled voices conversed: one gruff, another chirpy. Within minutes, the screen door squawked a greeting and here came Uncle Sparky. Little Claire rode on broad shoulders for the short trip to a little girl's haven. Water. Staccato dialog sufficed for morning salutations and departure prep, the exhilaration of a physical rush keenly anticipated.

Claire settled into the spotter's roost while the boys donned gear and plunked themselves through the smooth surface of a chill caldron. The succeeding two hours saw two young boys push limits of natural acumen for skimming, cutting, delving, jumping and sliding over the glassy sheen frosting their playground.

Dual ropes allowed for tandem skiing, effectively doubling their ski time. Experimentation laid bare formerly undreamt talents. Driver and spotter egged on youthful fearlessness. Derring-do throve. The elder teens were finding themselves in for more than they had bargained, Sparky considered. Small wonder they were sleeping in, again, the sage uncle snorted.

Following the first two weeks of the warm bonding amidst commonality of a therapeutic lake, Luke was melding readily into the circle of kinfolk with easy amity by a welcoming milieu of inclusion. Ella contemplated warmly, sipping coffee, enjoying two cousins' watery frolic from the big porch. Her nephew was literally blossoming before their eyes. The gurgly murmur of her big heart soared as marvel of it grew. The woman's confidence secured surety that this young man would hurdle his way into manhood despite trials still sure to be encountered after this summer had long lapsed.

October, 1991

"Chug."

The word hung between us in the thickness of the humid afternoon. I was distracted, as usual, and though peculiarity of the word did register, the activity occurring below sight lines made me less than communicative.

"Somethin' wrong with that?" The shirtless Asian boy queried me, art of defense clearly a familiar feature in the guy's personality. Sweat trickled down a smooth golden-skinned chest and stomach as he squinched the almond eyes cutting sharp holes through me. The intensity almost burned. I was upset with myself for leading this person to an unintentional inference.

"Heck no, dude. That's your name? Is it a nickname?" It scored belatedly in my fried brain that upon asking my name seconds before, the offer of his might reply. It hadn't been a sentence. So, as attention had fixed on two hairless golden arms angling together beneath foredrop of the army green plywood fence marking the edge of right field, separating us, I assumed the hands were in touch with his crotch snake.

The boy's initial gaze had appeared vacant when I looked up from my aimless trot his direction. It had taken a few moments for the both of us to gather details of the goings on, intent on our own business as we were. Supposedly, anyway.

Upon my realization the nice-looking male was draining the lizard, by body language exhibited, the cute boy apparently noticed my notice. He had recovered wits by demanding my name. I had proffered it reflexively even as I mentally pictured the hidden activity out of view. Obsession with the midsections of almost every male encountered was simply what it was. Slowly learning to hide the proclivity due to commonly untoward reactions, I now conjectured whether the present case would turn antagonistic.

No adjustment in stance, nor altering of nicely rounded bare shoulders feeding into muscled arms, informed me that, at the least, he wasn't shy. "No, it's a real name. Had it all my life. Dude." The emphasis on the 'dude' vernacular was meant to subdue. I read defensiveness by the method for a second time. Then hastened to lessen the tension.

"That's fly, man, I've never met anybody with that name--- I like it." Then, I added, "I'm an apostle." The attempt at levity took a moment, but upon registering, Chug broke into a close-lipped half smile, letting a bit of the guard slip.

"So, you're perfect? Or just Biblical?" He had wryly grasped the tactic usually employed to defray dislike for the burdensome name christened before I could raise objections about it. The ploy worked.

Curtly shaking something behind the fence, the boy snapped an elastic waistband. Two handsome golden hands raised up into sight. A wisp of sadness touched my teenage psyche as I lost the vicarious connection with what was conjuring curiosity by the hand moves. Ahem, I fantasized to myself. Another one eludes…

Sidling closer to the green divider, I nonchalantly gandered downward. We sized up one another, me visualizing the nether parts. Of course. As well-proportioned as the upper reaches already scrutinized, I now saw. Running briefs, jockstrap and cross-trainers framed nicely-curved thighs and calves. And the golden motif carried on there, too. Sexy.

"Neither, according to my folks. I'm the Devil's spawn." I hadn't meant to open up that much to this stranger, yet the words tumbled forth, unfiltered, in another manifestation of a plethora of tainted traits. Chachalaca. Chatterbox.

"Really? I ain't never met a bad Luke before. Wanna hang out?" The reply and offer somehow identified a kindred spirit and I prepared to expound on my badness when a screech of derision interrupted our repartee.

"Hey, Flash, you numbskull! Get your stupid mind back in the game and stop chasin' the damn butterflies!" This, from baseball-capped Coach Ribble. "You're not pickin' daisies out there… get your head outta your ass!" The vehemence stung. Tensing, I jerked around. Humiliated at my misfeasance, I chirruped a stuttered rejoinder of faked remorse.

Turned to re-focus on the boring baseball practice, it dawned on me that Chug remained. I could feel his gaze from beyond the fence. Calling over my shoulder, I abashedly offered a stunted apology. The Asian boy chortled that he would catch up with me after practice. Through the precipitous mental tumult, it flashed on me the guy wanted to continue talking. I grinned despite my doghouse status, happy that it was so. Chug seemed cool.

An hour or so later, after practice and another awkward trip through the realm of team showerland--- the fact that not a single pubic hair had yet popped up provided endless hilarity for my dratted teammates--- I emerged from a side dressing room door.

Having successfully blended into the wall by the darker back corner, avoiding coach's scrutiny of everything shower-related, it permitted uneventful escape yet one more day. Though still on high alert for torment tactics. The exit opened into a deserted administrative parking lot. I slipped under the tangle of bushes surrounding the little-used way toward blessed absentation from a despised team sport venue.

I had detested team sports ever since I could remember, ascribing only negative undertones to all things 'team'. It wasn't that I sucked at athletics, or didn't like playing them. Physicality was highly valued. It was simply that I had never taken to the model of group activities with kids my gender who, in packs, tended to be some of the vilest of blowhards and bullies. Teams equaled packs.

Lost in a reverie of these musings, I completely missed the furtive character crouching amongst the bushes. One second contemplating bully tricks, the next found my head and face wrapped in a ripe jockstrap. Ripping the thing off, I immediately assumed defensive posture employed more than once, fists raised, not knowing who or what to expect.

The giggle saluting a scheme well-met emanated from leafy bushes just passed. The source of it suffered a sharp reply from my still diminutive fifteen-year-old balled fist. Feelings of justified satisfaction for spoiling the fun of a tormentor lasted fractions of seconds--- right up to when a bloody-nosed Chug stumbled out of the hiding place, holding an abused body part in abject distress. I was instantly appalled by such a pugilistic response, too late recognizing a practical joke meant for fun.

"Whoa--- Chug! I am sorry, dude. I just reacted. I am soooo sorry. Here--- let me help," I offered helplessly. My blind punch had been perfectly targeted. Blood flowed from the boy's nose. I grabbed for his head and bent it up and back. Whipping off my t-shirt, I applied firm pressure to the offended appendage, receiving a brisk kick in the shin and jab in the ribs for my trouble. I didn't let go, though. Recognizing just deserts, I hung on.

"What a jerk, Luke," the golden-toned Asian gurgled. The raised head retrograded blood and mucous into my new acquaintance's mouth and throat, gagging him. Chug's hands came up, shoving the shirt aside to allow air through. I found myself inches from his face. As eyes met, emotions traded back and forth, conveying tortured opinions.

A sudden congestive ratcheting issued from his throat, presaging an explosive sneeze. The result drenched me with copious phlegm, blood, spittle and snot. Topping my freshly showered head, the rank mixture cascaded down my face, stinging my eyes and invading my mouth, then dribbling over my chest.

Still feeling this comeuppance was warranted, I used the soiled shirt to wipe myself down. Then, lacking anything else, I pulled off my shorts and proceeded re-applying pressure to Chug's still-flowing nose. It appeared crooked, I saw, withering me further by the comprehension of its dislocation. Or brokenness.

The next attempt, I more carefully tipped the ruined cartilage back, covering only the left nostril, which could now be seen as the side that was draining. Murmuring a constant stream of contrite euphemisms, I nonetheless remained attuned for additional hostile moves or volcanic eruptions. But, a spent Chug just sagged against me, losing steam and will simultaneously.

We stared each other down, closely approximated as we were, streaming persistent emotions. Loathing what had just gone down, concurrence infested me by the descriptive term this already ex-friend had assigned. Jerk.

What was wrong with me, the thought needled? Everything I did seemed to end badly. I was, indeed, evil spawn. And felt like clobbering my own nose in a loser attempt to make some kind of sorry-ass amends. Should rationalization have conceived it might have helped anything, I would have done. As it was, I just slumped down to the dirty curb with this Chug boy. There we sat, mulling private ideas.

After five counted minutes, I eased up on the gnarled nostril. Finding cessation of the noxious flow, for most part, I dabbed the thing sympathetically, jerk that I was. The look conveyed now was enigmatic. Chug's visage had changed to inscrutable. Only later did I learn about introversion, such as it was. An ages-old Vietnamese method for absorbing insults…or worse. In the moment, I felt he might still lash out, so remained on guard. Or hoped for more payback. Unsure which.

Out of the clear blue, I perceived a soft gurgle emerge from his throat. Tensing for a blow, or upsurge, incredulity washed through my confused brain as two sensuous lips curled slightly upwards in a whisper of a crooked smile.

"You sure as Hell liked that strap better when it was on me, Luke." The truth in the statement blew us both away. We melted into each other, quaking with inner laughter. My stupid eyes boiled over by the undeserved exculpation. Arms wrapped around each other and we knocked noggins in letting it all go.

The trip to the hospital for nasal reconstruction was both a long and a short sojourn. From then on, we were inseparable.

APRIL, 1992

"Dude. I don't think there's a right way or a wrong way. It's just the way it feels best." Chug inhaled the oddly palliative dung aroma as he shoveled shit while I pulled the wire curry through Joe's coarse mane. I could hear his familiarly raspy intake of breath from around the stall wall and mused over this explanatory slant.

"Really? You don't think they have rules about it? I mean, I thought there had to be some set standard for how it needs to happen--- and be right, I mean." I remained obsessed by intricacies involved with straight world sexual mores. Chug was my unfettered sounding board for such conundrums.

The snort arising out of Smokey's stall pulled me up short. I grinned in picturing my best friend's scathing glance sure to be piercing the wall in this direction. He was way too familiar with my prudish pronouncements and beyond exasperated by disbelief that anyone our age could be so unversed in the art of teenage sex.

Over the six months since we had met, and after the establishment of certain limits, Chug and I shared knowledge of one another that most boys our age would never have, were we typical fifteen-year-olds. But we weren't. Typical, that is. In any way.

"Well, it just seems that with so little variability in the ways you straight boys have at your disposal to please a woman in comparison to two guys doin' the deed, there must exist some list, or manifesto, or something, to keep you on the right track so's ya'll don't screw the whole thing up. You know how finicky girls are, now."

"Luke. Are you serious? My man, that is crazy--- you think there is a manual for how to get it on with a woman? You have to be kidding me." His strained rejoinder garnered nothing in return. The pregnant pause as I continued unknotting my Tobiano Pinto's long hair provided answer in itself.

I dearly loved pulling the Vietnamese boy's chain. Even though mystery truly shrouded methodology in heterosexual sex tactics, and more so, women's desires regarding the matter--- I had absolutely zilch in the first-hand knowledge factory on the subject--- it bamboozled that he could be so easily led down the primrose path as often as he allowed me to do so.

The soft crunch of our steeds' contented munching as they relished sweetfeed from wooden cribs seemed to stretch on and on. The air was chock full of moisture; my sticky skin prickled lightly in precipitous precognition.

Muted whir of air presaged a shovel full of horse manure as it angled around the corner into my line of vision. I was showered with a fecund mixture of straw, urine-soaked sand and horse turds. Rebuttal to my latest baiting perfidy by Chug's sudden epiphany.

The stuff rained over me, sticking in hair, clotting on exposed torso and arms and legs. Cutoff blue jean shorts offered precious little cover against the putrid mix. Bare feet were invisible under the crap settling around them. I stood immobile through the sloppy spattering, weirdly reveling in the communion we shared. Gross as it was, the mess proved our bond, I knew, and the small stitch in time stuck to my mind as much as the raiment of refuse now worn.

Seeing my non-response as he stared at the work of art from around the corner, Chug barreled into Joe's stall, riling my quarter horse in the doing. Smacking his smooth bare body against my own, our sweat mixed, sliming us both. He proceeded to smear the putrid mélange like a Sydney Pollack masterpiece, fingers and palms painting over my immobile form. Smooshed turds on my face, in my curls and down my shorts made an emerging toothy grin stand out, starkly contrasting brownness against white. Upon hesitantly opening eyes to check the scene out, my visage must have been hilarious, his own smile within inches of mine.

Anyone seeing these antics could never fathom friendliness as basis for the act. I puckered my lips and planted a smelly smooch smack on my friend's open mouth, further grossing us out. We giggled so hard together that we fell to the sandy floor, Joe sidling over to one side and arching his neck at us in an expression of pure equine disgust. As we surveyed the situation through the state of dishevelment to which we had been reduced, we saw Chug's dun pony, Smokey, peer tentatively around the corner in curiosity at such ridiculous display.

Our legs had gotten mixed together and we sat, facing each other in this organic guise, my fingers repaying my friend by slowly doing a little of their own body painting. A distinct 'click' sounded from a couple stalls away, down the central barn corridor. In seconds, both of us squinted around to see our fellow horse owner, Jill, poke a curious head into the scene playing out here.

Shock, disgust, disbelief, utter incredulity. All suffused her pretty face upon the beholding. We held still, guilelessly inert, as the girl busted our asses ignominiously. The fellow teenage equestrian was used to our impropriety and acting out, yet the present picture proved novel in her assessment.

Establishing the fact that our condition and positioning were resultant to neither a fight, nor off-the-wall kinky sexcapade, she simply rolled a set of emerald eyes at us, "How in the world do you two live with yourselves? You are totally uncouth! Truly." And with that, she disappeared back out of our visual field, tut-tutting in mock disdain for the mental picture she must now live with. We could feel her own resigned grin once out of sight as she audibly 'ewww'd' her way down the corridor to BelleStar's stall, her palomino.

The seventeen-year-old beauty queen had grasped the unusual bond we two shared within a few days after moving her horse into the utility co-op stretch of land snaking through the middle of the residential area adjoining it. Stable, barn, riding arena and large round shaded cement water trough, along with other rudimentary amenities, had been built on the land years before our arrival.

Tall metal matrix towers basing the electrical lines serving the area loomed benignly over all. While not upscale in the least, the dual function mode condoned by the electric co-op recouped a nominal sum monthly from the horses boarded here. Maintenance that renters such as ourselves did for the place in upkeep kept costs for the utility to a minimum. A win-win.

Eleven horses abided under the sturdily constructed barn at present. Most owners were residents of the surrounding suburban enclave. Chug, myself, and Jill were high schoolers who availed ourselves of cost-effective facilities, allowing a way to afford pleasures of equestrian pursuits in the quasi-urban setting we inhabited. Not to mention an escape from the tedium of home life. Chug had gamed into the set-up a month after we had met, purchasing Smokey and gravitating to the same advantages as I had done.

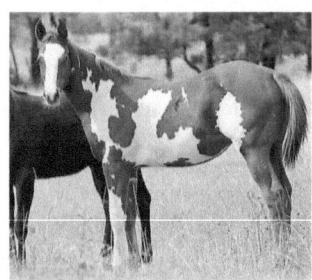

My parents had begrudgingly permitted purchase of the treasured brown and white paint horse a year before, using a bit of the proceeds accumulated over preceding years in saving for college costs sure to fall on my head in coming times. With three children, the youngest sibling status parlayed my options down the line of priority for Christian folk intent on scholarships to a devoutly religious college.

Gleaning that goal of theirs for me, plan B had been devised. Having figured out the definition of autonomy early in teenage life, I had grappled with the premise in an upfront manner. By merit of an unusually diplomatic approach, considering usual clumsiness regarding such matters, the promise of underwriting my own education had won their grudging acceptance.

Knowing that my life could not and would not follow edicts set by indoctrinated parents, and steeled by resolve to fly free of the lifestyle from the time of a thirteenth birthday, planning for escape had been carefully orchestrated. Mowing and trimming yards, grocery-shopping trips by bicycle for elderly homebounds, a part time job at Tinker's Auto-Body shop and odd jobs interspersed amongst these had supplied means to an end dear to my heart.

I purposely navigated the intricacies of evangelistic life born to in seemingly resigned fashion. But an underlying, unspoken strength of determination guided my path, dead ends and all. My mistakes were legion, yet it was Sophocles who had rationalized the truism that we never learn from our successes… by that yardstick, I must be very, very wise, indeed.

Presently sitting crotch-to-crotch, legs intertwined, sludged in shit as we were and busted royally in our antics, Chug pretended to be more grossed out by the feces-laden kiss planted on him moments before than the fact of our nasty condition. Yet neither of us attempted extrication. We sniggled happily, enjoying one another's proximity.

Though straight, Chug had never shied from bodily contact, even knowing my alternative proclivities. Having not yet acted on acknowledged predilections--- a couple of bizarre happenchances being summary of my sex realm to date--- this friend acceded to my bent nature. He had easily gaged me at our first meeting.

I found my best friend to be supremely sexy, and extremely desirable. We were inherently smart enough to know not to pursue a uselessly harmful fling. That path would destine quick dissolution of a deep friendship. So, while I teased him incessantly in ways leading to our current untidiness, he got back at me by tormenting my erogeneity. To distraction.

It commonly left me in a funk, these provocations arousing wild hormonal spikes. Confident in not only his effect on me, Chug also trusted that the ties binding us were rooted in non-sexual spheres of influence. No way would we ruin such an alliance by fatuous satisfaction. 'Friends-with-benefits' was not on the table for us. Thankfully.

Aware as he was, Chug now sat, almost dick-to-dick, with our legs layered, enjoying the state of all now between us. We conspired and confided betwixt ourselves, giddy in the connection. Predictably enough, as we rounded back to the previous conversation regarding straight boy rules when bedding a woman, the ever-ready snake between my legs took notice. The latent Pete gradually limbered himself awake, rising like a phoenix, unbidden. Up and toward Chug.

Never denying attraction for the beauty of my friend, I unabashedly allowed the engorgement. At the apogee of Pete's arching, Chug glanced down at the bluejean covered outline of him. Used to such reactions invoking my youthful indelicacies, he exhibited no consternation as the stupid, misguided thing once again made itself known. His own junk never responded in kind yet I nursed the belief that the boy was a bit over-curious about Pete.

Noting the enflamed appendage pointing directly up at him, within mere inches of bumping, conversation dwindled. I observed as Chug reached one hand tentatively toward the interloper. He grasped the denim fronting it, deliberately unzipped the dividing cover, then watched me as I watched him blatantly reach with the other hand, pulling the sides apart. His action allowed for escape of the serpent from its lair. Chug guffawed as the elastic junk snapped to attention between us.

Pete sat there, hovering and bobbling back and forth in all his glory. Chug, still totally unfazed, proceeded to examine the over-sized piece of equipment. In the semblance of an anatomy professor viewing a cadaver. While stiff, though, the organ was far from cold and lifeless. His interest interested me and I sat still, awaiting the next move.

A pearlescent bead appeared at the eye. To everlasting surprise, my bosom bud tipped the glob with a gold-toned finger, then raised the jewel to his horse turd rimmed lips. I was mesmerized; shocked by the unexpected move. His eyes returned my wide-eyed stare as he furthered the hamming by tonguing that finger. Then, he lowered the same finger--- just the one--- and curled it around the straining shaft embodying Pete.

The crowning head seizured at his touch. I liquefied as the eye spasmed, then felt, more than saw, the founts of juice erupt upward. Six or seven spurts landed on the gilt skin smoothly covering Chug's ripped belly, dripping down to pool in the sexy-as-hell bellybutton of which I was, oh, so vexedly familiar.

Chug watched all of this, evident enthrallment matching mine. As hot goop heated his umbilicus, he raised his head once more and uncurled the enwrapping middle finger. The resultant pitch upward slung remnants of creamy cum in an arc that roped both our filthy faces. The long dick smacked sharply on my flat belly. His shit-eating grin hang-dogged me in success.

"How long did you say it took you to grow that?"

We sized up this added quirk to the whole bizarre episode, filed it properly into a folder marked 'science experiment' and disentangled our mirthful selves from the other. During the brief trip to the nearby water trough, Pete languidly lolled before me, happy in his freedom. Submerging for an overdue cleansing, playing in the coolness of a constantly replenishing piped-in stream feeding the sizeable vat, we ducked under the galvanized waterfall for flushing of caked hair.

Returning to the stalls, we tidied up our areas, finished currying Joe and Smokey, ejected the friendly horses to pasture for the afternoon, completed raking and shoveling stalls, donned running shorts and shoes and locked tack rooms. Peeking in on Jill, busily braiding BelleStar's mane and tail, the girl again rolled her eyes toward us, smiling indulgently at our eccentricities. The way only a supremely confident pretty girl such as herself could. I took note of the second and third takes by Chug in her direction as we backed away. The straight boy was under a spell. And didn't know it.

Setting of a steady lope for winding a way home through tree-lined tracts of homes, enjoyment described our ease of association. I had up and quit the baseball team three weeks after the nose-breaking incident, much to my older brother, Elijah's, and Daddy's displeasure. It was, after all, America's Game. Figuring out that they were the solitary reason for my sticking with the sport, and honing in on the much preferable way my new friend spent his extracurricular time, the decision had been easy.

The cross-country track team added me to its roster soon thereafter. The word 'team' was a misnomer. Chug and I were partners. Plus, it had been one more act of passive-aggressive rebellion on my trajectory toward de-evangelized existence. Blissful release accompanied the pronouncement. The added factor of cementing a pledge between Chug and me had inked our marathon running pact. I was hooked. For life. I may not get to water ski often, but I could run forever. We wended our way home, secure in the verities.

Charles Ng Chug would beguile for years to come. Still, autonomy, I was figuring out, did become me.

May, 1992

"Luke... Luke? Are you there, honey? We have a bad connection... I'm having trouble hearing you, dear. This blasphemous new portable telephone is all static...Can you hear me, Luke?" Aunt Ella had been reaching out to me due to a report she heard through the grapevine. At home, we couldn't really talk, what with informative breathing on the bedroom party line. Dear Mama was listening in. So, I had taken a chance and called her from this payphone.

That had worked really well. Not a single word of mine had gotten through apart from the fraught, high pitched, 'Hello, Aunt Ella'. By her voice, it was clear she was damned worried. I tried yelling into the receiver from this phone booth outside school but noisy traffic from buses rumbling past stymied the effort.

I had a feeling connection problems came from my end of the call. The phone here was notoriously fickle. Being my prime source of private communication, I used it regularly. Many a quarter had been wasted by dropped calls and dial tone interruptions. Frustrated, I banged the thing, hard, back on to the hook. That sure should be beneficial to its future clarity, it crossed my mind. Tears welled up again, threatening to spill over. I huddled into the tiny free-standing booth surround in effort to make myself small. Or disappear. Or something.

Suddenly, a familiar tap to my left cheek signaled. Looking timidly up, I found Chug smiling at me. The smile faded as he took in my streaked face and red-rimmed eyes.

"What's up, LL?" He had recently taken to the new moniker upon finding out my middle name by chance when I lifted the birth certificate from Daddy's desk. They would never miss it, I had reasoned. In fact, they would probably extrapolate its disappearance to the next jump: I'd never been born. An option, at the moment, of which I perceived as preferable to the truth. Chug knew of my distaste for the name Luke. In an act of solidarity with me, he had opted for LL. Lucas Laughlin. He always had my back.

"Are you a'ight, boy? You look like shit," the only true confidant I had ever known asked.

That bit of sympathy was all it took. The welling up spilled bounds of ringed lids, flooding in deluge down my cheeks. I turned into my friend and buried face into chest, sobbing. His arms came up, gently encapsulating. Not a word. None were needed.

A scathing catcall flew out a bus window just rolling past, barking a single word, "Faggots!" Chug raised a middle finger salute toward the male voice. Pulling away from the vulnerable site, he led toward the nearby Dairy Queen. Entering, we slid into the closest booth to the door. While Chug ordered iced teas, I kept my head down. Using a shirt tail, I rubbed defenselessly expressive eyes, a constant giveaway of private feelings. My friend's bare leg rubbed mine under the table.

Thankfully, only a handful of students populated this common gathering spot now. Summer vacation fever was upon everyone, especially seniors, and the fast food joint wasn't the place to be seen. Chug didn't attempt conversing, feeling my pain. His leg just kept up the rhythmic stroking as assurance of presence.

After a few minutes, composed a bit, I glanced up for a second. Then immediately down. Awful wetness menaced again. I couldn't remember crying in his presence before…oh, except the first day we met when I had busted his nose…what a good memory to dredge up. Physical abuse at my hand…just great.

Chug's warm fingers finally reached over, taking mine, and pulled toward him. That worked. Lifting my head, I met his eyes. "Daddy told me not to come back home. Mama and he talked, he said, and they decided I couldn't stay anymore. I was too bad an influence on Eli and 'Bekkah, he told me: I break all the rules. So, I packed some things in my backpack and left for school this morning but couldn't go in. I've been over at Pygmalion Books all day. I just tried calling Aunt Ella, but we didn't get past hello…" My voice rasped low and monotone. Daddy-like.

"You mean Aunt Ella wouldn't talk to you?" He looked surprised, knowing how close she and I were.

"No, it was just a bad connection. I think I busted the payphone."

"Boy, I'll bet that took care o' curin' the problem," the deadpan reply made me smile in spite of myself. Which set him to doing it, too. In a minute, we were both tittering like schoolgirls--- or faggots--- and I felt like a ton of bricks had lifted off me. Chug could always do that.

"Y'know, Luke," reverting to my name without thinking, "you hate that house. Why don't you just come on home to the houseboat with me? My mom would be fine with it if you shared with us. My bed is big enough for two and my little brothers are pretty cool... for being just-past-rugrats."

I had met Mrs. Chug on several occasions, once Chug had gotten past the fact of embarrassment at living on a houseboat. I thought the idea of it was pretty neat, and I liked his mom and family. His Dad was always off in the Gulf of Mexico, shrimping. The only thing he knew.

The immigrant family was so obsessed with Americanizing themselves that I had been almost immediately lassoed into teaching the kids--- and her--- everything American. So, that option appealed greatly. A safe port, I thought. Ergo, one where I might earn my keep.

So, it had come to pass. The move was constructive. The Chugs were exceedingly gracious in their welcome. My mind cleared. Over the final weeks of my sophomore year, I devised a plan with aid from Mrs. Tipton, my counselor, which we took to Mr. Lade, the vice-principal. Achieving their blessing---both understood the home situation, having dealt with my folks--- the two bent over backwards to finagle the plan to fruition.

The best part was that upon hearing the strategy, Chug had bought into it. Hook, line and sinker. In two days, we were both allowed unusual leeway to proceed with the crazy scenario. On top of it all, Mrs. Chug and Aunt Ella had signed off on it. What a difference a day makes.

Through dumb luck or maybe some unrecognized foresight, advantage had been taken of a new feature at the high school equated to me by Mrs. Tipton in freshman year. The veteran counselor had seen something, I guessed, and taken me under her wing. Long story short, the process allowed exposure for a very few students to a crash-course curriculum.

The combination of being under-challenged by high school, along with a knack for speed-reading, permitted me onto the fast track. Mrs. Tipton lobbied hard for my inclusion. Only one other freshman had ever been included, administration deeming mental maturity a major force in reckoning for acceptance. That last point had been kept from me. Evidently, I met the bar.

By sophomore year, now about to be completed, I had accumulated enough credits through extracurricular study to graduate early. There were extra STEM course completions acceptable in the embryonic program, as well.

Two weeks after moving in with the Chug family, a Monday morning meeting with Mrs. Tipton concluded with information about my advanced placement through college credits totaling 31 hours. By this achievement, I would be allowed entrance to the University of Texas in Austin the coming fall semester. College sophomore status.

The whole thing hadn't really dawned on me when signing on, just gravitating toward getting away from the loathed duo of home and high school as quickly as possible. My parents had agreed to the program without really taking time to understand. Or, now that I thought on it… maybe they did. Things that make you go 'Hmmmmm'.

In very short order, the traumatic 'divorce' from family who deemed me a discardable child had transformed into a rainbow archway to the future.

Explaining the situation in bed with Chug that night, he had perked up at description of the stratagem fast track program. A confession followed. My friend had been inducted into the same program, at his mom's insistence. Chug was the other freshman. It had been the one secret between the two of us. Administration was careful to keep students on special track separated from one another in advanced classes, preferring acclimation to older students. Intent was to mitigate chances for young participants linking with one another in a clique that might stunt… yup… mental maturation.

Chug had been on a parallel track with his own counselor. We now understood the peculiar reason why we never shared any classes. Track team, the single exception. Desirous of not extending the perception of strangeness to which I was already sensitive sealed lips on the situation. Even with my confidant, Chug.

He harbored similar feelings. We now exulted over vacating the high school venue before it had been foreseen. Together. Double bliss. Unlike my parents, Mrs. Chug was busting her buttons in pride at her eldest boy's feat. My folks probably didn't even know. Chug's mom considered me a good influence, not Devil's spawn.

Exceptions not addressed in fast-tracking were the determination by administrators and school board demanding a base level of credit hours encompassing non-core courses---basically basket-weaving, home economics, etcetera --- be spread out over the progression of the modified high school event. A safeguard against exactly what the administrators feared: throwing students unready for college experience into a failing situation. These courses were to be completed in the coming summer by special dispensation. Powers-that-be had granted the first two-year graduation certificates so far endorsed.

"No, Dinh, Charlie is absolutely not a bad name or a bad word in America," I was addressing one of the nasty left-overs of the Viet Nam War. Known as the American War by the Chugs and other emigrants who were lucky enough to resettle here in the states after communist takeover in the 1970's. Thousands had escaped through the 80's and now, the '90's. My Uncle Sparky had served then and described the war of resistance fought by guerilla warfare methods. Namely: the Viet Cong; aka V. C. Hence, in American: Victor Charlie.

"Neither is Victor. Both were just a way for soldiers to refer to communist sympathizers they were fighting against back then. Charles and Victor are very respectable American names. Like your brothers." I hoped to dispel the notion associated with the names. Currently used by bullies, bigots and ignorant children in acting out xenophobic fear toward peoples new or different to this country.

My best boy, Chug, bore enough ill will for the fallout to go by his surname only, rebelling in a passive-aggressive manner the only way he knew how rather than hide behind an American name as a Vietnamese immigrant. Charles. His older brother had been named Victor years before in the Chug Family's effort to assimilate. The two male names were the only American ones they knew. By the time Dinh and Nguyen came along, the Chug's felt more comfortable using old family names instead. Good for them, I rooted.

Ten-year-old Dinh now had an American perspective to mull through. I hoped it would keep negativism at bay. His older brother had a heaping dose on his plate enough for all four brothers. Mrs. Chug came in with fresh spring rolls for a break from lessons being reviewed. Her old-world smile and manners endeared me more with the passing days. The woman was the epitome of what I pictured as a mother figure. Chug bumped the door behind her in entering and kissed her, then tousled Dinh's hair. Elder brothers were father figures while Father was away, by Vietnamese tradition.

Crunching the hot rolls and washing them down with Oolong tea, we sat on the side of the bed. Chug had sent his application to UT Austin two weeks before, much too early to expect any notification. Yet here he was, fretting over it big time. Since the two of us had day-tripped to the flagship campus a week before--- around our home eco and weaving classes--- in search of possible living space, he just couldn't contain himself on the undecided question.

No amount of reassurance placated him. Upping the ante, my application had been sent a year before for the fall semester a year from the coming term. Receiving acceptance earlier in the spring, admittance for the coming semester instead was mere administrative process. Mrs. Tipton had been ahead of the deadlines on my behalf. I would be ever grateful. Chug was intellectually advanced. Harvard or Yale would love to have him. If only I could convince him.

Even so, the two of us savored planning for academic life in Austin. On a night when the houseboat floated still and quiet, ex-rugrats finally silent on floor pallets outside our door, gentle jostle of wave action lulled us while we whispered conspiratorially. Chug's naked shoulder singed mine with each metronomic undulation. We contentedly drifted toward sleep, laying in the single bed.

"Do you think we can find a place for Smokey and Little Joe?" Chug was adamant about the subject. As hard as I had fallen for long-distance running, to which he had exposed me, my bud had fallen harder for the horse boys. He had never had a pet for which to care. Animals were workers--- or food--- in their home country. Our cross-over interests were welding more than bonding us. It was life-changing.

Sharing things in this manner provided an outlet never experienced with blood brother, Elijah. Total religious indoctrination had been replete with brainwashing of which middle-eastern madrassas could be envious. We did not communicate. Eli's initial fall college semester would come with a full scholarship to Bryan College in Tennessee, I knew. The fact of his being two years ahead of me in school by our age difference, but now concurrently entering college, held a particular irony.

The small evangelist college was the very one named in honor of W. J. Bryan--- that would be William Jennings Bryan--- he of Scopes Monkey Trial fame. From the 1920's when the battle over evolution had supposedly been fought. The same college which, in the last year, had changed its mission statement to permit teaching of only Intelligent Design and Creationism in the sciences. Nothing pertaining to the false prophet known as---horror of horrors--- Evolution. Go figure.

The entire science department and 25% of other departments' teaching staffs, including all department heads, had resigned in disgust. Still, full scholarship: good. That is, until I researched the school and found that 90% of the student body was there on full scholarship. All funds provided by Dominionists, Flat Earth Society, Oath Keepers, and the like. Translation: they needed acolytes.

Bugtussled at the premise, I re-focused my thoughts, "There's bound to be gobs of stables in Austin, Chug. Next time we're there we should look. I'd love to have the outlet of riding, dude. But, we have to remember what we're going to UT for. Will we have time for them by ourselves?"

"Yeah, I've thought about that, too, LL, but I don't know what we'd do without 'em if we don't take 'em. Or, what they'd do without us… y'think o' that?" My stalwart friend was nothing if not loyal.

"Well, what about Dinh and Nguyen? They could probably keep up the boys and learn new stuff by doing it, if we decide to leave them." My idea wasn't without merit. We had both seen how the youngsters took to the atmosphere at the stable when tagging along with us. An increase in responsibility would be good for them. Soft humming next to me made clear that Chug was turning the concept over another time. I let him have space for the process.

After a bit, he spoke, "That is smart, LL. They do need something to center them. Mom has been looking for a responsibility like that; she's worried about me leaving already. And Vic has his own interests." Victor, the eldest son, was head-over-heels in love with Cecile, the girl of his dreams. At almost eighteen, it was a ripe age for Vietnamese boys to start setting their future. And, Mrs. Chug wanted the next generation on board. Badly. A new American-born generation was all-important to her. The reality would set the family into sync with her adopted country's life stream. She hadn't minced words on the subject. Vic was vitally positioned in her eyes. Chug's mind churned.

"If we do find a place in Austin, any stable would have to be close to where we are, since we won't have wheels… and we would need to travel light. Just basics. We'd probably need to leave behind most of our tack… and saddles." My boy was really going now, I could tell. "When was the last time we saddled 'em up, anyway, Luke? That trail ride to Addick's Dam a few months ago?"

"That was it. Remember, we used the hackamores, and everything," I replied. "What a hassle. Had to take it all off to let 'em in the water, anyway. And they were so sweaty under the blankets and stuff. The boys do fine with halters, anyway. I like the feel of riding bareback better, so, maybe it would be best to leave all the bulk behind." I was rationalizing now, even though all was true. We both liked the feel of playing Indian over cowboy. Bareback and halters were a lot less encumbering.

"Oh, just admit it, Luke, you like feeling Pete rubbin' around on that backbone--- think I didn't see him perkin' up out there? You haven't put the saddle back on once since then. Ha. You get off on that stuff." He was teasing me. I hadn't noticed that he had spotted my discovery. I did like the effect. Pete was getting massaged regularly by the method.

Smiling, I rejoined the comment, "Funny, you seemed to enjoy it a little more than you admit, too, Chug. Little Chug was sittin' up and taking names as much as Pete, straight boy. I've never seen him so happy."

"Maybe, but Pete was leakin'. Dude. I watched all that wet he was spillin' inside those shorts. That wasn't all sweat. Dude." I could feel the smile around his words as he said them. His hand slid over Pete as he teased, never shy about touching. Pete jerked at the contact, immediately at attention. My barely sixteen-year-old hormones, combined with heat from Chug's palm, had proved a menace more than once.

Even though I was deeply aware of his sexuality, it mystified me at his penchant for 'crossing the line' in handling my junk. I knew it was just a way to reinforce influence over me, like my teasing manner was toward him. Still, lack of very many demonstrable limits for a future breeder, as I called him, threw me sometimes. Regardless of our steadfastness on the subject, if we hadn't staked out priorities from the start, I could probably fall--- hard--- for this person that I loved like a brother.

"Look at you, Luke. What is up with this thing?" As he fingered Pete, familiarly. Little Chug didn't respond in like fashion. I knew from firsthand testing. It kept me at bay.

I had concluded by this point that I fell into the category of well-hung. Rarely spying shower room snakes of equal size, it sure wasn't for lack of checking. Little Chug was two-thirds Pete's size. The morning stretches had proven the fact succinctly. As well, my hand had strayed over the beaut more than once upon wakening in nighttime hours, exploring nocturnal boners. While very nice, I thought, Chug's deliberate turning away had been enough to keep our few, but strict, limits where they were. For the best.

Nevertheless, the fact endured that Chug appeared innately drawn to Pete's size and shape. I felt that the ostensible front put up by teasing denoted just a tad more interest than admittable. Or admissible. His lack of inhibition proved multifaceted in the experience. I would never deny fondness that it occurred.

As if to punctuate the point, Pete began pulsing jism without any warning. Chug let it happen, feeling the sizzle drench his hand, snickering at his effect on me. Once again reinforced. With the other hand, he reached under the mattress and pulled out a towel stuffed there for just this contingency, as I had discovered. After cleaning himself, he draped it on still babbling Pete. My nocturnal emissions were well-documented in just the short time I had been a part of the household. Chug had armed himself. Flushing, more from release than embarrassment, I wiped as he chortled.

"Go to sleep. Horn Dog." And then rested his hand on my thigh. Wow, I liked having a real brother.

January, 1993

"Look at the teensy thing, Chug. She's freezing out here." The little black and white spotted puppy with a piebald face gazed forlornly into my eyes, recognizing a kindred spirit. The mite of a baby had been hanging around outside T.C. Jester dormitory tower for the past three days. I had delivered milk and crackers in a bowl twice already, hiding it around the corner amongst some bushes. She readily gobbled the mix, peering up appealingly both times after finishing, telling me, 'Please, Sir, I want some more.' Shades of Dickensian desire.

It had killed me to leave her then, on my way to physics and organic chemistry labs as I had been. But, the pipsqueak was still in place, waiting, on this brisk Saturday morning as Chug and I emerged for our weekend ten-mile loop. An hour later, the urchin bowed at me in playful invitation when we strode back up the steps, front paws splayed down and out, little butt wiggling out of control up and back, frenetic wiggle of coccygeal smiles daring me to pass her by. Chug reminded me of our commitments for the day. I regretfully scruffed her ears in a tacit pledge. The baby 'yip' tore me to pieces.

After the vanguard coolness had filtered through the Hill Country as augur of the main course to come, the predicted cold front blustered through the city in the coming night, winds howling around our tenth-floor windows. Frozen raindrops pinged icily off glass panes over ensuing hours, causing snowballing of angst at thoughts of the orphan shivering by a drafty corner of the big dorm complex. Finally, at 3:30 AM, I couldn't bear it any longer.

Rising, I noisily cavorted around our suite, bouncing and rattling in and out of the study carrel and closet, then the bathroom shared with our suitemates, Hamilton and Kevin. The two banged on the wall twice in signal to cut the shit out; Chug persisted in feigning sleep through my rudeness. He plainly preferred warmness of bed to a reckoning with the cold onslaught outside our windows.

Not a fan of such weather, hunkering down was his method for dealing with rare wintry snaps that reached Austin. Upon a third accidental ramming of his bedside, the last time carelessly yanking covers from his nude form, he had groaned and shivered. Grumbling mightily, nary a word passing his lips, he moodily acquiesced to plaints for an early Sunday run. I knew it to be my only viable option for possible success. It worked.

Body-stretching at Jester's cornerstone, I spied the quaking bundle of spots hunkering beneath some ventilated bushes. Ongoing lobbying efforts intensified. My harangue in her behalf was merciless. Still wordless, my roommate grimaced from her to me, finally shrugging in resignation. Brooking no chance for reneging on implicit acceptance, the tiny ball of fur was hastily bundled into my sweatshirt. We slinked back through the commons to north wing elevators, dinging the up button repeatedly until the slow machine finally admitted us, ascending once again to 1029.

Not a sound emanated from any room as we passed, even hardy partiers sacked out and snoring what with the monster storm now blowing. Entering the room, Chug sat and watched, sleepily acknowledging my ministrations for buffing the baby dog with a towel and then wrapping her in another. Exhausted, the little thing yawned contentedly at me as I placed her under my bed covers, tucking into warmth. Just ears and closed eyes remained visible. Asleep in seconds flat. I was finally mollified. Baby waif was safe.

Chug growled groggily, still miffed, "Are we going or not, you idiot?" It was not yet 4 AM.

Flipping up my hoodie, I strode to the door, backward glancing to assure myself of her sleep mode, then opened it. Sweeping an arm in a grandiose gesture, I beckoned a reluctant partner to join me.

Over 60 minutes, we made way south on Colorado Street to Town Lake, thence proceeding on well-trod trails over darkened paths marking a favorite loop. Not today, though, Chug's demeanor reflected. Uncharacteristically quiet, invitations to manhandle and horseplay went unanswered. I sulkily settled for the plodding pace set by our freezing feet, passing miles in stone cold silence. Weather was responsible for only a part of that chilliness.

Climbing graded inclines back up to campus, the gusty norther buffeted relentlessly. Sleet stung exposed faces and legs. By the time of return to the elevator, Chug stared me down frostily, "Can I go back to bed now, Massa?" It made me laugh out loud. He gave up a miniscule glimmer of a smile, according me understanding of forgiveness. Endorphin release had by now kicked him into a comfort zone. I ringed my elbow around his neck in gratitude. He punched me.

Entering the dorm room, my first glimpse locked on a knocked-out pup. Unmoved and unmoving. Nose tip barely visible from under blankets. I checked for breathing. Smelling puppy breath, sans shivers, I let the sleeping pup lie.

Chug stripped upon crossing the threshold, strewing frozen, ice-laden layers across the floor. His gilded skin glistened and Little Chug nestled in shriveled cloister, little guy doubling down on expressions of disapproval, mirroring an unsmiling topside mien. "Whadaya' starin' at, Godzilla? We ain't all horse hung." Voicing the opposite of my assessment. I thought the tyke was adorable as he was, telling him so. "Well, just don't be tryin' to wake HIM up, too. One of us is enough," he groused, disappearing into a hot shower. Steam was soon billowing from the communal area. I brewed strong coffee in our small pot and prepped a cup the way he liked it--- latte style.

Twenty minutes it took before the freshman re-emerged, rubbing his head with a towel in sniffing a path through the doorway, following his cute nose to steaming cup. Perusal of the pup brought a look of approval, softie that he was, "Boy, she is sacked, huh? Looks like Mary Magdalene after a Jesus fix." The sacrilegious connotation fit. She did look pretty blissful. "I don't know what you're plannin', though, LL. Ya' know she's not allowed in the dorm...right?"

That thought had bothered me since a first sighting days before, yet didn't change anything. She had to be helped. We would just figure something out. The little imp wasn't going to be put out. At least not unless I went with her, as the adage went. A remarkably prescient pledge as it turned out.

Over ensuing days, then weeks, the pup revived remarkably. I made a tiny sand box for her in a corner, assembling pet bowls and such from a secondhand thrift shop on Guadalupe Street. She owned them immediately, herding Chug and me towards the set every time we walked close. Oliver Twist had to be in her bloodline, I induced. She wasn't shy in the slightest.

While basically a quiet little thing, soft warbles and chirps grew demonstrative. Her head would cock like RCA Victor dog from days-of-yore in adorable relief, completely absconding with Chug's or my ability to ignore. She figured out buttons to push for whatever came into her bright-eyed little head. Expressions emoting from her were priceless.

Chug tried dubbing her Vicki for a while, but she and I both knew her proper name to be Magda Lena... after Lady Magdalene. She affirmed herself in it the first time it passed my lips. Chug persisted a bit longer but finally surrendered. Magda became a fixture. Not having to leave the dorm room for almost two months, except when we spirited her outside through nocturnally deserted hallways for runs with one or both of us, good luck held at first. Our suitemates noticed odd odors and funny emanations through our shared bathroom but held the confidence by unspoken obliviousness.

The kicker finally came, though, one morning when we were returning, pre-dawn, from a good loop around campus. Mr. Gladner was waiting at the double glass foyer doors when we arrived, Magda all over him in a quick second. The dorm manager, lenient and kindly most times, stood toe-tapping as she jumped him. "Ahh, so this is the clandestine virtuoso bedecking our edifice with mystery, of whom I have heard whispers. Hello, mighty mite-ress," he bent down and patted Magda a moment. Standing, he looked between the two of us, "You are aware, men, of rubrics set in stone regarding her presence. Correct?"

Dishonorably busted, we colored by flushing, saying nothing. What was there to say? Halfway through the semester, two days before Spring Break, facts spoke for themselves. We were allotted three days to place her elsewhere, or we, ourselves, would be in need of alternate accommodations.

Dejectedly entering the building after such an ultimatum, unsure of how to digest the dilemma, we were abruptly bowled over by a whirlwind figure bustling against our inward trajectory. A blond ponytail whipped back and forth in weaponized lashes, smacking Chug repeatedly across a surprised face. Then the whirling dervish came to a stop, realizing proximity to a victim just attacked.

"Oh, so sorry about that, I'm…" and in fractions of a second, Chug found himself face-to-face with our old stablemate, Jill. "I'm… oh my gosh, Chug! I am…blow me away…it is you… and you, too, Luke. Well, who is this--- cute as can be?" Magda hadn't been surprised in the least by this new presence, licking a tanned leg in greeting as if it belonged in her life.

Jill squatted down, wrapping the pup in her arms. Rising up, two tongues worked furiously, one wagging words, another slurping cheeks. Long lost chums, immediately, the girl cooed at her and then us. "What a surprise…actually a bunch of them. Do you guys live here? I didn't know they let dogs stay, too. My friend Emily is going to be happy to hear that--- she's missing her baby sooo much. She's in the coed wing up on seventh floor. Hates her roommate and is in new-found love with this boy, so she is wanting her dog a bunch right now. We're going out later this morning to look for a house." The bubbliness arrested us to stock still quiet, absorbing unexpected energy in a maelstrom of words. "It is so good to see you both." As her eyes locked onto Chug. Suddenly, I was an accoutrement.

We all took a collective breath before the two eye-latched people talked at once. "We just found out…," he began; she interposed, "Are you still cross-countrying?" They laughed together at the awkwardness, then backed off another second.

"Gee, Jill, you look amazing…like always. Sorry, I must stink baddd…we are just finishing a run," in an ungainly sniff at a ripe pit, he appeared ready to spill all his secrets to her in one-minute flat. I could tell by the gawping expression. He was bashful here in front of the most beautiful girl ever to cross his vision. As I knew, and he did but didn't. That's how nonplussed the boy was at the moment. Most definitely cross-eyed.

"That is so sweet, Chug, or are you going by Charles now?" She obviously had done her homework on my buddy. The high school homecoming queen who had graduated a year before us stood here, having matured from petite prettiness of prep days into a great beauty. New grace of carriage balanced by youthful glow and vivacity now imbued her with truly Miss America looks. Chug was noticeably tongue-tied and dick-headed.

I stood back as the two reacquainted, enjoying a view of two attractive persons, seeing more than either of them. Having always understood the look of puppy-doggedness in Chug's eyes when she came near, back in stable days, I presently saw similar characteristics flashing over hers. They liked each other. A lot.

Several minutes passed as they chatted, when suddenly, Magda gave a mini-whimper. Desiring to stand on her own. It burst the bubble enveloping them. Jill kissed the puppy, putting her down. The licks took up on my own legs and I leaned over to rub ears. "Oh, my goodness," Jill exclaimed, "How rude. Luke, we've just been ignoring you. That's so mean." The sincerity was filed away: this was a real person. Chug needed to know her. Go, boy, I shouted inwardly.

"No biggie. I'm breathless watching the two of you. I didn't know that many words could fit into so short a time. You two are amazing."

At the comment, both of them seemed to curl back from one another, making a space that hadn't been there a moment before. They became aware of more than just small-talk between themselves. It was cute as heck. I drew Magda to my side and told them I needed to get her in before morning traffic began. We were already in the proverbial doghouse, I said, and didn't want to compound things. Excusing myself, I hugged Jill and winked at Chug, pulling my own little girlfriend inside.

Over a slow, methodical, soaking shower, I contemplated these two friends. My best bud and past stable partner, Jill. There was chemistry there for anyone to see. It scared me a little, but brimmed me over at the same time. Sensations of something big were horizonal. I sat with Magda on my lap for an hour, studying physical properties of magnetism for physics. Metaphysical transference to psychological analogies kept invading my concentration, wrapping around magnetic qualities I had just witnessed, before Chug finally rattled our soon-to-be-ex-doorknob.

MARCH, 1994

"They are the cutest, most perky little nipple twins you could ever hope to squeeze and suckle, Luke," Chug was exuberant. After three Dos Equis' and half a dozen oysters, the boy was opened up like a jade gate on a wedding night. "Each morning when I wake up, the first thought in my head is that I've won the Trifecta."

"Well, by definition, Chug, you kinda have, dude." The wryness in my tone made him glance up from his preparation of the next straight-boy aphrodisiac, twinkling eyes aglitter. "Just thinking about her gets Little Chug a'fattenin' up, Luke. I'm gettin' more and better with each passing day. Damn, who would've ever thought? How's 'bout you, buddy, you stayin' happy? Any one rockin' your world right now?"

"I'm a monk, Chug. Ain't looking for nothin'. Nothin' looking for me. Magda and I are doing just fine, thank you very much. The books and stuff, plus runnin', that keeps us happy. Wish you and me could do some more miles, though. We're not that far apart, you know." My boy failed to respond.

I starkly missed that part of the two of us. He was mentor for that outlet of mine, after all. Now, what with him so pussy-whipped and our horse boys back home with Chug's younger brothers, there was a big hole where all that had thrived. Even after joining the university track team, without him along the ride was a little lonesome. I missed him.

Over the last year, scenery between us had changed. Elementally. Charlie Chug, my best man, was on the brink of putting that appellation on my shoulders. He and Jill had set a date and I was to be just that. His best man. Serendipity had burst the bubble of bachelorhood for my friend a year before on the early spring morning he and Jill bumped into one another. "She isn't pregnant, is she?" His ebullience brought the idea into my head.

"Hell, no, you know we're on 'the pill', and stayin' that way. It's gonna be years before we take that leap." The cocky confidence made me laugh. Where had we all heard those famous last words? But, I really did hold high hopes my two closest friends would do that. A family at this stage could change things even more than they already had. These two were head-over-heels in love enough to be twisted should expansion plans take root. Career courses might take on a different hue, if so. Surely, they were considering that. Chug was intent on an advanced degree in mechanical engineering and Jill was on track for a law degree. UT was Texas Mecca for both. Positioning couldn't be better. Hence, my hopes.

The crowd in Dry Dock had picked up in the last thirty minutes; noise levels intensified with it. We shared another beer and dozen oysters, then decided to call it an evening. I needed to study. And I missed my girl. Magda was my constant companion now that we had established a home on 28½th Street.

Bottom floor of the funky bungalow had come on my radar after a humiliating boot from Jester the previous year. What with Chug's move into Jill's new place--- a house on Greek Row she shared with Emily and Dave--- the little place had proved a godsend. The artists living upstairs from us were perfect housemates. Quiet and into their crafts. So, we were pretty much set.

"You doing anything new with the team, now? I know you run faster than anyone I've ever seen---in one place--- but you sure can go forever. They invite you to up the ante yet?" I just shook my head. He had encouraged me to take things to next level, but enjoyment of companionship with Magda and taxi team status were enough. I could keep focused on a medical degree better without hassles or interruptions. Study, my dog and home track meets were plenty. I was content.

"Just remember, Luke, all work and no play can turn you into a bitter young guy. You need an outlet for that little big man in those shorts. I know you too well. Want me to jack you off, or sumpin-sumpin?" He was pulling my leg, I was aware, but at mention of former chumminess on that score, my junk lurched of its own accord. Damn, that was another facet of our friendship I missed. For a straight man, he sure didn't have many hang ups. I'd never find that again, I thought. Never mind, though.

The five-finger jig was well-attuned for my needs. No prob, I reassured myself.

Turning away from him out on the street a half hour later, bewildering pangs of regret permeated me. Unexpectedly. I grasped the loss of familiarity as something for which my hand could never substitute. A lonesome tear rolled from my cheek to pavement as I turned back to see him fade into shadows. On the way home, I reflected on the callous twists and turns of Lady Fate.

October, 1995

A month into first semester of med school. I knew immediately that I was in the place and position meant to be. A natural acumen for the field emerged and with it, discovery of a scholastic home. The branch of learning birthed burdens of previously unfathomed responsibility due to erudite demands. Philosophies and theories unencountered prior to this exposure tasked me as never before. Finally.

It also awakened need for a strict abiding set of dictates guiding day-to-day routines, forcing development of a battle plan to keep on required track for successful navigation of challenges to capabilities. Adult strategies replaced simplistic teenage thought-processes. Different sets of trials and duties not apprehended in a more juvenile era now urged my conscience.

By developing abilities, subliminal fears harbored over the previous year regarding my young ward, the pointer Magda Lena, uncovered not only evidence of existential foundation for qualms, but also fresh avenues for comprehension of them. Surreptitious testing of Magda with the aid of a curious and sympathetic senior med student by clandestine means proved providential. And devastating.

Magda was discovered to be living with a genetic cardiac anomaly for which sole cure was a complete heart transplant. And that, only should I figure a way for her transmogrification to human status. Having noticed a few incidents of vague symptoms arousing worry genes in my brain, the set of diagnostics had been manipulated to establish or repudiate concerns. Results were definitive. Though not surprised, it still staggered. The girl was my life. She, and only she, knew me. Anticipated every move, read every mood, provided succor in time of need.

I found myself burdened by powerlessness to alleviate the threat in her defense. Confiding in a particularly benevolent cardiology professor, a dressing down delivered for unauthorized covert diagnostic workup was followed with heartbreaking confirmation that I might expect one to two years of relatively healthy time with her before a slow descent toward death would occur. And that, if there were no catastrophic events which could take her abruptly.

The furry light of my life remained unfazed. Bright eyes and smiling tail animated our days as reality settled in. Involving her in every aspect of my training regimen was my solution. Cardiopulmonary vestment and fortification could help extend her time. I was rationalizing, of course, yet the lifestyle suited us both, so daily protocol was made easy by acting on it. She thrived.

I savored every romp, run, playtime, naptime and love time inordinately. Every dawn, sunrise, morning, afternoon, evening, and nighttime were gifts. She returned everything fivefold. The dog had to know, I surmised. Somehow, this sprite of a being had demanded entry into my life just when she realized I would need it most. She was my rock. And, she now carried an expiration date.

Most of my early med school professors were charmed by the handsome pointer mix, letting her sit outside didactic classes in wait for my return, wagging and licking her way into hearts of classmates. The track coach made her our team's mascot, exampling her enthusiasm as a catalyst. Probably, I rationalized, she was the real reason I was allowed to remain on the taxi team, filling in for injured or ill regulars. It certainly could not be a result of my running forte. That didn't excel, at least on the collegiate level.

Whatever it was, it all worked to keep the girl contented… thus allowing the same for myself.

The time spent over an unforgettable summer on the shores of Lake Cutaway had opened me up to the art and benefits of all things massage. Minnesota Laughlin branch members of my family were heightened in their knowledge and practice of such modalities. Trade-out rubdowns were commonplace. I had gleaned then that the fine sense of touch was not the sin taught and reinforced at 'home' in the forsaken Evangelicalville of my upbringing.

Maintaining dedication even now, it was incorporated into our regimen for my favorite lady. Magda greedily assumed 'the position' upon gathering my intent each day, luxuriating in shared closeness and therapeutic profits from lymph clearance, circulatory stimulation and suppleness factors resultant to ministrations. Deepening our bond in the process. I gained as much from these intimacies as her. Hoping to extrapolate the practice to a wider range of beneficiaries in future times, I kept proficient.

Med School, indeed, proved to be my natural niche. Discipline instilled by the complexities involved both challenged and widened horizons. It was, as I already knew, where I should be. I felt way fortunate to have figured it out. Nimble reactions and dexterous rationality necessary to succeed with the principles and precepts made me tick. Puzzles with ramifications.

The youthful entry afforded me by an uncommon acceptance into a profession mostly reserved for older, more mature candidates hit my consciousness as the only aberration to a lifelong motif heretofore experienced: 'early to bud; late to bloom'.

Aunt Ella begged to differ. The wise lady confirmed and validated me, visiting Austin regularly in support of a boy's life course; the matriarchal figure missing from reality. Always taking a room at the quaint B&B around the corner from my bungalow, two of us ranged widely through topics meant to expand an intellectual radar over marathon coffee and tea rendezvous'. Starbucks profited by our patronage. She strongly reinforced the concept that the present road was a true calling. I grasped the conduit to a solid mission's province. Virtual blinders kept my brain straining forward, prize visible in the distance.

Unfortunate double-headedness peculiar to gender would come perilously close to spawning a derailment. The proverbial snake in the grass... err... pants... had yet to rear its own demanding, tunnel-visioned head. An erotic incident in oak woods off Zilker Park south of downtown Austin earlier that year had left indelible imprint. I would awaken in wee hours, Magda's head cradled in my arm, breaths puffing comfortingly over chest or shoulder, to aching engorgements consuming the celibate rascal Pete.

Nocturnal emissions increasingly soiled sheets, the quintuple jig unable to satisfy teenage hormonal spikes. Dreamscapes now encompassed recurrent variations on the erotic scenario played out that memorable morning. The sweetest short story on my porn-scope. When I had my rocks knocked off by the hairy satyr now torturing an overactive Id. Cravings of a missing link hounded me mercilessly, awakening unfulfilled desires barely tamped down by force of will since that incident. Until it all changed…

…An evening thunderstorm was not on weather radar. I had checked before leaving for an overdue running loop to clear my head and satisfy Magda's inherent need. We had just passed Dobie Mall on Guadalupe Street as the first big drops of rain hit sizzling pavement, super-heated by an Indian Summer hot wave. Steam and rain fragrance lofted over my nostrils. We zagged onto Pearl Street for detour under awnings known to line a less-traveled thruway.

We were soaked anyway by a sudden onslaught of wetness within another two blocks. Sopping curls plastered my face, impeding clear vision. Missing a large crack in the uneven sidewalk, an ankle caught an edge. The rain-slicked surface guided the unbraced joint to an angle, stretching a ligament to unsupportable limits. Tumbling down, I hit my hip, barely missing Magda on the way, ending in a heap. Knee scraped, hip aching and ankle unforgiving, I sat, massaging the injured locomotor. A low growl from Magda alerted me to presence. Glancing up, rain pelted my face in fuzzy visualization of a figure leaning over me.

"Looks like you bunged it up, by the swelling, boy. It's turning colors, too--- does it hurt?" The question didn't carry much tonal sympathy but the deepness struck a chord. Shushing Magda, I focused on the figure, putting together a picture of the familiar form identifying as the man of color often visiting my dreams since those lips of his had robbed Pete so ably, months before. The satyr.

"Yeah, it does. I hit a d-damn curb the wrong way and next thing I know, h-here I am," I griped. The goateed guy squatted down next to me

THE MANDRAKES · 73

and reached, touching the swollen joint. I winced at the contact. "Hey, c-careful, dude. That h-hurts."

'I think we oughta get you--- and her--- out of this storm, a'ight?" Rain splotched glasses, new to his look, cocked awkwardly at the tip of his broad nose. It cartooned his look. I laughed despite myself. "Good answer." The man had mistaken the response. With that, he handed my arm, hoisting upward in an easy move. Muscles in his forearm and bicep rasped against me on the way, reminding of the previous encounter by purposely provocative friction then. Pete noticed.

"Here, runner boy, let's go this way." Magda followed, wary in her distrust of this person, same as before. The manhandler guided us around a shrouded corner two buildings away. Accepting help, I leaned into the shorter man, causing further contact. By the time we reached a small metal door under a shallow overhang, cold rain was causing pinprickles by contrast to otherwise extremely hot weather. Added stimulus. I made out an innocuous sign over the door, 'Delivery Entrance for Pearl Street Warehouse: Austin's Premiere Dance Bar'.

Pounding on the door, he looked me up and down as we waited, "I DJ here some nights. We can get dried off and take a look," nodding downward at my black and blue ankle.

In a minute, a young guy opened, peeking out into the rain. Seeing my helper, he cracked a grin, "Marsh, hey bro. Get on in, I'm gettin' wet." He stood aside while we clumsily stepped up through the doorway, Magda hopping up behind. The guy looked surprised, "Hey, I don't think Jesse's gonna like that dog comin' in...maybe it should stay outside."

"Nah, Gerald, it's with us---well, him," gesturing at me, "found him a couple doors down with that."

The added gesture toward my ankle got lost in Gerald's track downward, alighting on my now swollen crotch. Pete was remembering, all right. And totally ignoring the more pressing matter of my injury, he had decided to make an appearance, obviously thinking re-acquaintance. Ahem, I reflected, flushing deeply at attention to the wrong joint. Gerald's eyes widened in astonishment as Pete's big crown took the liberty of peeking out from under suddenly inadequate coverage.

Grinning more, the black man named Marsh bounced looks in triangular fashion, noting Pete and my face before looking at Gerald, "Don't worry, Gerald, my man, I got this. We know each other. Could you get some ice and a clean towel...purty please?" The engrossed younger man turned slowly away--- at least his body did--- following the directive. Lips were licked by flicking of his tongue as the head only reluctantly followed along. It swiveled a couple times more as the body receded into a cross hallway behind.

"Wow, runner boy, glad to see me, huh?" His cockiness exuded the same confidence I remembered from the meadow those months ago. "Well, first-things-first, I always say," he joked. He led toward a small receiving counter, hoisting me effortlessly up and onto it. Leaning over, a burly shoulder purposely banged against my malcontented organ on the way down to loosen a shoelace. Again, on the way up with my sodden Tiger running shoe, the nappy familiarity of the ebony forearm jostled Pete.

The imbecile sproinged straight up into hover position from under the useless pouch enclosure of my shorts. Like a bobblehead doll. I watched, unable to even attempt covering the idiot. Not hesitating for a split second, this Marsh man deepthroated Pete in one fell swoop, throat rolling around the sensitive head, nose nuzzling pubes. The lightning bolt to my senses was not weather-related.

He stayed planted in that position for several seconds, until a scurrying Gerald burst around the corner carrying a cup of crushed ice and a hand towel. On his heels were two other people. One, a made-up, half-dressed male in a kimono, and another, a bluejeaned bearded man wearing a wife-beater undershirt. Shit, I thought, what in hell had I gotten myself into? As this question gelled in my head, the three bumped and grinded over one another through their headlong rush around the corner into the room. Apparently, Pete's precocious peeping had sent a message ahead with Gerald. Or else they didn't want the ice to melt.

The man called Marsh finally rose up off my companion. Not from an act of busted humility--- no, he just needed a breath of air. Pete preened in front of newcomers. A slimy rope of saliva mixed with several drips of precum slid by gravitational law onto rain-wet belly. Unlike an erstwhile thinker-in-chief formerly known as a brain, which reasoned my face to a quick place of reddened embarrassment--- it told me I was a total stranger here--- Pete waggled his way into boastful arch of conceit particularly preferred by his rarely seen blooded swell. The big-headed show-off.

"OK, let's see what we can do 'bout this swelling," nodding with a smirk toward the offended ankle below. He reached for ice and towel, rolling former into latter, then applied it wrap-fashion around the black-and-blueness. Reaching one-handed, he hoisted his t-shirt--- I recalled the signature move--- over his head, using it as a tie with which to secure the cold pack.

All this time, three sets of eyes ogled the cyclops. Like deer caught in headlights. What ankle? Their collective retinae pondered. My blushing arm mimicked the Marsh-man's move, using the single-swipe method in an overhead removal of soaked running singlet, shortly blotting out Pete's audacious dangle. Six eyes dropped in disappointment. The sculpted mowhawker's cocoa fingers encircled the shirt enwrapping a now-hidden shaft, grasping it like a stick shift.

"OK, folks, good of you to help, now let runner boy here have a minute to let the thing rest...'K?" The continued snarky grin acknowledged not a scintilla of self-effacement for his previous oral action.

"Really, Gerald, and Sonny... and Dee... pull 'em back inside your heads. I need to speak to the young man in private. Can you give us a second?" Even in my state of discombobulation, I questioned that. The three grumbled through an exit, but did so. Thank God, showtime was over. I sighed in relief.

"We really should get this elevated, boy." I mistook once again, what with his hand continuing to pulse Pete. "No, I mean the ankle. It needs to be raised up." The hand departed and repositioned under my knees, other arm and hand supporting my back. Cradling me now, he glanced down at Magda, good dog that she was, nodded to her, then proceeded to the cross hallway.

Instead of turning the way the three had just gone, he turned right. We went down a darkened way until an internal glass window appeared. In passing, I could see that it sided a DJ booth. Various sound-tracking and music-producing machines and devices littered the room, haphazardly strewn in a semi-semblance of functional disarray.

Jostling the knob on an adjacent door, he pushed it open, again signaling OK to my girl. Carefully leading with my dangling legs, we three entered. He headed for a couch on the far wall, covered in music paraphernalia, record and CD covers, etcetera. With one foot, Marsh swiped at the mess, sweeping stuff to the floor, then placed me gently on to threadbare cushions, backed up to one armrest.

Checking the tied ankle bandage once more and finding it adequate, he turned and twisted a plastic pull on window blinds. Magda settled into a corner, lying in a pose intent on keeping me in sight, watching as the shirtless helper came over and sat on the couch edge. A big hand braced itself as he leaned into me, strategically grazing Pete in pass by. Pete wasn't wilting at all; the compact muscle man seemed relieved by that fact. The hand stayed. Pete just throbbed.

"So, we meet again," the comment was monotone but meaningful. He looked into my eyes, locking on, again sizing me up, adding, "I knew it was just a matter of time. Just surprised it's at this place. You don't seem like the type to be around here. Name's Marsh--- yours?" The palm felt warm but my nipples were chilled, both tipping up in an erect posture by dichotomous effects.

"It's---uhh---it's uh, L-Luke…L-Luke, yeah, Luke…" Why did I stutter like this in the man's presence, I frowned? It was the more embarrassing of embarrassing things I had done in his company. Same as before, out on Zilker Park field.

"Ya' sure 'bout that, now…Luke, yeah, Luke?" His mocking was meant to confuse. The mimic exacerbated the act. Deepening my humiliation. At least we were alone. As thoughts burned through my degraded psyche, the hand wheedled Pete. Making intentions plain.

Seeing my transparency, he grinned another time, "Yeah, I'm a'gonna definitely do that." Slow squeeze. Covering singlet was pulled free by Marsh's dexterous snatch. Pete popped up, looking for something he'd mislaid. 'Ohhh, yes,' Pete mimed, 'it was that set of lips.' No more words, but those lips functioned in alternate mode, suckling the head, making it jump, then massaging their way southward. Ending in a sponge-lock of muscular mastery.

I forgot the aching ankle, eyes rolling back in my own signature move, completely under the man's spell. His sidelong stare at my face certainly milked the knowledge. We stayed rigidly joined, rhythmically jutting into one another, head to crotch, for a matter of three minutes--- tops--- before Pete spouted happily. Like a whale blowing. Spurting spume, hotly lining the oral cavity controlling me. The talented mouth never misplaced a single drop, repeating the glugging effect also memorable from our initial meeting.

The same look of contented repletion faced me when Marsh finally resurfaced, leaving me to wonder how anybody could enjoy the deed just finished. To my teenage mind, possibility of fulfilment in such a subservient role was alien. My prude self couldn't quite grasp the notion at this stage in life. Yet, there was no denying the absolute gratification Pete and I derived--- and badly wanted to re-visit.

A soft twittering of background noise following Pete's explosion alerted us to prurient eyes persistent in voyeuristic penchant. I was mortified by the audience through the 'closed' blinds; Marsh seemed proud by the display... go figure. I would need time to process that information.

As he wiped both of us with the wet singlet, a rap on the door interrupted. I hastily pulled up my shorts, attempted slapping Pete into submission, and observed Marsh's mouth raise in a smile. The man stood up, turned to the door, and opened it. Smeared lips, dishevelment and mostly bare naked state remained unadjusted, mysterious lump in the man's pants still unrevealed.

A Coolio-like personage entered the room, scanned the two of us, sniffed grungy odors pervading the close confines, then set down a stack of CD's in his arms. A wide mouth turned down in a way that still rolled up on the edges enough to equate an odd smile, haughtiness evident. "Well, it sho' do be a queer bar now, don' it, bitches? Which one did da'deed to who, now, yo?" He deliberately looked from us, then over to Magda from her place in the corner, then back...

...Marsh deposited Magda and me in our bungalow an hour after that, positioning me on the couch with the wrapped ankle propped on a pillow. The severe thunderstorm had deluged the city for the entirety of my second adult blowjob. Peeping toms, thomasina's and Coolio-types included.

"Still on the top-two dick list, runner boy. Been awhile, huh? You kinda torpedoed my tonsils by that e-rup-shun. Sweet stuff. Repeats to the front o' the line. Keep limber, runner boy." Straightening up, he cockily swaggered toward the door. The still bare muscle-laden back undulated with each step. Just before the door clicked closed behind him, I picked up on the parting quip. "Stay tuned."

Yup, the Devil Incarnate.

Three weeks had elapsed since the fartlek in the thunderstorm. Limiting myself to gym workouts and non-running cardio drills to keep Magda at least minimally satisfied, she and I suffered through the period. Dramatically. My mind wandered, studies lagged, nutrition was overlooked and even Pete was ignored. All not good. Magda exhibited cabin fever symptoms throughout the spell and by the time for the stabilizing ankle boot removal, both of us were near zombie state.

Mid-term exams were in the rearview mirror now, and imperfections regarding my performance had materialized. Dr. Bonnet, first year anatomy professor, and Dr. Nelson, intro physiology prof, had both called me in. Counsel with the two had led to takeaways that they wondered about readiness for the curriculum, even though both grades had come back as B's. Being the youngest class member, my inclusion had apparently been based on expectations of perfection; therefore, their concerns.

I assured the two of my complete dedication and wherewithal, assigning the bummed ankle a point of rationale for them. Their response that perhaps outside interests--- meaning running--- may need curtailment appalled my psyche, what with the investment and benefits drawn from the involvement. I promised, however, to adhere to a strict convalescence regimen and keep side-effects, i.e. injuries, to a minimum in the future. Whatever the reasons, I was informed, the subject may need revisiting.

I conveniently ignored mentioning the true distraction pulling on my concentration and drive because it was something refused admission even to myself. Looking back, if only Magda could have talked, perhaps things would have unfolded differently. I rehashed the recent three weeks, still in denial of truth, as I warmed to an elemental change without hearkening to facts of matters. It had all begun at the free weights gym within days of applying the ankle boot…

… I hoisted the curling barbells in supine repetitions and attempted to blot out the free weights gym now providing the majority of physical fitness work. This was definitely not my cup-o'-tea, I gritted teeth for an umpteenth time. A perpetual frown perfused not just my face, but my aura. I hated this. Poor Pitiful Pearl's sorry lot in life seemed jovial by comparison. The curling repetitions gnawed at me.

Magda must be frantic, alone at home yet again. The gym manager refused to allow her to even sit outside the doors to the free weights wing of the sprawling athletic complex on campus. She and I chalked up the snub to plain meanness by the words thrown at us when I had put in an insignificant dispensational request. Nastiness in utter refusal seemed awfully personal, somehow. I had given my word, though, and intended that to mean something. So, the suffering.

Now, centering on the fact I would be able to begin brief walking routines in coming days, incorporating this stupid and cumbersome boot, I welcomed a miniscule flicker of light at the end of the tunnel. Absorbed in aloofness and self-pity, I didn't notice a shadow darkening my own until the deep voice broke into a cloistered world.

"That's probably not the best use for those, runner boy." The intrusion made me wince as I jumped at the familiar sotto resonance, recognizing it at once. "Wow, sorry to wake your baby ass up, Champ. You look like death warmed over. Wassup?"

Marsh stood studying my technique, a few feet to my side, big arms pumped up by recent exertion. Blood vessels protruded like veritable garden hoses, snaking up and down the skin beneath the hairiness. Huge thighs and legs looked to be nearly ready to burst by their size. Tiny weight-lifter shorts bulged, as well, and my visage must've spoken volumes.

A toothy smile lit me up, teasing, "Damn, bro, you 'bout ready to get all up on this, or somethin'? That face o' yours is sure tellin' a story, now." Already red from my own exertion, I couldn't shade too much more—at least there was that, I thought. The heat of the blush still raised my temp, anyway.

"Hey, what'ya doin' here? Ain't never seen your ass on this side of 'da fence'. Thought you was a cross-country free spirit. Where's your track side at? You get banned, or sumpin'?" He was genuinely curious. It was the first time I could recall sincerity of any sort in his demeanor. I nervously stuttered through explaining the situation as he nodded comprehension.

"That's right, runner boy--- Luke, right? You done bunged up an ankle that day. Now I remember. When you came over to da' dark side, huh?" The mocking tone re-asserted itself. "The day I helped out with that ole' swelled joint, a'ight?"

Several dozen people were working out across the expansive weight gym. The man's allusion to our last meeting raised sudden fear that Pete might be listening; I felt a pang of anxiety. The little man between my legs had been unusually quiet and undemanding of late. Appearance of this man had brought tumult both times I had encountered him. Even though events had included distinct pleasure, I had no desire to broker a revisitation of previous situations. At least, not here.

The perceptive person scrutinizing me gathered as much. "Hey, how's 'bout we check outta here and catch some coffee. You should be getting' to know me some, a'ight?" Mixture of vernacular with an obvious ability at articulation was proving just another layer of confusing contrasts for me. I couldn't figure the person for what he truly was: thug or intellectual. The amalgam of evidence he broadcasted allowed for little categorization.

Without thinking, I responded, "OK, muscle-man, why don't we just do that? I'm finished anyway and can't stand any of this. Let's go." His look of surprise caught me. It wasn't what I expected. Again.

"Whoa, bronc. Now, where'd that come from, runner boy? You just showed me something new--- what about that?" That reply made me think. It took a minute to appreciate a sudden non-stuttering self in actual dialog with him. That had been a first. I felt bigger by the doing. And proud of myself.

He helped put misused weights back on racks, then we headed to the locker room. Unlike the track and field locker room, this one had private lockers and individual showers. I stripped, a bit warily, still unsure whether Pete might act out, and headed to an adjacent stall.

Marsh had disappeared around the corner on entering, saying he'd meet up at the exit in a few… giving me a modicum of confidence I could avoid embarrassing myself. No one else seemed to be close by at present, fractionally increasing my comfort level.

Soaped up head to toes, boot blessedly off, and eyes glued shut to keep soap out, I suddenly felt a whisper of breeze as the shower curtain moved. Next thing I knew, a fondling set of fingers were swirling around my nutsack. The feeling was indescribable. So said Pete. And with that, feelings of confidence plummeted, then soared, almost at the same time.

A familiar set of lips took to adding extra stimulus to the fingering, then began working their way up--- yes, Pete was by now pointed that direction--- arriving at the top of the shaft just as I got soap rinsed away. No surprise the lips belonged to Marsh, but the fact of his butt ass naked state did shock me.

The largest ostrich-egg sized balls I'd ever laid eyes on hung in pendulous continuity below a handsome ebony prick, currently aiming directly at me. Not as large as Pete, the thing was nonetheless sizeable.

Marsh slowly massaged the package as he peered up from around the swelling that was 'TopTwo'.

His mouth continued its work and I watched two sets of male equipment, both at full mast, centering my vision. An attempt to reach down and touch the wondrous balls met with a head shake and off-angled glance into my eyes, disabusing me of the attempt.

Sight of the man's ministrations cranked pleasure factors for me as I followed the live porn, vicariously sensing his hand stroke the swarthy junk. Damn, it made Pete better. True to form, only a few minutes were necessary to bring my wilding child to the edge. But this time, as I felt the release without seeing the spurts, I wide-eyed as his own dick eye suddenly did its own ejac-dance. Creamy stuff smeared my shins, dribbling downward, noticeably hotter than the shower spray.

Our eyes remained in coordinated contact. Another first--- my own eyes hadn't caromed upwards in the signature roll back under my upper lids, per usual. I got to see the man's stuff do what it did. Swell and spurt. It was satisfying.

Experiencing a throat-glugging reprise, Pete spasmed happily inside the mouth being test-driven yet another time. Blackbeard, a nickname that jumped into mind for his own piece, bobbed up at me in its own rendition of release. It answered things. I understood a bit better that look of repletion by the visualization. My bursting had made his respond in kind. Things that make you go 'Hmmmmm'.

He arose, letting Pete fend for himself, body-bumping me all the way up, then turned and flushed his mouth with hot spray serving us both just then. A hand curled around my left buttcheek and squeezed hard-packed roundness. Those eyes returned to mine and, now grinning, exuded approval in a single hissing word, "Nice." Drawing out the single syllable to a New Orleanian paragraph. Sending me sky-rocketing, the sexy-lipped man set his full set up against mine and sank that tongue through the connection, using teeth to lightly nip my lower one. He held it, quite still, and stared.

I was blown away. Never had such sensuousness enveloped me. The hook had been set and I was reeled in, then and there. We had to sneak our separate ways out the stall to avoid detection in a now populated wet area. Pete languidly bobbled, still half-engorged, past more than one set of curious eyes on my way to the nearby locker. For once, I couldn't have cared less. Let 'em look, I sighed.

Twenty minutes later, we sat together chatting amiably in leather chairs at the on-campus student union. Who in Hell was this enigma across from me? It was one query repeatedly trekking around my now vacuous brain.

He described for me a start-up home healthcare agency recently launched, boasting several government contracts as clients and currently negotiating more. Adding new employees weekly, I was enlightened to a shrewdness of entrepreneurial ambition. The DJ job was about to be scrapped as time needed to pursue that was fast diminishing. It was, after all, only a hobby. Other details opened new acquaintance with this fascinating man. Bedazzled was I.

Through all the information processing, I vaguely heard him ask, 'Would I like to be his guest for dinner this Saturday evening?' And heard the answer--- would love to--- pass my lips without thinking. Nary a stumbling stutter. Marsh acted impressed at new-found confidence. Only later did the peculiarity dawn on me about lack of questions regarding my own private life. It was all about him.

We parted at the entrance to the on-campus gathering spot with promises to meet at my front door this coming weekend night. Feet never once touched ground, restricting boot back in place but forgotten, as I limp-waltzed home to find Magda. Sensing an abruptly improved mood, the girl romped happy circles around me in the neighborhood park abutting our street, rhapsodizing in her and my gladly revived camaraderie. I told her I was in love.

Billy T's Bistro on 15th Street will remain a memory as inaugural dress-up dinner date for a newbie med student and accomplished man of color. His stylish ways and now entirely articulate manner melted my defenses as red wine suffused brain cells. The effect was amazing. I again wondered who was this person suddenly attaching to me? Hell, who was I?

The urbanity of the upscale restaurant and soft live jazz in a corner of the old converted home lent atmosphere to an evening the like which I had never once known existed. Acting the supreme gentleman, Marsh beguiled me through sublime instructions for choosing, swirling, inhaling and imbibing good wine, ordering hors d'oeuvres, experiencing entrees, naming the music and charming the wait staff. A Man of the World, he was.

Suave badinage flowed effortlessly. This time, all centered on me. I made a mark, I could tell, upon answering his question regarding plans and dreams. The fact of my present place in UT Medical School widened this handsome, talented, sexy male's dark eyes. I had taken him by surprise, too, gleaning an alteration in demeanor following the admission. Marsh played a flawlessly winning tack in granting me a dash of innocent gravitas by the fact. He seemed more impressed. I savored validation.

Over Baked Alaska--- necessarily ordered before dinner, I registered--- and Italian espresso, with a twist of lime, the paradox named Marsh further ambushed my wits by leaning conspiratorially over an immaculate white tablecloth. Sensuously, he whispered, "Hey, Big Boy, you are aware how damn handsome you look tonight, sitting there in your vest with those curls all ringling down alongside your pretty man face, now, right? Well, it is true. I'm going to take you home and make da' love to you… can you handle that, Luke?" I had most undoubtedly arrived. And could. Handle that.

Inexperienced as I was in matters of love, the 'digestif' back at the bungalow took a quirky turn which once again left me bemused. Yet, in a good way. I had long feared the act of submissive consummation more than a little, even though desiring it. My solely theoretical familiarity combined with total lack of experience made it that way.

Strong arms led a way into the den and made their dominating presence felt, erotically teasing me in ways untried. After a half hour of exotic foreplay, including a sensuous virgin fingering with an excited ejaculatory surprise, onslaught of masculine domination twerked.

Double boners waggling, bouncing and leaking over one another, Marsh placed me forcefully on my back. Raising and spreading my legs, he erogenously massaged my hole with that muscly tongue. This newest sensory initiation had me gibbering ecstatically, never having thought of back entry as a site for that action.

Whoa, I thought, as I melted in Sambo-esque swirlings. The big ballsack was bound to be bouncing off my cheeks within minutes. I steeled my senses for what was about to come---and cum--- into my virgin chute, curiosity tinging me, when Marsh unpredictably about-faced.

Releasing ankles and climbing up on my lap, he slid Pete smoothly up into his own tightness. Splendid heat engulfed me. Sight of eyes rolling up in his head took me aback. Rising and descending onto my smooth belly, the thick neck arched; buffed arms braced down and behind. Watching the man's certifiably excellent bulging abdominals and layered pectorals tense undulantly, Blackbeard and the fat ones bounced off and on in added provocation. The entirety brought me to climax twice more in the coming minutes.

Through synchronous riding, Blackbeard squeezed off his own spew each time Pete swelled inside him. Shooting over my face and trailing down my chest in encore, a second time augmented the first drenching which surprised us upon his saddling up. We experienced battling orgasms. I was overcome by multiplicity, not aware that was in the playbook between two consenting adults, either.

So, expected pain of anal entry, never experienced before, was not to be. We sank together, cuddling in shared simultaneity. Sleep overpowered amidst entwinement. Through the night, more mountings occurred. All manifested by Pete sinking inward to deep reaches he'd never plumbed until then. I was a top man, I reflected, falling into a stupor of sweetness. Now, a 'blooded' man.

Magda was odd one out in the scenario. Never having slept anywhere but in my bed, and what's more, in my arms, she woke me before daybreak, nosing my dangling hand from a lonesome spot on the floor. A soft whimper of confusion jerked me from reverie of repose, the sultry body beside me. I arose to smother her in hugs and kisses of apology.

"Good morning, Luke, my runner boy. Get back up here, I'm needin' some attention." The sexy-voiced bedmate called. A seductive blowjob, another saddling-up by the masculine bottom man and a leisurely breakfast over easy banter, shared in intimacy, next led to a communal romp with Magda. I felt pretty fulfilled by this point.

Daytime and evening were spent discussing plans for time together in coming weeks. This, despite niggling warning flags about loss of continuity of a purposely blindered existence focusing on important points of light--- namely, school and Magda.

Drift from her had begun the previous night. Monday morning Parasitology Lab marked the next chink in my armor, wresting precious little good from information not reviewed beforehand. A break in usual routine. I rationalized ways past both as Pete reminded me of the new force in my life. Marsh Robertson.

"What happened to your finger, Marsh?" I had noticed it our first morning together. The distal phalanx of his left middle finger was missing. A roughly healed scar covered the tip, uneven appositional edges poorly aligned. Had to be traumatic, obviously. Lawn mower? Cooking accident? I had wondered but never broached it until now when he had questioned the crooked little toe on my foot. The result of a running accident several years before. The thing had healed in misalignment, I had explained.

Now, I waited for a reply. A pause of several seconds lingered before an uncharacteristically tentative answer, "I was born without it." Nothing else. I didn't say anything, holding my peace. But now knew, for the first time, that this man would lie. Unnecessarily. When the truth would do. The warning would shadow me. Another slow, sensuous slide onto Pete made me forget.

Over the first two months dating Marsh, I was at least a physically full grown adult. Sexual experience increased by the week but stresses of school were beginning to weigh on me. Religious ardor of a sacrosanct routine lay in tatters and my girl, Magda Lena, had been relegated to benchwarmer. Her new spot on the floor by my bed was as close as Marsh would allow her to me--- us--- through nights we spent together.

The easy-natured, debonair male moved clothes into a spare closet. In the process, I found myself under a thumb by handfuls of little requests--- only suggestions--- for changes in heretofore ordered existence. Undemanding as they seemed, dull sullenness began a slow but steady creep into our interactions when resistance was mounted to any of these.

Over the months, classmates and Chug were steadily rebuffed in coldly emotionless fashion. Marsh gradually crescendoed disapproval of my relationships into open hostility. Should I cross him, he retaliated by vacating the premises. For days on end. No contact. Nothing.

After days of absence, concern mounting, he would turn up at the front door, grinning as if nothing untoward had gone down. Nary a proffered explanation. It was his private time, I was informed, and not acceptable fodder for discussion. I learned to keep quiet.

Those hiatuses, for all intents and purposes, yielded a blessing. After graduating from reviled ankle boot status, Magda and I were back to routine during his absences. Fartleks returned to the schema. Studies were engaged. Chug visited. Aunt Ella called.

With more passing months, the mood between us soured to a point that even Pete was not as interested. Periodically, Marsh would revert to full-scale pander pimp. Charm offensive on full display. Dinner and dancing with wine; teaching moments on subjects only he could impart.

Caving ignobly, time and again I disappointed not only Magda, my friends, aunt and classmates, but myself. I grew to read his modus operandi. Psychiatry courses depicted a manic-depressive characterization. Newly re-labelled as Bipolar Disorder.

The morning that I stumbled on imprinted pastel pills while searching for toothpaste in his overnight kit confirmed it. Paxil. Bouts of hatefulness finally ensued and six months into our 'relationship', I was first accused of cheating. With Chug. My married best man. The shrieking screams from an unreasonably illogical set of arguments backed by fictitious evidence and unnamed sources cornered me. He became unfriendly, then antagonistic, toward Magda. That proved unforgiveable. I never did.

When present, long silences became the norm, shouting fits his only mode of response. The day he cursed out Aunt Ella for her audacity in defending me was the final straw. I told him he must leave and stay away. Packing up clothes in the spare closet, I presented them to him one morning when the ear-to-ear grinning 'other guy' knocked. Contrast in personality display from one second to the next was shocking.

After that, I changed locks and barred windows. Magda and I made new running loops and varied our timing. I changed phone numbers and notified housemates, friends and classmates Marsh was now relegated to 'persona non-grata'.

Soon following, the stalking and dirty tricks began. I feared for my and Magda's safety. Marsh would show up at track meets, friendly as all get-out, or incongruently, creepy, with a full-body frown. And a black cloud hovering over his head. It was visible to me. I commenced looking for clues from a distance. I'd espy him watching from darkened corners. He showed up at restaurants or coffeehouses when sharing time with friends. Or at study sessions on campus, sending me scurrying to check on Magda.

The following late spring, about a year from our first encounter, on a predawn run around Town Lake, disaster struck. At a small footbridge over a narrow inlet edging the lake, Marsh dashed from around a shadowy corner where he had lain in wait, cold-cocking me in the ear. His powerful fist laid me out. The last thing I remembered was hearing a snarling Magda lunging to my defense and a sharp shrill scream of pain as he kicked or punched my girl. Blackness took me to a horrible place then.

An unknown amount of time later, I came to. Dazed and bleeding from the crushed ear, headache of epic proportions, blurred vision incapacitating me. Hearkening to the last memory--- Magda's pitiful scream, cut off precipitously, mid-sound--- I forced myself up, desperate to locate her.

What had he done? My mind shouted. Why? Stumbling over the bridge, I picked out a patch of fur floating in the water. A rope had been tied to an end post there; far end disappearing close to the patch. I sobbingly dove into the water, grasping the fur. Lovingly cradling my girl's still and flaccid body from under the surface, I began resuscitation efforts.

Opening an air passage, checking for vitals and breathing for her. There was no heartbeat. My cardiology patient love was not alive. Endless efforts brought no revival. I slowly sank into the shallow water's edge, forlornly coming to grips with the comprehension that I couldn't bring her back. In my arms, covered in tears of anguish, we sat.

My chest heaved in sudden nauseous spasms. Clutching her tight to me, I died inside. Morose bereftness invaded my heart. I felt it would stop like hers had. The beating in me registered as totally unfair. Why was mine working, yet hers was not? Feeling extra palpitations, I recognized that my heart was, indeed, breaking as I experienced it. I awaited the degenerative waves to slide me to a joining of us two on the Other Side.

Instead, the extra beats widened and strengthened, expanding my consciousness to a metaphysical state. Then, it dawned on me that the ectopic beats were not my own. A sharp beat bounced through my being. They weren't my own!

I grabbed the glimmering shred of hope and renewed efforts. Untold time passed, and then, miraculously, my girl precipitously coughed, slimy fluid flooding from her mouth. The last strangled scream, cut off by the vicious blow, gurgled up from her lungs. A remnant, now just the barest of faint whimpers. Her devoted eyes focused on mine. She had come back to me. The weak lick confirmed it was true.

June, 1996

I lounged, ruminating at my familiar haunt, Starbucks, on the corner of 30th and Lamar. The morning paper lay partially read in my lap. Tepid black coffee sat on a side table. Amidst a vacant gaze at the plate glass window, faraway eyes picked up on commotion of hands outside and pulled into focus. Chug and Jill smilingly gesticulated toward me.

Interrupted in their jog by sight of me through the window, new-fangled three-wheeled baby carriage leading, the two beamed as they slowed to a stop. Chug looked good. Golden skin glistened sexily, his toned body exuded good health. Jill was regaining svelteness sacrificed to bring Jillian Victoria into the world. Her beauty was unusual. Getting up, I walked to the door and joined the little family outside.

"I couldn't tell it was you for sure, Luke, the glare was strong. But Jill knew. How you been? Dude?" The jocularity remained and the traditional tease---dude--- still bore meaning. I felt suddenly older than my twenty years.

"Doing great, you two. How's the most beautiful baby in the world?" I cooed into the roller-stroller at the tiny gilt-skinned doll with almond eyes and Jill's nose, mouth, plus hair. The petite lips curled into a quick smile, laughing at my funny noise and face. "Gosh, she's pretty." Kissing both of my best friends, we chit-chatted for a few minutes, comparing notes. I hadn't spoken with them for a month. Studies now consumed me. It was my totality. And, I was regaining a form of contentment. Running again, the concussion side-effects remained in complete remission these past weeks. Clearance had been granted, so I had grappled bull's horns and stood up tall in a push for new normalcy.

"Well, you look like you're in the usual stellar shape, Luke. Look at that flat belly. We are jealous." This from Jill, little roll still pooching her middle. Her hand reached over and brushed sun-bleached ringlets, now hanging down past shoulder level, a wildness springing from my head in riot of auburn unruliness. "How do you do all that, Luke? It is so manly on you. Any girl would die to have these…or you," as she fingered the ends. I flushed at the compliment.

"Aww, shucks, girl, my head's swelling. You trying to unbend me again? It's a lost cause, Jill." The ongoing joke warmed me.

Chug joined in, tucking a pacifier into the little girl's puckering mouth, "Hell, Luke, you know my wife, always the matchmaker. But true, mighty danged eligible, my bud. You know you were my next choice if Jill hadn't hooked up with me." Smug smirk was wiped off his face by a sharp jab to ribs from his beauty queen. Wincing, he hang-dogged at me in surrender, but I noted the look in his eyes. And just wondered…

He straightened his face after a moment, "Really though, Luke, how you doin'? We know everything has been weighin' on you the past two months…lotsa stuff went down. Are you honestly coping OK?"

They were assured it was so, another time. Like the month before at our last meeting. True, I had dealt with a lot but while still disheartening, there certainly existed a lightening in the future. I meant to make for that place. In the meantime, the head would be trained straight ahead, with blinders. Making my way through med school was all that was truly needed. Along with my books.

Thankfully, nastiness that chaptered the time with Marsh had finally been put to rest. The malicious attack on Magda and myself had brought charges and quick incarceration. A restraining order was enabled.

Pending litigation, both criminal and civil, would follow the confused, sick man for years to come. Consultation with police and attorneys, as well as an associate D.A., had shed more light on nefarious ways of the man with whom I had come into a first adult relationship.

Turned out, the home healthcare agency had been a sham. Rife with counterfeit documents, faked home visits, calculated skimming of funds for illicit usage, and robbery of mentally-challenged people plus vulnerable retirees. Worse, actual visits had resulted in multiple elder-abuse allegations.

The detective involved revealed to me a story of morbid interest, equating basics of a violent liaison with another man. It seemed while living in California, that earlier lover had bitten off Marsh's middle finger in the midst of an altercation. After Marsh had strangled a pet cat. Authorities had put pieces together after several years of sleuthing, hampered by no help from the jilted lover. I was confident that when and if my ex-whatever--- lover, teacher, stalker--- managed to get through legal ramifications of his past, the IRS would be coming after him as well.

A short month after the lakeside attack, my dear Aunt Ella had suddenly, unexpectedly, succumbed to congestive heart failure. The wide-ranging, worldly relative with such an over-sized heart had fatally opted to take part in a niece's eccentric undersea wedding. The beloved woman's carefully secreted condition--- no one in the family had been made aware--- burst under the pressure. For a second time in weeks, mine had almost followed suit. The lady had been there at so many turns in my young life. Owing her almost everything ever achieved was such a trite truism. Overwhelming grief smothered my psyche.

Flying up for the funeral, I had spoken at her wake, choosing to relate the story of a time when she had been in Austin. Staying at the homey bed and breakfast as she did every visit, I told the Laughlin family and loved ones about one particular afternoon. On that day, upon arriving at the B&B, I had entered the front door to find Aunt Ella alone and laying on the midway landing of the stairs. Eyes closed as if asleep. Concerned, I hurried to her, asking if she needed any help. Unmoving and with eyes closed she calmly replied, 'No, Luke, dear. I don't. I can't decide whether to go up or down. So, I'm waiting here until I do.' From then on, when any Laughlin clan member couldn't make a decision about something, they simply said, 'I'm on the landing'.

Uncertain how to make my way without her, I succored belief that she would be waiting, when the time came, on that middle landing. The same as many others whose lives she touched.

Heavy-hearted, I then returned home, falling into my best girl's rejuvenated paws. Chug and Jill cared for her in my absence. Magda had revived after the trauma suffered in my defense, rebounding in a remarkable manner. I had hated leaving her behind for Aunt Ella's funeral, barely bearing separation from her for any amount of time after the incident. Our reversion to old running loops had made the girl extremely content. Nights together were full of sweet dreams once more. I awakened each morning to bright eyes of a licking fiend, as always.

On one particularly beautiful early morning, there had been a skip together down to Town Lake. Following a brisk 10K loop, we entered into a familiar game of hide-and-seek at Zilker Park field. Per usual, instigated by her. While the pointer studiously struck point at fictitious prey away from me, I had hunkered down, in a shallow depression across the wide-open meadow we both loved so much, to await her. Watching her dart out of bushes forty yards distant, her astute nose easily sniffed out my spot. Romping toward me, I lay stock still, enjoying my athletic companion as she bounded rapturously toward my prostrate form. She wasn't fooled in the slightest.

I could discern her smiling face, intent on reaching me when, within twenty feet, her eyes took on a puzzled expression. Her gait slowed, becoming uncoordinatedly out of character. I jumped and raced to her, barely reaching her as she sank drunkenly into my pleading arms. Cradling her there before she hit the grassy plain, we explored one another's eyes. Hers evoked a loving entreaty. 'Don't worry, Daddy, I love you.'

Registering the fact of what was occurring, I drew her into my lap, supporting and stroking her head as we longed back and forth. The private little jig, composed on the first morning of her warm awakening in the dorm room at Jester Tower, the one I had sung to her every morning of our time together, now arose haltingly from my lips. I sang it to her one final time. Absorbing the picture of her which would have to suffice me forever.

As I began the second verse, her glazing eyes fixed on mine and she reached out that long pink tongue in a face lick of reassurance. My hand over her big heart caressed the last beat as it reverberated through the both of us. Laying there together, celebrating our past and present, we were warmed by dawning rays of a peeking sun as they spread across the verdant field so fondly shared.

My mind meandered as Jill and Chug chatted on. They gradually noticed my distance. And one lone teardrop. A surreptitious glance they thought I didn't see signaled time to make an exit. With promises of get-togethers and plans to come, meaningful hugs fortified me. Jillian's little sniggle tinkled my ears as they picked up a departing pace.

Re-entering the coffeehouse, I gathered my things and now cold coffee, setting mental sights on this Sunday's itinerary. First stop, eclectic neighborhood bookstore, Half Price Books. Joe Wilkins, the proprietor, had alerted me to a recent Thursday delivery of books from a defunct monastery outside the little town of Blanco, south of Austin.

Joe's purchase acquisition had been fortuitous, he'd told me. At an estate auction, the rare book purveyor had taken possession of a number of the mission library's out-of-print early collections which had resided in the old Jesuit enclave these past three hundred years. As a budding collector, hopes persisted that in their perusal I might come across an elusive third volume of a three-book anthology for which I kept up a persevering search. Seeking completion.

Many spare hours had been spent combing upper reaches of musty shelves on a rickety ladder there at the funky old store. Planning to spend several more in quest of the uncommon tome, my feet headed out to do just that.

This might just be my lucky day, I conjectured, ambling down the shady sidewalk.

* * *

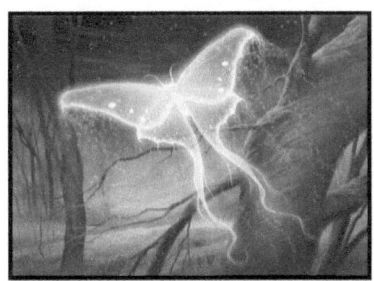

Volume II: One Clear Day

1992

"Mammay. What's a piccaninni?" Cal Al wanted to know.

The ten-year-old fixed a gaze on the elegantly slim neck as he asked, knowing truth of the matter would arise from that spot. Sure enough, at the same moment of the boy's last word, silky cocoa skin took on a tautness previously absent. Muscles beneath ribbed themselves in cords of sinewed potency though energy driving the display remained deliberately tamed.

No word had been spoken, yet the reaction informed Cal Al that the matter was, as he supposed, profound. The peculiar word was unknown to him; insight needed for meaning. He quietly awaited words to fill blanks in the question.

Cassandra Casseiopia Broadhearst continued measured peeling of carrots in preparation for dinner to come as her backside body language held son in check. While an already tall, slim youth remained still and mute, he inwardly summoned up basis for the query…

…An hour before, Cal hopped the gate outside the Roosevelt-era red brick schoolhouse across the Coosa River from his family home. The dull thud his cross-trainers made hitting ground muddled the word he heard from behind, "Piccaninni!"

Unsure if he had understood the alien term, he glanced over a shoulder. Ansley Hightower stood watching him from a few feet distant, just behind the bush bordering the gate and therefore out of sight. "Huh?" came Cal Al's request for clarification. He viewed the grimace marring a big seventh grader's pale features, thinking hot afternoon sun must be dazzling the older boy's eyes.

It wasn't. "I said, 'piccaninni', ya dumb darkie, cain't ya hear?" The grimace intensified up to a full scowl as thin lips spat the next words. "Lemme guess: ya don' be speakin' Anglish. 'Huh's the onliest word ya know how to say, I'm a'bettin."

Slow to rile, Cal Al nonetheless warmed at the low-rent vernacular; a little more by inclusion in a category of ignorance. He didn't know this boy, having only laid eyes on him before now when passing in the hallway a few times. Why the animosity? The fifth-grader tried defraying rising tension with a quick smile so commonly disarming to most. "No, I'm quite able to express myself. What might you be meaning was more my point. I couldn't quite make it out." Cal's diction was flawless. His truthfulness, a little less so. He had actually caught the new word; his footfall had only stepped on it a mite.

"Dumb as a stump, fo' sho'…what a idiot. Can't hear and dudn't un-nerstan' nuttin'. Just like all ya'll." The vituperation hit another nerve but Cal attempted placation yet again, invoking his parents' exemplary behavior and gentile manners as example. He was taught to respect elders and avoid violence. The fact that a lanky grade-schooler stood taller than the rest of his class still left him smaller by inches and tens-of-pounds in comparison to this blusterer, although the factor had not registered with the younger boy.

"I'm not dumb. I speak just fine. But never have heard that word, now, that is sure. Were you asking or telling something, sir?" Adding the term of respect, same way he'd heard Father intone with others.

Without further reply the blowhard suddenly rushed Cal, stooping to grab a handful of dusty sand then raising up in a fluid motion, slinging the decoy toward Cal's face. An opposite fist followed in roundhouse arc with coldcock intent.

Even at ten-years-old Cal was not fooled by a basic boxing tactic. He dodged the dirty shower, then easily blocked a curving wind-up blow with his forearm. The quick fist of his left arm darted reflexively at the bully's face, forcefully popping an exposed eye. The smack resounded around the almost empty school yard. A high-pitched yelp followed, bluster now replaced by a short blub on the way to sandy red dirt just sampled.

The fledgling self-defender assumed raised fists, leg-crouched position awaiting the next move. He quivered a little as adrenaline release hit. This was a first. In another second, seeing the bigger boy struggle, the youngster retracted fists and reached down to offer a hand up to the white boy.

"Stupid scum-bucket," the chubby ground rider chirped. He fumbled up, slapping away the proffered hand in the effort. Stumbling to his feet, Ansley bulled off down the cross street, palming a fast-bruising eye. Cal Al listened at a gradually diminishing spit of epithets as would-be bully distanced. Then brushed himself off and turned toward the river bridge to home…

…The memory receded as Mammay's soft voice broke in on the pregnant pause, "Child, wherever did you come upon the word…at school?" Cal related the episode just endured, with no little bit of trepidation in telling of the punch, knowing his mother's penchant for diplomacy. And he then…waited.

Still viewing the back of her head, no eyes to gauge, no lips to study, only the neck to judge what ground he might stand on just then, the boy was not fearful; only subdued. "Calumet Junior, my handsome and intelligent son. The word derives from an amalgamated contraction of terms through four centuries. Different meanings through varying times. Sometimes good, sometimes bad. Spelled one way one decade, another way the next." Her elegant southern lilt elucidated more than Miriam Webster's sound bite. The explanation was used as a lesson on more than one level, employing vocabulary meant to challenge her children's curiosity. It worked well. Her son would be soon researching at least one word she had utilized.

"In this day, my son, it is still cited, though rarely, as an epithetical term. A demeaning method exercised by weak-minded people to evince superiority as a brace against inner inferiority."

"In the language of Cameroon, from where our ancestors were stolen and enslaved, a precursor term once designated a Prince of the Hinterlands. And this, my son, is to what you must hearken whenever the word is uttered. Because your father has determined our own lineage arises from those same Hinterlands. You, my son, are born of the blood of Princes. And you must grow into a man able to fill the size of those shoes. With great gifts come great responsibility. Never, ever forget these tidings." She turned resolutely as she spoke those final five words, both eyes coming to laser focus on the ten-year-old son raptly alert to this delineation. Goosebumps pervaded him inside and out.

"When you have mulled the concept, your father and I will clarify any paradoxes raised. Now, off with you to change that filthy shirt. Find your brothers and mind that you finish homework before chores. Then play. My young prince." Fondness smiled in a perfusion of palpable affection. Calumet Alfrederic Broadhearst, Junior, hugged her tightly before hightailing it up the staircase.

The doorbell sounded at two minutes till dawn the following morning.

A yesteryear mechanism, the chime had been installed in the Civil War era. Having fallen into disrepair a hundred years before, the device had apparently been forgotten over ensuing time. Professor Calumet Broadhearst, Senior, had discovered the ancient extravagance while refurbishing the home in the first year after Cassandra and he acquired the old dilapidated estate.

Calumet's position at the local university as a Professor of Biochemistry was a milestone in newlywed lives eleven years before. The man meant to establish a home as complement to the station he had attained. Only by merit of an obliging friendship between a Rome City Clerk and the Broadhearst couple had the purchase been consummated. Sale of property in early 1980's between races was not common.

The clerk had smoothed transaction between a young couple of color and last remaining member of an old plantation family who had moved out amid losing the home place due to unpaid taxes and penalties. An old, destitute owner never knew of the buyer, only that the sale relieved her financial worries in age of dotage to which she had awakened one day. Assisted living was much preferred, and resultantly affordable, at this late stage in life.

History behind the ancient three story edifice on banks of a meandering Coosa River proved obscure, yet enough data remained in county archives to establish facts that the manse and outbuildings had housed only one family through many generations. Along with their slaves.

Several years, precious funds and much sweat equity had been expended but finally lustre of the antebellum mansion with iconic Corinthian columns adorning a spacious loggia had been reasserted. Every effort had been effected in discovering details and accoutrements crafting the grand house at its conception. Likewise, a contrasting exertion had been exhausted for uncovering history of it. Methodically, purposefully and quietly, all evidence of the macabre evil staining its fabric as a harbor for involuntary servitude was erased.

The outbuildings had been razed and ground plowed deeply under where slaves and livestock had once 'stabled'. Established century oaks were adorned with crape myrtle, magnolia and evergreen trees in major transplantation over the gently sloping river view expanse. Landscaping in Italianate style of the Renaissance Era was meticulously laid out beneath them.

Dumbwaiters were installed in place of slave closets which had functioned as hidden crannies for on-call servants in a past era. New fixtures updated all aspects of the home until it rivaled any in the Rome, Georgia region. Revitalizing the old estate, in conjunction with the couple's intellectual gravitas, marked the Broadhearsts as upscale denizens with whom to be reckoned.

Mindful of an edifying sentiment the doorbell apparatus might impart, Calumet Senior had taken trouble finding artisans capable of bringing about its resurrection. He discerned essence of his soulmate in the thing's rebirth. Repair of gong-like bells next to a grand front entry had been a final plum in the pudding rechristened as The Broadhearst Estate.

The doorbell system served, by serial synchronicity, multiple sites throughout the house and back verandah. Far Eastern flare of low, reverberative resonance reminisced an earlier period which Cassandra dearly cherished. Subtle tactility complemented audibility. By the effect, it endowed peaceful verisimilitude to an extant character of the worldly woman's refinement. Imbuing familial credence, it named the place 'Home'.

When it engaged so early in the morning, Cassandra detected a caveat of caution in its reverberations. She arose from her marriage bed, leaving a sleeping husband to drowse. Gathering a robe around herself, in slippered feet she descended to answer the bell's plaint. For, she sensed, such was what it must be.

On opening, the over-sized heartwood oak door gaped at three forms filling the entryway. Sheriff Lancaster, a deputy and the family lawyer were framed in a huddle which broke apart at her greeting. "May I help you gentlemen at such an early hour this day, Sirs?" Her charming manners counterbalanced somberness of both law officers; Counselor Black was previously familiar with her style.

"Good morning, Cassandra," Claudius Black began. "We regret calling at so obnoxious an hour," and at this, he cast a meaningful glower in the direction of two others, "yet I found myself duty-bound to accompany these gentlemen on an overstatedly urgent errand of which they first informed me an hour ago."

"Please, do come in, then, and let us see to it." Again, Cassandra assuaged sensibilities of the men by her grace. Standing aside, she ushered the three into a spacious foyer, offering seating which was refused.

"Mrs. Broadhearst," the sheriff removed his hat as he began, "I am afraid that there has come to the attention of the night magistrate a matter of some seriousness. The deputy and I have been dispatched to inform you of charges being filed against your oldest son, Calumet. And to escort him to the courthouse. We were informed of an incident at the school yesterday. Bodily harm was inflicted by him in a physical attack on Deacon Hightower's son, Ansley. The young man is presently in county hospital being treated for wounds from a blindside attack."

Cassandra's stiffening at roll out of these words altered the atmosphere in the room. A protective lioness could not have evinced more distinctive body language by response. Cold haughtiness now filled the voice that spoke, "I am very hopeful to hear that Mr. Ansley is not badly injured. That said, surely, Claudius, you have informed the local authorities and magistrate of several particulars which immediately spring to mind. Am I correct?"

Mr. Black nodded obsequious acquiescence and proceeded to summarize the situation, for obviously another time, in front of the law men. Due to the nature of the attack--- 'alleged attack', the lady interjected--- the sheriff had been instructed of need for bringing in young Cal for questioning. It seemed Deacon Hightower had pulled strings with the county judge, a family friend. Orders were plain, he explained.

"And am I to be informed as well that these gentlemen are fully aware of the age and nature of my son's minority status? It would be unsuitable for any reputable law system to approach such a matter in this way, or am I missing something?" Unruffled demeanor had become coldly detached from directly addressing two-thirds of the visitors to her home. A queen at court, reflected Claudius Black.

In that moment, Professor Broadhearst appeared. Wide awake, dressed and bright-minded, despite a recent bed-ridden state. Greeting the men, he shortly garnered tenor of the conversation. Astutely absorbing rare display of his wife's regal rancor, he took lead. Inquiring of the sheriff, it came to light that the boy, Ansley, had limped into his parents' home the previous evening following the school day. A badly blackened eye, a fractured arm and a deep head laceration with possible concussive effects had been brought along. Compliments, said Ansley, of a cowardly and unprovoked attack by a young black boy bent on violence. For unknown reasons, he had insisted.

Dr. and Mrs. Broadhearst traded glances, begged a private counsel with Mr. Black and retired to the kitchen for a pow-wow. Following a curt interchange, seeing no alternative, the three deemed it best to raise their son. All of them would accompany the law into town for a talk with the magistrate.

Two hours later, a confused ten-year-old and his thoroughly exasperated parents sat in a small windowless room at the courthouse in downtown Rome. Differing reconstructions of the altercation had been hashed and re-hashed before the night justice--- not the family friend of the Hightower's--- and decision to allow departure of the accused with parents had been summarily decided.

Evidence and deposition gathering were ordered, and, with a miffed tone, the magistrate informed the sheriff such should have been carried out before a precipitous move of detaining a pre-teen for allegations of unsubstantiated nature, short of charges involving homicide.

Young Calumet, remorseful at such turn of events, felt directly responsible for the bully's condition somehow. Even with firsthand knowledge that he held. It would seem a criminal justice system was intent on righting the wrong of an 'ethnic incident' in custom of a past century ethos. Could he be sent to prison? Were there prisons for ten-year-old felons? Might he be lynched, he fearfully considered? The boy had heard chilling stories about 'strange fruit'.

Reassurances had little effect, what with Cal Al's mastery of 1990's tech-driven information sources. Cable News, a nascent fixture in an apprehensive society, lent weight to implications regarding downfall of civilization by just such transgressions as Cal found himself presently accused. He concluded doom.

Arriving home an hour after that, the three were bombarded by five boyish mouths full of foreboding brainwaves. Via morning television news reports. Their saintly big brother had been demoted, in absentia, to lawless miscreant during the interim. They were in uproar. Sophie, lone little sister, lay asleep in her two-year-old dreams. Unfazed.

Parental remonstrance dissolved the kangaroo court in lieu of backyard landscape maintenance. Still, Cal Al had to deal with his twin later that Saturday evening as the two laid up amid sorry states of mind in their shared bed and bedroom, taking refuge from literal and figurative maelstroms around them. A deluge of rain, hail and winds had engulfed the riverside sanctuary in a fast-forming tropical storm. It provided perfect excuse for walling out the mess torturing Cal's small sphere.

Laying together familiarly, in fashion of twins, Coy Al begged the question, "How'd ya break his head and his arm with just one punch to his eye?" He could not come to grips with either the violent outburst or unbelievable talent for so great a damage quotient. The alter-ego twin both elevated and further debased Cal's tattered status, depending on gist, during seclusion together. "Why'd ya do it, Cal," provided recurrent refrain of the interlude.

The minutes-younger carbon copy rarely ever got under Cal's skin: their binding connection precluded most occasions for discord. The present scenario's confusing details, however, were trying his already thinned patience. "Coy, I already told you, none of that happened. The pea-brain guy is making it all up. Something else had to have happened after I saw him leave. No way I did any of what they're saying. Except the black eye…"

Having broken down the matter inside a nimble brain during flowerbed de-weeding a while before, Cal had cleared his bothered conscience. But if this twin brother couldn't grasp a sympathetic side, then there really must exist the proverbial creek without a paddle in the boat. Both boys started at a sharp clap of thunder, warm bodies pulling close in reflexive search.

Coy's dark brown leg wrapped through his brother's and he buzzed audibly as an inexperienced mind sought balance. Sense of angst between bosom brothers was palpable. The two were certain of sameness in feel of the other. Cal pushed a bush of hair onto his twin's chest; Coy responded by gathering closer. Each was a port in every mammay-less storm. They sensed things before the other knew it themselves. A two-way street regularly shared.

The next worry gelled in Cal's head. "Well, what do you think is going to come down at school on Monday? Am I gonna get gang-banged by the jerk's friends, ya think?" The idea wasn't pretty.

Coy let drop his previous line of questioning, quick to defend. "Bra, you know I got your back. Ain't no white boy militia gonna be houndin' on you, you know that. And Doy'll be there, too. We be good, Cal." His skinny arm pulled tighter.

The reassurance redounded inwardly, channeling a picture of three-musketeers facing off against forces of evil…it made things better. They soothed each other by communal closeness over the next hour. Falling into a peculiarly patterned shared body language, spoken words receded to mootness. Sleep settled and at least inner turbulence receded. No better place to be in a squall than their room, their bed… their bro.

Monday morning at school turned out to be more of the same. Virtual and tangible tempests. The weather-system hovered over the region in alliance with human dissonance. The minority faction of a recently consolidated grade school--- this despite decades-past judicial rulings--- found a few dozen students-of-color bastioned against coalesced raucousness effected by a 'put-upon' majority. The first black president's portrait, Mr. Clinton, might grace the principal's wall but a white student body reflected parents' stilted Jim Crow perspectives in perilous parallel to that supposedly bygone era.

Cal was hauled into the vice-principal's office a minute after arrival. Instructions by the Anglo administrator were concise and by-the-book. Every day upon arrival Cal was to report to the office. He wasn't to interact with other students. He was to conduct himself in a non-threatening manner. He must follow a teacher's aide assigned to 'assist' him these next days. Until an over-heated atmosphere cooled. In a condescendingly prejudicial lecture, Cal was also cautioned there was to be no further perpetuation of physicality. As if such a warning had either relevance or basis. Cal's lesson wasn't anything but abject humiliation...and that, he figured out, was the precise intent.

The boy found exceeding strangeness in the fact of lists of rules pertaining to himself and his conduct, but nary a one for the rest of the school. And the rules certainly didn't stop words.

For ensuing weeks, every turn accorded the youngster a new round of puerile reproach in some form or fashion. The white populace in school bandied their majority. Despite the aide's presence--- Cal's brothers were kept from him--- catcalls and belittling commentary sprouted. Even neutral adults exuded passive antagonism. 'Black attack' became the motif by which the issue was known; Cal was the lightning rod for a nodus of discontent.

A Friday morning dawned as day for the hearing. Not at school; at the courthouse. Judge Posner, the Hightower family ally, had speciously dictated a judicial hearing within sanctity of court confines. Translation: a trial. For a ten-year-old boy. Cal felt convicted before proceedings began. He and his stoic parents found themselves escorted everywhere, from the lane leading to the Broadhearst home to courtside seats provided by the judge.

Why a packed courthouse resulted was a mystery to the Professor, his wife and the ten-year-old accused. Counselor Black fronted the family, shielding them as much as possible, but harsh lights of media cameras simply exacerbated circumstances. The little group inwardly flailed. Never had the parents, let alone innocent child, ever been subjected to such public humiliation and scorn. Kangaroo court, indeed. Professor Broadhearst feared for his family.

Judge Posner, traditional southern throwback, began the hearing with ostensible words of admonition. His courtroom wasn't to be trifled with, order being of first and foremost concern. He fixed a gaze upon a congregated First Rome Baptistery surrounding the Hightower family. Pudgy Ansley sat in woebegone despair, head bandaged, arm splinted and strung, eye yellowish and brown in its slowly healing state of guiltless existence. Poor little white boy. The poster child for victimhood factions had been well coached.

An assigned child psychologist, Mrs. Newman, sat as bookend shield opposite Mammay. The judge hammered order at the crowd and the process progressed through a fraught morning. Little Cal wilted further down in a hard, sterile seat with each passing minute. Along unfortunately ethnic lines, opposing sides presented cases before 'court'. Bailiffs stood ready for any inkling of acting out. With only one lone, unnamed witness, a proverbial stand-off of 'hesaidhesaid' idiocy took darker turns by rotely ingrained attitudes of those in positions of authority.

As a third hour of monotonous testimony unfolded, the erstwhile quality of justice seemed unlikely to rescue the day. Cal Al began counting down final minutes of freedom toward inevitable incarcerated future as, one-by-one, God-fearing character witnesses, intoning a pious childhood to the plaintiff, overwhelmed the stand.

One bright spot, the unnamed witness, arrived in the wee form of DeWayne Smithers. The first grader had been straddled in a spread-limbed oak during the episode, quietly communing with a resident squirrel following emancipation by school bell.

Well, kind of. Emancipation, that is. Avoiding return to an abusive daddy and drunken mamma in a wrong-side-of-the-tracks abode 'sheltering' DeWayne and several sad siblings, the little guy sought daily succor hanging with the little tree rodent. From their hidden perch, boy and squirrel chewed over all matters schoolyard. That day, a seven-year-old had shared bird's eye view from a high leafy bower with Rocky, his bushy-tailed buddy.

Exuding boyish inelegance, DeWayne had bravely come forward on his own--- parents nowhere to be seen--- bravely equating a more truthful version of an ugly encounter than had been told to that point. Open guffaws and expressions of doubt met a little big man's courageous, stuttering stand. Unsympathetic presiding authority, Judge Posner, repeatedly admonished proper decorum in farcical display of neutrality. He frequently coached the tiny witness, "Speak up, young man."

Despite an antagonistic atmosphere, a stoic witness managed to lay out his testimony. Hope arose on defendant's row. Short-lived though it was upon discrediting by an astute prosecutor, wise to the ways of refutation. Disreputable home and background distracted from a truthful deposition. 'How could anyone in their right mind believe this little...?' An angry gavel and courtroom tittering drowned a derogatory descriptor. Nonetheless, the seven-year-old stood no chance.

Counselor Black presented a case worthy of mediocre merit, not a veteran of many courtroom trials and never expecting the pseudo one in this situation. Missing crucial points, overlooking salient objections, forgetting obvious inroads to repudiation of the plaintiff's case at multiple junctures, the several hours' waste of taxpayer money came down to a judge's final decision.

The interim called for while the judge absented himself in deliberative cloister was excruciating for Cal and his folks. Parents were still in shock state that the case had been allowed at all, perceptively aware of a ridiculous courtroom setting for such a complaint. Disrespect for normal protective safeguards considering Cal's age amounted to criminal negligence in not just their eyes.

The courtroom buzzed with negativity, only subsiding upon return of vested authority: Judge Posner. Black robe swirled with an air of resoluteness as spectacled magistrate seated himself, gaveling 'court' back into session.

Clearing an already clear throat, he almost uttered first final words when an abrupt whirlwind of commotion sliced through the hush.

A bailiff at the rear door started in surprise as a tall athletic form pulled it open and stood in profile. The resonance of high school wrestling coach, Randall Costner, reached the bench. "Judge Posner, please forgive my interruption, your Honor. I bear firsthand evidence needing exposure before the court and request your Honor's forbearance in order to provide it. May I approach, Sir?"

The judge, noticeably flustered, considered a moment before managing cautious assent. Middle-aged and crew-cut, the muscled figure of Coach Costner strode the aisle in confidence. All eyes followed as a harried bailiff scurried to keep up, barely reaching the swing gate demarcating gallery from pit before the intruder. He closed on the judge's bench and quietly conferred with his Honor for several minutes. Nervous buzz revived amidst a disconcerted crowd.

Though not a jury trial, Posner finally gestured toward the tall German-American in an assembly address. "It has come to my attention that we have not heard all relevant testimony in the matter before this court. In effort at fairness I have made a decision to allow testimony of Mr. Randall Costner. Bailiff, please show Coach Costner to the stand."

Showing no hesitation whatsoever, the tall athlete took the witness chair and settled for a moment. At Judge's beckoning, he began. "I am, as some of you know, wrestling team coach at Floyd County Consolidated High School. My family has been born and raised here these past thirty years and I am consummately gratified to be a citizen of this, my adopted country. My wife and I immigrated here at the time of President Kennedy's assassination. Pride fills us in observing the way America has rebounded to preeminence in its democratic experiment. Would that the world could learn by example." A ripple of assent bounded around the room in affirmation of an Aryan male's ringing elocution. Sanction was granted.

Continuing, Mr. Costner unveiled his account. "On the Friday in question, I visited the grade school for a conference with Principal Evans about establishment of both a computer science program and a developmental format for youth athletics. Both disciplines are sorely missing from the curriculum. I presented the cases in hope to establish new classes and extra-curricular involvement for priming grade-school children. Early exposure to important avenues of growth for this age group is my goal."

"Finishing presentations and receiving positive feedback for going forward, I loaded my project equipment. I was in a rush to get home, pack and then travel to Savannah for my brother's wedding. Serving as best man. Having put in for temporary sabbatical, my wife and I stayed on afterwards. We joined our small family circle in preparing an Old Town Savannah bungalow for my brother and his bride's return from their...doings...during an extended honeymoon in the old country." The knowing smile appearing on his lips brought chuckles of indulgence.

"I was taken by surprise yesterday morning upon coming across a wire story in the local Savannah paper outlining this very case. It jarred me. The account described a viciously malevolent and pre-meditated attack by a young man of ten against an unsuspecting thirteen-year-old. To see the gist of the article play on racial lines, picked up by the press and pushed in uproariously divisive fashion, gave me pause. Enough to cause a change of set plans." The blond man's hands motioned as he spoke, giving dimension to the account. The crowd was enthralled, but not yet comprehending. They were soon to be enlightened. Ansley Hightower now sat, alert, squirming fretfully in his seat.

"In my hurry to get out of town," the coach went on, "I exited by a rear doorway. Rounding the corner, I stumbled upon a familiar scenario playing out. It bore no resemblance to the story being heard here today. The newspaper summaries are sadly mistaken in their focus."

"You see, folks, I witnessed the very case before you. I noticed, because of the young man's" --- pointing out Cal Al--- "very athletic vault over a sizeable gate fronting an enclosed schoolyard. Not many children his age are capable of such a move. I was impressed, watching to see what next move he might make. The youth is just the type for whom I intend to provide focus by my athletic program."

"Imagine my surprise when I viewed, and overheard, a very racist epithet thrown, unprovoked, at the young boy here. By the Hightower boy over there. Having grown up in a country with a dark history of racism soaked in ethnic animosity--- which almost overtook an entire world--- I was not happy to behold yet another occasion for such incivility."

"But, before I could interrupt the situation, I observed a most diplomatic attempt, in multiples, as a well-spoken youth, Mr. Broadhearst, tried de-escalating the scene. Never once raising his voice, he artfully worked to make lemonade from the lemon being thrown at him. With a smile on his face. It was only after the older boy," here, the coach pointedly gestured at Ansley Hightower, "tried a truly cowardly blindside attack, did a much smaller defendant avail himself of a simple defensive move to block brutishness. He only punched once, in reflex, to avert further attack."

"The bigger boy--- a bully by any description--- fell to the dirt, then proceeded to further insult a regretful defender. I watched as this younger boy reached out a hand to help an aggressor rise. Still attempting to defray the unexpected foray. The gentlemanly offer was slapped away."

"Hauling himself upright in obvious embarrassment at a thwarting of bullying tactics, this boy departed in shame. On both legs, with both arms intact and absolutely no head wound besides a justifiably blackened eye. All the while shouting sordid curses I am certain would not be condoned by church members gathered here today in misguided support."

"Those hateful words made me cringe. Nonetheless, this boy simply watched to make certain of no more sneak attacks. Satisfied of this, he brushed himself off and headed an opposite direction over the Coosa bridge."

"I was taken aback on different levels at this display and never uttered a single word. Believing that similar situations have played out uncountable times over generations, I felt a proper ending and just comeuppance had been meted out, so went on with my rushed plans, leaving town directly. I harbored a desire to attempt identifying the youth on my return with offer to enter him into new programs I am hoping to guide. His athletic acumen and manners are commendable."

"More importantly, a true measure of character is best counted in the dark. With no one watching. There was, indeed, darkness that day. And I witnessed a measuring on both ends of the scale from my vantage point."

"It provided disbelief when I came across the news article yesterday. Because of twisted truth, I was instigated to act. You now hear my version of a boyhood experience gone awry and reasoning for hustling back here. Apparently, just in the nick of time."

"Whatever happened to young Ansley Hightower that day did not come at the hand of Calumet Broadhearst, Jr. And, by the young bully's display of true character, I rather doubt much truth would come from asking. Young Mr. Broadhearst should not be suffering in this manner for what occurred that day. He should be commended for strength of character."

"I beg the court and especially citizens of this community to all step back a moment, reassess, and come to grips with a hard fact of our contemporary culture. There is a jaundiced view being foisted on this country presently. In direct result, incidents such as this one are being misconstrued to unrecognizability. The wrongness serves only to divide this great country."

"That is all I have to say."

The atmosphere could have collapsed on itself in the opaque stillness. Silence deafened.

Finally, Judge Posner, chastened in his own right, uttered a simple phrase. "Case dismissed."

It let the air out of the room.

Back at the kitchen table, the entire Broadhearst family sat in reflection of the recent tumultuous events. The Professor reckoned a teachable moment. "Do any of you boys have ideas to take away from what we have just been through?" Cassandra sat with Sophie, listening to her soulmate.

"Yeah, that white boys lie," Doy Al offered.

"Not all white boys do. Look at Coach Costner. He did all that today and he didn't have to. You can't say that, Doy, even though coach isn't a boy." This from Coy. He had heard of the heroic intervention exonerating his twin, already lionizing the man.

"Well, I think that most people think what they wanna think and everybody takes the side they are on because of what their friends say." Roy Al piped up in his six-year-old capacity for profundity, glad to be able to offer an opinion with his older brothers. His own twin, Loy Al, nodded agreement. Ironically. The two were closer than any two people in the family and mirrored one another, to their parents' chagrin. Independent thinking pretty much topped the parents' list after unconditional love…they worried sometimes over the younger twins' exclusivity, even though understanding it.

"Want to…not wanna, young man." Cassandra offered grammar lessons regularly, intent that her children master the capacity to communicate properly in the real world. "But, you are right to cite the fact that many people just go along to get along. It is the easier path and requires little critical thought. Very good, Roy."

Cal Al, the target in the issue, was exhausted at having to rehash the over-analyzed event yet once again, but still had many questions. "Well, I don't understand why Ansley had to make all of it up. He knew what he did and he lied when the truth would have been better. Is there a difference between us and them, Dad? I mean, do you think his parents don't teach right and wrong? How did he end up getting hurt so bad? Was it fair, just because he did what he did to me?" All of it came out in a rush, now that the pressure was removed. He was in his safe place here.

The youngest brother, Voy Al, kept eyeing the fruit in the center of the table, uninterested in the whole affair at four-years-old. Food was more important. Especially the apple calling to him.

Waiting a bit for things to simmer, Professor Dad allowed the silence to permeate before making his point. "First of all, Doy, you must take away from this that any person in a given situation might tend to lie. There is no monopoly by anybody or any group for that bad habit. It be an easy trap to fall into and we must always stay on guard for it whether it comes from others or wells up to tempt oneself. It is a deceit which is infective and can take over the mind if not careful. The lie is like a snowball rolling downhill: it grows as it travels and gets out of control easily. And, keep in mind, a liar is never believed, nor respected. Once caught, it is very difficult to retrace one's steps. The trait undermines your conscience."

"Cal, you have experienced suffering by someone else's hand as well as their mind in this situation. I am proud of the way you conducted yourself through it all. We will probably never know the why of this affair. But, keep in mind that there were many underlying currents pulling that boy to decisions made. Even the first one which put you in a bullseye to begin with. Remember that we cannot force anything on others, nor may we be responsible for their mistakes. But we are able to rise above the frays in life and know in our heart that we did the right thing. Like Coach Costner."

"Coy, the man exhibits great strength of character and you would do well to emulate him. I do have a thought, though, which has stuck in my craw. As good a thing as the coach did, my dilemma remains why the court and attendees could not afford young DeWayne Smithers similar respect for the stance he took in Cal's behalf."

"Knowing what little we do about the boy's home life, I find a tougher row to hoe attempting to bolster the truth in light of so many obstacles. Yet he hurdled them. He had nothing tangible to gain and everything to lose, given his youth and station. Who do you imagine instilled such character traits in him? In the end, he was neither recognized, nor believed. Let alone thanked. We all should find food for thought in pondering the why of this over anything else before us, I do believe."

Cal turned inside himself at the premise. Leave it to his father to dissect to bare bones of a matter and expose the proverbial elephant in the room. The boy would debate the idea for years to come.

July, 1997

"Shhh. They be like da Barracuda and da Orca: 'lotta times like to hunt in da pairs or da packs and they tend to be on da shy side... exceptin' da teeth and claws, now." Tres whispered the admonitory message to Cal Al. From the boys' perch on a sun-etched boulder, under the lip shaded by a tall overarching breadfruit tree, Cal felt hidden even though the older boy assured him their body odor pervaded the entire area.

A cool mountain breeze caressed this early morning, making bare skin tingle by prickling tease. Whitewater crashed crisply a hundred feet below, where Privassion Creek rushed and tumbled through stacked highland rock ledges and alleyways. The arboreal conundrum of evergreens mixed with lowland commoners such as breadfruits offered a contrast of peculiarity to the landscape.

Cal combed the expanse with both ears and eyes alert in attempt at pinpointing elusive 'prey' the two early-risers sought. Since hearing the scream of a jungle cat the night before while sharing the huge bed with Tres, Quatro, Cinco and Coy Al, his curiosity had been piqued. Tres had noticed when Cal's head perked up from its nestled site inside the new friend's arm. Peeping between half-opened eyes, the lanky sixteen-year-old wordlessly signaled the visiting boy to meet at the wide, screened aperture demarcating indoor enclave from the deck outside.

Sneaking away without disturbing other crashed teenagers--- not a particularly difficult feat--- they had sat bent-kneed on the edge of the expansive deck in awe of myriad stars and crescent moon bathing the mountainous compound. Even without any more cat calls from a surrounding rainforest, the diorama was more than enough. Midnight hour tended toward the exotic, Cal had noticed, what with aroused and lurking nocturnal denizens inhabiting such remoteness. A lesson on strange flora and fauna was imparted to the young Georgia boy new to upland wilds of Blancaneaux Estate. Two boys were forging an easy bond despite a year-and-a-half age difference.

By Tres' tale of dichotomies, Cal learned how Nature had forced a combined contradiction of the tallest mountain range in Central America with a robust riparian treasure trove. Mixed alpine evergreens and rainforest attributes. Animal life drawn to such a fusion made the bizarre very commonplace. Wide variation in resident rodentia, by example, thrived alongside reptilian leftovers of bygone epochs. Flying squirrels, guinea pigs, voles and woodchucks existed with hog-sized capybara and coypu populations. These lived alongside and in competition with blue-jean frogs, barking geckos, basilisk lizards and tree iguanas. Coneys and hedgehogs flourished adorably beside defense-oriented tuco-tucos and porcupines. Marmots, chinchillas and, from the winged world, red Macaws, lent beauty to a unique ecosphere.

Diverse jumbles of animals had emigrated northward from a once-isolated South American continent as the bridge that became Central America arose during the Cenozoic Era. Rare predatory species like large cats, caimans and feared crocodiles had followed, all able to sustain their species by existence of the fore-mentioned. Cal was amazed to learn all this while Tres had been elated to meet an interested listener.

On that big deck under innumerable stars, it had felt like more than two days had elapsed since the Broadhearst family's arrival to a jungle-cleared airstrip via sputtering single engine Cessna piloted by the talkative family friend, Fred Lansing. Best man at Cal's parents' wedding, and Cal's shared godfather, the majordomo of Francis Coppola's estate had chattered amiably throughout an hour-long flight over rugged terrain between Belize City and Blancaneaux.

Tres had met the plane, guiding the landing in experienced fashion, then escorted the three oldest Broadhearst brothers to a roomy, thatched-roof boy lodge. The round cabana, constructed of huge mahogany timbers native to the area, sported a thirty-foot-tall pitched ceiling. A large open sleeping zone was furnished by round beds and flanked by a humongous walk-in pool-like shower with bath sector. A sitting area with adjacent bookshelves graced the remainder of the interior. Tiled in colorful Guatemalan mosaic, the sunken communal wet space took up a quarter of all square footage and lent itself more to a high school gymnasium shower room than private domicile. By fact of six regular occupants sharing the lodge with frequent visitors, it sufficed.

Cal, Coy and Doy were enthralled by exotic flavors of the place, not to mention the estate. Twelve-year-old Doy had latched on to his age-range Lansing 'cousins' from the outset. Namely: Seis, Siete, and Ocho. The middle set of a large Lansing brotherhood, ranging from eight to almost thirteen years, suited him fine. Elder twins had buddied up to the older boys, happily hanging with their teenage set.

Coy almost immediately disappeared with Quatro and Cinco, exploring the agrarian sector of a 75-acre estate. The cash crop cultivation drew his twin. That had perplexed Cal. He had never known Coy to like anything farm-related. The boy avoided yardwork back in Georgia at every turn. The oddity would bear exploring at some point, Cal sensed.

Recounting the introductory days to the spectacular place, Cal had sat, awash in silver-toned celestial-scape on an overhanging deck, going over it all in his head. Tres had brought focus back to the spangled scene that second night, furthering a riveting evolutionary tale by describing an existence amongst fifteen siblings--- and two more on the way--- over the next hour. Immersion of the large family with an amazing Belizean Maya Mountain sanctuary, which the tribe managed, was enigmatically interesting in its own right.

From an atypical set of two mothers and their seven daughters, who cooked and cleaned the multi-cabana compound, to eight brothers aiding Father Fred--- Papi--- in upkeep and oversight of the Coppola family's hidden gem, the Lansing clan led an idyllic lifestyle unknown to most of the wider world.

Tres told of tracking jaguar through mountainous terrain on a fairly common basis. Cal could not believe the strangely patterned feline really populated the area he was to call home over a coming six-week sojourn.

The roar of a large cat in dead of night had dispelled incredulity. Better than knowing of it, he had reveled in thoughts that in a short time from then, in dawn hour, Tres would fuel fantasy by trailing one of the elusive cats, Cal in tow...

...Cal's tracking buddy pulled the tall slim fourteen-year-old from a perusing lookout by a surreptitious finger-point across the small clearing the two presently overlooked. There, not thirty feet away, crouched a prowling form of dappled grandeur indigenous to this region: the fabled Jaguar. The big male seemed to be scoping out their very hiding place atop the boulder. Feline eyes, golden in hue, stared in slit hunt mode.

Were boys being stalked, instead of the reverse? Cal's nerves prickled in sudden wariness. The two watched with morbid fascination as a hundred-pound bundle of balled muscle silently commenced slinking straight in their direction. No words were spoken, but Cal noted the older comrade's hair raise slightly off his scalp as the beautiful cat closed the gap.

Without warning, the sinewy beast launched in a flurry of fur, covering remaining feet in three bounds before erupting into an arcing airborne missile apparently intent on human breakfast. Both boys rolled, instinctively, away from oncoming weaponry. As they somersaulted together to the sunny side of the big boulder, a magnificent hunter arrived at the spot just vacated.

Through a terse snarling growl, two carnivorous jaws clamped together. Razor sharp claws then assisted an athletic grab of a previously unseen three-foot tree iguana just a breadfruit limb height above where the duo had lay spying. Big cat crunched into leathery hide of a startled tree lizard, the doomed thing shrieking a death knell of reptilian horror, finding itself instantly dismembered in a vicious display of nature at its most raw. The cry of the cat's prey cut short as head and body were detached, Jaguar intent on ingesting this delicacy on the hoof… and on the spot.

Cal lay, spumed by syrupy green iguana guts and crimson blood in wretched disbelief of a cold-blooded kill. Occurring within two feet of them, the perspective proved morbidly riveting. Next thing he knew, the cat reached out a set of warning claws toward him, cautioning against interference. Tres seized his torso in a sharp yank outward and away from the 'crime scene'. Tumbling down five feet into a copse of flowering bushes, they luckily struck a soft-bedded landing.

Eyes met in wide-eyed terror of the close-up slaying. Open-mouthed, both absorbed the macabre exhibition in mute astonishment. Scrambling up, they hustled in clumsy retreat, back up the mountain path from whence they'd come a half hour before. Thoroughly freaked, the duo headlonged away from continued burbling scrunches narrating the hunt's finish.

So, Cal speculated again, who really had been the roleplaying entities just then? He struggled to make sense of the attack as Tres held tight to his fourteen-year-old guest. Newly enlightened artless trackers absconded with mostly unscathed hides intact. Mucked by butchery scents and juices, they absented themselves.

Fifteen minutes up a rough, rocky trail, the two dove into the benign confines of crystalline Big Rock Falls pool. Submerging, peering at one another from an underwater refuge, Cal and Tres sluiced around the watery hollow. Suspended breath permitted bubbly scrutiny of the other as they counted limbs and fingers, helping wipe stubborn gory entrails from naked bodies.

That interminable minute later, two breathless beings emerged. Scoping a perimeter of the pool for signs of proximate claws or fangs, newly bonded friends sank to frazzled respite on the edge of the bowl. Sheltered behind the fall's water curtain.

Cal fixedly jabbed Tres, "Shy, huh? I'm just glad he didn't order the main course."

"What is that smell?" Cal sniffed at cloying wisps wafting through air around them as they entered civilized edges of the compound two hours later. They let their guard relax now, having detected no sign of stalking predators since departing the blood-bath scene. Between the smell about which he was curious and a delicious aroma of grilled meat bathed by marinating Caribbean spices, both boys experienced salivary responses on steroids. Ladies in charge were obviously busy. Yet the sweeter smell of the smoke awakened Cal's curiosity. Unidentifiable.

Cocking his head, Tres sampled fragrances as well, patterning a discriminating look as he speculated. "That would be either... Alfred Ganga Khan or... maybe, Fredinand deSparkos." A couple of lip smacks refined the mental search. "Ye-yuh, it be deSparkos, a'ight." He smiled toward the younger boy, knowing of the goings-on by essence. Hiking drawerless shorts, he adjusted still damp junk and jostled Cal's shoulder, "Why, boy? Do you have permission for partaking o' da herb by your Papi?"

The funny return look brought him up short. "Ya don't even know if ya' do, now, do ya, Cal?' Another questioning face made Tres snicker. "Well, maybe we should be finding out before long, then. I imagine it'll be jus' fine, what with your and my Papi both partakers themselves. A mite early in da day to be doing, of course, though ya are company. And da Broadhearst elder boy... but newcomers be best warned o' da potent packin' our stuff carries... we should ask, first." Tres was plainly torn.

"Am I supposed to follow what you just said, Tres? None of that makes any sense. I'm wondering about the smell of that sweet smoke coming from over there. Somebody burning bananas?" He was head-pointing toward a copse of banana plants arching suspended clumps of unripe plantains a hundred yards from them, down a rolling lawn toward the rushing creek.

Gobs of colorful flowers surrounding the grouping were a draw by themselves, something else in which Cal was interested. Tres seemed quite desensitized to the beauty. Too commonplace in his eyes, the riot of pastels and bright hues were not a focus. However, as Cal began moving toward the funny scent, Tres followed, explaining.

"Cal, my bra, we do cultivating of da cash crop for da plantation here on da mountain. You are noticing our harvest. It's being da highest quality ganja found anywhere. Mr. Coppola been seeding da venture before I was born. Now, da enterprise be very fruitful indeed. Peoples from far and away come a'runnin to fill their stores with our wares, and we be a'fillin da coffers by da venture."

"Your true bro, Coy Al? He been helping my brothers in this work these past days--- it's da why for him not bein' around much. He is taken by da science." Tres smiled as he said this; Cal wanted to ask again about misunderstood Belizean dialect as the two edged around the banana grove.

On the far side, a breath intake accentuated the view before him. Wider, gently sloping lawns of St. Augustine grass flowed down into a pretty picture of multi-level water cascades: Privassion Creek on its cataracted traverse toward lower lands. Mature evergreens and other trees dotted the lawn, each perfectly manicured by flowerbeds rife with rainbow colors beneath. Large igneous boulders also populated the area, similar beds augmenting their edges as well.

One especially huge chair-shaped boulder lay silhouetted before Tres and Cal. This one pulled on Cal's eyes. Seated on the gargantuan plinth was his twin, Coy. Clutching a cannon-sized cigarette in his fingers, he reclined while seeming to gaze out on the vista expanding before him.

In leisure calm, he sprawled comfortably on discarded, sweated-out shorts and shirt, smooth dark legs hanging off one edge. Left flexed, right in full extension. Interestingly, Quatro and an aged gentleman were sharing the rock, too.

At least, Cal believed it was Quatro. A wild sprout of wavy hair flowed over his face, head laying across the man's chest. The swarthy older man's shock of silver curls flared around a grey-bearded visage. The pair lounged in adjacency to his twin. They were intent on what appeared to be adjustment of an old-fashioned shortwave radio. A long antenna stretched upward over the compact device which balanced on the gent's stomach.

Crackles and whistles distorted various stations in a noisy scrolling of airwaves. As Cal looked on, a strong signal was caught. One which focused loud and clear. "Ah, my Grea-oupa is with 'em. Dat answers da why of them doing da smokin' at this time of day. Papi doesn't allow smokin's during da daylight hours--- says it be too distractin' for everyone's concentration." By the look of Coy Al, such would appear to be truthful, Cal noted. He lazed, hypnotized.

"Oupa being the only other person besides Papi who might allow them to be doing it now…" The newcomers heard music jingle and call letters identifying a Johannesburg, South Africa station. A voice followed, welcoming listeners back in heavily accented Afrikaner pidgin English. Tres told Cal of the strange mixture resultant from centuries of Dutch, German, French and Zulu/ Xhosa influences, yet Cal found he could follow a good portion of the words.

Beside the facing rock stood a tiny mulatto male. Naked too, the darkskinned, skinny, pot-bellied youth watched in enthrallment while Quatro and Grea-oupa whisked across the radio spectrum and settled on the particular station. Like magic was being performed. Quatro, Oupa, Coy and the mulatto boy familiarly shared tokes on the large blunt.

"Well, be a'lookin' as if our blood brothers are acquaintin' well enough, doesn't it?" Tres grinned. "And da stray Guatemalan boy a'stumblin' on us last month--- Jyp--- I see is a'helpin' out. That boy be lucky he stopped here instead of keepin' on up the road through Mexico."

Cal's perplexed look prodded Tres to give background. "He ran away from all da gangs in Guatemala City as be takin' over down there, now. It's truly a question which be more dangerous: his hometown or da trip he was attempting… be very risky a'doin' that, now. Da boy was starvin' when he showed himself."

"He musta taken a lucky wrong turn when he popped out o' da forest into our ganja field awhile back. Da boy be amazingly backwards in his education, and not understandin' o' much in da ways o' da modern world, as you may see." Cal was grasping about half of all these goings-on at this point, so much was being presented of a sudden. He stayed quiet, listening and absorbing.

Tres waltzed closer. Hesitant to interrupt what Cal deemed an intemperate display, he nevertheless followed, though more slowly. The blunt in his twin's fingers was only a third burnt and upon reaching the engaged trio, Tres surprised Coy by tipping the fagot out of spellbound teen fingers.

Rather than a sky-high leap in busted embarrassment, which Cal anticipated, the twin dreamily angled his neck and face toward the new arrivals. A shit-eating grin lit up a blitzed mug upon recognition of his womb-mate. Not a shred of chagrin did the stoned boy evince. Quatro and tiny Jyp didn't even notice the arrivals. Their bemused faces, happily intent on a broadcasting radio interview, continued listening to an apparently engrossing show. Grea-oupa took note however, moving his great-grandson's head and radio from himself, sitting up.

A mostly unclothed octogenarian smiled warmly in arising, welcoming both boys. The rock occupants seemed recently freed from strenuous toil, disrobed and covered in caked saltiness. Cal deduced work had been finished and a break was in the making. Again, it dawned on him how unusual for Coy to be willfully involved in manual labor. Past tense, as observation showed.

Grea-oupa lithely slipped off the big boulder, hopping nimbly to grass. Also in an Afrikaner dialect, he elucidated new arrivals about the ongoing show. Letting them know of having arrived in time to share in the broadcast from his homeland. They were hearing the voice of a dear old friend's son--- or daughter--- as the case may be, he laughed.

Cal remained mystified…Tres just took a long toke. Obviously interested by what he was hearing. Turning to Cal, he exhaled a deep breath of some of the finest smoke in the Western Hemisphere. Already affected. Eyes dilated, shoulders slightly sagging as the stuff infused his brain, he handed the oversized roach to Cal in offer of an inaugural Blancaneaux hit. The fourteen-year-old wavered. He hadn't done this before and though the taboo scene no doubt tugged on him, he wasn't at all sure circumstances were right.

Tres placed a glowing blunt to Cal's lips, however, encouraging him. Cal tentatively took his first-of-a-lifetime toke. Harsh smoke made him cough. Instruction helped and by the third attempt he managed to hold a mid-size breath for several seconds. Tres and Coy silly-giggled at the inept tries. Quatro only squinted one eye toward them long enough to finally register their presence before resuming attentive infatuation.

Having had no significant communication with Grea-oupa heretofore, Cal was interested in knowing the elder. The laid-back atmosphere here seemed to be opportune, though he was unsure of the situation. Seeing Cal's bafflement, Oupa drew the new arrival under his wing and put him more at ease. While the others listened to both the show and great-grandfather, they were offered rudimentary synopsis of the foreign radio transmission.

He told of the interviewee, one Pieter-Dirk Uys. Aka: Evita Bezuidenhout. Son of his old friend, Hannes Uys, a fourth-generation South African of Dutch and Belgian Huguenot stock who was a musician and organist in Grea-Oupa's local church from long past days living at the tip of the Dark Continent.

Pieter's mother, Helga Bassel, was a German concert pianist whom the Nazis expelled from the Reichsmusikkammer in 1935 as part of their campaign to root out Jewish artists. She later escaped to South Africa where she met Hannes.

A very determined woman managed to pack her grand piano in hasty departure from Hitler's takeover, with which she taught her daughter, Pieter's sister, Tessa Uys, now an accomplished concert pianist based in London.

Bassel spoke little about a Jewish past to her children. It was only after her suicide that they discovered she was fully Jewish. Pieter-Dirk and his sister had an NG Kerk upbringing. Their mother encouraged embracing of Afrikaner culture. Upon reaching maturity, Pieter had rebelled against such strictness, making his way onto the volatile scene that was an ending period of apartheid in his country.

He crafted a way-of-life for himself, Oupa told Cal, even playing an instrumental role in apartheid's downfall. Taking to stage, he had assumed a preposterously edgy role as pioneer in an underworld of gay culture using the guise of a drag queen. Over several years, a young man developed the evolving persona who strangely captivated a country. Ergo, ersatz bombast betokening Evita Bezuidenhout.

The sassy South African patterned her version on iconic Australian drag diva, Dame Edna Everage, who provided a template. Evita, Grea-oupa explained, portrayed the former ambassadress of Bapetikosweti, from fictitious Bantustan--- or black homeland--- located outside her home in affluent, formerly whites-only suburbs of Johannesburg. Evita Bezuidenhout was named in honour of Eva Perón.

Under apartheid, Oupa waxed on, Uys used humour in comedy to criticize and expose absurdities of the South African government's racial policies. Much of his work was not censored, indicating closet approval of his views by many members of the ruling party, who were not so bold as to openly admit mistakes or criticize policies themselves.

Now, years afterward, the performer 'held court' as a Madame of considerable influence, currently weighing in on the new democracy through her popular television show and book, 'Funigalore'. It was this subject that Cal heard being discussed which so enthralled four youths bent over a shortwave radio.

All this information broadsided a fourteen-year-old boy as he ascended an inaugural climb into the clouds. Grea-Oupa's interest was understandable, he reflected. But were these teenagers truly interested in politics of an African nation a wide ocean away?

Oupa carried on, chatting insightfully about a confidant's progeny's direct effect on a hierarchy hastened toward demise at the ballot box two years ago, when President Mandela took office. Grasping basics of the explanation, Cal found himself interested despite disparate stimuli lambasting him all at once.

This was the first time to converse directly with Grea-Oupa, hear of a distant land's power machinations, or learn about this Evita character. In the air-headed state-of-mind now possessing him, he considered the whole of it queerly compelling.

Cal found himself concentrating on her interview and Oupa's paired narration, learning over the passing hour of Pieter-Dirk's activism, so revered throughout South Africa as well as much of Europe and Asia. The role of an outlandish cross-dressing transgendered personality had integrally aided transfer of power in the African nation from white elitist class to its first black president and government. The subject had never been broached in the narrow confines of the boy's history classes back in the States. He became spellbound by the subject and wondered for the first time about a wider world's affairs. This great-grandfather figure, so obviously respected by the Lansing youths, also caused conjecture.

All of it wrapped together: truly mysterious. Cal absorbed more than information during the time; he enjoyed listening to the elder man who had lived through so much. A boy's heightened awareness prompted question upon question after the radio show concluded. He wanted more from the font of wisdom before him.

As the others gradually became distracted by separate conversations, Cal found himself alone with Grea-oupa. His mind raced with ideas, feelings, thoughts. This seemed, indeed, a perfect time to pick the man's brain. He came away from the Oupa-narrated radio interview beguiled by an exotic land of Humanity's origins; particularly the southern country populated by such an odd polyglot.

Oupa, reading the boy's interest, graciously expounded for the inquisitive youngster, glad for attentiveness. The idea of a serendipitous alighting in Blancaneaux, just where he should be in this twilight portion of life, crossed a great-grandfather's sagacious mind. The deSparkos had opened a moment, he reckoned inwardly.

When the far-seeing man quizzed the jaguar tracker on the morning's harrowing experience, the query once more engendered clumps of spreading goosepimples across Cal's anatomy. A sensation becoming a common one in this mountainous retreat… for neither Tres nor Cal had mentioned the adventure to anyone. Things that make you go, 'hm-mmmm'.

Conversation gradually waned while the dissimilar pair rested back on the sunny rock. The others had forsaken the site, wandering in explorative haze. Quiet befell them and Cal became more introspective. He noticed the agedness of the great-grandfather. Crepe-like skin, manner of stretching and flexing old joints, raspy voice. It bumped against his consciousness that this was a rare experience: being so close to a person of such advanced age. His own grandparents lived far away from the Broadhearst Estate, seldom around. There were no great-grandparents living.

Out of the clear blue, Cal blurted a question. "Grea-oupa, what is it like being so old?" In such an uninhibited state of mind, the teenager found no insult in it. A bemused look infused Oupa's face. He sat taciturn for a few minutes, making Cal conjecture whether he had overstepped some boundary. The wizened countenance, at length, peered sidelong at a youthful interrogator.

"Well, Calumet Alfrederic, son of same... I guess it be like having a million gorgeous pieces o' life all floating around ma body--- and mind--- and I'm trying to reach out and grab them. There be great big bundles already clutched, stored away for me to try and search for where I put them; they get mislaid a lot more now."

"When I feel ma great-grandson's head resting on ma chest, I try to memorize the touch and rumble of his laughing voice as it rolls up from his throat, soaking through me. And the way my great-granddaughter falls asleep in my lap: I try to hold the feeling tight to me so not to lose it. I harken upon an old, long-lost friend and try to relive a certain shared tick in time."

"I reminisce and revel when someone actually hears me tell of that reminiscence." Here, the gray-hair stared deeply into Cal's eyes, "You see, no one of clear mind desires to depart this world without leaving at least a trace of where they have been... what they've experienced."

Cal felt his body nestle closer to the old man, inhaling the arresting aroma of age. A headful of youthful kinked coils scraped comfortably against an old man's bare chest. A wrinkled arm wrapped around his own, drawing him in welcome to an old man's lonesome, often touchless existence. Cal comprehended the octogenarian's unspoken sense that no person would any longer want his touch without acquiescence.

"But the pieces are flying faster now and I am unable to catch very many. I can feel a great number of them slipping right through my fingers. Soon, I know, those feelings and those gorgeous shards of life, they will flee me... and there will be nothing."

Gnarled fingertips prodded into Cal's silky skin, "I know how it must seem that you have all the time in the world, young mandrake," the unfamiliar word sent a tingle through Cal, "but you don't. Catch the moments of your life. Grab them while you are young and quick. Hold them close and savor the happenings. File them safely, with intent. Because faster than you think, you will look around and realize that you are old... and slow. Then, there will be no more of them to catch."

"And, Calumet Alfrederic, when you discover the person--- the one person--- that makes you whole, don't hesitate. Grab them the closest of all and hold tight. It is the luckiest person who ever finds that one. That one will send your roots deep." Gea-oupa fell silent. Cal focused on weathered breathing and feathery thump of the sage's heart. He felt unexpected tears spill from his fourteen-year-old eyes in regarding the idea and for an instant worried what Oupa felt by the spillage. Then he thought on the profound premise being discussed and divined differently. Silence spoke volumes between the pair; those watery wells bit by bit fluttered shut, losing the idyllic visual surrounds. Offering a yield of fragile inner bounty for the chest beneath him.

Cal's inverting mind's eye conjured distant things… things out of focus. Yet, somehow of great import. The young man grasped this, yielding himself to a trice of moment, then filed it away. An old man: even more. He grasped this lovely slice of life, gently clutching it close.*

Jyp roused Grea-oupa with a tug of the old man's leg. The napping pair finally arose and disengaged. The foundling drew Oupa toward the deserted field in search of tools left propped there. Cal drug his mind to focus. Still pondering profundity, he watched the wise elder disappear.

Tres and Quatro led the twins to the cascades, showing how to use a rushing torrent without being drug down into it. Heads' hazy, the four next wisely opted to relax on the lawn awhile before engaging others in conversation; something native god-cousins understood pretty well. Twins took the cue, seeing the reasoning for it.

Even so, the grass tickled as Cal stretched out. His mind wiggled in itches, still and again full of some zillion questions. Grea-oupa had awakened a cogitating monster. The cohorts were just about nodding off, exhausted and high as they were. Cal wasn't having it. The present zoned-high was now revving him, not putting him back to sleep. He had just resurfaced from there, thanks very much.

"So, this is a marijuana ranch?" He grilled. "Does that make you brothers pothandlers?" The witticism caused laughter, yet Cal had been purely serious. This had proven an unbelievable day so far. His curiosity was stoked.

Coy piped up, "Bro, that is funny. Have you missed that these whole first three days? Yo, you have some catchin' up to do. I'ma start a branch franchise up in Rome when we go back. Quatro's gonna supply me with the seeds… super, huh?" Even in continuing mental fog, Cal knew this to be a piss poor idea, but couldn't grasp proper syntax for making the point. So, he laid back and sunned, listening a minute now that he had incited the others.

Tres, always informative, picked up the idea now, explaining how this enterprise differed from Central and South American operations. Illegal ones. Belize law held no animus toward the propagation and sale of their product. Years before, the method for controlling illicit farming and therefore drug cartel operations had coalesced into workable policy. Without the illegality and downside black markets, the young country had avoided being ripped apart by underground forces such as had built up elsewhere in response to worldwide demand. Misguided attempts at control of it, undertaken by international powers-that-be, continued to miss the lesson.

There was no exportation of the quality produce. Notoriety of Blancaneaux's crop elevated the equation to similar market forces for a plethora of other high-end markets: buyers sought them out. The legality factor removed the onus of need for underground trafficking, hence the attainment of normalcy which surrounded the tiny, family-driven operation here.

The side effect of consistently hearty appetites melded well with growing bodies, yielding little downside consequence, what with parental oversight of the usage by minors here in the mountain enclave. "That meat is a'smellin' mighty hot-damn good, ain't it?" this from a stupidly high Quatro, not grasping which end was up yet. "Mater and Shady be grillin' da Caribe recipe, because o' our good cousins bein' here. We should go on up."

Tres nixed the idea immediately. "Quat, it won't be ready to munch for hours. You sure know who's gonna be haulin' and peelin' and who-knows-what else if we show our stoned butts anywhere near that cookhouse. We wouldn't get a nibble. Ya know how da mamas be 'bout their special feasts--- da Broadhearst feasts are the most special ones o' all. Give it up, my brother. By da by, we get busted for smokin' before da end o' da day, Grea-oupa or no, and Papi'll have our asses strung to da plane prop for take-off tomorrow. Settle those fat lips down a bit an' wait for da trangle, a'ight?"

Meaning the call-to-dinner triangle, Cal deduced. Not understanding the hierarchy here on the estate as yet, his mind wandered further. The last visit was when he and Coy had been five. There had been no nuance back then. Tres raised the idea by his comment. "I don't get the family ladder you guys have, Tres. You all keep talking about Mater and Shady, and how both of them are somebody's blood mother…what's up with that?" He had been puzzled by it while clear-headed. Now, in a fog of lost inhibitions, the question ate at him.

Tres smiled at that, looking at Quatro. The two traded funny looks. "Well, ya see, Cal, things be a tad different here in da uplands than back in your States, boy. Let's see, now…" and Tres internalized a minute before going on. Cal was totally taken by the lilting mixture of Creole and British accents. The aberrant thought hit him during the pause. He waited.

"Ya probably noticed da fact of things: that there be fifteen o' us Lansing sibs, a'ight? And, both Mater and Shady be getting ready to pop again in some months ahead. Then there be t'other fact o' da matter, if you pay attention, dat there be several of us who have da same age but not twins. Y'see, Papi has been married to Mater for all these years and Shady showed up five years after her. Da two of them made a pact to lasso da patriarch o' da family and share da duties…So, we're numberin' at fifteen and soon to be seventeen. Papi likes it--- he be trained proper now by da powers behind da throne but don't be even knowing it--- and da mamas bein' extra happy to not have all dat pressure.

Everybody is thinking it be Papi that did all da finaglin'. It ain't da case. These wise women thought this all through and made Papi think it's all his idea," Tres sniggled in the knowledge. Quatro concurred.

"OK, I get all that, it makes sense. But where did their names come from? And, how about all your names? Ya'll are numbered, right? What's up with that? I mean, it's good, I really like them, but…?" Cal's hanging question stood awhile before the Lansings continued. In amusement.

"Da wisdom and simplicity is a mighty wonder, be sure. Da truth is that Papi, whose name is Frederick, knew he be plannin' a big load o' baby makin' from da beginning. His idea was to make sure that we would all have a sense of family even with so many. That's why he made da rule: all o' da babies were to be named da same: Frederick. Fredericka for da girls. We don't any o' us have a middle name or a number after 'em, like da third o' da fourth. Just those."

"But, da mamas, they knew there had to be a system, so there ya have da number-names. And, da girls all got da letters, now. 'Twas Shady's idea to do it in Spanish…it threw Papi off da track for years before he figured it out. But he still calls us all: Fred. Girls and boys. And mamas. Oh, that's right--- da mamas are both named Fredericka--- Papi tells everyone he did that, too. But he didn't, either. We call Mater that because she's da Matriarch. Shady's da lady who be a'shadowin'."

"Oh, almost be a forgettin'. Papi names all da Rottweiler dawgs da same. Yup, Fred."

"Like I said: simple."

"Israel Silvas Osoriol, 6 Avenida Condesa, Caye Ambergris." Tres re-read the name and address out loud at the stop sign in San Ignacio. The fast friends were free, he thought, glancing at his young 'kissin-cousin', Cal, over in the passenger seat. Not only had his Papi signed off on the trip, Cal Al's Dad had also. Most importantly, the Mother Triad hashed it over for a few days before giving their blessing.

When that final hurdle had been tackled, the duo had packed and been ready for a predawn departure the following morning. The jeep was rough but dependable. What with the recent securing of an official license for driving without an adult, Tres had navigated the boys down a tortuous route to San Ignacio on their way to Belize City and then on to the Caye. Their Uncle, Israel, had resided there for a good six years now, purchasing a small Robles Beach home offering an unimpeded view looking out toward the barrier reef. Past that: the Atlantic, and then Africa. Water taxi from the City took them a final leg to the Caye. Escorted by a small pod of dolphins, much to their delight.

Uncle Israel stood at the dock awaiting them. A misnomer--- Uncle Israel was only twenty-six--- he slouched against a weathered dock post, huge straw hat shading his handsome visage, wavy black shoulder-length tresses blowing lazily. He wore only cargo shorts and old-fashioned high top sneakers. How retro, thought Cal. The man's slim physique filled the ugly 'straight-boy style' fashion statement in a way that was hard to mask.

Even at this point in his life, Cal recognized maleness in a way he knew was not the 'normal' one. He just didn't have courage or wherewithal to address such a verboten subject. Though he didn't shy from physical contact amidst the boys in the boy-lodge--- none of them did--- Cal had no ability at the age of fourteen to process hormonal flare-ups in any cogent manner regarding lifestyle choices. All the non-sexual body contact amongst brothers and these Belizean 'cousins' was just that. Body contact. Not a nasty or even hormonal thing; it wasn't given a second thought by anyone. Boners, notwithstanding.

So, when the youth noticed the svelte older male awaiting Tres and him, Cal registered only: pleasing. Tres obviously felt similarly, "My uncle be da bomb big man, now, just sayin'. Can ya believe we are here for a week, Cal?" The older boy was away from the estate for the first time since a parent chaperoned trip a couple years before. A parentless traveler for an initial time, Tres was feeling his oats... Cal smiled at the realization in his own right, too.

The taxi craft sidled expertly to floating halt at dockside, a dock boy securing it. Uncle Israel grinned greetings as he helped the two jump to the marina deck. Grabbing their sparse baggage---what did teenage boys at a beach-week need, after all--- the three headed for Robles Beach and bachelor pad existence enjoyed by Israel.

A late-in-life lovechild addition to Mater's family, the youngest had been doted on and spoiled. Israel had weathered that impediment without self-centered absorption commonly resultant with the type. Inherent magnanimity put family in the front-facing bedroom. Touring them for familiarization of the place, the all-important fridge, shower, can, and the surrounding area, he then informed that they were on their own for the day.

An unexpected call had come from Hol Chan Marine Reserve where a junior-level marine biologist such as himself passed typical work days. The 'work' obviously agreed with the man. He displayed easy congeniality and an unassuming nature around nephew and god-nephew, affording immodest views of his athletic self, disrobing in front of them while uniforming up.

Tres inadvertently licked lips, watching without compunction, in clear admiration for the idolized 'uncle' baring it all. The smooth-skinned man clearly felt no misgivings for doing so. Cal wondered a bit at their familiarity yet chalked it up to the familial thing he had accepted so easily among the large cadre of close-knit brothers in the boy lodge cabana. After all, he had five brothers as well.

"All right, now, you two. I hadn't planned leaving you on your own this soon after your arrival," the sexy-voiced college grad Britishly intoned, "but it is what it is, so... just be careful and don't do any stupid kid stuff while I'm gone, OK?" He grinned while saying it, but the message was clear: your parents entrusted me with your safety. Don't go kill yourselves. The boys got it. Their promise to be careful echoed back on them as the screen door slapped shut behind him.

Tres looked around, rubbing hands together in anticipation of a day on the beach. He was in heaven. The two unpacked in split seconds, pulled on speedos, then proceeded to explore. They found snorkeling equipment in an outdoor storage shed. Packing it and a sack lunch of pbj sandwiches from the pantry, the two took off. Several miles north, past any overt sign of civilization, they sat down in remarkably white sand, wiggling toes while scoping both reef and habitat of the spot.

Large sea boulders were strewn in attractive formations around them, not only on the beach and back past the dunes, but in the crystal-clear water. Several emergent islands rose and peaked jaggedly some fifty feet above water level. Bird life was rife around them. It was noted almost immediately how much dolphins liked the site. When the boys pulled on flippers and donned snorkels plus masks, they found themselves escorted into calmer sea past the surf line. Happy talk evinced by several aquatic clowns gave distinct conversational impressions. Cal quickly perceived the seeming friendship overtures were, indeed, that. And these new friends loved games.

Over the next hours, two boys swam and played with a pod numbering more than a dozen. They sought bodily contact with the teenagers, bumping, rubbing and flirting in their vivacity, even offering dorsal fins for exhilarating rides. Probing deeper into a diverse underwater biosphere uncovered richly teeming realms matrixed by the reef. Much color and blooming vitality surrounded them; an overarching rumble of ocean dialogue pervaded the boys' senses.

Tres pointed out elusive barracuda several times. Barely able to visualize the vicious-looking toothed denizens who hovered, inspecting, on the very perimeter of his vision, Cal became wary of sneak attack. As it turned out, the nasty looking 'hyenas of the sea' were notorious cowards, not known for hunting. The boys learned to ignore the timid scavengers who skittered away at slight provocation.

Labyrinthine coral beds proved delicately lethal. Quickly deduced by a few scrapes against the razor sharpness. Schools of rainbow-colored fish swarmed them in exhibitions of complete trust. Larger fish, manatees, sea turtles and even stingrays, with a couple good sized sharks, mingled with the boys as the afternoon transpired. All amazingly at ease with human presence. Acts of curiosity were frequent, as if introducing themselves. Cal was charmed.

Ultimately needing a break, they beached it again. Sharing drinks and sandwiches plus fresh mangoes off trees behind the dunes satisfied growing bodies. A dozy stretch under beating rays extended the idyll by a sun nap in repose on wave beaten rocks, drowsing between conscious study of stupefying natural artwork and meandering dreams. Cal had never fancied such splendor could exist. The bridge between wakefulness and fantastical imaginings wrought during the daydreams grew blurred by an astounding array of catalysts. He was overawed by the encounter.

That first evening, drained by events and activities of a full day under taxing sun, the two found themselves feted to a veritable seafood feast by Israel. Teasing mercilessly until they dropped the 'uncle' moniker, he insisted he wasn't old enough to be saddled that way. Besides, he alluded, many fewer rules and restrictions might deem merit-able in absence of the term... Absorbing the advantages, an opt for acceding to his preference was ultimately granted.

Coal-baked, succulently flaky whole tilapia and amber jack, prepared on an open fire at the beachside El Norte Bar and Grill, augmented by fresh local vegetables and wild rice, were washed down with locally brewed tea and ale. It satisfied ravenous appetites. Israel snickered pleasurably while listening to the reggae band and observing the wolfing of several fish each. He gathered a friendly competition was in play and sat back in disbelief as the two gorged themselves.

Under a rising golden gibbous moon, nursing full-bodied dark ale, Israel lounged contentedly in contemplation of a day's hard, satisfying efforts. Familiarizing anew with this surprisingly mature nephew frosted his day. How gratifying was the revelation. The younger American, Calumet, came across appealingly inquisitive and articulate, too.

Engaging and pleasant by emerging self-awareness, the effect was enhanced with vicarious sharing of innocence. Revisiting the day's events from their fresh, unblemished perspective renewed his spirit. It was alluring to regain sense of novelty in a day-to-day world... exactly why the family baby had settled here. Time and routine had dulled some of the pleasure.

The week's stay unfolded in continuation of the theme. Daily discoveries whammed the visiting youths with something else unbelievably eye-popping at almost every turn. Dolphin friends became a daily diversion. Names evolved for pod members. It is said to be a facile ability for young minds to absorb alien languages into which they are immersed. The concept was certainly cogent regarding Cal and Tres, acquiring sea mammals' language nuances by the hour.

The dolphins mentored the process. After all, their mental abilities far outstripped humankind. Only simpleminded ignorance and a touch of human arrogance denied the fact. Cal was heart-warmed to hearken upon the dolphins' dubbing of himself. A poetic lyric reprising a peculiar staccato click and twirl combination broadsided the youth to shocking clarity when Flipp and Flex performed it at him time after time… until enough. He had a name amongst the dolphins. Things that make you go, 'hmmmmm'.

"Dr. Tyson says that there are more stars in the universe than there are people on Earth, Tres." Cal was contemplative under the myriads above them as they waned together sleepily. The beach blanket was secured at each corner by rocks for inhibition of the resolute night breeze's attempt to muss it.

Prostrate and sprawled, his propped head undulated with each of Tres' slow breaths. Cal enjoyed the draped arm wrapping him and fingers languidly rubbing his belly. Having worn themselves out during another filled day in sun and water, tacit agreement had been reached for passing a night peaceably on the blanket rather than expending energy to relocate indoors. That they both failed to dress after showering earlier was a luxury. Israel had decamped to the house after a leisurely dinner of boiled eggs, fruit, cheese and crunchy-crusted potatoes baked to inner fluffiness on beachside campfire coals.

Speculating on profound things, they considered the winking moon's halo. Wispy clouds caused the effect in drifting past during nocturnal progress. Twitters and chirps arose from nearby night creatures scurrying frenetically on obscure quests. The wholeness of it lent a soothing quality of melding tranquility. "I believe it to be da truth," Tres whispered drowsily, mouth an inch from Cal's ear. "Do you think they be talking with each other--- da stars?" The premise was interesting.

"I don't know... but I always wonder if each galaxy, with millions of stars; and each star, with its own planets; are just specks in another existing universe. And, if each grain of sand has its own teeny universe somehow fitting inside of it, too. Like a big nested pack of little-to-bigger universes all intertwined and ignorant of others. If I ever meet Neil deGrasse, I'm going to ask him." Cal was casually firm in the intent. Two drowsed into contented oblivion. The night sky traversed...

...Cal's dreamscape unfolded in lifelike parallel. In it, he turned away from Tres, re-positioning for comfort. But, in doing, his big piece slipped over the hand fingering his belly. An immediate unintentional response was spawned. The big boa involuntarily filled with blood, inching upward, rubbing over the hand just bumped.

"You be talkin' to me, now, Cal?" Tres' dream speech couldn't miss the heat of the appendage arising. He grasped it lightly. The thing bounced to rigidity by that digitalization, now straining against the hand. In fluid motion, Tres rolled out from under Cal's shaggy head. His own leaned down over the now-arching organ, peering at a draping cowl as it receded lazily from a barely visible eye with ever-present pearl of adolescent goo.

After another second, a seeking tongue tipped the thing clean. Lips caressed phattening elasticity, causing it to jump even more by the touch. Another warm hand cupped the tight dark ball sack, torqueing gently, raising the pole to a more convenient angle. Then the shaft slipped inside an oral cavern begging for company. Tonsils were pushed aside in sliding passage to a deeper place; succulent labia felt hairless pubes and balls nudge them.

Cal's hands lifted up and over silky skin covering Tres' back and neck, coming to rest, one each, on head and cheek. Synchrony of opposing movements wended upward in a slow arc toward mutual climax, Tres' own piece never leaving the proximity of his companion's rasping calf. Copious eruptions juiced them both, inside and out, as the next period felt pleasurable drippings ease past paroxysmal stages of pulsing satisfaction.

Wordless reverie banked the fantasized episode. After, even with less-than-conscious awareness of only dream-state virtuality, the two relaxed back to repose, luxuriating in slippery ooze. Breathing resumed normal flow... four heads slooped downward into deep, slaked slumber...

...Fifteen degrees of moon arc later, Tres awoke. It must be close to dawn, he drowsed. Cal was still nestled into the crook of his arm, deep asleep, never having budged once. Tres' eyes lifted to a shifted moon. Night breeze wafted more gently than before, still caressing bare skin. Illuminated puffy clouds danced a slow jig around the pregnant lunar body. Eerie silhouettes of radar-guided bats dipped and dove in careening pursuit of night-flying insects.

A faint scraping sound chafed his left ear. Peering to the side, he viewed a tiny struggling turtle. Its nose was strangely hooked, like a bird's beak. Miniature flippers furiously attempted a rowing climb up Tres' face. The close-up gave a weird view of the little face set in determination for achieving an uphill goal. The boy watched the misguided ordeal, then observed three more of the pygmies come flippering toward him on the heels of their leader. Each appendage was tipped by double teensy claws, aiding their efforts.

Tres was certain he and Cal had seen and swam with bigger versions of these--- the adults had stretched to over two-feet in length, more colorfully marked in bright greens, yellows and reds on a dark carapace. The denizens of the reef had been feasting on sponges amongst coral, deftly extracting delicious morsels with large, talented hooked beaks.

Jostling his sleeping god-cousin, Tres urged, "Cal, wake it up. Ya gotta see what's chasing us now." He elbowed the boy's neck up, rotating his chest onto the sand to force the issue.

Call sprang from sleep, wary of sea monsters, "What is it?" He vainly struggled to rise and flee from whatever was upon them. The grin caught him and he elevated to tiptoes upon Tres' warning to trod carefully. The boy softened as focus on the tiny beings registered. A dozen more of the sprites had paddled on to the blanket, whirring those little flippers as they swarmed the two.

"Wow, Tres, aren't they flyin' the shade?" Studying them a bit more, he broke out, "Hey... aren't these the babies Israel told us about in the big project he keeps getting called to help out on? We need to tell him!" Saying this, his eyes suddenly widened in disbelief at seeing a strange raccoon-like animal at vision's edge, unmistakably slobbering over the mini-meals-on-the-move.

Too wary to chance a direct encounter with humans, it nevertheless expressed every bit of the desire by its body language. Then, the bristly beast darted suddenly at one corner of the blanket, nabbing a lagging tyke, racing off with the snack already disappearing down an open gullet.

"Quick, Tres, go get Israel! I'll get him away," Cal was frantic to stop a massacre in the making. He hopped upright, junk flopping around his crotch. Tres reflected that a good weapon was present right here before him--- just sling it around some more. The mental picture made him guffaw despite himself, scarpering for the nearby house.

Cal proceeded gathering little turtles into the blanket's safety net, shouting and gesticulating at the predator. By peripheral vision, he espied glowing red eyes of several more hunters. Apparitional as Sherlock Holmes fiends. The eyes evinced malevolence in unblinking scowls. A few remaining coals in the fire ring allowed just enough glow to give reflection to a strange 'Lion King' re-enactment of Scar's hyenas. So ugly.

Coatimundi. The name of the animal sprang to mind. Known as a hog-nosed coon, the avid hunters were common to the area, but Cal had only seen pictures. The thing hissed at him in dismay at being blocked, bottle-brush tail switching in frustration. It appeared ferocious, looking more like it would overcome its fear and attack any second. The beast eyed toiling babies with determined purpose.

Dozens of flailing thrashers were all moving like a herd of cats toward edges, on various paths, forcing Cal to leap multiple directions for collecting them. Coati wasn't pleased. Raising blanket corners together in net fashion kept them somewhat bunched. This move tumbled little ones toward the center, buying Cal time. He continued shouting and waving, grabbing more of the crawling herd as he worked. Some outliers weren't lucky enough to reach the safety net.

At the very moment Cal observed several sets of darting red eyes lowering toward the sand, as if gathering for a group launch, bright lights harshly burnt across the setting. Upsetting a concerted plan. From behind, there came a running Tres, with Israel. Both waved powerful beams like laser weapons, scaring and dispersing now visible night predators. Not only the coatis, but traditional raccoons, night birds and rodents of sizeable stature dashed for shadows, only reluctantly giving up a moving feast. At least for the present.

"Cal, keep rolling up the blanket--- we'll get the stragglers. You're doing great!" The young marine biologist took control of the situation, instructing both boys in succinct fashion. Mere minutes transpired as a greater majority of just-hatched nestlings were rounded up. Next, they were carried closer to their distant goal: the safer waves and reef. Israel named them as Hawksbill Sea Turtles, a severely endangered species imprinted to Robles Beach for untold generations.

Protection was a must, Israel told them. Not only natural predatory danger but human trophy hunters, too, were swiftly wiping out the beautiful creatures. Getting hatchlings to water was a giant step. Though still hunted even there by humans and sea predators, it was all the three protectors could provide. Israel emptied the blanket twenty feet from surf's edge, explaining the need for all hatchlings to imprint on beach itself to assure return in two to three years for repeating the breeding and nesting process. The Cycle of Life.

Taking Tres' light, he next floodlit the mess of babies, drawing their attention. Then he used candlepower to direct a path toward waves. First one, then a dozen, then the entire herd turned to a track paved for them. The scientist explained during the odd traffic duty how normally, glints of reflective stars and moon off water provided instinctive pull for untried neonates.

A major factor decreasing survival rates for many different sea turtle species arose from manmade light sources which misdirected babies away from water. Sending the boy's outward on either side of the queue, reef-bound, they waved away the alert and hovering land predators. Protected passage, at least to the water, was secured.

Afterwards, seated lifeguards huddled in satisfaction by the impromptu Underground Turtle Railroad, jesting over success and the scenario leading to it. "It is way lucky that you two decided to camp this night of all nights, Tres and Cal," Israel was elated by the fortuitous favor.

Statistically, one in a thousand hatchling turtles survived to maturity. Though only a short part of the tough road, the three could feel extremely gratified to attain such a high rate of survival for the herd of almost one-hundred and fifty on this leg of their journey.

"Well, the bigger luck was that they didn't hatch two or three hours earlier… we may not have noticed them," Tres smiled over at Cal as he spoke.

"Think you would have slept through them, huh?" Israel seemed oblivious, scribbling notes into a log.

"You could say that, ah-yah," came the dreamy reply.

April, 2000

"Go, big Cal! Make us proud!" The pretty cheerleader's pom-poms bounced in rhythm to the marching band's drum cadence. Other cheerleaders picked up the chorus and in seconds, the surrounding send-off crowd picked up the chant. If Cal could have, he would've blushed. Deeply. Liking attention as much as any eighteen-year-old boy, especially adoration, the good-looking youth nevertheless had deeper emotions than desire for being singled out in the current scenario.

The senior class valedictorian, student body president, All-State wide receiver, cleanup-hitting center-fielder and self-deprecating class clown stayed in line behind the wrestling team captain, Josh Reynolds, his good friend Melvin Watson, and younger brother Doy. Only one of the close group of wrestling team partners. In the middle of the pack.

No acknowledgment of the elevated regard rendered by the shout-out over his teammates escaped Cal. Rather, he was ill at ease by the chant. Teammates and coaches couldn't miss the chant, but also noticed the non-response. And the modesty. They were accustomed to his innate humility.

The whole wrestling team had qualified for regionals two weeks before, after all, and he was but one member. The six-foot-three growing teenager was ever mindful of his friends' and teammates' sensibilities, disdaining personal illumination. Not that he lacked pride in himself, simply that there was plenty of attention to share. He was anything but a limelight hog.

Yes, had his dark complexion allowed for it, the blush would've been noticeable. As it was, a faint head-down toothless smile provided the sole acknowledgment of Jenny's declaration. That and rib punches delivered on the bus registering good-natured envy at attention from the class beauty. Almost any boy in school would be bowled over by the compliment. Calumet was not one of them. More, he remained the single unattached team member. He wasn't let to forget that fact, either.

On the bus, the boys absorbed new-found popularity afforded a typically lackluster sport by advancement to state wrestling competition. Coach Costner bounded up entry steps after a few moments delay by a brief address to the throng. Scanning now-seated occupants, the mentor let them all know in clearly certain terms where they stood.

"Ain't a single thing been accomplished yet, men. Keep your eyes on the prize. You are all aware of what we talked about first week of school last fall. The state finals. As a team. No one carries us alone. All-for-one and one-for-all! Hup, hup! Let's focus on what's important. Drag your eyes back into all of those swollen heads--- the upstairs ones--- and think. OK?" The lifelong teacher was strictly authoritarian. And highly respected.

He was consummate coach and mentor to the team, having ushered them into the sport years before, grooming each one along the way. Community followed the man's career and family like a celebrity. Accolades were but fluff to him. He intended to mold these young men until they were graduated and away from his guidance. Like teams preceding this one. And those to follow.

Cal contemplated the coming meet on the way into Rome Civic Auditorium where regional finals were to be staged. Others failed to draw him out. They were used to his trances. When he was open to it, the boy was ultra-gregarious. But when like this, all knew to let him have space.

Through the bus ride, unpacking and locker room change into red and gold jump suits, Cal Al introspected. He had a method before meets and this was it. Focus was the aim. Today, though, there existed an added reason for the zoned effect. His competition. Namely, Billy Westfall. It struck a chord in Cal's mind. For several reasons. Not least was the fact that the blond Atlanta-area senior was the last opponent to take Cal down. Though a technical take down, a take down, nonetheless. Three months before. A split decision, it was a losing one. Leaving him lacking. The challenge to rectify that loss was overpowering this day, yet Cal felt other, more private reasons just as strongly.

He found himself strangely drawn to the boy. Golden boy. The blonde bombshell in no way mirrored Cal and his approach to sports or life: loving and basking in every bit of attention he could point toward himself. Billy Westfall had nurtured a name in the metropolitan area and meant to harvest rave reviews any way possible. Multiple girls revolved through his world, even college co-eds. An entourage tagged him as lead dog in every venue the young sports star chose. He played to the hilt all manner of attention-grabbing ploys and knew full well the effect reckoned by the mantra.

The string of successes in every sport undertaken had made the high schooler a prime target for multiple college programs bent on recruiting the cream of the crop for collegiate stardom. Billy was anything but half-and-half. One had only to ask him, if there were any doubt. The senior wasn't shy.

So, he was on Cal's mind. There were other things nagging in the background, too, like his erstwhile twin, Coy Al, who had ditched the team months before. He approached life differently than Cal. As well, upcoming SAT's for college entrance placement had him concerned. Not to mention final exams and the niggling question of a prom date. But those things were all secondary now.

A bop to the short-cropped head brought him to reality. "Met-Man, you gonna pout the whole damn day, now?" Mel grinned as he alternately poked and pushed on his close buddy, ready to interact before the meet. Melvin styled himself a lady's man and wanted to drag his virgin buddy along on the trail he traveled, sampling wares of a growing stable of options he found looking back at most every turn. As tall as Calumet, five pounds heftier and sporting a retro 'fro, the buff schoolboy knew his own strengths and pushed limits exploring them. He was commonly frustrated by an introverted personality intermittent to his best friend.

"Nah, Mel, just zonin' the warm-up. I plan to burn some bridges today, what's up? You ready for what's comin' down at us?" Cal was quietly laying out the approach he was tracking and not easily distracted, even by Melvin's ebullience. Mel took a friendly hint, brushing his friend off and turning to seek other stimuli. He knew better than to try prying Cal loose when he sensed the mood now evident. Cal went back inward.

The meet began with weigh-in and med checks followed by bracket settings. Due to the fact the regional meet included no female entrants and no female meet officials this year, coaches agreed on an easier uniform-less set-up phase, relegated to privacy of the communal locker room. Entrants catcalled and teased incessantly throughout this naked prelude, what with high school mentalities involved. Then each member tacked his strategy and huddled with coach or trainers for last minute advice. Pep talks were over.

Matches proceeded throughout morning. By merit of a strong showing from the Floyd County school, culminating matches came down to half a dozen which pitted Cal against several foes he had met before. Running his bracket, like the entire team, it came down to Central High against Floyd County High in the finals. Cal wondered if he would meet Billy Westfall in the final singles match.

Plenty of extracurricular crowd interaction by the flamboyant team had most definitely enlivened the meet. Billy brought his typical hangers-on, a mish-mash of mixed sexes, genders and lifestyles, all intent on being close to the star factor Billy radiated. Catching up to Cal and Mel at one point, Billy razzed the two on their lonesome selves, sans acolytes.

"Dudes, ya'll done been blackballed, or what? No bitches followin' ya'll, huh? No homies' keepin' you relevant? Wassup with that, boys? You thinkin' we done knuckled down outta fear up against ya'lls' podunk school, or you just got a heavy thumb a'pressin' on ya, yo?" He head-flicked toward Coach Costner, knowing full well the strictness Floyd coaching demanded. They were, indeed, 'under the thumb'. Like all matches.

Billy's coach, Whitaker Daniels, was a free-spirit himself, allowing latitude to his team, and especially Billy Westfall, in recognzance of market play it gave him with media. Billy had it good. Or so Mel thought, jealously taking exception to freedoms boasted across the arena.

"Damn that dude. He be gettin' on my last nerve with all that trash, Met Man. Ain't no sense in not wipin' his pale ass out 'da door when we gets to do it, now… what you say?" The rivalry was good, even with talk going on, and the two knew it. But as luck would have it, Simon Graeber ended up matching with Billy in the final, by rote of unusually allocated team points rather than wins, pins or take downs. Technical falls determined matchups this day.

In the end, despite a sizeable team lead Floyd took to the final match, Billy managed to pin Graeber, in shut-out style, resulting in narrow victory. For Central High.

Downcast, the team still knew State Invitational was just that: invitational. Due to point accumulation, Floyd County CHS's passage on to the state meet was automatic, pushing Floyd vs Central into contention yet one more time. A boisterous crowd accompanied the team home in jubilance even though they were runners-up instead of regional champions. After all, Coach Costner stressed, the team would see another day by their chance at State Meet, in Atlanta, two weeks ahead. They took heart in that fact and would buckle down for the readying interim.

"Ewwwww…" Cal Al winked open one squinty eye to envision Billy Westfall's flaxen dutchboy haircut framing the exclaiming visage in throes of rapture. The 'O' shape of the blond hunk's lips evinced the expression in coordination with his aroused state, presently bobbing up and down on Cal's smeared stomach--- the blonde's stuff still roping copiously from the one-eyed prong jutting from sexy paleness. Cal's wrestling nemesis grinned down at him from saddle position, astride Cal's straining pelvis.

Cal lay still, feeling pulse after pulse gush the boy's innards to exclamatory welcome. "Ewwwww…" He was loving this, Cal exulted to himself. If this was losing, it wasn't so bad after all, he supposed, on this early Saturday morning after the team's second place bridesmaid finish. Matching hues with towhead blondeness upstairs, bouncing around an animated face, a curly encircling patch downstairs seemed to bridle the buoyant thing draining onto the flat hairlessness of Cal's ebony stomach. He reveled in that color contrast. Coffee and cream.

Disappointingly, the angelic face faded into a blur when Cal's second eye peaked through the murk, giving dimension. Even so, Cal's pulsing continued and as the blurring pale face phased into a ceiling fan, Cal's consciousness joined with his pipedream.

The sound blended its multisyllabic elongation with rising ebony features of his twin. "Ewwwww...," and the two fixed their stare on one another. Coy grinned lewdly, licking his lips as he stared into Cal's eyes, then rotated downward to his brother's midsection. Following Coy's ocular move, he found the presence of yet another brother.

Doy Al's sleeping face lay in repose on Cal's stomach. His face slathered in a flight-of-fancy's beaming ten-inch arch of satisfaction. Satisfaction for the subconscious success at nocturnal transmissions. Cal delighted in the release even as he hearkened on reality. Truth be damned. Spasming teemed.

Coy's grinning visage passed from Cal's face to Doy's. He reached a tentative finger down to the third brother's slimed cheek. Tipping one pearly glob dripping slowly downward, he deliberately raised it back to his nose, inhaling the smell of it. All the while drawing Cal's eyes like a hypnotized moth to light. Cracking his own matching ear-to-ear grin, Cal jostled his pelvis, rousing the sleeping Doy.

Over a slow-motion few-second time lapse, the twins spied together as Doy's eyes fluttered open, causing a sticky string to spread with the wavering lids. Mindfulness gripped the younger boy only incrementally, in typical teenage emergence from deep REM sleep stage. Doy engaged. Fuzzily. Then puzzlingly. His own fingers came up to test the foreign gel. His tongue tentatively licked smudged lips, smacking lightly.

Mirthful waves of laughing fits consumed Cal and Coy. They whooped at the crass male-centric joke, studying younger bro's recognition of the situation.

In a fit of repugnance, Doy Al darted upward from his big brother's brownness, ricocheting the biggie among the six Broadhearst boys by the abrupt action. Up and down off a taut belly. A few final pulses strung from Doy's face to cyclopean eye. The corona nodded independently, plainly glad to have enjoined as it had done.

But, the fiddler had left the roof. Ensuing howls of laughter engulfed the twins. Infecting Doy, the third brother gradually commingled into his older siblings' joviality, abashed perception melting into acceptance of the unexpected and involuntary display. Sticky fingers attempted wiping slimed cheeks but succeeded in only authoring a finger-painting tour de force by the moves. In curious teenage crudeness.

"Whoa, Bro," Coy broke into the wordless awakening, "What was that all about? You lose like that very often and we may all drown.

Maybe we'll sleep somewhere else." He finger-plunked the turgid arch and sat back against the headboard. "Doy, you need to clean that off, boy. Really. Before someone comes in."

Getting the message, Doy jumped up to retrieve a t-shirt slung haphazardly across a chair. Turning, wiping his face and ruining the organic chef-d'œuvre just wrought, he posed the obvious, "Cal was that 'cause I fell asleep there, or were you dreamin' somethin' hot?" The two youngers burst out, now heckling their big brother. But the noticeable non-response by their example-setting sibling pulled both up short.

"Who was it, Cal?" Doy had to know. His oldest brother was the most transparent member of the family. Coy and he knew without doubt a fantasy had set the eruption off. They just didn't know who triggered it. "Come on, bro, tell us...was it Jenny?" His nosiness couldn't be quelled. "She's gonna be hurting bro, if it is--- that junk isn't going in easy, for sure, when she gives it up," the poke to the subsiding volcano accented what he was picturing.

At that, one too many undesired references signaled a next move. Cal pulled the sheet up over the thing, finally removing the trigger for the uncomfortable turn talk had taken. "Guys, I'm hungry. Let's get up, 'K?" Disappointed, the third-degree men backed off, lightening Cal's load. He sighed in relief as Doy headed out to the shower across the hall. Rustlings of morning routines were filtering up from the first floor.

With Doy gone, Cal sat back. He gathered thoughts, recalling the mounted fantasy ride of a while before, eyes glazing over at the recall. Coy, observing quietly, introspected in the peculiar manner his twinship status allowed. Bridging the mental gap as only he could do regarding Cal. After a moment, elucidation flooded his features. The surprise deduction left the younger of the two both perplexed and clarified.

Whether his brother would find confidence to open up to him, of all people, was a question only time would tell. Yet, by data now figured through, Coy had the enigma solved. And, it was not alien to his own feelings. Cal and he were on one more plane of parallel. Now that he, Coy, knew of it, he simply had to help Cal come to peace with the sticky situation.

Two weeks had passed too quickly. And not nearly fast enough.

Cal's prom question still confounded him. He realized the expectations but felt ambivalence over a recent lightning bolt of self-discovery.

Did he admit to himself the emerging truth and deal with it? Or fall in line with everyone's anticipations?

On another subject, SAT's were not particularly study-able; what had been accumulated over twelve years of school would have to suffice. The tests would not adequately address the life's pursuit he meant for himself. Computer programming and software development. Yet the way to his future traveled certain unavoidable paths, therefore the necessity for college admittance. Angst over their approach persisted.

Senioritis was prevalent amongst the class. His friends all tugged him different directions. Pandora's Box was pressuring more than one cohort and even Cal was feeling a call to explore expanding boundaries.

His parents sat back, content in the preparation of their eldest, knowingly confident Cal would navigate things with good sense. Little pressure came from that quarter. Cassandra and the Professor remained the quasi-graduate's biggest fans, looking forward to commencement speeches as much as State Meet. Now, Coy, that boy was a different story altogether, Mammay considered. Somewhere along the line, his tracks had shifted. She worried because the new ones appeared founded on sand.

Amidst thoughts on all this hubbub, Cal found himself and the team bussing into Atlanta the month before graduation. Zoned, per usual, in preparation for coming challenges. He could sense change in the wind but was mystified by just what was niggling inside his gut and brain. Extrasensory perceptions were tangled in too many layers. Deep introspection on the trip was called up in order to cope.

Atlanta Convention Center Arena was boisterously loud on entry, mounting energies infectious to the team. Even Coach Costner's iron will found itself hard-pressed to constrain his team amidst the infused atmosphere. After prelims of weigh-in, bracket settings, meet rules and the like, entrant teams were sectioned off on the arena floor.

Excess of dynamism slammed Floyd County's small town entourage. The packed house roiled in rival expressions of spirit and competitive displays. Uniformed pep bands and drill team squads mingled in camaraderie only manifested at this time each year. Cal and Mel sized up opponents. The two huddled in joint effort to strategize for the coming onslaught. Mel, the coolest of heads, was flashing nerves under the current venue conditions.

"Damn, Met Man, you catchin' all this craziness?" The duo was seeing the full panoply of a carnival-like environment but having trouble absorbing it all. "Hey, yo, look over there--- see who just came in? Looks like the big man is lettin' everyone know who has arrived. Puttin' us all on notice... the asshole."

Cal followed his finger point, coming to rest on an extravagantly decked-out team across the floor, marching in a big spiral toward the center spot. Central High's top-seeded team cavorted into the ruckus flanked by vaulting cheerleaders and perfect drumline. Billy Westfall's unmistakable supremacy reined front and center. The large group flaunted frenetic activity around his blue and silver robed personage. The athlete lacked only a crown to proclaim suzerainty before which all might dutifully genuflect.

Several mobile-cam teams from local Metroplex TV stations flanked the group. All pointing Billy's direction. The arresting blonde wallowed in the center of attention, projecting justifiable desert by his swagger. Smugness oozed from the consummate showman. Undefeated gladiator had taken the stage.

Coronation was written all over him, Cal reflected. Mel was disgusted.

"Can you believe all that shit, my man? That's just over-the-top wrong. He needs to be taken down a notch. A full helpin' o' some ole' fashion humble pie whoop-ass. And, it's gonna have to be one of us that feeds it to him... you know that, right, Met Man? No one else here hefting balls big enough to do it, but us."

Cal observed the comparatively reserved display from Floyd County's side of the floor. In partly mesmerized awe, he nodded in almost dubious agreement. Conflicting emotions and urges flooded over him. Cal was weirdly drawn and consciously repelled at the same time. He felt his junk lurch as the golden boy turned, granting a glimpse of the ripped physique partially visible under the Rocky-esque robe.

The champ's eyes, sweeping the arena, caught and linked with Cal's at that moment. The normally confident boy-man found odd comfort, one more time, by the dark complexion into which he had been born. It saved an embarrassing betrayal by the full body flush enveloping him. A snarky smirk filled the face of his archrival. As Mel and he watched, their nemesis purposefully strode across the floor toward the two.

In audible proximity, he greeted them. The eyes were only on Cal. "Dudes! Ya'll ready to rumble?" The braggadocio carried him close.

With several sycophants trailing, he came within smell range. "Good day for a competition, huh, boys? If you call it that. Hope ya'll ready for the big finale. I'm looking forward to lookin'--- down--- at you chumps. From the winner's stand." The boy's chutzpah was enthralling. Even Mel was rendered speechless.

Catching a whiff of erogenous musk exuding from him, Cal stood hypnotized. Puppet-like. Leaning even closer, Billy whispered into Cal's ear, "Dude, you behave good today and I just might let you have a lick o' all this. Your mouth outta be just about at the right level when we finish up. Mind yo' manners, now, hear?" And with that, he deliberately reached down to cup the sizeable mound tenting the jumpsuit inside the gaping robe. Intentionally brushing Cal's crotch on the way.

Another lurch of the junk brought Cal back to reality, freeing him. The smarmy grin remained. Cal recoiled at the obviously disrespectful move, fists balling instinctively. But the autonomous junk yawed of its own accord. Billy glanced downward perceptively, adding, "Sure seems to me like you needin' a prom date, dude. Bad. Lizard is takin' note, looks like. Happens most times when I get this close. See ya' soon… girlfriend."

Mel came out of his freeze at that. Small town wrestler pushed hard against the overly close invasion. The alpha male flailed backward in mock exaggeration. Like he had been struck. "That is plain uncalled for, boy. Just teasin' a little, now. Only a friendly rivalry here. Get hold o' yourself…chump number two."

Cal barely snagged Mel's balled fist before forward trajectory began, but the damage was done. TV cams were focused and recording. Three angles caught the mini altercation in full-blown audio-visual detail.

Just then, a strong arm wrapped each boy around the chest, pulling forcefully. Coach Costner yanked Cal and Mel away and out of camera range, "What is this going on here, men?" He was livid. "That is NOT the way either of you have been taught. Get a grip and fall in." Disgustedly whipping around, he stalked away from the scene, not totally sure his charges would follow. Gesturing to the remaining members, all huddled around the tall German. Looking from one to the next, the seasoned mentor re-established command.

A booming laugh behind them dug deep as the loose cannon named Billy Westfall assured rolling cameras that there was no problem to be seen here. Knowing full well all would play out on 6 pm news. He snorted in condescension as he and his followers retreated to their own wedge of allotted arena floor. Their own coach was still nowhere to be seen. The party continued there.

"OK. Now, I get what just went down. We all saw it. But, the optics are bad, boys, very bad. This is no way to conduct ourselves on the very first trip to State. Everyone, into the locker room." Heads down, tails tucked, all high-tailed it out of the fishbowl. Ten minutes and a thorough drubbing later, the cream of Floyd High's wrestling program reentered the competition arena.

Color guard made the call-to-order and matches were underway.

Being in opposite brackets, Floyd and Central didn't match up in early rounds. The team settled down and methodically carried on with wiping away competition, head and shoulders above the rest. Their confidence returned. Cal's parents beamed at him and his younger brother Doy from across the floor in third row seats. Coy's seat remained empty. He caught Jenny studying him wistfully--- what's up with that, he wondered--- for the first time through the day.

Match points flashed running tallies up on the jumbotron scoreboards around the center and Mel commented periodically to Cal on the collision course setting up between the archrival schools. Floyd County Consolidated and Central High. Country yokels vs Metro urbanites.

It was during a semi-final match between Mel and Macon High's Charles Gatti when calamity hit. During the third and unnecessary set--- Mel had swiped the first two with simple ease--- Gatti posted an illegal takedown on Melvin, flipping to his offside in a brazenly dangerous move. Frustration finally got the better of the opponent by the mastery Mel had imposed over him through the first rounds. A hard landing dealt by an illicit maneuver resulted in a head blow to hardwood. Off mat.

Meet officials threw the book at the competitor. He was escorted from the arena, forcing a forfeit by the whole team. A resultant concussion left Mel dazed and confused. Officials remanded him to treatment and observation in the medical area. Though points went to Floyd County, the team was bordering on demoralized. Mel was their psychic leader, revving everyone else to top form by his enthusiasm. The loss of him stunned the group. Luckily, their captain, Josh Reynolds, filled the vacancy in the final match of the semis, allowing for maintenance of a comfortable bracket lead.

An interim between semis and finals allowed Coach Costner and his assistants to rally their troops. Rehydration by IV's and rubdowns by trainers helped. Pulling Cal aside, Coach informed him of match-ups now set. Calumet--- Met Man--- would take Mel's lead, matching against Billy Westfall in the final of the state meet.

Floyd County's boys performed in stellar fashion for staging Cal's finale. Gratified at the way they had coalesced in the face of Mel's loss, he observed the positioning giving Floyd County a chance at something special. He could see the Westfall boy on the opposing sideline off-handedly joking with reporters intent on inevitability of a third straight state wrestling title.

Though holding but a slim lead, Central High team members were already gunning up for imminent jubilation. Billy Westfall, reigning individual champion two years running was pitted against Cal Broadhearst, a previously defeated and outmatched opponent who didn't stand a chance in the eyes of odds-makers.

The team bolstered Cal as he was rubbed down a final time. His eyes hardened on Billy. The champ was focused back on him, too. The zone of tension was a feeling typically invigorating for Cal. If not for this particular opponent, and a creeping self-doubt, it would have been the same this time, as well. Instead, Cal evinced a beleaguered visage as he stepped onto the mat.

The state final singles match mandated a neutral start. Both competitors faced off in standing position. Billy wryly alluded to an unavoidable outcome as the two stood together. Cal may as well just give it up, he was told.

Indeed, the first of three rounds ended almost as quickly as it began. A nimble takedown move surprised Cal. It was a professional maneuver and one which high schoolers rarely employed. Or encountered. Cal escaped before a pin could be scored, but just barely. The two faced off twice more when a sudden pivot allowed Billy to revive another takedown. A near fall scored for him. Cal was stunned. No one had succeeded so adroitly and so quickly against him in years. Even in the most recent loss against Billy, to which Cal was now hearkening. He wavered. Round one ended in a significant point disadvantage.

With sound but hurried advice, Coach Costner righted Cal's balance, instructing him on a countermove for the pro-maneuver shocker. The second round began in referee's stance, Cal allotted the bottom position.

He had lost the first round. Whispering under his breath, Billy wrapped over Cal in the opening grip, "Get used to it, girlfriend. This'll be your assumed position from now on when you're with me. Bitch." He spat the last word.

At the bell, he attempted an unusual pro-maneuver of yet a different sort, again catching an unsuspecting Cal. A takedown and near fall resulted, but by quick reaction and agile defensive response, an escape and smoothly athletic reversal caught the defending champ unawares. Rather than by an alien move, Cal managed to surprise Billy in his own right by sheer extraordinary athleticism. Scoring his own takedown, he flipped the champ and the tide.

A near fall was recorded, and along with an escape and reversal points, the score disparity evened out. Billy was not pleased. No one took him down. In two years, it hadn't happened. Though still outwardly confident, Billy couldn't quite keep the barest wisp of concern from his features by the turn of events in the round. Three minutes belled out with the two in a dead heat.

The crowd was fanatical all around them. Though far distant from the two on the mat. They existed on an alternate plane: one dominated by a suspension of time and space. In full view of everyone, all eyes locked and loaded on two center-stagers. Neither competitor was aware of anything except one other person. Zoned.

Third round began in role reversal. Referee's stance with Cal now top. Billy in unheard-of bottom position. He was more than miffed. It was demeaning, exposing a chink in an impervious aura of invincibility carefully constructed through three seasons. Not since a first title three years before, as an untested underdog sophomore, had he endured an overarching body enwrap him the way Cal did now.

Subservient was the term that flitted through the champ's mind. Cal remained stoically mute. His code. Never let 'em see you blink. Billy puffed up in indignity at feeling the ebony hand girdle his lower belly. "Don't get comfortable, now, choker," he whispered upward, "You ain't fit to scratch my nuts, bitch. Get ready now, I can feel your black dick fillin' up, girlfriend. Touchin' yo' Daddy like this gots yo' uppity-ass self all 'bout to fail. Big time. Watch that your big old giveaway boner don't tell everyone what be happenin' down here close and heavy, boy. Don't lose your cool, now. Nigger."

Patronizing as hell and intentionally racist, Cal heard every word from his inner zone. The distant roar could've been the crowd surrounding them or it could have been blood coursing through his brain. Whichever, Calumet called to a place deep inside himself. Summoning up a reserve never known to be. The debasing words were impelling.

Upon registering the third-round bell, he felt the escape move take shape from below him as Billy exerted every ounce of ability and strength for affording himself a technical reversal, a takedown, and a quick pin. How dare this colored upstart challenge him.

In response, Cal reacted rather than strategized. He expertly blocked a leg maneuver capable of taking down any other wrestler in the state. Unleashing a ploy he had never used, let alone contemplated, he incorporated a superbly toned, honed body in hoisting the maddening blond fantasy beneath him.

Rising up in gargantuan effort of will, and a fluid movement, Cal twirled Billy Westfall over in a slow-motion ballet of rippling musculature, slapping the champ decisively to the mat. One fell swoop.

Falling on him, Cal pinned the stunned boy, holding creamy shoulders against sweat-soaked surface for a full five second count. His entire torso covered the dumbfounded state champion. Faces immobile, within millimeters of one another. Eyes wide shut. Noses tipping. An almost erotic embrace.

As the referee called pin and match, Cal opened his dark, smoldering eyes to the baby blues of a dream fuck fantasized multiple times over preceding weeks. The shock reflecting in them was priceless. "Need a date? Bitch?" So softly, Cal wasn't certain he had uttered the words. But Billy heard them.

Then the moment was past.

The official referee hauled Cal up from Billy's defeated form, intimate contact broken. A sinewy ebony bicep was hoisted above his head and skyward in verification of the victorious full pin securing Floyd County Consolidated High School its inaugural state wrestling championship.

Cal stood proudly erect, straddling the vanquished blowhard. The crowd of thousands had fallen silent in collective disbelief. A diminutive whisper wafted through the convention center, gradually rumbling to a giant crescendo of reverberating proportion in acclamation of the dethroning.

It wasn't until thirty seconds into it, when Cal hazarded a glance downward at poor Billy Westfall, that he noticed what everybody else had already seen. The entirety of the ten-inch black anaconda, so denigrated by the crestfallen loser presently peering up at him, arched in fully engorged glory before his eyes, lazily drooling a long, roping string of precum on to a just-pinned shoulder. Very happily sharing in the celebration.

Leaving absolutely nothing to the imagination.

"You just have to be the most difficult person in school to talk with," Jenny was smiling prettily, but her sparkling gray-green eyes were saying something different.

"Gosh, Jenny, I can't believe you think that," Cal Al abashedly fished two books from his locker, trying to come across friendly with this popular girl. While they spoke commonly, and shared several classes, he had never felt he was avoiding her before this. "If I've been rude, or something, I am so sorry. It was sure not intentional."

"No, silly, that's not what I meant. It's that there is always a dozen people around you." As she said this, Cal was side-swiped by a beaming Mel stalking past. Out of Jenny's vision, his bud turned to hook a double thumbs-up. Coming the other direction, Coy and Doy slapped their brother's butt, teasing him too. Noticing who he was talking to, they sped past instead of stopping. "See what I mean?" She practically winked at him inside of the wide smile and he wondered for a second.

"Oh. Wow. I didn't get you. Sorry again, Jenny." This, as two catcalls from across the hallway yelled his name. Truthfully a little nervous in her presence, it wasn't for reasons anybody had induced.

"Well, if you can spare the time, I'd like to talk with you after biology review. Big Boy..." she was teasing him and it simply raised the anxiety level in Cal's brain. He didn't like being anything but straightforward with people. Yet, around Jenny, he found himself reticent to allow much to open between them. He felt like a total coward sometimes; a complete jerk at others. A little of both at the moment. Besides, the recent dichotomy of pride and mortification besieging his psyche and life was plaguing him. The term 'Big Boy' implicated way too much innuendo to allow decipher as good or bad right now.

Sure, I'd like that. Meet you after, then?" He felt awkward as hell, wanting to get away to collect himself. And make a plan. Like that was a new concept...dealing with the quandary had been ever present in his mind recently. He just couldn't come up with a practical solution.

Excusing himself to hit the bathroom, he succeeded in escaping. But only in getting free of the 'Jenny dilemma'. The bathroom was filled with students. Ever since state meet, the previous safe place would never again serve as either a quiet spot or a waste disposal area. Anybody present evidenced either inordinate curiosity--- aka: getting a look at the infamous snake--- or harangued him lewdly for the unique victory pose exhibition. He got out fast, brooding the ever-present 'other dilemma'...

...Written accounts were obtuse, of course, and pictures plastered on every form of public media in business sported a smudged circle around his pelvic region. But the fact remained of several thousand firsthand accounts circulating to the stratosphere and back since the unveiling.

There existed obscenity laws on the books in the state of Georgia, Cal had chewed over. The past week, he felt as if at any moment, the morality police were going to descend and haul him away in cuffs. He even dreamt one time of a triple cuffing: wrists and big piece together. All because of the public act of indecency playing out at the very moment of his biggest triumph. Sportscasters and writers statewide--- probably farther, he reflected--- had had a field day over the whole affair. To the point that Cal had avoided school, church and social settings for four days after the meet. Holed up at home; mostly in his room. Under both his father's and mother's benevolent tending.

His Dad had taken him aside in the study. Father and son sat quietly commiserating for a long period. Letting the tension wear off. Then, he'd related a fractionally similar episode he, himself, had endured at about the same age of eighteen. The scenario wasn't all that unique, the wiser man had let him know. Cal had just suffered ill luck for it to happen in front of such a large audience, was all.

And lest Cal forget, Senior reminded Junior, by jiggedy, his eldest son had just completed the biggest upset in schoolboy history on the way to cornering the title of State Champ. He couldn't be more proud. The Professor assured Cal that the present furor would wear off with time; annals of history would have only his top head in the picture for sake of posterity. The two spent an hour relishing more glorious parts of the day.

Feeling the edge had lifted, Professor Dad finally deemed it best to get the monkey off his son's back. He forged a clearer perspective for the item he knew to be peculiarly pertinent to the teenager. The axiomatic nightmare of finding oneself exposed in front of a multitude with nowhere to hide. Addressing the fragment darkening the day for Cal right then, he broke things down to the vernacular, man-to-man.

As it spilled out, the two were gradually reduced to hoots and hiccups in reliving the 'close-up' from the vanquished boy's vantage. They had finally agreed that the look of unmitigated horror and falsetto shriek passing Billy Westfall's lips as some mighty viscous juice had made its way in a slow-motion trail to his body had to be the absolute best of the bad part. That boy would never be quite right in the head again.

If Cal had been mortified, the Professor chortled, think what the ex-champ must be undergoing. The jackass--- Cal had never heard that word from his Dad's mouth--- had not only guaranteed a victory in front of a packed house, he celebrated prematurely and insulted anybody and everybody on the way. And then, 'The Pin' had happened. Yes, the phrase 'just comeuppance' had never been so aptly imposed, by his daddy's reckoning. Cal was going to survive, he realized, after that talk.

Mammay had taken a different tack. She would refuse to let anybody denigrate her son over the matter. If pushed too far, she had explained, she would not fail to tell any busybodies bold enough to bring it up that there was not a person in sight that day who hadn't felt some level of envy at the 'unmasking'. Male, female, student, adult, parent, fan. Nobody, she emphasized. "And don't you ever let anyone tell you different, my son," adding that she had already done so. Twice. That was how she framed it. It blew him away.

His brothers were the unqualified worst. Not giving him a second's peace, Mammay had finally banned all talk of wrestling meets, then included almost every conversational subject known to teen boys as the days progressed. It seemed anything at all could cause a segue way to the subject. That kind of worked, except for nights in bed with Coy. Other brothers were exiled from their room after the first two days.

It grew old for Coy in only a short time. First, he had quit the wrestling team for reasons unknown the previous fall. Just not feeling the team thing, he had pretended to Cal. But, as a twin, in this situation, he could very much relate. They shared almost everything. Second, the sight of the big boner was not new to him and since Cal didn't surpass him but by a bare fraction in the meat department, anyway, what was the deal? If you got it then show it, Coy had already deduced... and he did, Cal was to later learn. That premise made Cal think, too. Things that make you go 'hmmmm.'

Teachers had been understanding, mostly. The principal had even set back the normal celebratory pep rally considering Cal's 'situation'. What with end of semester and graduation in less than two weeks, however, the calendar date had been rather forced into the schedule for the coming Monday. A schoolwide assembly would supersede homeroom period. Cal was pretty certain he could feel a cold coming on by the knowledge.

This forced link between highest and lowest points in his life was plain galling, Cal railed inwardly. On the other hand, the whole thing did set a future for a much-lowered bar in the modesty department. He figured that no possible embarrassment could…ever…rival this. What the hell? Why be shy of something he was discovering to be a definite asset… full-scale pun intended. He matured some in the moment.

"In summary, natural processes do occur and proceed in a direction toward equilibrium. This is the basic conclusion for the second law of thermodynamics. Entropy. All interacting entities seek an equilibrium state…. OK, everybody, material discussed today should be all that is necessary as far as the comprehensive exam goes. Know these principles and you should be well-enough prepared. Thank you, class, and good luck to you all." As Mr. Salvano finished, the bell rang. The man was an illusion of perfection, Cal thought. How did he always do that? No one could end a lecture at the exact moment the bell rang like this. Yet, he couldn't remember a single time that anything else had resulted the entire semester. Remarkable.

A tap on the right shoulder pushed his neck to turn left. Par for the course, he glanced that way as Willim Jennerle snickered at Cal's adroitness, "How do you do that, dude? I can't ever fool your ass. You are like my mom. Eyes in the back of her head." Changing subjects, he went on, "Can you believe this is the last lecture? Ever? Hot damn, never could believe this day'd get here."

"Yeah, hard to believe, huh?" Cal liked this geeky guy, his lab partner. More so because the boy never knew local gossip and didn't follow sports. He must be the only person in the tristate area who didn't know the story of Cal's debacle. And couldn't care less. The best person in school to hang out with right now, Cal figured.

"But, just so you know, Will, the shoulder tap thing? You've only done the same thing every single class this semester…OK? It wasn't too hard to figure out. I even know your touch by now." The smile made sure Willim understood Cal's friendliness was sincere. As if his lab partner would think any different regardless. The guy was guileless. Another good thing from Cal's standpoint. What you saw was what you got. He was disarmed by the virtue.

"Oh. Yeah. I guess that's true… you know my touch? That's amazing, dude." Again, the genuineness factor. He pushed his wire rims up his nose and looked over Cal's shoulder. "Hey, Calumet, there's somebody tryin' to signal you, I think." It was always 'Calumet' with Will. As Cal looked up, Will pointed behind him.

Turning to look, Cal caught sight of Jenny. She was at the door, books in hand, wide-eying him. Her forefinger crooked up and inward. He smiled, remembering his promise from earlier to get together, raising his own finger up in arched eyebrow acknowledgement to hold on. Turning back again to Willim, "How'd you know she was signaling me, Will? She could have been waving at you, y'know."

"Right, Calumet. Fat chance. Girls don't wave at me. Especially ones like Jenny Sampras. Yeah, she's signaling you, all right. Well, dude, you gonna be good? I mean, for the final? I think I'm ready, but if you wanna hook up to study, you know where I am. Call, 'K?" And he sidled off, pointing one more time toward Jenny. Cal grinned a 'see you later'.

The moment the geek turned away, smiling as usual, Cal was bounced sideways and over the desk just vacated. The push knocked off his backpack and he stumbled back into his seat. "Met Man. Bra, you be done, right? Let's scat to the gym, how 'bout? We got plans to make." Mel was stoked. Ever since the end of high school had crystallized in his mind, the usual hyped energy level had skyrocketed. "There's a dread plan goin' down with some of the team for prom…we gotta get on it. It's secret. So, let's hit it." He head-rubbed Cal, one arm around his neck, the other knuckle-nuggyin' the nap. Always handsy. Cal resisted, ineffectually. It was nice to be treated normal.

"Mel, bro. Hey, yes. I'm finished. But I've---"before he could get the sentence out, the dropped backpack swung in on the edge of his peripheral vision, lambasting him in a dull 'thwunkk'. A surprised Mel grabbed the missile, too late. Yanking it back, Cal's friend tossed it away again, and Cal saw it skid three rows distant, the open top spilling contents.

"Josh, that wasn't funny, bud," Cal focused on the newest assailant, shaking his head to clear it.

"Well then, champ, get your wild ass up and let's get going. Mel and me want in on this and you be holdin' us up. Now, get up," the toothy grin from his worthless team captain reminded Cal of the value of these teammates. He suddenly wanted to go with them. Next second, he remembered--- cutting a look to the door, he viewed an empty archway. Jenny wasn't anywhere to be seen.

"C'mon, Met Man, let's go," Mel was adamant.

Cal sagged in the chair. "Guys, I can't right now…really. I can meet you later, but I made a promise I can't break. How about I catch up with you in a while, after I finish? I may already be in trouble--- give me a little space, OK?" Both friends groaned together. But they backed off.

Watching his friends depart, he heaved a sigh of relief…or maybe regret. He wasn't sure which. Stooping to retrieve the spilled pack, Cal wondered if he had caused a problem with Jenny. He needed to go look for her. Stuffing books and things back into the bag, he spied a piece of folded red paper. Not his. Unfolding it, he read, 'Varsity field, visitor's dugout'. Whoa. What was coming down here, he cringed?

Zipping it closed, he deliberated only a second, slung the pack over his shoulder and headed out.

The afternoon outside was dark. An approaching front pushed thunderheads ahead of it; roiling clouds pitched and swirled overhead. Varsity field was away from the rest of the old school, separated by a railroad track. Sequestered with other sports fields, the complex stood silently foreboding. Angst level ratcheted up as he rounded the end of first base side dugout. Peering into shadowy depth, he was hit by a blast of cool, rain-rich wind, hindering his view momentarily.

A female voice cut through, "Hi, Cal. I'm glad you found the note. I didn't think you'd want me to butt in so I left it. I'm down here. At the end." Jenny's gray form silhouetted against the darker anchored bench where she sat. A flash of lightning slashed from a billowing cloud over left field. "You look worried, Cal, come on down. Everything is fine. It's not going to get wet in here, I don't think."

Cal descended the steps and headed toward her. "I owe you another apology it looks like, Jenny. Hope I didn't insult you. How you doing?" His nerves were on display. He could hear it and kicked himself inside. What is up, idiot? You got this. Settle the heck down. All this passed through his mind as he stopped before the sitting girl. Rain drops began pattering the corrugated metal roof. Cal plopped down beside her.

"No, you don't Cal. I think I owe you one. The spy movie stuff here. I'm probably freaking you out. I didn't mean to. You don't need to be worried at all. I'm not going to come on to you or anything. So, relax." The soothing tone and words did take the edge off a bit.

"I've wanted to talk with you for a while, Cal, and got it in my head it should be private because of how everyone is into everybody's business. I know you get that. My friends have been driving me nuts to get all up in your face and that's... well, I just don't do that." Her earnestness lowered the tension level further. Cal did relax. Then, it spiked to astronomical levels again when she blurted, "Cal, I wanted to know if you would go to prom with me."

Shocked, Cal stammered a reply, "Wha-what?" He inadvertently scooted back down a little to create space.

An impish grin spread over Jenny's face. "Thought I might get that response. Look at me, Cal. I am smiling. But I am not joking. And, I am not trying to rock your world, boy. I want to go to the prom and no one has asked me. Nobody has asked you, either. Both of us could have a great time and without any strings attached. It might just take some of the pressure off us. Don't you think?" Cal stared in mystified disbelief at all this. His mind was screeching in maxed-out mode. His mouth wasn't even close to functional.

So, the two sat, listening to the rain increasing in intensity and volume, the thunder rolls rousting above them and periodic lightning strikes flashing over them in bright relief. The seconds passed. Then minutes. The musings were out-shouting the storm.

Finally, Jenny broke into the building maelstrom, "Oh, boy. I do think I've really put my foot in my mouth. Maybe I should just go…" her voice trailed off.

Cal cornered his dark eyes at the girl and sized her up. His voice came cautiously, unsure and certain simultaneously. "Jenny Sampras. I have been noticing you a long time. There is something about you that makes me look… and wonder. For some reason, we haven't ever gotten to know each other. My friends have sure been bugging the heck out of me, too. They are convinced we are destined to be together. There's only one problem in the equation. And it's bothering me more now. Especially since I just figured out why it bothers me… I'd like to know you, Jenny. But there's a situation that I should let you know about because most likely, it is a deal breaker, girl. You see… umm… you should know…"

"You mean the part about you being gay?" Impatience made her blurt it out. As she said it, Jenny watched Cal's jaw drop. His eyes went dull and his shoulders sagged.

"You know that…how? Damn, am I that bad at hiding it?" Jenny saw a devastated face.

"Cal. No. No, it isn't at all like that. Oh, I am so sorry. I'm making a mess of this. Haven't you ever heard of Gaydar before? Well, it doesn't work for just boy-on-boy, or girl-on-girl. I've noticed it because I am too. Please don't feel like that."

An ear-shattering peel of thunder blasted them at that moment. Cal looked up at Jenny. They stared back and forth through several ensuing lightning strikes. Facial changes exhibiting stark serial fluctuations flared before them both. Like a Freudian mime show. When the series ended,

Cal cracked a smile with his head down, knowing somehow that she was doing the same.

In a second, he heard her giggle. He followed suit. Before the next round of thunder rolled over them, they were themselves rolling. Breaking down the ridiculous walls so carefully erected. Raindrops and tears of laughter mixed and the two fell together in a hug that met the second law of thermodynamics. Equilibrium happened by their connected embrace. Entropy reigned.

Backing off after a minute, Cal peered shyly down into Jenny's huge gray-green eyes, "Yes, I will go with you. To the prom. If you'll have me, Jenny Sampras."

Sweet release.

Giddy now, Jenny took Cal's hand and drew him up the dugout steps to the grass, then the muddy first base path. Cal followed, absorbing pelting rain amid growing feelings of twenty-first century emancipatory freedom. Head tilted upward to face the rain, Jenny stopped at first base. Then, she walked the baseline out to second. Head straight up. Turning around, the pretty senior reached up and abruptly kissed Cal smack on the lips. Not in an erogenous way. More like a glorified peck. From a cousin. Then, they stood next to each other and studied the sky, soaking up the wetness.

The rain came down so hard, it filled their grinning open mouths and then their pockets. It was that hard. And oh, so cleansing.

Cal took Jenny's hand this time, crooking her into him. Still cloud watching. "Why are we here, getting soaked?"

"So that you can tell your friends you got me to second base."

"Bro, I told you that thing at State would end up bein' a plus. No damn wonder you didn't want to come with us yesterday. Now, we can double to prom. Aliea is going to love this, my boy. She's been non-stop yakkin' at me to get you hooked up. I'ma call her now." Melvin was ecstatic. Cal had a hard time getting him to focus.

"You need to chill, Mel. It's not that big a deal. We hardly know each other and it's a first date. Don't blow this all up." Didn't have the slightest effect. Mel was recording a message sure to go viral within fractions of seconds. Cal commented wryly, "Well, you may as well tell her we're engaged and the date is July 4th, as long as you're doing it." The look coming back could've melted rock.

"Seriously Cal, Aliea is all into this stuff. You are lettin' me off da' hook. You're not foggin' me, right? Because if you are, I be the one ain't getting nuttin-nuttin' else until after July 4th. At least. Don't be shadin', a'ight?

I am not shadin', Mel. Just don't want more attention. Can't you just wait until you see her and let her know that? Please?" Cal really didn't want to see the references to State in relation to this sudden prom date with Jenny. It couldn't end well for Jenny, what with the wagging tongues network as coordinated as it was. And for an interracial couple, the air was already tainted by white-girl man-napping and size queen allusions, as it was. This kind of put the lurid details into another class entirely.

Cal extracted the promise and headed home. Traipsing the gravel lane to the house thirty minutes later, Cal was broadsided by the imp, Sophie. The nine-year-old ball of energy tumbled from a hidden alcove in the bushes, almost succeeding in tackling her big brother. She climbed his leg, up into his accepting arms, clinging around his neck. Girly breath was pfuffing into Cal's face in her exhilaration.

The tiny tornado couldn't get her words out fast enough, "Are you gettin' married, Cal? I heard you already bought a ring and that you're in love with Jenny Sampras, and your rehearsal dinner is on the night of the prom. Are you gonna wear your wrestling uniform or are we buying you a... tennessee tuxedo with tails? ...Well, are you?" The precocious only little sis was always full of information and forever adding to her collection.

"Whoa, there, Senorita Sophonsiba Rill, just take a breath and chill a second. Where did you hear all that mess of disinformation, little missy?" An indulgent big bro was blindsided by the massive gossip dump. If this little thing had hold of it, what else was circulating? That was just the tip of his consternation... the worst of his bad feelings were suddenly materializing before his apprehensive eyes. Already. What the...? "You've been to Aunt Maizie's today, haven't you? All right, spill the beans, Soph."

Nodding, shaking her head, opening and closing her mouth like a cod fish, gulping breaths in between--- all combined to make both of their heads spin. Cal couldn't help but laugh in her face. It didn't slow her down a bit. "Jocelyn said that you were just about married and that when you graduate, ya'll are packing up and moving to Barbados--- where's

Barbados? --- and that Jenny was gonna have striped qua-dripple-palets because Mr. Johnson is the biggest guppy donor---what's that? --- in the county... and everybody knows that. What does it all mean, Cal?"

Red flags were sailing full mast through Cal's head now. Alarm bells signaled 'danger' and 'tread lightly' and a million other suddenly fearsome warnings. He tossled the pig-tailed urchin in his arms while sizing up the explosion on the horizon. "Soph, you know very well that Jocelyn never gets anything right, and what's more, Aunt Maizie's mouth is one conduit shy of the gutter...nothing at all that you have just bombarded me with holds one single shred of truth. You need to talk to Mammay about all of this and I think the two of us should do that right now."

The ensuing wiggles aimed at extrication made plain the fact that his little sis knew full well the sources from which she was spewing tripe was more than questionable. But Cal wouldn't put her down. He nuzzled and tickled the whole trip in distractive effort. Unsuccessfully.

They trudged in tandem to the front verandah and proceeded directly to the kitchen where their Mammay was stirring a pot of beef stew for dinner. The wise woman turned upon their entry, perused both faces for a total of one-half second, and then turned back to replace the kettle lid.

"Well, now. It would appear that my bookend chillun's" --- she only used the colloquialism when a teaching moment was coming on--- "have been parlaying together and may have things a little topsy-turvy, by the stories painting their faces." Cal stood Sophie down on the floor and took a seat at the kitchen table. Sophie eyed both doors deciding which way to run. "Sophonsiba, please do sit down with your brother." Cassandra knew the effect of four syllables versus two when intoning her only daughter's name. The method saved many breaths. Sure enough, Sophie huffed to the table, scowled up at the big Brother so blameworthy and sat. Opposite him. The farthest seat away.

Spending a little more time checking stove top and utensils, Mammay allowed the stretch of the silence to marinate. Four eyes watched the back of the head, and neck, so busily dedicated to ignoring the duo before finally rounding once more, seating herself between them. "What, pray tell, might be scurrying through my two most astutely attuned offspring's brains?"

From Cal, a simple nod toward Soph engendered reprising kicks to his shins under the table. It also opened dialogue. The three proceeded to sift the blunderbuss of information fiddling in a little girl's brain as the older two soaked in words, nuances and flatly hilarious details that she had gleaned while at Aunt Maizie's an hour before. Mammay's eyes widened a tad at mention of 'Mr. Johnson's guppy factory'. A miniscule upturn to her lips was only read by Cal, who had a like response.

Sophie was genuinely desirous of information in plain terms. Between the trio, a détente of partial blank-filling and 'splainin' played out. When Roy and Loy busted through the back door, immersed in some hieroglyphic sign language conversation of immense import, the little twister tied herself to their wake. Having accumulated enough information to satisfy her curiosity for the time being, she received Mammay's nod and vanished.

Cal and Cassie continued a while longer in the soothing percolating stew. Another brewing summer squall rattled through, swaying trees outside. Blustering thunderheads invaded the sky past curtained windows. "Mammay, you do believe me when I say that none of the stuff those scuttlebutts are spreading is even remotely true…right?"

"Oh, please, Child of Mine. You are talking about the younger sister who once spread the word that her Uncle Charlie had taken up with Marilyn Monroe. In the White House. With JFK. Lord, that girl could whip a dog dead with a snake and never see or touch either. So, yes." She smiled and covered his huge dark hand as she said this, continuing, "However, I am a mite perplexed at the news of the prom coming up. You were adamant about not going up to three days ago. Care to fill me in?" Mammay never minced words despite her diplomatic shrewdness.

Cal told her of his new inclusion in the coming high school social event of the year. Explaining the date with Jenny as he had to Mel fell flat, though. He should have seen that coming. "Might I know who asked whom, dear?" Sometimes the woman's clairvoyance made Cal tingle. It did so now. Deciding how to frame it, he fairly stammered his way through the stormy interlude at the baseball field.

"So, my son is going on a first date with an unfamiliar white girl who asked him at second base on a stormy baseball infield. Calumet. You know I have absolutely no qualms about where, who, how or when. Yet, the why continues to pose a puzzle. You know I know you better than anybody in this world, now, correct? Even your father and Coy Alfrederic. And, there is not a single thing in this wide world that could change my love for you. Again correct?" Cal's curt nod allowed her to go on. "Well, then, what say we two just clear out the cottony blather filling up this kitchen and make a bit of room for to maneuver…?" Her arched eyebrows brooked no dissent. The finger-tapping to the back of his hand spoke volumes. So, Cal took a deep breath and let it all out.

The next minutes were a mish-mash of disjointed half-stories, memories and meditations, all of which lent cogent thought process to a total of no one at all. After several minutes of beating a 360-degree circle around the kitchen mulberry bush, Mammay held up her hand. "Enough, my child." The blinking shut of her violet eyes and dipping of her head cut him off abruptly.

When she raised up, opening them again, the look there pulled Cal back to a forgotten time. A time when visions of those eyes and the two breasts below filled the totality of the world where, as a baby, he throve in safe haven. Long tucked away to a lost place. An overwhelming sense of love enveloped him in a velvety pillow of reminiscence. The emotion almost scared Cal, such was its overpowering aura. This woman, his mother, did indeed know him as no other being could. Including himself.

"My love child. We two were one for nine long months. Just like Coy and myself. Your beginning washed through me in a rush of awareness. I bore you. I nurtured you. The bond between a mother and her firstborn is like no other. Keep in mind that the old carol, 'Silent Night' was not originally written in honor of a virgin birth."

"I have been awaiting the day you come to fulfillment of your true spirit. Having watched the years pass as you grew into this intelligent, strong, handsome specimen of a man, I have known the vantage you command from where any other man would be envious to view the world. I have seen the inner strife over which the selves vying for your soul have fought. I feel the turmoil, Calumet, and have cried in the deep dark hours of many nights, controlling the desire to offer guidance through the storm that has been brewing. You needed to find inner guidance on your sojourn to manhood. It was not my role to do so."

"Not until now. When I see that you may be forcing an alien aura into your spirit. My boy, you must be aware of what I have known since you were suckling. I cannot simply stand by now and let you walk a path which might require years, even a lifetime, to retrace."

"We needn't say the words, Calumet Alfrederic. We both know what exists here," her warm hand raised to his chest, "and I think you know the tale you shall tell. With one other. It is not by the present path you travel, by mistake, that will find the sanctuary sundered upon your weaning. Now, think on this some, my dearest. You will infer I am right. It may be a harder and more burdensome road. But, it is the true one." Their tears mingled in the ensuing embrace.

After the timeless share of emotion, thunder again bowled around the Broadhearst Estate, matching the intensity in Cal's heart and head. He pulled back a smidgeon, absorbing 'the look' one more moment. "Mammay, you are my shining star. I will never be able to thank you. And neither will he, when he shows himself."

March, 2004

Why do they put these bruised bananas up for sale, Cal groused? Unless a person was going to take the old mushy things home and dump them into a mixing bowl to make banana nut bread, it just didn't make sense. And only Mammay would do that anyway. He was perturbed at once again trying and failing to procure fresh bananas for his morning smoothies. Whole Foods should be ashamed of themselves. Cal continued his mental tirade, railing at the store, then the parking lot's lack of bicycle lock spots, the small efficiency apartment's rusting outdoor steps and the cockroach doorman guarding entrance to the small domicile he inhabited.

Putting down the two sacks of precious groceries--- how could a starving student keep nutritionally fit with the prices the college town grocery store charged for staple items--- he grumbled through the small apartment to the bathroom. The mirror reflected his chagrin in living color. He shouldn't frown like this, the advice occurred to him. It made him look 30. Damn. He was just pissed.

The mail had delivered the rotten news a couple hours before that now left the tall, lean, ex-Sig Ep member stewing. After waiting patiently for months to hear from the next dot com start-up firm about his umpteenth application--- why did they require snail mail communication anyway--- the rude, one sentence denial note had set Cal off. All the time spent and meticulous preparation undertaken…relegated to a wadded up trashed state in milliseconds. Yes, he was pissed, all right. Enough to skip classes for the Wednesday he now spent, alone, in less than 600 square feet of suddenly prison-like confines.

Stripping disgustedly in front of the cheap wall mirror gave him time to study the familiarly dark outline of ebony-skinned litheness staring back. Dropping the sweat-caked drawers to the floor, the deflated leg lizard even wiggled in vexation. Sexy foreskin covering the eye blocked commiseration between the topside set. Cal bore exasperation towards him, too. They weren't speaking. Nothing was quite satisfactory in the world now.

By way of blind response, the bugger began swelling in signal complaint for separation anxiety the forlorn thing felt. Cal had tried in vain satisfying the one trick pony--- he only echoed one blatant message---stroking to rapid-fire completion six and eight times daily for a whole month with hopes to ignore him for the next. To maybe get some relief from the thing. One day he'd topped the baker's dozen mark.

Did that satisfy the over-sized baby? Hell, to the no. The snake mimicked a heroin addict. More, more, always more. Exactly like an addict, the climactic eruptions were always ecstasy-inducing… for a quick minute. Shucks, Cal thought, he could sink to the depths of that science experiment involving the monkey programmed, Pavlovian fashion, to climax via self-induced electrostimulation with the flick of a hand-held switch. As often as desired. Yet, Cheetah's craving never waned. The monkey had obsessed to the point of starving itself slowly in repetitious orgasmic ad infinitum.

So, Cal had gone on strike. He was ignoring the ingrate. For three weeks, now, the swelling come-ons and boner states had played Siren to him, lustily begging sweet satisfaction. And for three weeks and one day, he had successfully fought the urge to yield. Damn it.

Fondling the silkiness of smooth cocoa skin, he idly explored creases and crevices in distracted fashion, still carping about the newest rejection letter. The sleek feel assuaged the bitterness a little, but upon refocusing, he found the cobra staring up in arching, eye-peaking entreaty to, 'Oh… please, please, please do something to help me…' Cal slapped him instead, stepped into the shower and coldly soaked the sorry sycophant into submission.

Thirty minutes later, still in deep chunter at the eleventieth tech rebuff, the lean jock trekked up hill to The Drag--- Guadalupe Street--- edging UT campus. Destination: old dollar movie theatre. Wallowing in unfamiliar self-pity, Cal had recollected the marquee announcing the playbill of Vincent Minelli's, 'On a Clear Day'. Having seen it before, the ditzy panache of early Streisand with appearances by a youthful

Nicholson and Newhart, offered an air of inane fancy he somehow needed right now.

The cloudless day insinuated densely packed, dark, low-hanging billows of misty fog by his present mood. Maybe this momentary escape would allow assuagement? Paying the old-fashioned ticket window matron, Cal followed a darkened aisle to a midway seat three deep to the end. Maybe two others were inside on such a sunny weekday.

Considering the title of the movie and his gloomy temper, it struck a chord of irony. A smile surprised him. See, he told himself, it was already helpful. Screw the missed argumentation lecture. He was certainly in no mood for that branch of learning. Presuming more chance for implementing fists over Cicero in the present mindset, another morose grin surfaced.

A throw-back pre-show cartoon, a 'la the old days, featuring Chip deluging Dale with acorns bolstered his escape decision. Who the hell needed a stupid MBA anyway? Maybe he would just take up abode here in the third seat, order take-in and pay rent for a couple months. The fantasy world sounded better and better by the moment. He scrunched down further in the seat as the movie started, intending to memorize lines for old times' sake in memory of another viewing of the cavorting Babs when he and Jenny had slipped away to the Rome Adelphi Theatre a rainy day forever ago.

The bygone friend would like this, he reflected. He missed the pretty blonde lesbian. She and he had entered UT together under guise of a dating couple back in 2000, anteing up rhetoric of jabber-wenches throughout Rome by their 'elopement'. While Mammay and Dad knew the story, Mel and Aliea, Aunt Maizie and others had all been convinced of the affair that wasn't... so much the better, Cal thought.

The two had snickered conspiratorially over the clever ruse, comfortable that the distance would keep their secret. Friendship had grown strong. For more than two years the two were bosom-buddies, confidants, roommates and pseudo-lovers for all to see. An exotic duo of flavor which, even on the progressive campus of UT, tended to draw attention. Both drew strength from an agreeable arrangement and for those years, even they almost bought into the fakery.

Then, Celeste Devereux had happened on their scene. A buxom Coco Chanel La Boheme, she had figuratively knocked Jenny Sampras' socks off. Jenny and Celeste were soulmates before a month had passed. The duo became a trio, many deducing Calumet Broadhearst had begun a twenty-first century harem for himself. The svelte figures of two raving beauties on his arm elevated the enigmatic relationship to near legend status for the better part of a year. Men ogled the sight of the three inseparables in their Toulouse-Lautrec chic. Celeste evinced the height of French suavity, bending both Jenny and Cal to the polished style she portrayed. The campus adored their élan.

Until duty had called. Celeste's Father, back in the Loire Valley chateaux, called with news of her Mother's contracting of a rare cancer. By abrupt dénouement of the agreeable pact, the idyllic period ended. As the saddened French girl had packed for an immediate return to her home country, she had packed not only her belongings but Jenny as well. The two were besotted. Cal was devastated. Jenny's sobbing adieu still caused him to tear up.

No longer feeling the little shared bungalow or the Greek social life--- his Sigma Phi Epsilon fraternity brothers had been kicked to the curb--- Cal hid away in the little studio efficiency off Lamar Avenue between Pease Park and Town Lake. Tucked behind a grocery store, for God's sake.

The hermit's life now justified him, in direct contrast to the previous bon vivant bravura. School ascended to prime focus, an MBA the goal. His astute penchant for computer programming and technology invention accorded the twenty-year-old an aside to the mundanity of business school. It had proven a boon.

Broadening a distinct perspicacity for the cyberworld, Cal had delved an embryonic talent only skirted as a hobby until that point. Other interests and Jenny, then Celeste, had previously headlined him. The nascent tech science field, introduced by Coach Costner, was implemented with vigor.

Inventing more than one uniquely useful hardware innovation during this veiled existence, he had forged a reputation, albeit small in scope. Another failed quest to bowl over Silicon Valley as informed via this day's mail brought him back to earth. With a reverberative thud. Cal was still convinced that his freshly devised method of down-sizing pc chassis size and revolutionizing the co-adaptation of the server to encompass power, cooling, storage and connectivity, thereby mobilizing the journeyman's pc reach, was sound.

He had dubbed it a 'blade server'. IBM and Intel had not been impressed. Desktops were the future, they felt. Who needed to carry a tiny, awkwardly manipulated keyboard on a mobile computer with them, they shortsightedly insisted? Cal mightily disagreed. Maybe he would just take the idea to Mr. Dell or Mr. Jobs instead. The two were much more forward-thinking. And one's headquarters were but 30 miles distant.

Kicking himself for the oversight now, he attempted concentrating on Babs wafting her silly self through a flower garden… the split personality character was seeing the clearness of the day he had utterly missed. He spread his legs and scrunched further, pulling his baseball cap further down on his head.

As the girl warbled her way through the title song, Cal noted a late arrival out of the corner of his eye. Movement indicated approach of a person who came within two seats of his before plopping down. A glance identified a small younger guy who nodded toward him congenially. Odd. With all these seats empty, he apparently liked the one only two from himself. The other two moviegoers were ten rows behind him and twenty rows over. Out of each other's spheres.

Over the next half hour, Cal was distracted more than once by the little guy's fidgeting. Not wanting to look, he could nevertheless feel eyes checking him out. A fully-haired Bob Newhart awkwardly staged his career brand of stammering innocence as the shuffling persisted. Finally hazarding a sidelong look toward the wiggler, Cal was astounded to see the diminutive Hispanic boy with his pants dropped to the floor. Legs were spread and stiff prick was slowly being stroked up, then down, in deliberate display.

Seeing Cal's eyes on him, the jerker grinned lewdly, turning a slight bit to allow a better view of the proceedings. Not shy in the slightest. Cal tried focusing back to the screen and Babs, but rhythmic undulation to the songs, slowly steady, kept pulling him back. The boy signaled something after the third glance--- now close to a stare--- and Cal jerked back forward to block the visual, not wanting acknowledgement of contact.

The next thing Cal knew, the boy had slunk down out of his seat and crawled over two chair widths on the cement floor. The kid's hard piece rubbed enticingly on Cal's bare calf as he slid past. His hand tentatively hovered over Cal's abruptly expanding pant snake, the tenting going on inside quite unmistakable. Cal sat up quickly to escape the touch he knew was coming, turning nervously around to see the person behind and the only other on the opposite side apparently absorbed and oblivious. The small hand's heat suddenly scorched the snake through pants and drawers both. What the hell, Cal realized. This pint-sized fiend was going to get freaky if he let him. Right here.

As the offer sank in, the little person settled deftly between Cal's legs, further scorching his bare legs by contact with olive-skinned arms and shoulders. The hand called to its mate and as Cal watched, enthralled, the paired team expertly unzipped, spread, gripped and then pulled both shorts and drawers down in a concerted effort to expose what he was plainly seeking.

Cal couldn't believe himself when his own slim hips elevated in absence of any brainwaves. Just a fraction of an inch aided the shorts to slide free. The anaconda was on the prowl. Snapping loose of the elastic band sliding past, it slapped up and off Cal's exposed belly. The six pack which the whopping thing smacked against felt the heat. Every rippling abdominal muscle tensed under the feel and sound. The sharp report must surely have alerted the theatre and surrounding neighborhood but he forgot that concern the second those sizzling hands reasserted themselves.

Sliding sensuously up his smooth thighs, erotically slipping past the big balls tightly retracting against the long phallus they abutted, the fingers didn't miss anything. Their talent began a slow dance, testing different parts of exposed anatomy. Two black eyes peering up from between widely spread legs twinkled in mischievous resolve.

He would have noted the smile accompanying them but for the shadows. As he observed, wide-eyed, the lips parted and gradually raised up to the tip of the cowled corona topping a huge shaft. A crooked forefinger enwrapped the base of it and pulled toward the lips. All ten inches were on red-alert. Completely forgetting about the hands more commonly caressing this part of him. After all, Cal reflected, those two--- his own--- had been neglectful in their duty of late. Fuck them, the cobra informed the higher head.

And then, the enormous black dick sighed in exaggerated liberation upon linking the sight of the approaching lips with tactile sensation.

The mouth took it all in by a slow, deep slide crotchward. Only stopping when the oral anatomy had been stretched past normal capacity. Little Cal acquainted with the boy's Adam's apple, from the inside, as it gently massaged the phatted head. Perception was excruciatingly hot and honeyed. Not ninety seconds and several dozen cavernous strokes passed before Cal felt upsurge of three weeks….and one day… worth of baby juice pulse in an ejaculatory explosion of almost unrivaled scale.

Surprise arrested the blow job aficionado swallowing him whole. The widened eyes darted up to connect with his own. As the four stared back and forth, Cal could see the peripheral image of a gallon of creamy jism seep out around the cute boy's full lips, be-smudging the three-day stubble. It struck Cal that at least this dickboy wasn't jail bait.

The little digits came up, greedily scooping ambrosial goo into cupped palms. But, he never elevated from the fixed position as he rhythmically massaged the spewing eye and spasming head by deepthroat golluming. Tremors shooting around Cal's body infected the dark boy. A blackly sleek head mop fluffed poofily about his face as Cal sensed an answering eruption. Day-umm. Cal disseminated in a stupefaction of sensate heaven.

Unaccountable lost moments spent themselves in regaining sense of surround. Finally, the boy slowly and deliberately ascended from his planted spot. The lips plopped free of the thickness; he licked to save the prize. Next, the boy raised the hands still cradling escaped spillage. All through the slurping, the pequeño whizz took time to survey Cal's reaction to the picnicking going on between his rangy legs.

An impish smile blossomed in vague evanescence. He whisper-garbled, "Quiero este otra vez, por favor, Señor Gigante?" Cal got the gist of it. Patting the boy's silky head, he motioned that it was time for him to go. The boy slumped his disappointment--- he had apparently meant doing it again right this minute. Fuzz of the episode was still numbing Cal's senses but he knew he needed to leave. Dr. Chabot would simply have to court Daisy…or Melinda… without his help. The girl's clairvoyance surely ascertained the same ending as before.

As the tall sexy brother began to rise, a still kneeling boy braced sticky hands on Cal's legs, "No, senor, por mucho favor… el gusto es mio." And pulled a moist cloth from a hidden pocket. Cleverly prepared. The explorer boy scout carefully, lovingly, caressed the famous johnson --- in Rome, Georgia, anyway--- detailing a cleansing of both it and associated parts like a race car driver polishing fenders. He didn't overlook the muscled thighs or calves. Leading to another unavoidable boner. But Cal firmly refused, smiling. Resisting one more plaintive request.

Tucking the swollen junk back inside raised shorts, and lowering his t-shirt, the sated stud did finally arise and take leave. Jack Nicholson was preparing an incestuous proposal to his ex-step-sister--- was that even a thing, it struck Cal--- as he turned away.

Walking carefully up the dim aisle, Cal caught glimpse of the person seated ten rows back. Tears flowed freely down a profoundly absorbed youthful face. Light emanating from the screen illuminated a classic cherubic mien of Raphaelian loveliness.

Framed by a riotous mass of dark golden curls, striking wide eyes watched the movie in tunnel-visioned focus. Thickly sensuous, pouting lips under an exquisite pug nose, itself sprouting from between the most beautiful large doe eyes of indeterminate hue, all water-colored into a descript being amongst Cal's brain cells. Long-lashed eyelids blinked in hypnotized erogeneity… and sheer innocence.

For a second time inside the darkened confines of the seedy old vaudeville-era theatre, Cal felt broadsided. First by hormonally-induced volcanic rapture. In this fleeting stitch of time, however, he was overcome by marvel of prickly déjà vu. Regarding this beguiling, vulnerable young man of inordinate familiarity. Somewhere from deep within, a mental mime reached up, seeking. Yet lacking words.

In forcing himself to not stop or make address, awareness surfaced of something profound about this person which would haunt Cal's Id for time to come. In augur for an event of momentous impact. He was staggered by the power from the vibe. Cal barely managed to exit ornate old doors without making a fool of himself.

A move soon to be branded as pure blunder.

January, 2006

One more damnably interminable semester. Cal put the laptop pc on to the library kiosk desk and lowered long bluejeaned legs from their propped position. He was seeing stars from screen strain and still, the context of the thesis stretched on and on. The research, while interesting, had ceased to motivate him. He wanted out. Or in. Whichever term was more appropriate. By merit of his newest--- patented--- offering in the computer technology field garnering some lukewarm interest, entrepreneurial enterprise was much the preferred subject these days.

Having learned a hard lesson about beggars and choosers long before, the multiple-venue trial balloon method certainly had instilled more respect in smaller dot com start-ups striving to corral that one mercurial breakthrough. Even feedback from megalodons in the computer industry had upgraded under pressure by modern competition. Cal knew there were eyes on him, now, at the least. In spite of it, or maybe resultant to it, necessity for a completed MBA both hung over his head and dangled from around his neck. With any luck, the next two or three months would see to its culmination. Cal couldn't wait.

Scratching his head and rearranging balls, he gazed distractedly around the fourth floor of Ransom Center. Archives section. The bustling place wouldn't close for another two hours, yet he was ready to clear out now. B-O-R.... I-N-G played in his subconscious to the cadence of Aretha's 'Respect' while he tapped pencil eraser on desk.

Snippets of low conversations drifted around him as he tried deciding whether to continue or pack up. From a near corner, a conversation arose as a male and female voice combo closed in on his cubicle, "Jake, you need to get out more. All you ever do is study or sneak away to that dumpy old theatre on the Drag. It's right next to that looney Scientology church and one of these days, those crazy people are going to kidnap you... I'll wake up one day and you'll be gone. Boy, think about it. School and that place shouldn't be your whole life." Although faint, the trill of her voice cut through to him. He wondered why people didn't whisper in libraries anymore.

"Well, Abby, it's top of my list to get through med school and I don't like missing classes--- it wastes money. Maybe if you were paying your own way, you'd be better about showing up, girl... besides I don't have a photographic memory like some people." The mellifluous male voice sounded like a Pachelbel melody. So musical... Cal honed in on it. "And, I don't get what you have against the Bijou. It plays all the old classics and hardly anyone goes there. For a measly buck I feel like I'm in my own little world." The flow drew Cal's notice for some reason.

"Boy, now pay attention to me. Someday soon I am going to drag your ass out to experience some of the world. Pledge week is coming up and Delta Gamma puts on good parties. They network with the Greek men, too. There is a real world, you know, and Jack Nicholson said that 'all work and no play, makes you a dull boy'...or something..." the girly giggle faded as the two walked on. The couple had turned away from him, voices diminishing as they continued on between stacks of bookshelves.

Suddenly hitting on the words, and the actor's name, Cal jumped to his feet, peering down one aisle then the next, seeking them. As he came on a distant row, he barely glimpsed a boy and girl turning again at the far end, a hundred feet away. A ski parka topped a set of muscular legs sprouting downward from a delectable little round ass, washed-out blue jeans form-fitting the sexy curves. A headband of some sort tamed a riot of dark golden curls... almost. Above and below the knotted wrap, those ringlets poked and spiraled every direction, splaying around it, long enough to bounce off the parka collar. The Raphael boy, Cal established. It was him!

For close to two years now, Cal had felt sure he would run across the mysterious boy someplace around campus, certain he was a student. He just had to be. But in all that time, never once had similar curls proven quite so untamed, quite so dark golden, or… well… Him. As Cal grabbed his stuff and packed it all inside the canvas shoulder bag, he mentally reprised words just overheard. Paying his own way…Med School… Bijou…old classics… And that voice. Cal's junk jumped again as he replayed the clip of a chance conversation, absolutely convinced it was the same boy. He dashed down the aisle after them, determined not to let another chance pass by. There was something about him. He just felt it.

Sliding on the polished floor, he barreled past the corner at the far end of the aisle they had passed through. A cursory 360 around the open area of fourth floor found no evidence of the couple's presence. Where had they gone, he hollered in his head? They must still be here! Flying to plate glass windows overlooking the piazza outside, lamp lit darkness shadowed numerous people walking--- together and separate--- on their ways to somewhere. None were the two he sought.

He raced to the adjoining wall of windows, searching harder, heart sinking with his hope. Then--- there, just disappearing into a glass foyer of the Union Building across the mall--- he caught sight of the shining halo of curls. He recognized them from just the two sightings and appearances in recurring dreams. The Raphael Boy. There he went. Disappearing, in obliviousness to Cal, inside.

Tearing to the stairway, he clambered down four flights, taking three and four steps at a gallop. Bursting into the crisp night, Cal realized he had left his hoodie up at the kiosk and cussed himself. But didn't stop. Reaching the Union, he yanked open the doors and blasted inside. People scattered out of the tall ebony man's path as he helter-skeltered every different direction through the building. From cozy fireplace rooms with big easy chairs, to cathedral-ceilinged commons, through food court and adjoining bookstore, back to the lobby and around the whole big place. Up and down three of five levels and the underground parking garage. Twice. Nothing. People were staring. Wondering out loud what the crazy black guy was up to. Cal could not care less. He had to find him…

...But no amount of searching turned up the mystery youth. After thirty minutes of hunting he finally sat down to catch stymied breath. Damn and double damn. Not again...

Arriving at the little efficiency behind Whole Foods grocery after eleven, Cal tossed his pack and the day's mail on the threadbare couch, flopping down next to it. Deflated. Well, he conjectured, at least this time he came away with more knowledge than the last. He was now aware the boy's name was Jake--- Jacob, maybe? What a sexy name. And Jake went to the Bijou sometimes, where Cal had seen him that one time. He'd go back, now, even though that tactic hadn't reaped benefits before. Cal now knew he was a Medical School student. Had he been accepted at the age of twelve, Cal speculated? He couldn't be more than sixteen, by his looks. So. Sexy as hell and intelligent. Cal's mind bounced from one place to the next in formulating a plan, probing for additional details, racking his brain through another hour.

At midnight-thirty, Cal noticed the stack of mail strewn over pack and sofa. Absentmindedly gathering and sorting it, still obsessing with newly identified Jake, he suddenly focused on an envelope addressed to his 'Full Name, Esquire'. Not common. The return address denoted 'Intel, Incorporated'. The rejection notices all had been addressed to 'Cal Broadhearst'. Period. His heart leaped.

Ripping open the vellum quality packet--- another anomaly--- he quickly scanned the cover page. A yelp of flabbergasted delight erupted from his lungs, deep-chested whoop sure to waken neighbors. His latest patented invention had been picked up by the computer giant.

He had come up with a method for coordinating home media centers with a regulated concept ratifying manufacturer standards. It would streamline media pc connectivity. The details provided here informed him the technology would more than likely be named ViiV Tech. The company was welcoming him into the corporate world. Cal was ecstatic. This could mean multiple lucrative future contracts. And, millions of dollars.

Calumet Alfrederic Broadhearst II was on his way.

With renewed vigor, Cal set to finishing the thesis for his MBA. Having researched and posed the central question to be addressed, set primary sources, shaped the outline and contextualized a great portion of the work, Cal tweaked the whole project by narrowly focusing on newly marketed technology now contracted to Intel. It eased his struggles by fine-tuning the research to a newly valuable modality. The conclusion and defense became moot points by the success he had achieved, verifying the thesis by real time means.

By March, Cal had polished up supplemental info, verified UT requirements and proofed all. The final version was impressive. At submission, committee members sitting in review were duly swayed and charmed. Positivity for opening future spin-off science in the field added a major boon. Cal felt validated. Graduation at May Commencement was virtually assured. On schedule.

Pressure now lifted and Cal was fortified by a new sense of being. The contracted inventor began feeling out old friendships. Revisiting old haunts and even reinitiating ties with UT Sig Ep House. Confidence soared and he lightened up. BMOC returned as a term used in conjunction with his name; he was close to fulfillment. With one exception.

John Gilbert, Sig Ep brother and current president, a past close confidant, emerged once again. After the ballyhooed 'harem' deserted a few years before, Cal had retreated into isolation. Now, the UT Greek world was again including Cal Broadhearst back in the social circuit. His charisma, always infectious, lured pledges by underclassmen in droves. Everyone was taken by the tall, ripped Don Juan; they wanted a piece of him. Cal was responsive. But only on certain levels.

"Cal, the mixer next Wednesday is going to be killer. I'm pretty sure we have everything covered." John and Cal shared a beer while summarizing the itinerary. "Thirty-three pledges are invited, dude, and that is our biggest group in three years. Whoa. We gonna get down, now, bro." John was ebullient. He recognized that Cal's presence had been instrumental and was gratified by his old friend's reappearance.

Yet he remained perplexed at the sudden rejuvenation. While he grasped the fact of Cal feeling bummed after getting dumped, and identified with buckling down on the study aspect, John had picked up on a piece that wasn't fitting. Something was not quite adding up but it couldn't be pinpointed. Maybe he was still just missing his ladies... who wouldn't?

Cal hadn't told anyone---anyone at all--- about the Intel contract. Nor was it his intention. There would be time for that later. In the meantime, fun was the guiding light. He was gradually recalling how to make that happen. "It's all good, John. I'm stoked. Be here at 5 on Wednesday for set-up?" He hopped down off the bar in the big makeshift main floor party room and headed for the door. There was a matinee at the Bijou on Cal's search schedule. Funny Girl was showing.

"Sure, Cal. We'll be ready," John replied. The thoughtful half-grin pensively studied his friend even after the latch clicked shut.

True to his word, Cal knocked on the chapter house front door the following Wednesday. Three matinees over four days during the week of Spring Break, such as it was, had been nostalgic. At least there was that, he rationalized.

The kegs were arriving; the slip-n-slide was already wet down and sluicing in back by the pool. The bar was fully stocked, bartender taking inventory, and fresh ice was on its way. House dwellers were trickling down from their residence rooms above and the DJ joined Cal as Schultz opened. Cal made certain to put in his two cents of advice for the tune-spinner--- excuse him: Musicologist--- knowing what music he wanted to hear. Like the guy would listen. That was OK, thought Cal, he could dance to anything.

Four hours later, five Negro Modelos downed and a girl on each side, Cal waltzed to the DJ booth. His tastes were eclectic, to say the least, but put on the spot, the disc jockey succumbed. Then, before hearing the request played, he was pulled outside. Passing the pool on the way to a group around the fire pit, two conspiring girls proceeded to push in synchrony ever so slightly, on a mission. Equilibrium impaired by the beer, tipsiness propelled him head over heels into the deep-end. A lazy underwater sortie around the pool cleared his head a little. Sputtering upon surfacing and threatening retaliation, Cal climbed out in amusement as two dozen partiers followed suit. Voluntarily. The pool was filled with fully clothed disrobers in seconds.

The temperature notched up as clothes came off, not the fewest of which were shed by Cal. Just as the girls had intended. From their vantage point in the now well-populated pool, Cal put on a slow striptease for their benefit, slinging clothing different directions. Then hopped back in the pool. A few minutes later, bulging biceps bracing the pool edge, the big man accepted a primo blunt. He inhaled deeply before passing it on. Yes, he sighed contentedly, what a contrast between pre-and-post thesis author mindset. Pushing away from the tiled side, a leisurely backstroke offered momentary respite. He desultorily arced pool water from his mouth, mind fuzzy and meandering.

Emerging after a twenty-minute swim, the slip-n-slide was graced as well. By now, clad in only the dripping wet skin tight drawers which covered very little and disguised less, the fire pit again called out. Warming up before it, the contents were anatomically sketched in erotic detail by flickering flames. Men and women alike were captivated. But after another deep hit, this time from a power hit offering, Cal caught the onset of the call tune he had asked of the DJ earlier.

Departing the bogarting tokers, the smooth and dripping big barefoot stud made his way back inside, stopping to peruse the room for a moment at the doorway. Then, without more hesitation, the six-foot-six frame vaulted lightly up on the twenty-foot mahogany bar in an agile bound, feeling the tune. Every eye in the big party room became fixated. Most mouths were salivating. The pledges were raptly awed to be rushing the Sig Ep Chapter which claimed this member as brother. The drawers clung graphically around junk filling the pouch, limber length and girth quite discernible. Even the sexy foreskinned cowl stood out plainly through sopping cloth.

Cal was not only aware; he was working the knowledge. The wall mirror behind the bar allowed for indulgent self-appraisal more than one time. He felt like an unabashed hedonist by the deed. Erogenous body gyrations projected the cocky attitude being cultivated. 'Why not, for once?' the giddy party animal theorized. 'Hell, if you got it, go ahead and flaunt it'. An inflating super-ego caroused with abandon.

Swinging in a wide arc, arms and belly rippling, he felt acutely aware of an ongoing metamorphosis from introverted grad student to abounding extrovert on the edge. Cal's dark eyes roved the crowd egging him on. Grinning, ear-to-ear, he observed almost every eye locked on to some part of his anatomy. The awareness grew a slow swell...

Then, abruptly, his vision wavered.

On the far corner wall, nursing a glass with a curled straw no less, arms drawn up and crossed as if in defense of something, stood a boy. By himself. Pouting lips sucked on the straw as long-lashed sea green eyes stared, unblinking, directly at Cal. Myopic in their lovely intense scrutiny. Scrutiny of Cal. Everything slowed to pause. The music muddled in his ears and Cal suddenly felt over-exposed.

A breeze wafting through the open window raised a ruckus amongst the dark golden ringlets fluttering about the cherubic face. The Raphael boy appeared as he had while tunnel-visioning Barbra on one long ago clear day in a dark theatre. Sans tears this time.

Cal didn't quit dancing--- hell, for the first time, he had the youth's attention. The erotic boogie and prance now intimated a private invitation for the angel. His eyes completed a steady loop with the boy named Jake. He wasn't about to let go. The next few minutes passed trapped in surreal suspension. Everything went still in Cal's psyche. Raucous surroundings existed only on a parallel plane; beat of the music sustained a lone connection to reality. Cal knew he looked good and he was damn well gonna milk that fact. Jake hadn't taken his eyes from him. Not once.

A static eternity later, the tune melded to a less strident beat of another carrying on. Without breaking eye contact, Cal bounced nimbly from bar top, straight-lining toward him. Interested roisterers lining the path he took grabbed and grasped for attention. Cal made his way, undeterred, having eyes for no one... but Him.

Desperately eager to not screw up this chance, a split-second decision stuck with the aura of cocky confidence. He took a gamble, swooping in on the doe-eyed target, brazenly sliding to within a bare inch of the adorable pug nose. A flush of epic proportion permeated the tanned young face. Wisps of Irish Spring emanated from him, altering Cal's first choice in soap at that moment.

Cal felt strangely vulnerable in his presence, aware that his own musky body odor must surely be assaulting the boy.

Despite hidden misgivings, he leaned in close, cheekily querying, "Hey sexy, come here often?"

* * *

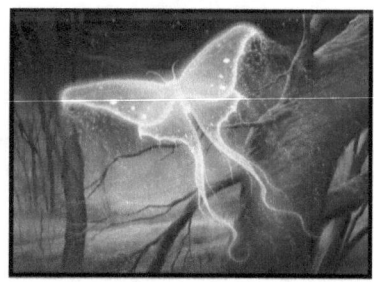

Volume III: Call of the Loon

June, 1991

"Noooooooooooo!" The crescendo of the long, woebegone wail was meant to make a point. And split eardrums. From a head-covered position and squinch-faced demeanor, I hazarded a single-eyed peek from inside protective hands, surveying the damage. All three persons in the room appeared in ear-covered distress. I deemed the broadside successful.

It proved only temporary, however. After a minute's recovery, the man in the striped shirt with the sharp weaponry--- who had strapped me into position for the beheading--- came again. This time, the broom sweeper aide and Mamma plastered my shoulders against the swiveling death chair in apparent collusion with the beast's murderous intent. Pointed scissors waved ever closer while dastardly abettors attempted reassurance by the most transparent of felonious lies, saying anything they thought might engender cessation of attempting salvage of my head.

I wasn't at all certain my body would do well detached from the familiar anatomy, and less, that it wouldn't leave a scar... a bad one. Could it even be put back, it occurred to me to worry? I needed to alert an authority of the cruelty threatening me. The banshee shriek was the last-ditch effort left in my sparse arsenal of protections for self-preservation. So, I tried it again.

"Nooooooooooooooo!!" Under the heavy hands pressing me into the death seat it was all I could do to inflate five-year-old lungs with enough air to get the message out but even then, the effect was not near as shrill as would've been preferred.

Mamma tried soothing me with obviously faked compassion, "Jake, Jake... listen to me, honey. This is for your own good. It has just gotten too out-of-control, my little one, and we are trying to make things easier.

That is all. It won't hurt in the slightest. But it must be cut. Your Daddy says we must and it will be a whole lot better. Now calm down and sit still for us, or it really could hurt you, dear."

Well... that sure worked, I screeched inside. Not!

Easier? Better? For whom? Duh, I reflected, insanely ill-at-ease, you really think so? Of course, it will hurt. And that man--- Wilbur, or whatever you call him--- is NOT my Daddy. My Daddy would never try something like this. And he would surely be here to save me from this Devil with the sharp scissors. Totally freaked, I opened my mouth to renew complaints.

A sweaty palm clamped suddenly over mouth and nose, immediately cutting off the attempt, but worse, my breath as well. Big eyes widened in terror as I realized now that the broom sweeper's nasty paw was only an additional method for inflicting torture. It would be better for them, my mind reasoned, to render me unconscious--- or worse--- before implementing the decapitation process just verified as coming.

I had to do something.

Much as I didn't want to, I pushed my tongue through pressed lips, wiggling it against the gross out palm bearing the warts which I had seen layering it upon entering the death chamber. All red and gooey with thick pus, or something. I had been nearly nauseous by the glimpse. The feel of them against my tongue was far, far worse.

"Yuckkk!" came the outcry from the mouth attached to the warty-palmed man. Boy, I thought, did that gripe have it backwards. It was my tongue on those revulsions. Yet, he did loosen his grip a tad. It gave me just enough of an angle to open my teeth and chomp down on one finger. "Ouch! That hurts, ya little turd bucket. Leggo!" I held fast, clamping down as hard as possible, hoping to sever the stupid thing. I could already taste blood, and dearly hoped it wasn't my own. Scissor man was out of view...

Shrieking now, in his own banshee rendition, the glass-eyed sweeper wailed in agony.

Just as I thought I was making progress, Mamma's hand slapped the bejeebers out of me. I let go in shock. She had never before struck me. I was more forlorn than ever in knowledge that evil intent had invaded all those present.

"Jacob Winslow! You stop this. Right this instant! I will not have this kind of behavior from you, young man. Just wait until we get you home and I tell your Father!" She was almost frothing as she hurled this at me. The wild-eyed look scared me almost as much as Mouth-clamper and Head-chopper. I pulled up short and sat deathly still, staring from one to the next in sheer horror that three grown adults would do such things.

Watching, quietly now, I saw the bleeding pinky rushed to the nearby sink and stuck under a streaming faucet. Mamma implored the two executioners, "Please forgive me. I don't understand what has gotten into him." Her sidelong hard look daggered me with venom, as surely as if I had been bitten by a pit viper. It hurt. Bad.

Head-chopper went to a cabinet, removing bandage and nursing materials. Returning to help the injured--- but not enough--- warthog who was now blotting a blood-seeping gash. The two worked at medicating and securing the wound.

Mamma came back and bent down over me, hissing not at all kindly through clenched teeth, "This is just abominable behavior Jacob. I will not have it. Now sit up straight and act like a big boy. Mind your manners. I cannot believe you would do this to these nice men. Your Father is going to be angry when we tell him."

That broke through my arrested psyche. "Well, I'm sure not gonna tell him. And, he is NOT my Father, and you know it, Mamma. You should be ashamed of yourself--- all of you," looking from one of them to the next, "you shouldn't be trying to knock me off just to get me out of the way. He hates me! And you know that, too! Just let me out of here and I promise to leave and never come back!"

All the words just tumbled out in a heap. I pulled up short again, amazed at myself for the very grown-up response to this barbary. Scissor-wielder cocked his head at Mamma as he taped a bandage on the wart-covered pinky. "Ma'am. Mrs. Howard. I don't think I am going to be able to help you and your son today. There seem to be issues that may be needing more attention than just a haircut will help." He glanced my direction. "What's more, we won't be incurring any more damages at this time. So, if you would be so kind as to remove my barber drape, you and your son can take off. That would probably be for the best." The man's jaw set decisively.

Firmness in the tone left no real basis for debate. Mamma huffed her way through doing as requested, removing the death cape from its snug tightness around my neck--- no doubt meant to keep blood from dripping down my headless body and making a mess--- then hustling the two of us out the front door.

I focused on the red, white and blue whirly cylinder on the pole outside, trembling at the near-death experience and wincing by the hard grip of Mamma's hand over my wrist. She dragged me with her to our station wagon parked in front, loaded me ungently into the restrictive child seat without so much as a word, started the old car and screeched out of the strip-center lot.

Thirty minutes later found us sitting in the bathroom at the forest home. Me on a closed commode seat, boosted by a telephone book; Mamma on the kitchen stool, bending my head back over an adjacent sink edge. She wielded Spotty's dog clippers and fairly spat the first words from her mouth since the chamber of horrors. "Now, Jacob Winslow Howard, I don't want a single movement or word from you. Keep your head leaning back into the sink, just like it is."

With that, and the fear of God paralyzing me, she proceeded to strip the wild mess of curls in curved path after curved path by progressive arcs from brow, up over the crown and down my neck. Within seconds, my riot of lifelong ringlets lay orphaned in the porcelain sink. Limply staring up at me as if to say, 'What did we do, Jake?' I turned my neck when given license to move, peering from there up to the mirror. The bald pate staring back bespoke naked overexposure; my face lent credence to tragedy. In unspoken defiance, I yelled mindfully: It is NOT Howard. It is Marshall!

But, I also sighed in relief. My head was still attached to my shoulders. At least there was that.

Later that evening, 'Father' arrived home. Indeed, the man was more than unhappy. "He bit the barber?" The shouted sentence resonated through the house, alerting us four to take shelter in the basement.

Not waiting to hear Mamma make the moot point, "No Burt, he only bit the helper," we abandoned ship. Luckily, the basement door was right next to our bedrooms and coast was clear for scurrying down steep dark stairs. Shelves bearing preserves, drying produce and herbs provided a hiding spot, yet we all knew it would provide very little more than a temporary respite.

Jill, Michael and Avery all conspired, right there in front of me, to throw the guilty one of us--- me--- out into the open area when He came bellowing. The voice alone was monstrously scary; feared belt medieval in its efficiency. My little butt bore scarred witness.

Reading the writing on the wall, I came to a snap decision. Making myself very small, I silently slipped down the back-shelf line. A handful of freshly pulled carrots and potatoes, some drying apples, a plastic bag and several bottles of water were collected. Heading for 'The Place'.

Guarding against being seen by conniving sibs, I scrambled inconspicuously behind wall shelves to a secret pocket first stumbled on in grieving search for hidden haven the previous spring. When I was only four. Under circumstances more dire than those presently building: that time when Real Daddy had left.

Prying plywood backing from the wall, I squeezed soundlessly through a narrow cleft. Carefully drawing the shelf back into place after entry, a pitch black five-foot track toward the earthy smell marking the broken cement bulwark was crawled.

A foot-wide hole where ancient concrete had disintegrated offered a worm-riddled pouch of a cubby. The fecund odor of rich earth was not horrible. I didn't like the occasional worm or tiny critter as they strayed over me on their travels but the alternative seemed grimmer.

From previous sequestrations, I had left a moth-eaten blanket. The thing smelled a bit worse for the wear. I felt around it for alien inhabitants. Thankfully finding none, the bagged produce was poked into a corner. Wrapped into the blanket, I planned on 'laying up sorry'. In hopes the storm would blow over without my presence.

Last time, Wilbur had departed on a salesman's road trip during the self-imposed banishment. Mamma had been so relieved my dead body hadn't washed up downstream from the forest home on Elkin Brook that I had been spared bodily harm. A result worth repeating.

The first time discovering the site, I was bereft with sorrow. It was late in the night, having withdrawn to solitary confinement upon forced comprehension that Daddy--- my dearest hero and real Daddy--- had left. Never to return. And without saying goodbye.

I had crawled by sheer accident between shelf and wall, burrowing my sorrowful self deep from reality. There had been no goal, just determination to get away. The narrow wedge of an opening had presented itself and without reasoning, I pushed past it. Reaching the unlit little lair, I curled up and slept. Then, stayed in the cozy little hole in the wall for a better part of six days. Until I had felt like Daddy looked. Mamma was distraught by the act, thinking she had lost two family members. She almost did. Though hounded for weeks, I resolved to never let go of my secret. She had finally given up probing.

Earlier in the day leading to that night, Mamma informed us that Daddy had 'gone to Heaven' after a Blackhawk helicopter crash over in a land named Ethiopia. Somewhere far away. He wouldn't be coming home. Even at four years old I was aware that didn't add up. She couldn't just erase the fact that he had been there only hours before.

I had found out the truth.

Eavesdropping a conversation between Mamma and Dr. Aston late in that dreary afternoon following her telling us that story, it came clear to me that Daddy had gotten sick a long time before and the reason was a cause for shame. I didn't understand. As told by Dr. Aston, after returning from a tour of duty a year before, a sickness carried by green monkeys and 'unnatural' men had sneaked in and overwhelmed him.

I remembered observing it all. Month after month, he lost more and more weight, eating next to nothing and shriveling before my sad young eyes. From the tall, vibrant, fearless protector who sang to me, took me fishing and hoisted me on broad shoulders for romps around the yard with a leaping Spotty, Daddy had diminished to a sunken-eyed ghoul who rarely spoke. When he did, he sucked air in through crusty nostrils. Concave cheeks had puffed out words in stuttered phrases.

All over his once strong body there blossomed dark blotchy circles that hurt... and sometimes drained a smelly stew. A broken-hearted promise was pledged to him then that I would grow up--- fast--- to become a doctor. I would save him. He hugged me and smiled at that pronouncement, promising in return. He would hold me to it.

Mamma hated him though. I could tell. Under her breath, she muttered once, disgustedly, that he deserved it all. I heard.

We were finally barred from going to him or even speaking. So, he lay there. By himself. Withering and rasping in the darkened spare room. Alone.

One somber gray morning, a long black station wagon had rumbled into our driveway, backing up to the garage. Peeking unseen through front window curtains, I beheld a narrow bed roll out of the garage opening. A lumpy mass lay on it, covered by a sheet. The whole thing was loaded by two uniformed men into the back of the strangely shaped vehicle. It then slipped away into mist. Sad, wispy, swirling fog trails arose behind it, gathering as if by a witch's spell, to gradually obscure the entire silhouette. Like a dissolving spectre.

We were told nothing at first. While fearing the worst, we held out hope he would get up from bed and come out of the gloomy, reeking room. After hours of terrible waiting, Mamma tearfully described a tragic helicopter wreck with another craft, crying as she affirmed Daddy would not be coming back home. One thing I knew for certain was that last sentence. The rest, I had gleaned, was a big fib. The overheard conversation later that afternoon cut deep.

It was not long afterwards--- only a few unhappy months--- that replacement Daddy, Wilbur Howard, had come into our grieving lives and sorry home. A poor substitute who disliked all things children. Even Spotty was despised. I figured all that out in ten minutes flat. The man knew that I knew, too. Spotty never once set foot inside again.

Now, ensconced in my portal to underground, I listened to sisters and brother plan my sacrifice, then bore their aggravation at yet another discovery of my ghosting. They detested me for doing it, spying incessantly in trying to figure what I did and where I went. But without success. Covering my tracks well, no one ever guessed.

True to form, within thirty minutes, three exposed children sat shivering in their boots as the trumpeting baritone voice of evil traipsed on leaden feet around and around rooms upstairs. Demanding obeisance. Mamma finally slithered downstairs, ushering the three upstairs to face the music. I listened as they were excoriated in 'covering' for me.

Threats of dire consequences led to nothing, of course. Finally, the house quieted to an uneasy peace.

I spent the next five days in that spot, only coming out to relieve myself at the open septic tank vat in a far corner and to gather more food and water. Recognizing my strange method, the five gradually went about their normal routine, deducing that somehow an outdoor hiding place offered refuge which they could not locate. It proved baffling to them that even Spotty couldn't track me. They commonly sent the furry friend of mine on wild goose chases around the acreage in the Green Mountain Forest tract. Without success. Never was my friend and confidant let to search the basement, for some reason. Else, I would have probably been outed.

After those days, my creeping trip up the stairs, clandestine escape to outdoors and subsequent hike through surrounding woods over a day with nature brought me, roundtrip, to the back door. A sullen welcome was met as the sun was setting. A disgusted Wilbur ignored my reappearance. Not even deigning to acknowledge the return. Boy, this was the best answer to problems, I rationalized. Success was measured in this fashion and I went to bed exhausted, hungry, bald and alone. Perfectly whole, I reflected. Without a mark.

I was a quick learner. With a good memory.

May, 1994

"Hold still, you old coot. You've gotten it caught in your collar." The two old guys were close, almost in a hug, as the speaker reached his arms around old coot's neck, trying to unravel tangled fishing line. It wrapped the silver-haired man in at least three complete loops, spiraling upwards from ankles to neck. The freshly baited hook stuck insistently in the collar of the red and black plaid Land's End jacket. A writhing, hook-impaled nightcrawler whished, in agonal throes, on and off the adjacent bare neck. Old coot did not like the slimy texture.

"Chad, get the horrid thing off me. It's shitting and pissing all over me, goddamit. Ewwww…get it off!" The pitched voice lent urgency to a scene that Jake and Spotty were having a hard time deciphering. Dog and boy grinned together at the fix the couple were engaged in, watching from behind a big old hemlock tree screening them.

The old-fashioned three-tiered cane pole attached to the line now entered the fray, its end flicking around four booted feet, successfully lassoing both men through two minutes of a silly, twirling dance. Jake channeled an old 'I Love Lucy' episode when Fred and Ricky were wrapped in a similar imbroglio and stifled a laugh by covering his mouth with a free hand.

The other, bracing Spotty's chest, rose by simple rote function, covering the dog's mouth, too. As if to stop a second guffaw. Spotty licked the hand, but sat still, tail wagging in enjoyment of all the goings on around him. Jake saw that his buddy's canine lips were also raised in a tickled grin, apparently absorbing the scene and Jake's mirth. The two shared much.

"I've almost got it, Derrick, if you'll quit your prancing and give me a chance. Hold still, will you?" Chad remonstrated in vain. A fraught Derrick--- the old coot--- was either unable or unwilling to control himself. Two pale wrinkled hands fluttered helplessly in nervous circles around their bodies, expressing abject horror that the greasy annelid dared intimacy as it did.

A startling falsetto shriek erupted as wormed hook pricked tender skin, poking through the jacket collar. "I've been bitten! I am done in... by a worm!" Derrick's neck arched dramatically skyward. The next thing Jake knew, the victim raised a limp wrist to brow, emitted a grumbling sigh... and sank. The rest of his body followed the wrist's suit. He timbered limply toward the ground, eyes rolling up in a blood-drained face. The inelegant swoon dragged the enmeshed fishermen to a thumping bump on the grassy edge of Elkin Pond.

Silence ensued. For the next seconds, nobody moved. The conscious elder, boy and spotted dog all took stock of the situation, viewing the fainted Derrick in an unconscious sprawl. Chad's eyes rolled shut and he began heaving hoarse breaths from his trapped, wrapped position atop his companion. Jake was certain somebody was dying. Or had already. He was familiar with death, after all.

Then, he witnessed a huge sucking of air by old coot, laboring to inspire air from under the stout body smothering his own. The expressive hands began snaking a peculiar snakelike jig all around--- but not touching--- Chad's form.

This disturbed Jake. He felt he must inveigle himself into the scenario, in order to render CPR. Or something. One or the other seemed to be in need. Jumping up from behind the massive tree trunk, Spotty sprang into action as well. Savior duo proceeded to aid the unlucky fisher people. First checking for other signs of life, then unsticking and unwrapping the confused, exhausted, laboring men.

This took more than several minutes, what with the thrashing, passive resistance and gurgling anguish exhibited throughout the process. Finally, separating the friends--- Jake assumed they were--- Spotty and he managed to nudge the pudgers to semi-sitting positions. Facing one another.

Jake stood back and watched as first Chad's eyes opened slightly, then Derrick the Coot's fluttered and focused. A sharp cry and staccato palm slap emerged from his mouth and hand, in that order, seeing upon whom his eyes wavered to convergence. "Dreadful! I say, a blemish on the compassionate side of Humanity you are... you... you... ingrate!"

At this new outburst, and apparently unsure how long he had been rendered cataleptic, Chad the Ingrate winced away from the blow--- way too late for believability--- and harped, "Me? An ingrate? Why, I have lain insensate for no telling how long here amidst cold vile filth of this pigsty, most probably been raped or pillaged while in that state, and surely had wild animals drool on me in marking my face for a snack… and all because I risked everything to save the likes of you?" He stumbled feetward in ungainly manner, continuing to glare at the still slumped Derrick. Fire swords were erupting from his eyes.

These were met by a contrasting ice-daggered stare from Derrick, who persisted in wounded damsel mode. "Well, I knew I should never have taken up with the likes of you, as my ex-wives have always told me. You are no good and good for nothing." Then, just to be mean, "For pity's sake, I don't even like anybody who likes you."

Following suit, the old gent struggled to arise, falling several times, until old Chad--- the Ingrate--- reached out and helped hoist unsteady feet beneath him. It was then that Derrick recalled the slimy nightcrawler, feeling tentatively up and around his head and neck for evidence of the gross thing. He just knew the thing must be masturbating, or something else awful, in his hair.

Having stood silently aside and taking all of this in, unnoticed, Jake meekly intervened. Softly clearing his eight-year-old throat, the diminutive mop head timidly spoke up, "Umm, excuse me, Sirs. I think you both got tangled up and fell. It's all right, though, because me and Spotty got the line off and turned you over and made sure you were… alive. Oh, and here's your worm… err, bait." The big-eyed youth handed up a hooked and still wiggling sufferer toward the couple.

If Jake's emerald eyes were naturally big, long-lashed and engrossing, the elderly gentlemen matched them in size as they turned to little guy and spotted dog in utter surprise. Both immediately smiled, attempted straightening and brushing themselves, simultaneously transforming from grumpy demeanors at recognition of new presences. Portraying two exactly opposite personas.

"Well, my, my, look at this, Chad. If it isn't the most adorable boy and his dog. What is his name, little man?" Jake's innate wariness of all adults raised to high alert, previously inculcated to changeling behavior of grown-ups. As tickled by the two crusty old curmudgeons as he had been when observing them in unassuming natural states, so too was he now stand-offish by the affected alteration.

Chad, likewise transformed, now came across more like Hansel and Gretel's wicked witch. Offering toffee and divinity. Fake. At least so thought Jake. "Uhh, his name is Spotty. But watch out, he doesn't take to strangers very nice. If he thinks I'm in trouble, he'd probably get mad." This, as the tail-wagger smiled good-natured acceptance of the geriatric people. The dog had obviously already sized them up. Maybe he was wrong, the thought crossed young Jake's mind.

"Then I think that we should maneuver very carefully around the gallant protector, shouldn't we, Chad?" Derrick posed this. "After all, it isn't very often that a person can count on another to back them up in a pinch." He winked over at his friend munificently, all previous animosity forgotten. Amazingly, the former drama queen reached out, taking the proffered line and hook with a now limp worm, deliberately winding the long length of heretofore shackling entangler around his fingers. Jake was extra-perplexed at such change.

"That would certainly appear to be the prudent thing to do, Derrick," Chad sat down on a nearby stump, apparently a fisherman's stoop by the smoothness and wear, and put a friendly hand out in greeting to the dog. "Hello, there, Sir Spottiswood. And how are you this fine Vermont morning?" Spotty responded without hesitation. Coming forward, he offered a paw and accepted a friendly ear scratch, open-mouthed, tongue tipping out and nose sniffing of the man.

Jake was a bit mollified. If Spotty trusted them, he should probably as well. Animals in general, and his canine buddy in particular, had secured Jake's unshakeable trust. In distinct dissimilarity to humans. The latter, not so much. "Sir Spottiswood? Who's that?" Jake was warily curious.

"Why, Lord John Spottiswood was a Scottish peer of the seventeenth century. A trusted advisor to King James I of England, the man was. This noble dog may just be related, eh?" The man smiled warmly in praising Jake's best buddy, thereby winning the first foray. Spotty thumped the tail harder on listening to these words. Jake was enthralled. He came closer, now interested in hearing more.

"Did he have dogs, too?" An obvious question. If the possible relative did so, then another link would seem to be forged in the eight-year-old's mind.

"Well, of course, young man. He kept a bevy of hunters. And a few that even slept with him. But, we are remiss, Sir," --- here, he bowed ever so slightly, glancing back at Derrick as he did--- "We have not been properly introduced. That should be rectified, post haste, eh? I am Chadwick Elkin, born, raised and recently returned resident of this domain encompassing Elkin Pond. And this be Mr. Derrick Diogene, my bosom friend and confidant... and sometimes blood brother..." The emerging grin exuded benevolence toward the gent.

His friend edged forward, extending a slim hand in offer of friendship. "Yes, we are that, Chad. Blood brothers, in that we sometimes do draw blood, figuratively and otherwise, I am abashedly afraid. But that is another story for different time." Looking at Jake, he added, "We are, indeed, bosom friends. And very glad to be meeting you, uhh...?"

Jake raised his own hand in greeting, now, satisfied by the words. At least for the moment. "I'm Jake. Jake Marshall. Me and Spotty live across the pond, over where the brook is. We are out hunting today. Spotty heard you. We watched for a little bit while you were... talking." Jake said all this in more openness than normally allowed around grownups. For reasons well-grounded in experience. These two now seemed harmless; the dog's reaction a great deal of the reason for his impression.

"It be certainly nice to make your acquaintance, young Jake Marshall, and we count it as our great good fortune by the chance." Chad disarmed the boy further by a charming ease of manner. Jake relaxed. The three entered a dialogue bridging generations over the subsequent time, trading tidbits and opinions, comparing notes and observations, discussing the pond and its environs.

Jake was astounded to hear of the fact that old Chad's great grandfather times nine, Thomas Elkin, was the progenitor for whom the pond was named. Before that, it was explained, the Iroquois Nation--- specifically, the Mohicans--- had held loose hegemony over the region now dubbed the Green Mountain National Forest. The Elkin Family holdings intertwined with forest boundaries while the small acreage platted by Jake's real Daddy, twelve years before, was surrounded on three sides by the national set aside. A fourth side, Jake now knew, bordered old Chad's land.

"That makes us neighbors, Jake Marshall. I suppose we should be a mite more neighborly in the future and get to know each other, eh?" The elder used quirky words and phrases unfamiliar to the boy, yet he was responding positively by the nuance and tone imparted in the delivery. Generational bridging. Jake liked these men. He readily agreed to come back soon, and regularly, to make that acquaintance happen. He had no other true friends, being a total loner at the small school in Grafton town, five miles distant. The boy warmed to a new friendship possibility.

Over succeeding weeks, then months, the three became close. A comfortable camaraderie developed as Jake's trust grew. The gentlemen were taken by the sharp-minded youth and captivated by his boyish beauty, not the least of which began with a crowning mess of re-grown curls topping him. The boy's enlivening personality and vigor brought the best out of the two. Their sometimes-rough relationship, when alone together, smoothed remarkably to an evenness not enjoyed between them since an earlier era.

Jake took to bouncing in on the duo without forewarning at the ancient, yet newly refurbished, family compound on the opposite side of the pond from where he resided. Spritely appearances both tickled the older men and engendered superlative behavior. They were still a little embarrassed by the initial meeting's circumstance: the fishing hook episode.

By guarding against another of similar nature, the couple unintentionally regained an ease of temperament which had been their basis for years. And the reason they had fallen in love. The appearance of Jake, and Sir Spottiswood, reinvigorated a stale and stodgy existence. One slipped into through plain lack of care.

"Derrick, do you and Chad always sleep together?" Jake had picked up on the proclivity by astute eight-year-old patterns of observation, and was inquisitive. At the query, Derrick dropped the coffee cup he was sipping, totally flummoxed by the temerity of it. The contents sprayed and sprinkled into nooks and corners, but the sturdy mug remained unscathed. No one ever asked things like that, he reasoned. But he should've been ready: Jake was not shy and did keep both on their toes regarding traditionally touchy subjects.

Choking on poorly swallowed coffee and whirling suddenly nervous hands, the old queen sputtered inanities attempting a reply. In total failure. While Chad and he were comfortable in their relationship and at ease with themselves, harsh light of reality crashed a serene scene by the innocent question. Derrick pulled himself together as he righted the cup and blotted the mess with a napkin, assessing the best way to address such forwardness.

"Well, I guess, Jake... ummm, well, you see... actually, dear lad... oh, goodness... yes. Yes, we do. Indeed. We do share the big poster bed. Unless he acts out. Then he gets to spend nights on the couch." The curt woodpecker-esque nodding was reassurance more for himself than the boy. Why, he reflected, should he lie about something like that in his own home? It wasn't an issue of which he was ashamed; simply a verboten subject abiding as an elephant in the room even amongst familiars.

"I figured that. But I just needed to know." Jake's innocence once again blew the older man's mind. The younger set seemed so much more at ease in the present day with things unspoken by older generations, Derrick ruminated. How refreshing. He couldn't wait to tell Chad. "How many wives do you have?" Again, the directness. This one made Derrick think for another minute. More for whether he should answer than how.

"Umm-Hmmm. That one may take a little longer, young man. Why don't we fix some more coffee and cocoa, and we will discuss the matter?" Derrick almost looked forward to the enlightenment as they trod the kitchen hallway.

Over the three months Jake had been visiting, Chad and Derrick had grown fond of the precocious boy. Much more mature than his years, with a quiet touch of somber, the couple had discussed an approach to the moldable lad. A decision had been made for taking the inquisitive youth under their wise wings.

Perceiving an insatiable appetite for knowledge, Chad began by opening discussions all things historical and medical. His areas of prime interest. Dialogue flourished about the region of Vermont with its rich past. Jake listened endlessly to legends and stories during fishing interludes at various pondside spots, shooting back with pertinent and impertinent probes. The choice of fishing as a venue proved a perfect multifaceted boon for the confabs.

While Chad dearly loved the sedentary pursuit, Derrick barely tolerated a messy, smelly, tedious distraction. Fishing: ick. Boy and dog embraced the pastime with barely contained gusto. Both remembered their idyllic period with real Daddy and were animated by a renewal. By the fact of old Professor Chad having been born in the big old pondside home, there existed in his memories tales rife with significance which he had begun fearing might die with him, childless as he was. In Jake, he found an assiduous recipient.

Long periods of bait and bobber watching buoyed roving discussions ranging from family anecdotes to the American chronicle. Iroquois Nation lore and colonial sagas, and especially horses, all awakened a nascent yearning to explore intriguing genres. Jake borrowed multiple books from the Elkin library in augmentation to the narratives. He devoured many tomes but favorited 'The Leatherstocking Tales' in rapt zeal. A never-ending quest for everything relatable to James Fenimore Cooper's Natty Bumppo, Chingachgook, Uncas and all matters equestrian engaged the boy into adulthood.

As much as these forays into the past fed fast friends' appetites, it proved only secondary by relation to another subject tantamount in import to them both, although from opposite ends of the spectrum.

Consummating a forty-year career practicing medicine at Weill Cornell Medical College as a tenured Professor of Physiology and Surgery, Chad Elkin had fallen into his purely true calling: instructive pursuit of the artful science. Entrance into well-earned retirement, while relieving, left a brilliant educator dispirited by bittersweet existence. Satisfaction, the tenet on which all true teachers thrive, had left a void by its loss.

It only made sense, then, that at the moment of little Jake's enlightenment to the man's august station in the restorative profession, the look of wonderment on his face commenced a tacit pact between them.

The subject of medicine had been grabbed by Jake with both hands, both ears and both big eyes. His spacious young mind proved the readiest of receptacles. What surprised Chad simply fascinated Jake. After all, Jake had made a solemn oath meant to be kept.

The venerable educator awakened to the fact of a swan song mentorship remaining on his plate. Awaiting fulfillment. He fed the fire of a ravenous appetite for knowledge, overjoyed at the young mind craving intellectual illumination. And was left downright astounded by an astute ability to hoard knowledge at the ripe age of eight. The term wunderkind regularly leapt to mind.

During the older couple's re-established day-ending reveries, Chad related the boy's prowess in daily excerpts to a soulmate who lavished nurture upon the young prodigy as his own investment. The role proved palliative for the old coot whose rudder had been sadly faltering until Jake appeared on the scene.

Through two years of refurbishment fervor at the all-but-abandoned homestead, achievement of definitive completion had left Derrick drained. The stakes involved with a career in high finance had instilled him with a sense of the frenetic. A need for constant activity. Design and remodeling efforts had furnished the fast pace for the time it lasted.

Once the endless projects ceased thrumming his motor, however, the seventy-year-old engine of energy had revved on, tractionless. Slumping into an easy chair to heave huge sighs of relief while surveying success had consumed all of two weeks. Attempted rendezvous with his life-partner amidst shared endeavors of patrician gentlemen had careened the duo perilously close to double homicide. Realizing only discord and lost harmony, he hearkened on the need for an outside interest.

Only so many old musicals could fill a day without driving one batso-cuckoo. Delving into the world of arts and crafts had been appealing but held no sense of accomplishment. Bead stringing, basket weaving and macramé braiding amongst bored contemporaries provoked impressions of God's waiting room. Gardening provided some relief and he kept at it, yet remained unfulfilled. Other quests had left a similar emptiness.

Sheer process of elimination led to pursuit of the physical. He had never expended energy that way. But doctor's recommendations--- no: demands--- borderline diagnostic test results and a waning verve for life pushed Derrick toward untried disciplines. Long walks, calisthenics, aerobics, yoga, Tai-Chi. These and others whelmed him in motivational routines which grew a sense of endorphined ease.

On a low-sky dawn morning, Derrick surged exertive breaths as he turned the bend marking Elkin Brook, approaching the little foot bridge spanning the robust rapids draining the namesake pond in a constant flow. He was approaching the now-recognizable stage of effort where a flood of calm would suffuse him. Assigning a new meaning for bated breath, he reflected, giggling to himself.

Suddenly from behind came a sense of company. Glancing back, he viewed first Spotty then Jake come bounding from a swathe of undergrowth. Spotty saw him immediately and wagged a furious greeting while Jake eyed the rear, perusing a trail joining the one which Derrick now traversed. His long, tangled mass of untamed curls bounced, almost nervously, while he progressed heedlessly forward.

When the boy finally turned toward him, his face reflected an angst never seen until then. He caught sight of Derrick and darted an evanescent grin. Friends joined up in seconds, the youngster's pace outstripping the exerciser's significantly. He hastened to keep up.

"Master Jake. So good to run into you, sir. Are you enjoying the morning energy?" He noted the blue jean workout get-up. A peculiar choice, it occurred to the stylish exercise newbie. His own two-piece warm-up suit in burgundy with blue leg stripes and high-performance cross trainers contrasted with 1960's style white-tipped black track shoes and a tattered, dusty t-shirt.

"Hi, Derrick. Spotty told me we might be being tracked, so I was lookin' out," the worried demeanor projected concern. Still peeping over his shoulder, he slowed a little to match the walker's stride, falling in next to him. Spotty took the other side, licking the older man's swinging hand.

"You've mentioned you and Spottiswood commonly run together in the morning. Do you have routines and trails for it? Or are you more the free spirit type who follows his nose?" More questions were forming in the elder man's mind. He held his tongue to see what might be offered.

"Spotty likes certain ways but we try to visit new places every time we can, so unless there's something after us I guess we're kinda noser's. What about you? I've never seen you down on this side of the pond." The intermittent glances behind continued.

"Oh, I am branching out, young Jake. Extending my footprint if you will. My wind is getting better and the distances are lengthening." Derrick wiggled his fingers in response to the continuing Spot licks, the day gone by when he retracted in distaste for the wet tongue. He presently found it almost pleasant. The increasing testosterone levels must be flooding him with masculine attributes, the retiree presumed. Part of the rejuvenation process, he ventured. And it felt so... manly. Derrick wondered why he hadn't perceived the effect before.

Focusing on the earlier comment, he queried, "Something after you... like maybe a bear, or the like? Should it be a source for alarm? I have mace," this as he reached for the inside pocket to reassure its presence.

"Naw. Nothin' like that. My sisters and brother sometimes tail us. They don't like that we disappear and are always tryin' to see where we go off to." Jake's reconnoitering was intent...Derrick noted that the boy disliked the idea it was needed.

"Are you supposed to be somewhere else? Or do they just want to join you?" Derrick knew of the siblings, but details had never been divulged and he was wondering about an unknown home life. He had overlooked the fact of the Marshall home's existence here when he had set out on this earlier-than-normal exercise loop. It was one of only four houses bordering the good-sized private pond.

"They are spies for my parents. Neither of them can figure where I go when I leave and they want to keep me under their control. But not because they like me... just because they don't like not knowing. Pretty sure they wish I wasn't there. And I wish that too. So, I leave." The words pierced Derrick. The visage of angst just envisioned moments before returned. It was disturbing and warped the youth's outer beauty. The older man's heart ached by the knowledge. He conjectured how the negative flow must be affecting the boy's inner beauty.

"But, Jake, I thought you loved the time you spent with your Dad. You have spoken more than once how you and Spottiswood enjoy doing things with him." The busy tongue went into high gear upon hearing the familiar rendition of his name.

The three kept stride around the several mile perimeter of Elkin Pond as the exchange withered. Morning sounds were breaking out and Derrick fixed on the plaintive calls of the black-throated loons as they sought one another. He awaited the boy's response. Jake cocked an ear at the song, as well, pondering the haunting tune.

"Mr. Derrick, my real Daddy died four years ago. He was real sick and we weren't supposed to talk about it. Mamma's new husband is Wilbur--- he almost spat the name--- and he hates me and Spotty. I don't think he likes Jill or Michael or Avery either, but they try to get him to... I don't. He's evil. I hide from him a lot of times and Mamma too, because she does only what he wants. She's not the same anymore. I think she's getting sick, like my Daddy, but she won't say anything. I just see it."

All this unseemly information poured over Derrick. The inward cringe almost conjured tears. He could feel the little boy's emotions streaming in increasing waves of fear and revulsion, just by voicing these things. It hurt his soft soul to know of so much pain. Gathering the boy under his arm, he hugged the boy close, kneading tiny, tense shoulders. The act shook something loose. Jake sagged into him, suddenly sobbing in release of the pretend strength he projected. Spotty whined and came to his side, nuzzling empathetically.

It was all Derrick Diogene could do to keep composure, aware he must. Steeling himself, he reached to Jake's chin and turned it tenderly upward, taking in tear-stained cheeks. "This Wilbur. He doesn't hurt you, does he?" His defense mechanisms were on quick alert by the notion. The mother hen in him feather-ruffled at the thought.

Two huge moist eyes peered into his, wallowing in the sympathy, and shook his head. "No. Not anymore. He used to get out his belt when he first came. To all four of us. But Mamma stopped that. Now, he just pretty much ignores me. But he tries to kick Spotty. I tell Spotty to stay away at night when I am in my bedroom, 'cause he isn't allowed inside anymore. Even though he used to sleep with me and Michael. I'm afraid Wilbur might do something to him when I'm not there. So, he sleeps somewhere in the woods. He's very smart." The dog nuzzled harder at repeating intonations of his name.

Another sharp glance darted back. Jake pulled away from Derrick, signaling Spotty. Looking up, he pronounced, "Derrick, we have to go now. But thank you for listening, and…" Trailing off, the two high-tailed it off the path into the nearby underbrush again, disappearing in fractions of a second. It shocked the older man. He was confounded by this sad information.

Turning backward himself, he saw a dark-haired boy, a bit older than Jake, thirty yards behind. The furtive movements let Derick know it must be Michael. Had he seen his brother? More, had he seen the two sharing that sorrowful moment?

His background made him wary of contact with children, what with the current social climate, priest debacles, and antipathy borne by many toward his ilk. A wave of anxiety coursed through him. He attempted cover by a friendly wave, receiving a half-hearted response with a limp-wristed pre-teen mannerism toward all things adult. By body language, it appeared he hadn't come upon the two before Jake had escaped. Thank goodness.

Reaching a large smooth sitting rock, a little further ahead, just a short way off the path and almost out of sight, Derrick halted. He had visited it before and found comfort. The shaken man sank to it. Both boys were gone, along with the dog.

He propped knees to chin and clasped arms around them, introverting to a familiarly remote place. There, on previous occasions, he had contemplated deep thoughts…and always found succor. The melancholy call of the loons cajoled from offshoot angles as profound musings inundated a wise old mind.

"Chad. I was so affected by it. The boy has been putting up a brave front since we met him, never once letting on what he is carrying around. At least, until now. What may we do, Dearest?" Derrick was distraught by the morning's tidings. Both the conversation, the mangled emotions and the stalking were combining to wilt his defenses. He needed his own back-up for wherewithal to deal with it. That back-up sat across the cozy study from him.

Professor Elkin, emeritus faculty of one of the most prestigious universities in the world, had grown grave and serious upon hearing of the 'confession' by Jake hours earlier. For that was what it was. Along with a cry for help. Albeit a chance one, a cry, nonetheless. The two mulled things by firelight as the merry flames warmed the familiar nest shared by the men. It was inner sanctum of their sanctum sanctorum. Where all subjects of moment and import were debated.

This was both momentous and important. In the three short months of knowing little Jake Marshall, the couple had fallen heavily for him. He could not comprehend the depth of their feelings. They had purposely kept the times as light and airy, or as 'teachable moment' as possible with the youth to protect all three. His person had taken on that much magnitude of meaning with them; there was no desire to compromise the budding relationship. Or the boy's phenomenal potential.

Acute awareness existed of the optics now holding sway in the present day and age. Too many naysayers and ne'er-do-wells with malevolent intentions were abiding in the world, probably nearby, who would dearly love to infer nasty, small-minded meaning to the triple friendship. With corruption of so many things religious in these modern times, tradition had been turned on its head and good objectives skewed topsy-turvy.

Chad reflected on historical times past when age and wisdom had maintained gravitas as a force for improving the world. Youth were immersed into settings of older, wiser, preparatory settings for the exact goal of furthering the progression of Humanity.

Now, however, a rank cynicism had taken hold of great swaths of society. Not unprecedented: the stutter step of human progression had surfaced multiple times before--- just look at the Spanish Inquisition, for one--- when powerful interests had succumbed to the basest of fearful instincts. Yes, it did occur through history, he mused.

But that it was taking form now under the guise of 'protecting' the younger generations remained particularly galling to the two sage retirees. How had it happened that they must now shield themselves, and a youthfully promising protégé, from callously misguided malcontents bent on pursuing another agenda of hegemony in the name of God? Which One, they understood all too well, did not really matter. Any religion's deity could be bent toward narrow-minded human-based methodologies in pursuit of influence over others. Such was happening now. A crying damn shame.

Because a small number of deviants had been outed in their improper malfeasances, a far greater group of ill-advised fools with little or no education, let alone common sense, had taken up arms in the name of 'defending the innocents'. So, sadly, prodigies like Jake must suffer consequences of people unable or unwilling to separate sexuality and life experience.

More and more, Chad and Derrick bemoaned the fact that those who were at the forefront of the movement were very often sexually stunted. Understanding nothing of the balance of learning with the fullness of life. Conjuring wickedness from innocence and using it for perpetrating nothing but ambitions of supremacy.

All this they had hashed over before. Hence, now, reposed in the haven of their lair, the pair of wise persons pondered options for effecting benevolent intent with regards to the young man. Without upsetting the proverbial applecart.

'Ahem', they both evinced together. Glancing into each other's eyes at the same moment threw both into fits of hilarity. They were just too much alike... birds of a feather. La cage aux folles.

The moan of the night breeze through the cracked window and the prickling of Jake's neck by its arrival proved prescient. The boy awakened with a start. Instantly, he felt something was awry. Sixth sense on alert, the boy just knew.

Glancing to his side, the view of his older brother, Michael, verified no wakeful commonality in the signal. Closed eyes, open mouth, light eleven-year-old snore, body strewn in childish haphazardness; all assured that Jake was alone in awareness. The boy was keen to the need for getting out of the house. Unseen and unnoticed. His brother was a heavy sleeper yet had been known to sabotage his little brother by booby-trapping the bed with triggers sure to arouse the elder one in case of surreptitious leave-takings just such as Jake now aimed.

He silently traced fingers in a path around his naked body--- he had taken to the clotheless sleep mode to lessen chances for traps--- until he had completely circled himself, verifying no string attachments. Then, carefully but quickly, the boy touched feet to floor, testing for IED's--- aka: trip wires--- and maneuvered to the chair bearing his shed clothing. Sneakers were double-checked for encumbrances of any sort. Boxers--- check. Socks--- check. T-shirt... jeans... both missing. Darn it, the boy swore inwardly. He should've seen that coming.

Well, he figured, he'd just have to make do. Who needed pants and shirt? At least the shoes were here. Creeping to the cracked window, Jake ran fingers along the sill and up over the top pane. Ah-ha! He tipped the glass gewgaw--- normally sitting on the living room end table--- as it leaned precariously against the glass. Barely catching the fragile thing before it crashed noisily to the wood floor, he set it aside, then inched the window open. Using the unobtrusive dime hidden close by, the screen was unscrewed. A light hop through the cleared path to cool grass beneath and… freedom.

The new moon left him shadowless and light cloud cover provided easy escape to the adjacent tree line one hundred yards away. The forest of dense hardwoods, as well as birch, spruce and pine, hugged familiarly as he was enveloped within. Hurrying, he made for the shrouded clearing Spotty holed up most nights, the dog being prime concern.

A soft whistle brought no response. Not waiting, he made his way along a covered wildlife pathway to the next most common lay-up site. Again, no answer. Now, Jake was worried. His best friend always showed himself lickety-split anytime he went looking, as though his dog radar was synced to the boy's frequency. That Spotty hadn't responded was a bad sign.

As he stood, deciding his next move, there came a low reverberative rhythm of human conversation. The buzz of anxious voices remained unintelligible, but discordant waxing and waning injected a sense of anger and anxiety to the speakers. He headed for the sound.

Less than a quarter mile to the east, Jake came upon the more than three-century-old county line rock fence which marked the Marshall property. The voices were low and masked, evidently on the other side of the five-foot wall.

It stood three feet thick. Constructed of smooth river rocks by old time Vermonters from the seventeenth century, the boundary had stood the test of time. Not a smidgeon of mortar bonded big building blocks, yet the solid fit was masterful. Jake crept next to the ancient structure. Finding a free stone of some size resting by it, the boy boosted up to peek over.

There came a dim light from the far side. Standing slowly, allowing his eyes to accustom properly, he beheld a gut-wrenching sight. Below and ten-feet to the side were three men and a woman. They stood circled in conversation, discussing something disagreeable.

The appearance of each was disheveled and creepy. Unkempt greasy hair, rags for clothes, ropes for belts, unlaced boots or shoes described all four. The smell of them was horrendous, bodily funk ripely rife around the small clearing where they stood.

Much worse, a few feet to their far side sat a wire cage. Inside, Jake regarded a forlorn Spotty. Corralled and roped, tightly bound to the heavy metal enclosure. So tight was the restricting truss that Spotty exhibited distress. His tongue hung out one side of his mouth, lips red and swollen. The poor loving eyes bulged mournfully. The proud tail was tucked between muscled hind legs and he could barely tiptoe the cage floor with front ones, leaving him virtually suspended by the neck. On the floor of the cage lay a scrap of raw meat, answering the baiting method used to trap him.

Jake almost cried out at this but caught himself. That would do no good whatsoever. He had to devise a way to get to his friend and free him. As he took stock, the kidnappers conversation became more distinct. "O'sK. Try it again. We's a got the mutt. Gotta get it to the road to Grafton before 2 AM. Ah still says we's outta jus' up an grab the cage an' a'haul it through them woods yonder, an' get 'er done." This from the obese big man with oily cords of shoulder-length matted hair. His horribly dirty pocked skin bore open sores visible from Jake's vantage, reminding him of his real Daddy's sickened body.

The ugly woman disagreed. "Buzz, ah bein' tellin' ya agin: you maybe can but we cain't be a'pickin' that damn cage all up fer long. It be all solid steel, or sumpin', and heavy as Hell. Ain't no way we's gonna get that damn thing all's the way a mile an' a half through them woods, thick as they is. Ain't a single trail through 'em, and it ain't a option."

The greaseball hag appeared to be de facto leader. A cigarette hung from her lips, wagging throughout the harangue. Of course, she was right, Jake shouted to himself. There were no practicable traces except for the hidden tracks of deer and other wildlife passing anywhere near a line heading for the distant farm-to-market road into Grafton.

She continued. "I's be a'thinkin' it's a gonna be best if'n we just slay and butcher the bitch right here an' now, an' carry it out in pieces. We still collect on the bounty. That idiot Howard ain't a'gonna be a'carin whether the beastie's on the hoof or pieced up anyhow. So, let's jus' do it."

No! Jake almost shrieked at the horrible idea. He could see Spotty trembling in the cage, soulful eyes bulging more by the minute. The hanging tongue seemed more swollen and turning purple, too. The boy was frantic.

One of the other lowlifes, a scrawny mugwart of a fellow piped up. "Ya does 'member, Gladys, don' ya now, that the jerk tol' us that he'd pay extry for the return o' the cage, right? He bein' wantin' the damn thing back. Why don' we jus' take it on down the damn creek like we said?" The nasal voice cut irritatingly, grating the others' nerves.

"Jus' shaddup, scrawnbone, who done a'asked ya sorry ass anyways? We's bein' mighty tired o' hearin' ya pipsqueak ass voice. The creek be takin' us a mile the wrong way an' we gonna' havin' ta be doublin' back then. We's gonna miss the van if'n we don't get a goin. An' now!" She was adamant.

The men wanted the extra pay the cage promised and insisted on the point, so the hag was forced to back away from her perceived easier method. The closer wooded direction was agreed upon. Within minutes the four had hoisted the weighty and bulky cage to their shoulders in heading toward the dark perimeter, apparently meaning to blaze a trail as they went. Spotty was tossed back and forth, increasing the dog's distress with each step.

The two smaller men had machetes slung to waists and unsheathed them as they got close to the underbrush. It occurred to Jake to wonder how the four had transported the bulky cage here in the first place until discerning hinges, figuring it must collapse on itself... but still. Precious little space to maneuver even in a flattened state. The thing would sure be easier hauled if it were collapsed... and empty. Hopefully the stupid people wouldn't figure that out, he prayed to himself.

Wielding the dull tools made for slow progress in hacking through dense brambles and thorny bushes. This would take a while, Jake surmised. If Spotty could hold on, maybe, just maybe, the boy could devise a way to distract the group and get his friend out and away.

Thirty minutes later, Jake lay prone, hidden in a small covered path along what he hoped was the trajectory of the kidnapper's progress. He was having serious misgivings for the measly plan he'd come up with but figured it would have to suffice. A quick trip back to the house and storage shed had secured several items. He'd managed to stay quiet enough to not rouse the still-darkened house, then stolen away again through the woods. Now, laying on the little-used moss-covered animal trail, he willed things to work out.

In the near distance, progress of the bungling band could be heard, cussing and griping at obstacles, and one another, in drawing closer. Jake apprehended that he had, indeed, guessed the proper path after a fast scouting of the area. As dark as the night was, a lot was left to chance.

Several strategically placed good-sized rocks had been positioned in a wedge formation, gradually narrowing in their placement. Meant to force a rough course toward the spot he now waited. By simply stumbling into tactically placed stones, the lead men had veered inward in the manner Jake desired, seeking a path of least resistance.

A long piece of strong twine had been secured to a suitable tree trunk. The diminutive size of the boy had allowed stringing of it in a transverse fashion across the hoped-for path. He was able to access the woods in ways adults could not easily navigate. Loose end now pulled taut, the twine encumbrance hovered at a ten-inch height above the forest floor.

The vague arc of weakening flashlights wavered unsteadily toward the trap. As the troupe neared, the front two stumbled over the stretched rope. One tumbled forward, sticking himself in an eye by catching branches on the way down, dropping his light in the process. The thing blinked out as a fallen miscreant's high-pitched scream pierced the others.

The second fell sideways, twisting an ankle in failed attempt to regain footing lost to the unseen snare. Buzz and Gladys, in the back, stumbled over the two in front, capsizing the cage. The second light was doused by its smash-landing. Jake couldn't visualize Spotty, but heard him grunt in strangled anguish as the thing toppled.

At the same moment, the little boy snapped the 'on' button to the cassette player, begging for it to play. He had the volume set to maximum. A split second passed. Suddenly, harsh sounds of a soundtrack from the horror movie, 'Cujo' stabbed through darkness, compounding the first man's cries of anguish. He'd pre-set it for a several minute scene when the rabid St. Bernard attacked mama and little boy in their stalled car. It sounded ferocious in the close, unfriendly woods. Raving dog, mad in its diseased state, and shrieks of both the victims plus their own compatriot, provoked a sense of panic in the men. Even Gladys was freaked. Just as Jake had hoped. Not knowing what could be attacking them in the murkiness made for quick chaos.

The cage lay forgotten as the greasers fled in states of fearful uncertainty, tripping over each other amidst the unexpected din. Jake listened for a few moments as the clashing clatter of smelly scoundrels diminished steadily back down the path they'd cut. Then, he whipped out the fish-cleaning knife gifted him by Chad and hastened to the deserted cage.

Quickly accessing the door and breaking into it, he severed the nasty rope encircling a nearly unconscious Spotty. Pulling the suffering dog out by hind legs, the two lay together for a few moments gathering wits. The dog gasped air and the boy massaged his buddy's tender neck, watching to see if the beautiful dog would have strength to respond. Horrible swelling of tongue and jowls along with bugged-out eyes made him appear cartoonish.

Jake knew they would have only a few minutes at most to vacate the site and get safely away. As the eight-year-old cried tears of pain and relief, his best friend looked up at him. He weakly thumped an exhausted tail in recognition. A sluggish tongue attempted a weak lick of the familiar face. Jake bawled into the dog's head, hugging him.

Recognizing continuing threat, both struggled up together. Acquiring bearings and cocking heads toward still raucous sounds of close-by shouted curses, the boy realized they were out of sight. Prodding Spotty, the two crept in the opposite direction using another burrowing animal track for an escape route.

Spotty struggled mightily but managed to keep up with his rescuer. Only upon reaching the rock wall and boosting awkwardly over did they feel a little more secure. Without stopping, they kept heading away. Ears perked for any sounds of pursuit, the friends trekked to the easier track around the pond. Carefully keeping to darkened edges, the pair finally reached Elkin Lodge.

With a huge sigh at reaching the place, Jake rattled its door with a pounding knock. And waited. After a seeming eternity, a nightlight peeked on inside. Jake could see the countenance of a groggy Chad. Spying the night visitors, surprise overtook grogginess and the door opened in a fast second. "Jake? And… Spottiswood? You look awful. What's happened, my boys? Get on in here right away." The two scurried inside and collapsed as the lock clicked into place.

By Jake's insistence that Spotty get looked at first, Chad put together a cold epsom salt compress, mixed in lemon and honey, and salved the still badly misshapen face. A similar poultice was prepped and wrapped tenderly around the dog's neck, with added baking soda. Then an injection of a quick-acting steroid was administered in conjunction with an antibiotic from the ever-ready first-aid kit. After a nerve-jangling time, Jake finally fathomed an effect. Swelling and inflammation began to recede; his friend was breathing easier.

Only then did he loosen up. At Chad's continued chiding, a wracked little boy tearfully summarized what had just occurred. A mug of soothing hot cocoa appeared in little hands. Chad just sat, listening. Smoldering in rising anger at the attack.

In the middle of this sordid tale, a dazed Derrick wandered into the kitchen, unaware of any urgency. He had slept through the pounding, raised voices and hubbub during the nursing care. Stumbling on to the situation, he frazzled himself to a tizzy in trying to make sense of the meanness.

Spotty fairly purred his approval of the attention, accepting Derrick's maternal intervention and coddling. The tongue looked more like it could return to normal; within the hour all three heaved another sigh of collective relief. Looks of consternation passed between elders as they appraised awfulness. Next on the agenda, though, was quest of rest for the taxed little guys.

A guest bedroom embraced dog and boy within minutes after that. Providing a nest of security, tucked into warmth of fresh sheets and fluffy comforter. Together. The men insisted Spottiswood climb in with his boy. The two fell asleep in seconds. One another's arms and legs intertwined in adorable repose. They remained unmoving over several hours under watchful eyes of a very worried couple.

"Yes, dear, it is what must be done at this point. This is horrendous. But I emphasize vigilant need regarding Jacob's well-being. If the stepfather is capable of such a dastardly deed, what's to assure that a next step won't be assault on the boy himself? We have seen studies demonstrating parallels between animal cruelty and human cruelty. Even though the ogre didn't perpetrate it himself, there is little difference by the intent. Do you agree?" Derrick hadn't slept a wink after the deplorable event the night before. Every few minutes he was tiptoeing to peek at two angels through a door left ajar. Hackles were up and Katie-bar-the-door should he intuit any further hooliganism. Not if he could help it… and he could.

"We are in agreement, Derrick. On all. Though we must tread carefully. Ramifications of an overstep could be disastrous. The plan must be comprehensive, yet sublime. We have both connections and wherewithal. What we lack is legal standing." Dr. Elkin was as resolute as his partner, though acutely aware of necessity for nuance.

Derrick arose. Coming across the study to his beloved, he circled behind the big leather easy chair and rested his hand on Chad's neck. He kissed the top of his head as he whispered, "And this, Professor, is why I cherish you so." The two followed the flickers of flame dancing before them as they contemplated the coming possibilities. Hoping to avoid a maelstrom.

July, 1998

"Mrs. Eton? Would you mind joining me for a moment, please?" Dr. Elkin could hear the matronly woman rummaging in the solarium next to the study and decided now would probably be as good as any for the discussion. Windows were all wide open and a summer breeze lifted curtains in pervading the rich maple wood room. The fireplace, of course, was cold. At least until evening when the pond chilled the air even on high summer days. Close to eighty degrees Fahrenheit presently, the breeze did its job of securing summertime comfort quite well.

The silver-headed gentleman squire sat back from the solid heartwood cherry replica of the Resolute Desk, a piece of furniture the man valued highly. He put down his pen and awaited the lady's appearance. After a moment, an aproned woman appeared around the corner. Her hair was pulled up in a loose bun, reddish tresses wisping around her face and shoulders in partially successful attempt at escape. Whisk broom and polishing rag in one hand, a finger of the opposing one pushed an errant strand behind her middle-aged ear.

She entered wearing a kindly pensive smile. "Yes, Doctor?" She insisted on the title, despite many attempts at getting her to drop the formality. To no avail. Chad was aware that the housekeeper kept to it more for her own sensibilities than his, yet failure to break through still gnawed at him. Well, never mind it, he thought, she was who she was.

Stoutly built, the handsome woman was wife to Headmaster of the Collegiate School for Boys in upper Manhattan: Habersham Eton. For twenty-five years, the couple had exemplified Vermont traditionalism. Ten of those had been in close confidence with Chadwick Elkin while serving as headmaster of the oldest and most prestigious preparatory school in New York. Weill Cornell Medical College recruited regularly from the esteemed institution.

Collegiate School for Boys predated New York City itself, having been founded circa 1628 in Nieuw Amsterdam as a Dutch West India Company school. In coordination with the Dutch Reformed Church. Now secular, the private boys' establishment existed as the oldest independent school in North America.

Having entered into a two-year sabbatical during Habersham's convalescence from lingering illness, the couple had settled, after persuasive insistence from Dr. Elkin and Mr. Diogene, in the carriage house adjacent to Elkin Lodge.

The place sat back away from the pond in a small copse of cherry, maple, hemlock and spruce trees, opposite the home lodge which lay situated pondside amongst old growth oaks and hickory. It had been remodeled simultaneously with the main home and endured as a charming cottage from where the two based themselves.

After a year of abiding there, Mrs. Eton had requested, firmly, to take up housekeeping duties for both houses. Suffering feelings of need for recompense, since the retired male couple refused payment for such a living space, she kept the main lodge spotless and functioned as chief cook plus laundress. Her childless status in combination with strong, unrequited maternal instincts made for an arrangement which worked.

"Mrs. Eton, sit with me, will you?" Chad wanted her comfortable as well as settled to discourage a brush-off should the coming topic prove unnerving for her. Derrick had purposely vacated the premises, accompanying young Jake in his hired capacity as pantry stocker to the Grafton Dry Goods and Grocery, choosing avoidance of overwhelming her by similar reasoning. Spottiswood lay curled on the hearth and lifted his head at the lady he liked as she turned the corner. The friendly thumping of his tail always disarmed her, big brown eyes following as she alighted on the loveseat divan.

"As you are aware, Master Jacob will all too soon be gearing up a departure for the prep school in commencement of his fourth year. Or seventh, should we measure by scholastic accomplishment." Chad beamed as he extoled achievements already accrued by the young prodigy. By the current scale, Jake would graduate the prep school in the coming year. At a projected age of only thirteen, the boy would rank amongst the top ten youngest graduates, age-wise, in the entire long history of the institution.

Her curt nod expressed contentment at the boy's mention, having become as attached to him as the same-sex retiree couple. Chad continued, "Though he doesn't live under our roof, and we have no familial ties, there thrive strong sentiments for ensuring the young man's chance of success."

"As you also know, he abides amidst rather trying circumstances at the family home across the pond from us during summers away from school. Hence, the in-session living arrangements at the West End boarding home in the City. You may not have been mindful of the extent of our role in way-paving for the boy." Not blowing his own horn, he nevertheless felt necessity to lay proper foundation in order to impart proper import to the coming query.

The woman signaled cognizance of a moment of consequence by straightening her apron and posture. Habit again pulled a finger to taming one ever free-spirited lock. Dr. Elkin read trepidation by the shift and worried inwardly. He did not desire alienating the matron, yet knew that to continue their present course her blessing was crucial. Habersham was already on board with the men's proposal but would not speak for his wife.

"Your husband operated in my behalf several years ago, securing a spot at Collegiate for Jacob. Both of us are deeply indebted for that effort. The young man's potential has been well-documented since that time. Should present rate of advancement continue, need for decisions involving placement into an institution of higher learning may be upon us before any had anticipated."

"Rarely has Collegiate provided a student of such promise with the foundation for as early a passage on to the next level. In that endeavour, the coming months' groundwork will be key. Unfortunately, hindrances posed by the boy's erstwhile family lay as a major barrier toward advancement of that aim." The poignant point in the soliloquy had been reached. Chad drew a deep breath, then barreled into it.

"The fact that Jacob's patronage is underwritten by an alternative lifestyle couple might prove an undesired encumbrance. At least from the perspective of the boy's mother and stepfather." He studied the woman's features for signs of antagonism. "I am hopeful that Mr. Diogene and I may count on you and your husband to sponsor our protégé, only titularly, in light of your established respectability not only in the realm of education but in this community as well." Having said maybe too much, Dr. Elkin now quieted to await a response.

He sat externally calm yet percolated uncertainty on the inside. Having been overtaken too many times throughout his long career by unexpected, and sometimes untoward, reactions when opening a vulnerability in the present manner, consternation was palpable. He felt like an untried kid at a first recital.

Mrs. Eton remained poised, immobile and worse, inscrutable, before the old professor's gaze. Body language gave away nothing. Ensuing silence stretched to minutes. Even Spottiswood absorbed an increasing level of anxiety invading the study. Sitting up, the dog peered back and forth between the two people. Chad noted this action as well and took it as a negative sign, though continuing still and mute. Determined to wait the woman out. Had he totally overestimated the matron's character heretofore? It took every bit of self-control to hold in check.

Finally, Mrs. Eton blinked. The far-off gaze faded and she centered up to Chad's face. "Dr. Elkin. Forgive my introspection, Sir. I needed a few moments to assess the words and idea proposed."

"In frankness, Mr. Eton and I have had conversation on the very subject you have broached. Though behind the scenes, I spent years at Collegiate passively grooming students passing through the doors in their transition to adulthood. In all the time there, my husband and I agree that Jacob Marshall is a rare entity indeed. Seldom, if ever, have we encountered a more roughened jewel with less roundedness than him. The youth holds a peculiar mishmash of traits we find befuddling and enthralling at once."

"Much of the uncouthness derives from the fact of so severe a lacking in his home life. This was easily determined. One of many advantages gleaned from the generosity of our inclusion here these past two years has been a vantage of observation as the boy has been exposed to the civil and cultured ways by which you and Mr. Diogene live. Not to mention the school's ambience. He fairly inhales this way of life, so contrastingly alien and yet of seeming second nature. Our hearts have been wounded and warmed by dichotomies of his reality. The two of us are convinced that should the youth be given free rein to fly, heights attainable should be limitless."

"I must confess taking a liberty ungiven. Perusing public records and sifting verifiable information, I have already evaluated the background and circumstances young Jacob has been--- and is--- allotted. Appalling is the word that summarizes my conclusion after surreptitious study. I may be knowledgeable of things even you and Mr. Diogene are not. It is with no little discomfiture that I confess this. And may address the long pause rejoined before making reply now. Even so, our erudition of the situation has served only to burnish the youth's exceptional promise by its perception."

Here, Mrs. Eton took a breath, focusing in on the professor's eyes. "The shorter answer to your noble mission and enquiry is that Habersham and I would not only accede to the invitation for sponsorship, we would consider it a singular honor." The deliberate blink and nod accentuated the declaration.

The long explanation and quick acquiescence took the man aback. Not once through all of that, Chad reflected, had she alluded to the one stymying subject so feared. Derrick and his relationship. By merit of omission, he garnered intended relegation to superfluous status. It made no difference to her…

A tear of gratitude involuntarily escaped an eyelid as he blinked to squelch the inadvertency.

"I can't figure this out, Burt." Lois was mystified. By many things, to be sure, but presently by the fortuitous circumstances surrounding her younger son. The one living at a boarding house in New York City. Her youngest boy kept the woman in a perpetual state of an emotional rollercoaster. And now, by merit of a missive arriving with the day's post, she was unsure whether to feel blessed in the sight of the Almighty or fearful for her immortal soul. One could never be quite certain when dealing with godforsaken secular humanist schools to where she had given permission for his attendance. Why had she done that, it was wondered again? No telling what the boy was being exposed to. But, by the act,

God had provided a way for things to even out around the house, so there was that blessing.

Glancing over, she saw that her husband hadn't heard her comment. Or was ignoring her again. He reclined in the birthday gift she'd gotten him two months before: the faux-leather Barcalounger. There were times when she thought that he loved the rocker-recliner better than he did his own wife. The man certainly shared more intimacy with it than her. If she wasn't such a God-fearing woman it would just make her cross, she thought.

"Burt. Burt… can you hear me? Burt?" Nothing. "Wilbur. Jenkins. Howard!" Only by intoning the man's God-given name did one eyeball make a belated showing in her general direction. That lazy eye of his amazed her in the way it could do that, she marveled. The ways He worked were shrewd, to be sure.

"Whaddayawant?" came the reticent response. At least Lois thought it was a response. It was hard to hear over the roar of engines as hotrods raced in circles at the NASCAR stadium festooned with ads pushing guns, liquor and… duh… auto parts. The occasional Dixie Flag completed bedecking of the stands filled with rabid auto-racing fanatics. Lois could not for the life of her find anything redeeming in the noisy 'sport'. It befuddled the woman that it was even classified as such… a sport.

For goodness sake, the stars, or drivers, sat on their fat rear ends through the whole endlessly circular ordeal. The most exercise expended was by pit crews when fixing or replacing something or dashing to avoid being run down by other race cars. Even the winning of the puzzling events was unfathomable. One could never tell when the race was finished or if a declared winner would remain so after interminable challenges by the losers…amen, she tittered. God give her strength.

"I said, I cannot figure this letter out. Could you come and take a look at it and tell me if you can?" She received the expected reply--- well, bring it over here. Don't make me get up again--- and obediently arose, doing so. Heaving a bored sigh as he took the paper, the man was clearly put out to be interrupted during the 'race of the century', as she had discovered all NASCAR events were dubbed.

Putting on the RiteAid over-the-counter reading glasses, the unshaven weekender reluctantly skimmed the official letter. Lois had noted the return address bearing the 'Collegiate School for Boys' insignia. But the wordage eluded the high school graduate. Why she felt that her less-educated second husband would fare any better did not occur to her, except possibly by the adage of 'two-heads-better-than-one'.

Anyway, he was the husband, and the man of the house was the power-that-be, so... she genuflected to his overlordship. Lois certainly recognized the teachings of the most read and revered Book ever written. The rules were plain. She stood, waiting.

"Well, Hell, woman, this must be another one o' them notices from that place the devil's spawn is at. They sends at least one ever dangdable month. Says here, the boy done got given some 'nother useless paper-chaser A-ward. It isn't asking for money, at least, so what difference does it make? He don't try to explain none o' this stuff when we do hear from him, so what's the fuss? Are you that crazy 'bout making sense of it, now? Lemme get back to the race--- this is one that'll never happen again. It's once in a lifetime. And can I get another beer--- dear--- a cold one this time, maybe?"

He was adept at two things, Lois noted for the umpteenth time: orders and sarcasm. He didn't mean the 'dear' part, she knew. It simply rhymed and he remained impressed by his own witty abilities. Just ask him, she deadpanned. Wordlessly, of course.

For a minute, on her way to the fridge, fleeting memory of an earlier time flitted through her head. One picturing a robust figure of Beck--- Beckham--- her first husband, as he shouldered baby Jake around the backyard on his shoulders, capering with the leaping dog--- Spotty, she seemed to remember, wasn't it? --- and her deflated heart leapt for a second at the energy and love evoked from that temporary time of happiness back in the far reaches of her dulled mind.

The thought thread continued in regards to the bad ending for that dog. The flea-bitten thing had taken to a life outdoors after being let to live a life of luxury in the beginning. Inside the house, sleeping with the boys... everything laid out on a silver platter for the ungrateful mongrel.

Then, suddenly, all Hades broke loose when Beck had taken ill and died--- she preferred suppressing that sorry period once the perverted nature of that man had come out--- to be replaced soon enough by God's gracious blessing of Burt's appearance. God had provided rescue from the lassitude of life as a single mother in lonely widowhood. The dumb critter had shown its gratitude following that by revealing itself only when Jake went to find him in the forest.

She remembered the day that Burt had come in the back door, sorrowfully announcing he had come across the poor thing's torn, lifeless body in deep woods. Apparently attacked and partially devoured by wild animals… he hadn't the heart to allow innocent children sight of horribly mangled remains. Having done his best by the thankless beast, he'd informed the family, a burial was carried out beside the brook. Such a man of compassion was he.

Lois had felt badly on hearing of it, yet she noted that none of the children were particularly upset by the loss. Even little Jake had acted peculiarly detached at the news, disappearing, per his usual wont, for a day or so. The boy was a total puzzle to her. It was as if the boy covered his emotions in a shell of deceit, she surmised.

The idea had crossed her mind that perhaps the boy might be a chip-off-the-old-block, in the vein of the sinful, and dead, husband. God have mercy on his errant soul. Well, she decided, if so, best that it stayed buried and not be brought into light of day. God would not put up with such malfeasance, as she had already witnessed. His immutable ways of forcing atonement upon sinners, such as they were, were just that: immutable.

Pulling her mind back to reality, Lois wondered anew at the mysterious methods through which He worked. How else could it be explained in any rational manner that her younger son had seemingly fallen into a life of book-learning as had turned out? It boggled her brain.

The day that the Grafton schoolmarm, Rita Johnson, had knocked on the Howard front door next recurred to her. Bearing news of surprise acceptance into an exclusive boy's school down in Manhattan, of all places. Where in the world had that all come from, she still pondered? Mrs. Johnson had been baffled, too. Something about a work-study program for deserving youths was the explanation. As the ambiguity had allowed for one less out-of-pocket expense with which to deal, the concept had appealed to her. God be praised.

Signatures allowing Jake's admittance had been delivered along with the difficult boy. He was to be housed in a respectable boarding home, at a church, less than a block from school. And would only be home for summers.

All of it became official once assurance was procured that there would be no bills appearing in the Howard mailbox to cover unforeseen costs. In writing. Wilbur had been vehement on that score. He'd even had foresight to insist on a notarized statement of guarantee. Strength of the Godly man's will once again had won out. She had borne witness. It amplified the sense of awe in which she held the pedestrian man who saved her. In actuality.

He might have his shortcomings, the good Lord knew, but the wherewithal he brought to table in dealing with hard questions of life were a Godsend. And she was properly thankful. What would she ever do without him? She set the chilled beer can next to his recliner and sat back down.

"I coulda' sworn that I read something about medical school in that thing, but I must be mixed up, like usual, I guess." Lois quite sensibly deduced that that was a misprint. Or her misunderstanding. Only a dunce would think that a twelve-year-old could be associated with medical school. That was for college and doctors, for heaven's sake. People older than herself, she rationalized. Wilbur hadn't seen that, so of course it had to be some sort of mix-up.

As she laid the letter aside again, there came a knock at the front door. Who would be interrupting the Sabbath, Lois thought? Didn't anyone respect the holy day anymore? She 'hrrumphed' her way to her feet and went to answer, affixing her Sunday-go-to-meeting visage in place. The severe demeanor would bear more impact, she reflected, without the background noise of revving engines.

Opening just a crack, she found a respectable looking well-dressed couple on the step. Looking a bit nervous, she noticed. "Yes, may we help you on a Sunday afternoon, such as it is?" Lois meant to milk the moment, a bit cross by the intrusion. But, the couple did seem quite decent in appearance. Not selling anything, either. She opened the door a tad wider, brushing her hair down at the same time.

"Mrs. Howard?" The well-heeled female spoke up. At Lois' affirmation, she went on. "Hello, and so sorry to burst upon you unannounced. We were unable to locate a working telephone number and decided to take a chance." Pleasant-looking, the woman appeared dressed for late church service, as did the gentleman with her, mollifying the matron of the house. But she still didn't reply, wanting to know why they had come before expending energy in any sort of welcome.

"If you please, I am Olivia Eton and this is my husband, Habersham Eton. We come from the far side of the pond and desire to greet you and your husband, if we might. It has been far too long that we have been in residence as far-side neighbors. And, thought to rectify that. As well, we do have an additional reason for dropping by. May we have a few moments of your time, please, to do so? If it is not too inopportune?" The cultured eloquence defused Lois' defensiveness. And the name of the couple struck a chord. The Etons.

Changing disposition, Lois now smiled and opened the door wide. "Well, I'll be. Mr. and Mrs. Eton. I had no idea we were neighbors. Won't you come in?" She stepped aside and further patted her disheveled hair in haphazard welcome. Half turning, she hollered back toward her husband. "Wilbur? Dear? We have company. Why don't you turn down the television a smidge and see who has stopped by for a visit?"

Wilbur, visibly unhappy, grumped up and ratcheted down the volume, just a little, then edged toward the door. Eyes still glued to the screen. His ribbed undershirt sported stains of spilled food and a few chip remnants, Lois saw. She reached to brush the crumbs away. Thin, rumpled, unwashed hair spiked around his head. And remained that way.

Finally deigning to pull eyes from the race, he grudgingly greeted the two slicked-up people interrupting his Sunday. "And just who might you be?" Totally unimpressed.

"Why, Wilbur, this is Deacon Eton and his wife, of the First Missionary Methodist Church of Brattleboro, and our neighbors from other side of the pond, Dear. Surely, you remember us speaking of them before?" God always forgave white lies, she reminded herself. Looking back, she ushered the couple to seats in the cluttered room. "We have had it in our own minds to come visit services at Missionary but keep so busy... time just seems to fly by." Lois was now nervous as the gravity of such a respected couple paying a visit hit her. She was prattling.

"It would be a distinct pleasure to see you there, should timing become right," Olivia was overflowing in her affected pleasure, showing nothing of the distaste fueling her brain as she took in the unkempt couple and home. She did not like the place in the slightest, especially in light of the fact that young Jacob must suffer living here. Even if for only part of the year.

She made small talk over the next quarter hour, looking to carry through the mission upon which the two had set out on, yet not wanting to come across rushed or uncaring. To her credit, Lois kept up a welcoming manner, attempting repeatedly to draw Burt into the conversation. Olivia continued in her professional mode, quite able to affect the desired front, after years of having to do so in undesirable circumstances. This ranked right up there, she assessed.

Acquainting and conversing finally ran its course, however, and the deacon delicately broached the subject for which they had truly come. "You may be aware, Mrs. Howard, that we are intimately involved with Collegiate School in New York City. Jacob, your son, is presently a student there. A commendable one, at that, I might add." Habersham's eloquent articulation held attention without need for volume, even amidst auto engines in the background.

"We are certain that the two of you must be so very proud of the young man. It is actually for this reason that we would ask your forbearance, if we may." He watched the faces of both people as he spoke, noticing the appearance of mild distaste at mention of the boy. How odd, he thought. "On sabbatical, as I am presently, I nevertheless keep close tabs with goings-on at Collegiate. Your prodigy of a son is high on the list of those for whom I keep those tabs."

"He's done something bad, I am figuring, then? Am I gonna have to come fetch him from the place? You know I still have those papers guaranteein' no financial responsibility for him, even if he acts out. Right?" This from Wilbur, who was confusing prodigy with prodigal. Sourness in the man's face spoke volumes, matching the man's breath. Habersham, like Olivia, was less and less impressed.

"Why, on the contrary, Mr. Howard," Olivia smoothly cut in, "Have you not received mailings the school regularly sends to communicate with parents? Young master Jacob is at the top of his fourth-year class. More than that, the lad has set himself apart from the rest of his classmates as a role model of exceptional acumen, already having attained scholastic status of a junior year student. On his present trajectory, he shall finish all requirements and then some, by the end of next session. The boy will have completed an eight-year curriculum in a span of only four years. An unheard of four-year-early graduation accomplishment. Hasn't he informed either of you?"

Not pausing to wait for a reply, she went on, "Never in my husband's tenure has a student achieved so much in so short a timeframe. We couldn't be more pleased by his performance. The maturity and scholarly attributes the boy displays have put him into the upper echelon of students ever to have attended the institution. You are only to be applauded for having foresight to send him our way."

The atmosphere in the room could have been cut with a knife, so thick was it.

Mrs. Howard, nonplussed past the point of cogency, stared from one to the other of the visitors, looking for all to see as if she had swallowed the proverbial canary. Wilbur had nothing to say. Period.

Seeing the two in their speechless state, Mr. Eton continued. "We are here today, besides our desire to acquaint with the two of you, for the purpose of asking a favor in your son's behalf. You see, he has expressed ongoing interest for three years now of intent to enter medical school. He holds an almost unique position for choosing where he would like to attend, rather than being chosen, as is the traditional method."

"There is an increasing list of medical schools around the country, as well as two in Europe, who are actively pursuing the young man's entry to their programs. Eight of the institutions have interviewed your boy at the Collegiate campus in Manhattan. All of them show exceeding interest in having him. This, despite his age."

"Our quest today is bent toward the idea of sponsoring your young man, as guardian mentors, due to his minority status. There would be, of course, no obligation whatsoever put on either of you for underwriting such a venture. The boy has earned his way to placement in unprecedented fashion. Any additional financial obligation would be of no concern, should you allow us this honor." Now, finally finished, the cultured gentleman sat back, content.

Olivia was not finished, however. "I am so very regretful that neither of you is apparently current with any of this information. Should we find that the school has been remiss in sharing all of this good news over the previous three years, I fully intend that there be an investigation into reasons for such a lackluster performance." This was stated as she fairly glared at the open letter on the end table next to Lois' chair. Implication purely apparent. Looking from the letter up to Jake's mother's face, she plastered a sickeningly sweet smile in place. And sat stock still, staring holes through the woman.

Even through the haze of her slowness, Lois reaped the meaning. She straightened up and cleared her throat with as much dignity as she could muster. "No, Mrs. Eton, we have sure been receiving letters from that school. We are very much proud of my son's progress, of course. As much as a good Christian has the right to be. Pride being a sinful attribute, as we all well know. But, we were just not quite understanding all these other things and all of my Jake's accomplishments. We are only country folk, I am afraid, and some of this highfalutin language may be just a little above our heads."

She had enough sense to be slightly embarrassed, at least, thought Olivia, and could see she was proud. On the other hand, Mr. Howard was simply distracted. The blank look and continual glances toward the television made the man's true interest all too obvious.

The stepson factored to nil, by the look of things. Not even a true stepson, she reminded herself, as the public records showed no proactivity toward attaining guardianship of any of four children here. Seeing this, she thought best to push the point right away rather than allowing any time for puerile mercenary purposes. This man would surely hold the boy's future for ransom, given the slightest chance. She didn't intend for that to happen.

Reaching into her purse, she withdrew a stack of papers. Then proceeded to browbeat the mousy woman in the sweetest fashion fathomable. Headmaster Eton sat back in mute disbelief at the whole scenario, from parents' ignorance to his wife's hutzpah.

Within minutes, she had obtained all proper signatures necessary for the purposes of the couple, and their elder retiree friends, in furtherance of securing Jacob Marshall's future. Then and there. No compunction for remorse was registered by the technique. She found herself almost surprised when Wilbur, in his apathy, did not sign the dotted line with X's.

As she and her husband reiterated their firm desire to see the two in Brattleboro for services very soon, Mr. and Mrs. Habersham Eton, headmaster-in-absentia of Collegiate School for Boys and his wife, took their respectful leave. Now, newly designated legal sponsors of the youngest graduate from the prep school in more than a century and a half.

November, 1998

"What? No green cheese?" Simon was dead serious and perplexed. What a sheltered life he led, thought Jake. A home-school education by helicopter parents living in a 56th story Fifth Avenue apartment for the first five school years had left the boy lost in real world scenarios. Now, at eleven-years-of-age, the first-year enrollee sixth grader had little basis for comparison in measuring the experience of most boys at Collegiate. Though only a year-and-a-half younger than Jake, the kid was psychologically miles and years distant in regards to maturity level.

Jake continued currying Diego as he contemplated the silly reply to the posit made about the recent verification by NASA that the moon provably harbored water. The core studies of the lunar samples collected by the Athena probe had stoked Jake's interest in space travel and such subjects. Mixed with lunar 'soil', and in frozen state, it was nevertheless H2O. The discovery would revolutionize planning for extraterrestrial travel in decades to come. Water could be 'harvested' from the lunar surface rather than transported from Earth. Of that, Jake was certain.

A little less so was how 'simple Si' reached the age he had still holding the belief that the moon was made of cheese--- green, cheddar or gorgonzola. But this had to be measured alongside the surprise the boy exhibited upon being made aware that the ponies masquerading as unicorns during birthday parties here at the stable were not truly unicorns. So, he quietly reassessed before answering.

"Well, Simon, maybe there is still hope for the far side of the moon hiding something from us but the Sea of Tranquility has officially been designated as non-dairy." He smirked inwardly a little as he pulled tangles from the donkey's coarse mane. Grooming the draft horses, ponies and this particularly precocious Provence Donkey, misnamed with a

Spanish appellation such as he was, provided a savored and soothing pastime for Jake.

He had sought out Chateau Stables a year before during Thanksgiving break in search of diversion during his first solitary holiday. Some thirty blocks south of his boarding house at the church on 77th, he had run across the urban horse stable during a morning run a year-and-a-half before and made mental note of the place.

An intensely antagonistic atmosphere at the family home on Elkin Pond left the boy with little desire to return. He felt sure the feeling was mutual by the non-committal reply to the decision upon informing his mother and step-father. The boy hardened a resolve to ignore apathetic emanations from there. His friends, Chad and Derrick, were away on a European holiday. Without the older gentlemen at home on their side of the pond and by the fact of Spotty accompanying the Etons to upstate New York for the break, the rural setting provoked little appeal. No big deal, he reminded himself. More than once.

So, finagling a volunteer position at the venerable equine stable close to Central Park, adjoining Tavern on the Green, the then almost twelve-year-old boy had been conciliated to familiarize with yet another new animal family. A nonjudgmental one at that. Continuing working on intermittent weekends and some other off-days, too, it had been only a few months before Mrs. McGill offered Jake a part time caregiver position. Quite enchanted with the gentle resident equidae, especially this non-rideable 'pet', Diego, he had jumped at the chance. This much enjoyment and he got paid for it…? What could be better?

The donkey and boy had struck up a rapport which the stable owners were stumped to understand. On the first day of Jake's tenure, while grooming the big loveable old French Percheron, Blackjack, an inquiring set of curling lips and large velvety nostrils had appeared through the wooden slats dividing stalls. Comically twitching and blowing his direction, the invitation toward the strange-smelling newcomer had been unmistakable. Expressing interest in the boy combing the donkey's sole friend and comrade. Everybody agreed the common French heritage had to be the reason for the friendship, hence the side-by-side quarters.

Jake had approached the beast and tickled the presented anatomy. A friendly snort later and the two had taken to a game of hide-and-seek up and down the narrow openings. The little bugger liked the tweaks and tickles as Jake extended fingers in boyish acquaintance.

After minutes of the game, he had purloined some carrots and an apple from the tack room, then slipped into Diego's forbidden corner stall. Without hesitation or second thought the eleven-year-old proffered the delectable tidbits and progressed to brushing the little guy's body. The donkey shuddered in delight at the gentle, brazen, heretofore unexperienced handling by anyone, let alone an obvious innocent.

By the time Nick, veteran overseer, guide and handler, had returned from lunch break, the two were enmeshed in prankster one-upmanship. The handle-bar mustache residing above the surprised upper lip had jolted in disbelief upon rounding a corner to a view of long-lost buddies.

No one had befriended the mercurial beast to that point; something unbeknownst to Jake. Nick unobtrusively observed as the little reprobate bent his neck around to nuzzle Jake's belly, setting up a giggling fit which the two proceeded to share. The donkey and boy danced a jig of camaraderie, alternately poking, prodding, rubbing, needling and just touching together in humorous conviviality.

Brought in years before as a guard for the stable, the diminutive big-eared lout had not exactly endeared himself with the staff. More than just stubborn, donkeys can be certifiably territorial, vocal and defensive. Often cantankerous. The disagreeable young cuss dubbed Diego quickly instituted a practice of non-discriminatory aggression toward friend, foe, familiars and strangers alike, from the outset.

The obnoxious temperament was only tolerated because of a defined proclivity for fending off interloping bandits and thugs who periodically targeted the enterprise. He was let to wander the stable yard during off hours. As word spread of an irascible ass's presence, break-ins had declined and stopped over the past two years. A routine had been developed for corralling the biting, kicking, pitching devil-of-a-security-guard each and every morning before functionality could be established. The inscribed nameplate above his stall was emblazoned appropriately. 'Diego: Attack Donkey'.

For some unfathomable reason, the loner had imprinted immediately on Jake during that first Thanksgiving holiday. Within three days, whinnies of greeting informed all present of Jake's arrival. The two bonded. Closely. Love nips devolved to just that; previous damaging bites suffered by all in proximate reach diminished to gentle nips by the donkey's recalibration to his new love: Jake. This Thanksgiving break, untangling the mane and tail had achieved status of a recurring love tryst.

Diego contentedly munched timothy while Jake and Si carried on with their tasks. "So, are you telling me that the tests eliminated cheese as a moon element?" Simon had vocabulary to come across informed at times, yet instances like this reinforced lack of concomitant knowledge to back it up.

"Really, Simon? You do get the premise that cheese comes from milk, which derives most commonly from cows, right? Where would be the source?" As much as the option presented itself, Jake chose not to be derisive. He had no desire to ridicule the fellow student, who he liked. But this was difficult to believe. "Not to mention," he added, "milk is not an element. It is a complex organic molecule."

"Well, you do know, Jake, that milk comes from other sources, too, don't you?" The pre-teen was coming right back at his older friend, not giving an inch. "Like goats and deer and monkeys… and mothers? Just figuring that the old Man-in-the-Moon's wife has to feed her kids somehow. And the kids gotta have pets. It's only logical. So, maybe, they make a lot more up there because of less gravity. I bet they store it. There's lots of free space…huh?"

Jake had no ability to reply on that level of illogic and gave up. As he smiled quietly, working through a tough knot, Nick, the stable guide came into the stalls. "Hey, Jake, can you come up to the office in a minute? Anita wants to talk with you." Jake signaled he'd be right there. Patting Diego affectionately, he put away the curry and de-tangling comb. Knowing he would not be left alone with the donkey, Simon did the same. The two headed to the front office.

Taking the steps three at a time, Jake finished the run home, nicely winded, on the rock staircase entrancing the old West End Collegiate Church where he stayed. He raised a bent leg onto a rock finial for post-run stretching, mind still centered on the conversation with Anita. The two boys had been released early from afternoon chores at Chateau without much explanation. Only that there was news sent by Collegiate which needed Jake's presence.

Simon's parents had been called for a pick-up of both boys, but Jake had declined so as to get in an early evening run back to the boarding house. A signed release by his guardians allowed for just such forays. Independence which he dearly appreciated, the boy regularly availed himself of the perk. Running permitted him an autonomy not common for those in his age group.

The salt-caked running sweats and upscale cross trainers which Derrick insisted on replenishing twice yearly ensnared him in a clamminess of which he'd soon be shed. He methodically worked through the regimen set for cooling down in accustomed manner after exercise jaunts. The big city had been a bit scary at the beginning, Jake remembered. Second nature to be absorbed by its energy now, the boy reveled in it. So many people and sights.

Slowly stretching a tightening left quadriceps muscle group, he wondered again about what his advisor and the headmaster had to discuss. During a holiday break, no less. Finishing calf extensions and flexions, he made way through the heavy brass doors in ascent to home. Upstairs, the lock clicked familiarly as the door fell shut and Jake stripped casually on the way to the closet.

Robing up--- he had gotten used to the 'no nudity in the halls' rule over three and a half years--- Jake grabbed a clean towel, soap and flip-flops for a trek to the communal shower down at the end of the hall. Deserted now, the holiday break gave Jake a reprieve from almost the entire Collegiate student body. Of 600+ boys, about a hundred of whom resided in this church boarding house, maybe six had been sighted these past two days. He liked the solitude.

The heat of targeted double spigots hitting him was another cherished perk when others were away. Jake immersed a curl-sprigged head under their confluence, leaning against smooth bricks in splendid plenitude. No shortage of hot water right now, he basked, breathing deeply of heavy steam building in the spacious shower area.

Lights were dimmed for the break. Without any windows, a resultant gloominess felt cozy. His ears were useless under the streaming spray. Smelling fresh pine-sol application for control of fungal-challenged male shower surfaces, he kicked off flip-flops. Another comfort, he thought. Total privacy... and totally nude: no drawers for modesty, per usual. He remained ensconced for a good quarter hour, reflecting on multiple things...school, stable, Vermont, the moon experiments, the new movie Titanic, and then the sudden uncalled-for hearkening... Thelonius.

The prickly heat of the water bathed his groin in a deluge of aphrodisiacal bombast. Nascent hormonal release exacerbated the effect, augmenting quick onset engorgement. In downright unbounded indulgence, Jake felt his junk swell precipitously with the conjuring of his favorite and feared erogenous picture-thought.

Thelonius. Basketball captain and teammate. And, now: biochemistry lab partner. The darkly handsome sixteen-year-old junior had chosen the youngest classmate out of twelve in lab class on first day of fall semester, ensuring the youthful Jake's absolute loyalty by the respect paid him in the act.

If Jake hadn't been both nervous and enthralled before, he was from then on. Every time he was near the mature, accepted leader-of-boys who was Thelonius, there came similar effects. Hard-ons sprang awkwardly unsolicited; problematic by cumbersome noticeability.

The twelve-year-old did not understand. Not at all to say he didn't enjoy the effect, just plain didn't get it. Biology class had illuminated 'normal' over preceding three semesters. The male: female bond had been the only sex-ed option broached, so what Jake felt when the older boy came within proximity was bewildering. It wasn't something that was supposed to happen. And, it never had... until Thelonius.

By that standard, when school was in session, Jake never allowed contemplation of the sexy name, let alone mind's eye provocations, whenever his developing young mind wandered. Surrounds such as this were potentially ruinous. But he allowed it now.

The video-streaming memory, tucked deeply away, remained crystal-clear. At the time, the humiliating event had been extremely disturbing by its public context, happening in the middle of a practice as it had. But now it hovered subconsciously as a talisman of profound impact.

He had innocently initiated contact by merit of a missed attempt at a steal. Thelonius' superior athleticism had guessed the move and dribbled away from the darting hand which mistakenly grasped the older boy's crotch--- in a fully encircling grope--- by mistake. Thelonius had pulled up short, locking eyes on Jake's, as errant fingers had snatched a feel of the fleshy shaft and balls nestled deep inside those shorts. An intense shared moment had ensued. Then it was over as Jake hastily extracted girdling fingers. Through a full body flush, there erupted a stammered apology for the misdeed.

"No problem, little dude." That was all he'd said. And the episode was past. Gone and forgotten. By Thelonius... but not Jake. Subsequent reenactments erotically invaded randomly blossoming dreamscapes deep in the night when his mind would revisit that instant. Usually, though, in those closed-eye scenarios, the ebony junk was not covered by anything, the half-second was elongated to seconds or minutes, the shaft always stretched out to an amazing darkly pigmented foot-long hotdog and once, very recently, the ante had been upped when he'd made dreamy contact with the whopper as it wiped a lewd path back and forth across his cheeks.

Upon finally surfacing from those uncalled yet begged-for recurrences, he most commonly awoke to find himself smeared in stickiness. Salty-sweet smell of the obnoxiously unmannered stuff had a name, learned theoretically, several years before. Sperm. A viscous fluid filled with tiny wiggly spermatozoa. Millions of them.

The reality of the gooey mess was not how he had pictured it in that academic introduction. The pre-teen worried he may suffer some exotic condition needing medical attention but was too ashamed to address the matter with anyone, coming on the heels of such iniquitous dreams as it did.

The unpleasantness required stealthy intervention. To cover the guilt. Copious rinsing in the dorm room sink, surreptitious Clorox soaks to cut the smell, Febreze soakings afterwards to minimize multiple odors. Such a giveaway. Hanging huge white sheets anywhere and everywhere after his roommate departed grew to be hazardous and anxiety-inducing. Much worse, it was snowballing. In both frequency and volume. He lost precious hours of sleep by time wasted, as well as needful hassles for de rigueur cover-up.

The morning his roommate, Garth, busted his ass bigger than Dallas would rank right up there with the worst in his short life. That is, if the fourteen-year-old hadn't empathized.

"What's up with this, Jake?" The boy melted of mortification upon hustling back to the room, returning from a fast clean up down the hall. Garth had arisen earlier than normal and found stickily soiled sheets wadded by his bed. Rushing around the corner, Jake nearly smacked chest-to-chest into the amiable roommate who stood holding the dripping things above his head near the doorway. Examining it. The stains looked a lot worse under lights.

Stuttering a nonsensical reply, Garth drilled him with a curious look, "I didn't mean that, Jake. I meant, what are these nasty things doing wadded up here, drenched? Why didn't you put 'em down the laundry chute instead? You savin' it for something?" The light bulb figuratively burst in both boys' heads almost simultaneously. "You didn't know to do that, did you, Curly?"

Still faltering in a trapped state and flabbergasted to have overlooked the oh-so-apparent solution in a twelve-year-old mind before this moment, Garth chortled at Jake's overt discomfort. "How long you been at this? Didn't anyone ever tell you? You sure don't want that around stinkin' everything up, right?"

Another bulb popped. "Wait, dude…Jake… You don't get any of this, do you? No wonder I've been smelling all that bleach and Febreze when I come back to the room. Hey, bud, sit down a sec. You're shakin'." He patted his rumpled bed, inviting. "Jake, nobody's talked with you about this, have they?" The nervous head shake said it all. "You do realize that we are in Collegiate--- you know--- Boy's School. Almost all of us here are doin' the nighttime gush. It's normal, bud. There's no reason to be embarrassed. Here, let me show you."

With that excruciating scene came a teachable moment. Garth walked through the accepted method for disposal of offending bedding. A running dialogue shed light on a bunch of mysteries. By the time they re-entered the room, grinning had infected both.

So, it was a boy thing, huh? He wasn't dying, after all. Jake's relief made him giddy.

Finally piping up, "Wow, I feel better, Garth. Thanks. I was losing sleep doing that every night… couldn'ta kept it up much longer, I… don't…… think." One totally astounded roommate's face made Jake trail off.

"You mean you weren't saving that sheet up? That was just one load? What the hell are you… a damn volcano?"

All these discordantly tumultuous thoughts cascaded through Jake's mind in tandem and parallel at the pleasantness provided by hot water and bouncing boner. The pendulous thing was enjoying this rare freedom of expression. Closed eyes amplified the erogenous episode and rush of the water over his head made a virtual cocoon from which to suspend time for a short interlude of private excess. Such an extraordinary extravagance.

His fingers massaged in heavenly swirls up and around smoothly soaped pubescent groin, stomach and chest, exciting sproinging twerks from a ready organ between youthful runner's legs. Knowing that any touch of the tumescent appendage would result in immediate cresting, he avoided direct contact with the independent-minded member, letting himself slide slowly to the shower floor. It felt absolutely divine just the way it was. The desire for prolongation was paramount at the remarkably sensate moment.

A sudden realization butted him. Imagination could enable anything a horndog mind might devise in the heated circumstance now unfolding. Naturally, the latent Thelonius illusion bubbled up through the deepness, in rich virtuality. Jake concocted his fantasy's slow, creeping approach across the wet area. Smooth espresso hand and fingers stretched forward and around him--- no: those luscious full dark lips surrounded him--- in his pipedream caprice: Thelonius.

The full thickness of his lab partner's sexy pair wrapped sensuously around the virgin shaft now bobbing for the unattainable. Something so obviously verboten that Jake shuddered in the sinfulness of the idea. And, with such a superbly wicked thought, the simulated effect pinpointed every hot dot of illusioned contact. The massive boner gave way to surging capitulation, fruitful eye spewing copiously.

Now, in release, Jake's fingers finally came up to offer guidance and succor to the unmatchable effect roiling his body. A cry of surprise in the middle of this pleasure erupted from Jake's own lips as his fingers encountered not the expected spasming shaft, but Thelonius' cheek instead.

Seizing back reality, he popped to standing again, out from under the shower's cascade. Flooded eyes opened to the sight of actual lips--- though not Thelonius' set--- busy at the treasure trove.

The almond-eyed youth attached to those spongy chops stared straight into Jake's astounded eyes. The full mouth, having followed the ascension, obligated itself to an oblong-shape by the enormity of its prey. Jake recognized the janitorial boy commonly cleaning up after messy students' routine sullying of the wet area. Having engaged short friendly dialogue with the diminutive teenager, he knew the boy worked part-time alongside his dad, Wang Ho, to augment family financial needs. The two enjoyed an affable acquaintance. This scenario stepped past that level, assigning new meaning to 'sullying'.

Jake remained in thrall to the mouth currently favoring him with the sweetest satisfaction ever experienced, seeing rolling expressions waltz across Junior's face in evocative fulfilment. He clearly liked the present position. And, Jake deduced, was not new to it. Greedy lips availed themselves of the harvest from the rigidness presently obsessing him. Had the event proven less gratifying, Jake would have felt used. Or something. As it was, he simply endorsed the idea that whatever had just occurred, it could just keep right on occurring. Thank-you-very-much.

After an indeterminate time, a sapped fantasist leaned against the smooth tiled wall. Incredulous of that just experienced. Discerning that the newest look from young Wang Ho was now auguring oncoming communication of other than that which had spoken wordless volumes already, Jake watched a slow, inching retreat.

Smiling almond eyes peered diffidently upwards, accompanying a look of repletion. "Excuse me, but you appeared to be in need of assistance. Nobody else was around, so the onus was mine to render aid. Hopefully not delivering insult." The ancient art of Chinese diplomacy made Jake cede control by the disarming effect. He slumped in a sliding plop back down to the shower room floor, putting the boys on eye-level with one another. The curling of his lips informed the eastern boy of, at least, no anger. When the toothy grin emerged next, he knew all was probably good between the two.

"What the hell just happened?" Jake's warbling voice pitched in skewed vocal conflict. The funny trill of sounds made Wang Ho giggle. The two boys relaxed, Jake unabashedly naked and Ho only a little self-conscious in his besmirched condition.

The next bit of time found the two conversing on a level not achieved to that point. Both recognized that by the event just shared, no need for much in the way of obfuscation or affectation was either necessary or appropriate. In true teenage fashion, they assumed a familiarity which Jake felt would persist for the remainder of his tenure.

Arising, Ho braced a hand familiarly against Jake, who watched as he turned into the spray still waterfalling them both. Already wet, he drenched himself under cleansing spray, pulling the drawstring from his stomach to allow it to wash telltale stickiness down insides of pant legs. Jake realized the boy had peaked, too.

Next saturated was the silky black shoulder-length mop of hair. Backing away from the cascade, he shook his head and body in a markedly canine fashion. Jake's turn to laugh, he arose too, rinsing off. Ho removed his sopping clothes and they dried together, sharing a towel.

The reveal of his body exposed Jake to a new idea of maleness as he took in the golden-shaded skin, complementing almond eyes. Smooth hairlessness and the compactness of build was very pleasing, Jake thought. A fast friendship had been forged. Retrieving discarded flip-flops, he toweled-up as Ho dressed. Then the cleanly sated boys exited the shower area together, Jake's robe shouldered and Ho wearing the damply wrung-out outfit in which he'd entered.

As they neared Jake's door, Ho's father rounded the corner, obviously surprised to see friendliness so evident between his wet son and the towel-draped American student. It caused some muddle. Jake introduced himself, quickly winning over the older man by mannerly respect and elocutionary skill; attributes highly prized in the father's country. He told Jake so. The boys parted amidst promises to keep touch and get together.

Turning the key in the knob to his room, Jake sensed, more than heard, a dull, pummeling racket from inside. Pushing carefully to peek, he was rudely blasted by a hot spray of water. Puzzled, he widened the crack, exacerbating the effect, and visualized the dorm sink. The faucet had somehow blown off the spigot, permitting an eruption of hot spray to pelt him directly in the face, head-on.

He squinted into the strong stream, palming his hands out to thwart the inundation. Rushing inward, he whipped off the now-sopping towel, ineffectually covering the geyser smashing into his face and body. It only diverted the flow. So, he leaned over in blind search for the shut-off valve beneath. Locating the handle, Jake twisted it hard, clockwise. The blasted hardware broke off in his hand, leaving the cascade still deluging him.

Sinking to the floor, the spray seemed to follow his descent, never letting him escape from its flooding blitzkrieg. Frustrated beyond coping, he wiped a hand down head and face to clear his vision just a smidgeon. Then, he peeked through the torrent to try assessing another solution. The view confounded him. There, from floor level where he had sunk, he visualized the faucet, somehow back in place, jetting directly onto him.

Focus on the conundrum--- how did the stupid thing get back on--- compounded itself as he found it not only back on the spigot, the spigot no longer emerged from the sink. Instead, it was attached to the wall. What was more, the cinder block wall had transformed into subway tile... the same kind as in the shower... down the hall. Whoa, Jake mused, this is just plain weird.

Shaking to clear his groggy head, the youngest senior dipped to the side, finally managing to move from under the frustrating spray jet. His eyesight cleared. And, there, he found himself. Staring at the still spewing double wall jets, just where he had positioned them. He was, to be sure, in the big communal shower. On the floor, all right... and alone. The familiarly tapering leg snake lay there, bouncing languidly on and off one thigh. Dribbling, like always, it occurred to him.

The dawning was a strange one as he grasped the reality. All that had gone on before, fantastical as it was, was just that. Fantasy. A night dream, very normal, but during the middle of the day. He had blown a fuse, for sure. Sweet feelings verified that. Wow, he thought. And, no sheets to strip or deliver to the chute... he should shoot for this again.

Picking himself up, Jake rinsed off again, rotated the handles on both shower heads to closed, reached over for the waiting dry towel... and purred. All the way back to the room. The dry room...

Residual buzz waxed through Jake's body as he dressed and descended to the walkway connecting the church to quadrangle on his way to the headmaster's office. Never having been through such a powerful release, pheromone saturation left him flushed in unprecedented mellowness.

He walked into the secretary's foyer guarding the headmaster's own office and found a busy young woman. Chrissie, as the student recalled from previous visits, sat deluged in stacks of records around her cluttered desk. With two phones ringing and a borderline frantic look about her, a perfunctory smile greeted him from this vantage and a quick hand gesture indicated for him to go right on in through the closed door.

Jake opened it hesitantly, stopping in the doorway before entering. Before him sat Mr. Readoner behind his big antique desk. The man was engaged in conversation with Mrs. Bonnier, the dean of students, who was also his advisor. Mr. Eton's fill-in as interim headmaster and formerly the assistant headmaster, Mr. Readoner looked every bit the part.

Long silver locks combed straight back over his head, a wool plaid vest with immaculate white shirt and perfectly knotted bowtie: the man exuded academic gravitas.

Seeing Jake appear, he interrupted the conversation. "Greetings, young Master Marshall. We have been awaiting you, Sir. Do come in and take a seat." His and the dean's friendly demeanors dispelled Jake's rising trepidation, still ignorant to the reason for a Thanksgiving break summons. It eased his mind that at least he wasn't in trouble and nobody had died. Not with this evident good mood. He came in and took the proffered seat.

"Jacob, it appears by your appearance that the physical labor with Chateau agrees with you. You are fairly beaming. Am I under a correct assumption?" Everybody was aware of the headmaster's ability for sizing things up. Jake nodded, momentarily questioning whether the man also guessed his recent upstairs pastime. That thought was a little jarring.

Assuring the man of his positivity regarding the riding stable, he waited expectantly, looking back and forth between the two administrators. Dean Bonnier opened dialogue to the subject at hand. "Jacob, it's good to see you doing so well. We do have hopes that you are finding some enjoyment over the quietude of the break." Again, Jake debated the allusion, innocent as it seemed. He rationalized it must be only paranoia.

"There has been news this morning of some significance concerning you. We felt it best to have you in straight away to discuss it. Don't worry, it is all very good news, so relax," she added, apparently picking up on Jake's underlying consternation, despite the 'beaming'. If only she really knew, he thought.

"As you are no doubt aware, we have been receiving communications over past months, and will continue to do so over coming ones, regarding our students' various applications and interviews with higher institutions." A look of satisfaction was unmistakable. Master Readoner went on.

"We are presently in possession of four different institutions' positive responses to applications sent in your behalf. Your state of age minority required special dispensations from the school for contravention of normal protocol. Nearly perfect scores on the MCAT facilitated a concession. Well, that and the status of personal comportment noticed at your interviews, of course."

"Head of the respondents are Princeton and Yale. There remain several others outstanding. It would seem we all have some weighing to do…" The smile on both administrators' faces were effusive. And contagious. Jake lit up at the news.

The subsequent hour was spent mapping a plan for evaluating alternatives, a list of pros and cons drawn up. Besides the Ivy League schools, Stanford had replied, as had The University of Texas at Austin. Harvard, Cornell, Cambridge, Leipzig and others were yet to send news of their determinations. Jake, indeed, had choices.

All four of the first institutions would require three to four years of pre-med programs to ascertain Jake's disposition for medical curriculum, which was fine by the boy. His own uncertainty on the state of readiness had been a dogging concern. Fear of underperforming hit the overly young candidate like a ton of bricks. He wanted to confer with Derrick and Chad, along with the Etons. But he was nonetheless ecstatic at the possibilities.

In his heart, he already recognized a decision, though unready to let it be known. Something in the deepest reaches of his Id had informed him. A warm sentience on the mind's veiled horizon provided assurance. That, and some youthful heart palpitations.

Leaving the headmaster's office, he floated to his room, then lay levitated in bed, contemplating the future. His real Daddy had to be happy at the news. After long absence, dreams of shoulder romps with Spotty nipping ankles pervaded a boy's dreams that night.

May, 1999

"Texas? That is your verdict, Jake?" This from Derrick after an in-depth discussion of the matter once again before them. Graduation would be upon their young ward within weeks and the boy had pondered the dilemma for months. With input of much sought-after advice, all his wiser confidants had presumed pronouncement for an Ivy League institution entry. Up to now, Jake had been almost maddeningly non-committal. This declaration surprised the couple. Chad and he looked equally puzzled by it but sat quietly, pondering ramifications.

It was Chad who broke the silence. "You have done your homework on all this, we are sure, but this is unexpected, Jake. Care to fill us in?" Chad was secretly pleased. Were he in a similar position, he would like to think he would've struck out in such a free-spirited manner. Points unknown. Totally new perspectives.

And after all, he reasoned, the Texas flagship Tier One University ranked in upper echelons of America's premier medical colleges, so there was no lessening in quality by this decision. Just the fact of the destination made him think. A 'hinterlands' venue riled his paternal instincts somewhat. But, good for the boy, he reiterated to himself. He thought to bone-up on the capitol of the Lone Star State.

Jake sat tacitly a few more moments. Deliberately, he looked first to Derrick and then to Chad. Correctly deducing the one rooting for this decision. "I know I'm probably too young to be going so far away," this was directed at Derrick, "but it is true; I have been really meditating about it."

"There are a lot of things favorable for me here. Mainly, the two of you. I know I would never be in this position were it not for you both. But, I hope you can understand the feelings going on inside me."

"I watch the things you share when we are together. I've seen the other side by the goodness that you have brought my way and will be forever grateful. With no means of ever re-paying either of you. Money isn't what I am referring to, though there is that, too. It is the love and compassion you have demonstrated to and for me. I would still be fighting from a dark hole in the basement wall if it weren't for your involvement. You gave Spotty his best home, too," as he patted the graying friend at his feet. Thumping that tail softly.

Derrick was blubbing by this time. Even Chad felt a rare tear course his cheek at the maturity the youth exuded. The penchant was becoming a habit in this regard, he reflected. Knowledge of the boy's recognition of their feelings for him was the best of all... They grasped he felt the same in return. The boy went on.

"Ever since the name of the Austin university came into the options, I have had a feeling about it. I can't put it into words. But it is there. Something to do with the way I see you when you don't know I'm watching. You have an ease of existence between yourselves. I haven't ever seen that between two people, not even the Etons. The best part is that you don't seem aware of it."

"Something in my future is connected to Austin, Texas. I feel it holds a prospect like yours there for me. Don't ask me how. I have to go there. Someone is waiting. Does that make any sense at all, do you think?"

Jake knew he saw things others couldn't. He had always paid attention to the inner facet of himself. Difficulty making the present decision derived from self-doubt of following indecipherable innatism to such an extreme end. Not whether the feeling was correct or incorrect. He already knew it was. Could these special men ever understand that? Jake was very fearful to leave all that was familiar and comfortable, yet if he were to live to the potential which his inner being assured could exist, he realized he must. So, there it was. He observed the men now, awaiting their thoughts.

"Jake, you are way too young in my eyes to leave us. I just can't get away from that thought. But I--- no, we--- are also mindful that you are an uncommonly unique person. We will have to recognize and deal with that. Know that both of us feel blessed to play a role in your life. That it may set in motion events which put you on your Life's path makes us very much desirous of respecting that. But I am going to blubber the whole way, regardless." And he did. Sinking over into Chad's shoulder.

"You go, big boy," was all that an almost-sniffling Chad managed.

And so, the die was cast.

December, 2002

"Tell me again why you signed up for an entomology course? It's not like it's a requirement for med school--- are you changing majors?" Cullen wasn't accepting the logic. In his second year of college, the sophomore hadn't yet contemplated elective courses. Pre-requisites dominated his academic life. That somebody might take a course just for jollies remained outside his rationality. Girls and social life collectively constituted anything close to electives in Jake's roommate's world. They were sometimes more important than classes. Jake had figured that out early on. Luckily, the sophomore was serious about school and a degree, so all was good.

"I've always liked insects, Cullen. They're really fly beasts. Don't forget, they make up most species that inhabit Earth. And, to boot, there's bunches more yet to discover. More are identified every day." Jake was studying taxonomic charts in readying for a final exam two days hence. It was more fun than work and he laughed with Cullen more than at him for misunderstanding. It was a way to divert attention from the approach of more pressing matters.

The two boys sat across the dorm room from one another, breaking off for a minute from dead week studies as finals week loomed. Jake could see out the twenty-seventh-floor window of Dobie Center high rise. Memorial Stadium stood statuesque in the distance. The campus spread out below them as he contemplated the recent turn of events. Beginning with this new roommate. Easy friendship had budded between the duo over the previous year since they met one late afternoon at nearby Town Lake…

…Dusk was arriving as Jake had finished his daily run at Congress Avenue Bridge that late summer day, intending to take in the fascinating phenomenon about to erupt. He loved awaiting the daily event, enjoying assignment of make-believe life stories and circumstances to interesting characters converging on the site for the same purpose. Austin was chock full of weird inhabitants. The process provided appealing amusement in which Jake had taken pleasure over two years since settling in the central Texas capitol. Strangeness always drew the young misfit. This place he frequented accessed a venue availing nourishment for two appetites at once.

As the western drop of the sun advanced, the fiery orb hypnotized him. Using the waiting minutes, he methodically stretched used muscles. Per habit, since engaging the running hobby as a very young kid intent on vacating an unpleasant home life on Elkin Pond back in his home state of Vermont. The mainstay recreational diversion followed him faithfully though all that time. Presently, he hiked a sweat-socked ankle by the crook of an elbow up behind back and butt, toe-touching his mid-dorsum. It loosened quad muscles before spasms ensued, thereby draining lactic acid and avoiding painful charley horses.

Balancing on the stairway railing, absorbed in thoughts and blinded by the quickly sinking sun, he was abruptly bumped, hard, off the step, when another runner back-slid stepwise down the stairs without so much as a glance. Jake barely caught himself as the blond boy turned in surprise at the obstruction. He reached to help balance Jake upon seeing what he had done.

"Whoa, sorry, man. Didn't see you there. I was just doin' my moon-walk-downs to loosen up. You OK?" He obviously meant no insult and the boy's hand-brace kept Jake from toppling one-legged down eight steps to the gravel trail below. A smile accompanied the surprise and concern, lessening any chagrin maybe engendered by the collision.

"Nah. I'm good. It's all right. I should have been keeping an eye out anyway. The sun's bright." He took in the handsome face and athletic form of an obvious running acolyte like himself, further allaying any umbrage.

The steadying hand grasped his tricep and the two pulled close in the save, evaluating each other. Jake thought at first he might have detected interest but after a couple minutes of banal banter he deduced this straight boy was not of his own persuasion. No biggie. All good-looking men aren't gay. Just the majority. He wouldn't hold it against the guy. The thought made Jake smile. The two continued a dialogue as the sun disappeared. Comparing running shoes, cool down techniques, running apparel and loop preferences, they became a little familiar. Dusk set in unobtrusively during their chat.

Suddenly, a swoosh of black wings engulfed the pair, along with other gathered watchers, causing a low upsurge of excited murmurs amidst a flapping torrent. It took the new boy by utter surprise. He ducked and dropped to the steps as if under attack, covering his head, wondering what the hell was happening.

Jake's turn to help the other boy. He reached out, grinning, and handed him up, reassuring that the onset of the dusk occurrence now unfolding was one not only expected, but anticipated. The boy rose only warily, despite the explanation. The rush of passing wings continued in a seemingly never-ending flow. Chirping and clucking noises added quirkiness to anyone happening upon the phenomenon. As this runner plainly had done. "What is it? Birds?"

His anxious visage tried vainly to control an emanating fear, seeing others around them affected in a positive way but still unable to come to grips with an unknown entity.

"It's the bats, dude. Aren't you here for their emergence? Everyone else is. If this is your first time, don't worry, they don't bite or sting or anything. They won't even touch you. We're just like a tree or bush to them. They have great radar. They're on the way up to hunt all night." Jake explained all of this as the guy collected and settled himself, gradually accepting Jake's words. A bit hard to do under the circumstances.

A few minutes helped, along with calm clarification. Ooh's and ahh's all around them convinced him finally that all was well and he stood straighter, observing the winged maelstrom wax over the succeeding minutes, then gradually begin to wane.

When the fluttering receded to just a few stragglers at a time, the boy took in the whole situation and fixed Jake with a stare. "You say this happens every night? Where do all those things stay? And why aren't they attacking? I always thought bats bit and that we caught rabies from the buggers. We kill 'em quick when they show up back home, but then there's never any more than one or two at a time and they're usually lost, or something, seems like."

Jake replied, "This is a colony of nearly two million that predates the bridge. They've lived here in caves for eons. We are the interlopers. Not them. The colony took up under this bridge after the last caves were closed off. Everyone used to think the same way you do but now recognize the super-coolness of it. Hundreds of people come here to watch every summer day."

"These smart mammals--- they're not birds--- eat night insects. If you let them alone, there's a whole lot fewer mosquitoes to suck your blood after sunset. You get bit a lot, I bet." A quick nod of surprise acknowledged that fact. "Yeah, vampire bats live only in Central and South America in the Western Hemisphere, so blood-sucking isn't an issue. And, since mosquitoes much prefer blondes…and kids… you're a prime target."

This comment brought a defensive response. "Me? A kid? Hell, man, I'm blond, sure, but I'm legal--- turned eighteen in May. Hardly a kid. Look who's talkin'. You and your big ole' fourteen-year-old self." The great smile warmed Jake. A notorious loner and hermit, he preferred solitude, running and books to people. Precisely because of his kid-like looks. He tired quickly of explaining the age thing. By the fact that those his age almost always lagged in educational accomplishment, Jake was overly careful to display confidence and communicative skill beyond his years. The disparate factors left little common ground. It rankled him to be pre-judged. Therefore, he most often kept to himself.

But he liked this guy. "Wow, thanks a lot. I'm seventeen next January. So, go on with your own stuck-up person." Smiling as he joked. "I'm only a year back… or so. You live here? In Austin, I mean?"

"Yeah… well I do now. I'm from south of here--- Cotulla--- and I go to UT. I live in Brackenridge Hall on campus. Just about to finish freshman year. You?" Jake's nod engendered more. "So, if you're only sixteen, man, how'd you get in early? Are you at UT, even? Or ACC... or St Edwards?"

Jake was used to this, so proceeded cautiously. Responses varied from surprise to disbelief or even derision. He generally shied from the subject. ACC was an eastside community college for remedial work before applying to more established schools while St. Edwards University was a small private school to the south of where the two now stood.

"No, I go to UT. I live at Prather Hall now, but am not happy there and hope to move for fall semester. I have a roommate-from-hell who never studies and party's non-stop. It makes me spend most of the time in Library or at Ransom Center to get anything done." He left it there, hoping to change subjects, but the boy wasn't having it.

"So, UT... at sixteen. That's pretty good. What are you taking? I'm going into Business Admin and in the fall, I'm gonna move, too. Wanna get outta Brackenridge Hall. It's prehistoric. Built in the 1930's or something. Prather is too, huh? Just over from Brack. So, what's your major, man?" He must want to know, by the repeat. "And, where you from?"

Well, so what, thought Jake... here goes. "I'm from Vermont and in pre-med. It's a long slog." Jake conveniently left out that he was finishing his junior year, not desiring to bring attention to the fact. "How do you like business admin? You working for an MBA?" He noted bat-watchers thinning out. The two were less jostled now. They sat down on a nearby bench looking at the lake. Jake awaited an inevitable third-degree.

"Oh. OK. Vermont? Up by New Hampshire, right? Why'd you come to Texas? Had to be a Longhorn, huh?" He joked. But didn't third-degree. What a relief. "Hey, wanna go over to Starbucks and get a latte? You can tell me about these blasted insect-eating birds some more. It's kinda straight-up. 'Specially that they miss you when they fly by. Oh, by the way, my name is Cullen. Cullen Porter."

An hour of chit-chatting at the coffeehouse left Jake 'in like' with the freshman. Personable but not nosy; self-deprecatingly congenial. The two began running miles together after that, usually ending at Congress Bridge, then walking up to the dorms through downtown. By end of term the boys had agreed to keep in touch over summer and try finding a room together for fall term when Cullen returned. Jake was gung-ho at a chance to pick a roommate after five semesters and five roommates assigned by Prather Dorm RA's.

Summer sessions flashed by quickly. August arrived and Cullen turned up with his mom who needed to meet this new boy wanting to be her baby's roommate. A protective woman, she wasn't having any more of the types her son had been stuck with his first year. By the end of the dorm search weekend, the svelte country mom turned to Cullen and, right in front of Jake, issued a statement, "Honey, this young man has his head on straight and knows where he is going. I think you should take the Dobie Center room and be done with looking."

The sweet smile informed Jake he'd passed muster. Cullen hated the parental acceptance, but liked Jake enough to overlook the invasion into newly sprouting autonomy, so acquiesced. Besides, the two ran well together: like paces, like loops, like timing, like habits. So, it happened. Three months into teaming up, the match was proving a good one…

… "Jake, we Texans are brought up to hate insects. They're all pests down here. The only good insect is a dead insect." He was adamant about it. In a semi-arid region, the mindset was understandable. Insects killed crops. Fast. But Jake still loved the tiny beasts, actively seeking them when he was on runs or hikes, anything taking him outside.

"You have to admit that they are pretty cool-looking even if you don't like them, though, right?" The colors, the exotic anatomical and locomotive diversity, all stoked Jake's curiosity. "Do you know that in one square mile of forest there are more insects than there are people on earth?" He thought that factoid amazing. "And, also, an ant can carry fifty times its body weight? That's like if you weigh a hundred and fifty pounds, you could carry your own car around… gnarly, huh?" How could that fail to impress, Jake reflected.

"Boy, oh boy. Yeah, man. Think of the gas money I'd save…" Cullen, with no car, remained unenthusiastic. "But, seriously, you took it on purpose and didn't need to. Is that right?"

"Yes. That is correct. I like insects."

"All of 'em? Even the bad ones? You know there are a bunch that only do bad things and spread disease and stuff. How is that interesting?" He was at least trying to relate.

"The more we understand them, the more we are able to control them and limit any damage they do. That makes sense, right?" He was glad Cullen was picking his brain, needing a break.

"So, you think bugs like black widows and brown recluse spiders and damnable blood-suckin' ticks are cool? I knew a guy who put his boot on with a recluse spider in it and the thing bit him. In three days, his whole calf rotted off. He's never been the same since. What's up with that?"

"For the major point, none of those are insects, Cull. They are arachnids. I'm not studying those. But, dang, those are killing machines, aren't they?" Cullen was mystified at that exuberant comment. "Probably the most interesting thing about the insect world is the way medical science can harness toxins, anatomical oddities and other things for good purposes. Like medicines and orthopedic devices. So, there is that. What if the recluse toxin could be targeted somehow to eat cancerous tumors?"

"OK, I'll give you that point. Keep your friends close and your enemies closer, huh? Well, check this out. What about those bugs that the wife eats the husband? Right after he gives the bitch the goods? That is sick. Where's anything good there, now?"

Jake thought about that a minute. He debated amongst 'himselves' and decided to. "Well, I agree, not a whole lot of good to be seen there--- at least from the male's standpoint. But there's a little bit of a story I read on that, if you want to hear it." Cullen nodded OK. "You may not like it. But here goes."

"I read about a study done by a grad student in Arkansas who observed habits of praying mantises--- or mantids--- in the wild. First one ever done. It encompassed two years. Results showed the females didn't always eat their mates after mating. Sometimes, he would eat her. And other times, when a group of males surrounded the female, vying to be her mate, she would snap all their heads off in a big serial-beheading and then mate with all of them. Headless. They gave her the goods even after that… pretty skanky, huh? That happened in about 2% of wild-setting matings. In those cases, after the babies hatched and Mom died, too, the siblings all came out fighting. They devoured each other. Last mantid standing, so to speak."

"Damn, Jake. That really is cold-blooded. They could still get it up? There must be bug Viagra, I'm guessin'. That's what I call fucking your brains out!"

"Yep," Jake replied, "and they are truly cold-blooded." To himself, he thought, it also made a good case for 'it pays to be gay'. But didn't say so.

April, 2004

The odor of formaldehyde was overwhelming. Jake could see people walk wide paths of avoidance whenever he approached, wrinkled nostrils offended a block distant if winds were right. Upon happening on others unbeknownst, many exclaimed in gagging vexation. Were it possible, he would avoid himself, he considered, hoofing his way by back paths to Dobie Center following the thrice weekly introductory anatomy laboratory session.

As a first-year med student, he had taken to waiting patiently a fair distance from the elevators until a lull in riders happened. Traveling in close proximity had prompted bouts of heaving fits within such close confines. He found himself praying that no one would hitch a ride somewhere along the traverse from the lobby up to the twenty-seventh-floor domicile where he bided time with his near-mutinous friend and roommate, Cullen.

The three-hour marathons, while remarkably interest-provoking, left all those departing the clammy, smelly cadaver-laden settings open to ostracism and occasional threat to physical safety by disdain for the stench absorbed along with knowledge in the macabre venue.

The putrid pong permeated not just clothing during hours of exposure. In its molecular state formalin penetrated skin, resulting in cadres of walking pariahs throughout the four semesters required for a foundation to medical training. It remained the bane of every first and second-year med student's existence.

Everything involved with medicine derived in some manner from the noxious laboratories housing preserved and dissected bodies so magnanimously bequeathed prior to departing the physical vessels we all inhabit until we don't. 'Donating one's body to science' holds a ring of dedication to perpetuation of humankind. How noble, think the masses. Right, Jake wincingly deduced, after the revelation broadsided the incoming class on the first day of their noble pursuit.

Medical students the world around thought of it in an entirely different way. One which the remainder of humanity would, as well, were they to be subjected to reality of such an ignobly messy demise. Rending of one's former unique bodily components to pored-over, separated, dissected and torn-apart-limb-by-limb methodology was what accurately occurred.

Enlightenment would likely make the most honorable of beings rethink themselves. Should they ever hover as a proverbial fly-on-the-wall in watching green medical apprentices wade through the process, that is. The process shaded students with a greenish tinge over the course of study. Yuck, Jake reasoned.

Yet, what could be any viable alternative? He, like all who had preceded him, would therefore simply carry on. Unable to partake in common day-to-day activities by merit of reviling ripeness. Ahem, he conceded.

Approaching the door to room 2713 where he and Cullen had called home these past school years, familiarity drew him. Thankfully, the hallway was deserted. The reality that he would most probably revive upon entering caused foreboding. He disliked the antipathy arising from his presently loathsome state. It had taken the boy thirty minutes to maneuver his way here from the lobby. Now, Cullen's distaste loomed.

Before entering, Jake unleashed his latest stratagem for battling the dilemma. Unzipping the flight suit procured from the Army Surplus store the previous day, he pulled out the also newly purchased heavy parachute-silk backpack dedicated to the cause. He hoped the impervious nature of it might stifle some stink.

Stripping off the new 'travel attire' for the hike through campus along with the more offensive lab coverall underneath, he turned both inside-out and wadded them into the Air Force issue bag. The protective suit donned upon departing lab had noticeably smothered the aroma on traverse to Dobie and that was a good thing. Hopefully this method would mitigate the noxious effect enough to salvage his longtime roommate's goodwill.

Grasping the doorknob, he turned it and pushed, expecting an onslaught of dissent to the bouquet he shepherded. Every other day, now.

Waiting a pregnant moment before entering, nothing greeted him. Peeping in to Cullen's side of the room, he found a napping blonde, book open on his chest, hands gripped behind his head.

Whew, he exhaled. Quickly, Jake moved to hide the pack deep in his emptied closet, closing the door securely. All his sparse wardrobe now resided in stacks under the desk along with running shoes. Next, he stripped off underclothes, hiding them in yet another dedicated bag. Putting it into the closet also. The downstairs laundromat would see a triple vinegar soak and wash late that night. His newest plan was a go.

Clean drawers later, along with the signature headband, used for years now in taming riotous sprigging curlicues covering him, Jake settled on his bed with a book on parasitology to review for a didactic lecture the coming morning. Not too bad, he reflected. This was the best entry after a lab to date. Maybe he could make it work after all and save driving his friend to other accommodations.

A good three hours passed before Cullen snorted to consciousness. He knocked the business tome to the floor and sat up abruptly. "Hey, Jake... man. You snuck in, huh? I was waiting up for you." A glance out the narrow window as he swiped his wavy blond locks back from a groggy face informed him of not having done so. "Wow, what time is it?" The digital clock stared up at him. "9:30? Already? Can't believe it. I was gonna be finished studying by now. How come you didn't get me up?" He finally focused over at his settled partner.

"You were sleeping like a baby. I didn't have the heart to do it. You haven't been doing much of that lately, I noticed. That's why." He avoided mentioning the elephant in the room. The pervasive preservative was only very mildly perceptible and Jake was hopeful it wasn't just his inured sense of smell missing it. The non-response proved telltale. Cullen hadn't even remarked on lack of smells or that Jake had taken drastic action. Great news, sighed a relieved anatomist.

"So, why were you trying to wait up, you night owl you?" Looking pointedly at the clock, he glanced back. Teasing him always provided Jake fun in the watching. It took a minute to dawn on the blonde. He grinned and rose, heading to his desk. The briefs he preferred were hiked and twisted up on his hips and crack a bit, leaving round ass cheeks delectably exposed. It was a cute visual. Way too cute for a straight boy. Jake chewed on that premise regularly.

Cullen's current main squeeze, Ashleigh, commonly commented on the boy's globular pair of tight cheeks. The couple drug Jake along to meals downstairs sometimes in the food court or at one of the affordable student hangout restaurants on the infrequent chance that he was not in class or studying. He pictured her slapping the taut buns in public venues like that and wished for the chance himself... "Jake? You hear me?" He was looking back over his shoulder, matching orbs flexing sexily in the turn. "You checkin' out my butt, man? Ha. You must be hard up. Need to get you some pussy. You know that, right?"

He never let the subject rest; hadn't for the whole tenure of their friendship. Jake had never shown predilection toward persons of either sex in a romantic context. Cullen apparently worried about the lack. Though he didn't boast his sexual prowess, Cullen didn't hide his appetites. More than once, Jake had walked in on his roommate in the sack with more than one pretty female.

Jake had suggested the old sock-on-the-doorknob as signal after each of those episodes to spare everyone's sensibilities, but never had he been forewarned. It was his estimation that the guy wanted to be walked in on during the action. Jake'd probably never know, but it sure made him wonder.

"No, I really did want to talk to you, man." Neglecting to rearrange the skewed briefs, on turning around, the primo buns disappeared and the nestled junk rotated into view, exhibiting some residual effect of just awakening. Remnants of swelling still bloomed inside, tenting the front in lewd demonstration.

Cullen let all stay where stuff posed, walking four steps toward him, holding out a news clipping. "Did you know we stay in the same room--- 2713--- where Michael Dell stayed when he was enrolled at UT? I couldn't believe it. But I checked it out at Ransom and downloaded this."

Jake was surprised by the fact and perused the clipping. Sure enough, he skimmed a bit of an interview Dell had done a couple years before.

Now, the CEO and sole owner of Dell, Incorporated, resided in opulence befitting billionaire status, having made his mark over the time since then. But sure enough, here was the evidence, in print, verifying it. "Pretty cool. How did you figure this out, Cull?" Jake was still glancing sidelong at the half-awake basket snake. Having seen it bare several times--- even partially hard--- he was still drawn to the sight presently leaving something to the imagination through those sexy white briefs. Cullen seemed oblivious to Jake's further browsing.

"That's the funny thing, Jake. A guy came by our room about noontime today, knockin'. He asked me if I knew it. Said he just wanted to see the spot the big man had stayed. He came in and we talked a while. Sat right there on your bed. Dude looked like a big jock but said he was an MBA candidate--- pretty gnarly, huh? He's got some inventions in the works trying to be the next Mr. Dell, I think. Nice guy. Hope he gets some of them going. He gave me some advice on my degree plan. I told him he could stop back by if he wanted. Anyway, that's when I went over to the Center and downloaded the info from UT Housing records."

"That is pretty neat, Cullen. So, the guy's ahead of you toward his MBA? And a jock, too? That combo is pretty unusual, huh?" Jake watched as Cullen's hand nonchalantly rearranged the junk-store while looking in his desk. Delicious looking, Jake still thought. "What was his name?" Only half-listening.

"Yeah, said he was about to start his dissertation. Couple of more years, maybe three, and he says he'll be golden. Big guy, like I said. Tall--- like 6'6" or so. I thought he was a basketballer or a wide receiver or something. Said no, though. Cal. Yeah, I think he said his name was Cal...something."

Junk flopped over inside those shorts as the good roommate laid back and picked up his capsized book from the floor. "Hey, what happened to the damn smell? It didn't follow you in today, huh? You quit that crap, or what?" He smirked at Jake as he settled back.

"Abigail Van Stavern! You are incorrigible, girl! I can't believe you just said that!" Jake grinned at his best girlfriend, amazed.

"What... you mean to try and tell me it isn't so?" She was grinning, too, but the two were miles apart on thought process. "You know perfectly well that it wasn't when we went to sleep and when we woke up it was rock-ripped rigid. I didn't just see it--- I even felt it. Tell me that wasn't in your mind. You just aren't willing to admit that those luscious boy buns get that big thing all excited. I'm glad you aren't into girls because that is one fearsome weapon." Pointing between his legs. "Don't be looking at me like that, boy, you know I am right. Girls have a feel for these things…just like gay boys do… so there!"

Jake had to admit--- inwardly--- the girl was spot on. Though he wasn't about to give an inch. "Abby, you have no idea what goes on in this head. For all you know, I was dreaming about waking up in the Delta House naked with three sisters giving me head." Though both knew there was fat chance of that. Jake had been busted by the girl as he nearly drooled over a video of Puff Daddy yanking his shirt off at the finish line of the NYC Marathon months before. Unbeknownst to him, she had observed his behavior. And then confronted the subject. Though Jake had been mortified, blushing five shades of purple, it had finally put to rest her scenarios of the two hooking up. Abby had harbored secret ideas of such silliness to that point.

Now, the pair fairly reveled in the sharing of tete-a-tete's such as that currently happening. Both loved the idea of the 'secret' between them. Like now, as they sat cloistered in a private study carrel inside Ransom Center where they studied together. Abby had been teasing Jake about his shyness to come out to his longtime roommate. She contended that the lengths to which he went covering up reality were patently ridiculous.

The time, only a week before, when he had begged her to be 'caught' together in his dorm bed when Cullen walked in was just the latest source of amusement. Hatched as Jake's attempt to divert Cullen's innuendoes about Jake checking out his 'stuff' on more than one occasion, the scenario had been staged. Very successfully, it might be added.

Late that afternoon, the disrobed, platonic couple had lain, entwined, in the single bed on the twenty-seventh-floor dorm room. Napping together until the key in the lock had alerted them of Cullen's arrival. Assuming positions and locking lips, the roommate had been confronted by the surprise hook-up upon walking in. By lucky circumstance, Jake had awakened from napping with a huge boner hovering over his bare belly, engendered by something from a dream playing out inside his subconscious. Cullen couldn't have missed sight of it. A faint gasp had escaped the unassuming blonde's lips seeing the entanglement.

The business major ladies' man thought he was unheard by fakery of noise accompanying the shadowy act 'occurring' before him. And, in fine straight boy fashion, backed unobtrusively out the door, quietly clicking the lock as he gave them space. A thoroughly bemused look as he tiptoed away was not seen by the lovers.

Abby continued teasing her bosom bud over appearance of the boned-up appendage so squishily inert between the two prior to that preparatory naptime. "You know better, Jacob Winslow Marshall. How long have I known you? We are both very aware of the triggers for Rowdy there," again implicating the white-boy behemoth living between his legs.

"I am not any sort of liverwurst when it comes to looks and you damn well get that. If there had been any inkling of interest in my gender, it would've 'come up' before this. God knows, I gave it a shot…" She smirked in allusion to the charade that had played too long between them from their meeting that first day of medical school. Now, Jake determined the pretense may as well just be shucked.

"OK…OK... uncle, already. I give in. Let me alone, woman. So, I get my rocks off over the same thing as you. It's not like you have competition. Straight boys aren't exactly abandoning the fairer sex to get into my pants, you know. The boys I am scoping out are simply not on the map yet. I've got an agenda. And I intend to follow it through. Just because some of us are able to juggle a social life while navigating med school doesn't mean the rest of us can. Give me a break, 'K?"

She did hound him mercilessly on two scores. Coming out was the major one. Getting laid was the second. It was antithetical to Jake's perception of what he knew about women. Men were the constant horn-hounds, he conjectured, while girls were supposed to fit roles of centered and reasonable on the topic of sex. Not so much with this girl, he had deduced. Abby seemed bent on getting Jake's sexual needs met. Even without knowing what those may be. And she read way too much into a lot of things that weren't real, too, he inferred.

The girl worried over his lack of a sexual outlet yet at the same time fantasized a very active and covert sex life for him. His mind remained boggled by where that all came from. Other than off-handed comments and chance occurrences, she had no actual basis for knowledge of his appetites in that field. Were these truly the conversational proclivities women had amongst themselves when apart from the male gender, he considered? If so, then by jiminy, girls were every bit the horndogs men were. They just covered it better.

"Well, I still say, you'd better watch out boy. I've seen some mighty interested glances by that 'super straight stud' roommate of yours. It wouldn't surprise me a bit if he jumps your bones one of these days. Like when there is a pussy drought, or something. Mark my words."

Some women can be so blind, it occurred to Jake. Did she really think that the faked sexcapade for Cullen's benefit hadn't assured the boy of Jake's tendencies? That man didn't have the slightest intent regarding him. They'd been rooming for years now, in the same place... seen each other's junk at various compromising stages of inadvertent arousal... showered together regularly and slept within feet of each other. If that possibility was relevant it sure would have happened before now. How ridiculous.

"Man, you must not be plowin' da' furrow lately, huh?" Cullen was curious. Again. For the previous two weeks, multiple allusions to Jake's sex life with Abby had been plaguing the running buddy's mind. Jake was puzzled by it. Now, as they rounded the bend by Zackary-Scott Theatre off Lamar Avenue, their pre-dawn run had been peppered by the blond boy's continuing dialogue on the subject.

"What? Why do you keep saying things like that, Cull? Abby and I are just fine; no problems. We're doing great." Jake grasped neither the reasoning behind the reiterative comments nor the conclusions.

"Well, ya'll sure haven't been shaggin' up in the room or nothin', man. When you getting the goods? Just 'cause me and Ashleigh are kaput doesn't mean I want to see both of us living a monk's life. Dude, you need to fill me in... I ain't getting' nothing these past weeks. Blue ain't my favorite color and it's soakin' into my damn balls. Gotta get me some kinda input to stoke the fire. You need to at least lemme in on the 411 how ya been sewin' the seed..." A five-second pause, then, "So, things are good and ya getting' what ya need, huh? Spill it, bud."

The line of thought was bizarre, thought Jake. "I'm tellin' you Cull, there's nothing but good between Abby and me. And who's to say we're not getting it on at her Delta House? Or the study carrels? Or, hell, the alley? You think we're only capable of the deed in our dorm, or what?" That should put it to rest. And, indeed, Cullen seemed placated, introverting to a quietly subdued state over the ensuing couple of miles. Jake contemplated things he might be able to do to help the poor guy out. A couple thoughts came to mind, mostly involving the supple roundness of the twins residing trunkside in the nylon running shorts beside him. Damn, those buns were cute.

Descending a small hill at a lake-feeding tributary filled with quacking ducks, they followed beside clear green spring water sluicing through it, burbling riff muffling ever-present background city sounds. Crossing the footbridge, the boys turned a corner trail back from water's edge in making toward an underbridge traverse beneath MoPac Expressway.

The water sounds themselves were now drowned out by motors whizzing over them on the busy bypass. The roar gradually diminished as distance was traveled from it. Morning sounds of awakening animals and birds became discernible. Quiet padding of four cadenced feet, matching gait, provided both with comforting regularity of the physical exertion so enjoyed.

A more raucous birdcall signaled from ahead, around a bend in the trail. They keened to see what species made the call, not recognizing it as familiar. It rose and fell, undulant and almost plaintive, like a mating call maybe. The sound increased in volume as they neared the source. Emerging up a small rise centered by a shrouding copse of trees, all four running shoes clopped to a sudden halt. Both sets of eyes widened in surprise and disbelief as the sweaty pair beheld a peculiar and unusual sight. Blurry in dim pre-dawn shadows.

Before them were a pair of men. A toned white guy kneeled in bent position over a tree stump. A tall, muscular mahogany-colored athlete hugged close behind him. Both wore cross trainers. Nothing more. The tight round set of curving buttglobes backing the man-of-color rotated in a deliberate rolling fashion, melding with the white ass directly in front of it. The elastic white melons, perked upwards, bounced to a beat. The whiteness was edged by deep tan lines demarcating the torso and smoothly muscled legs above and below them.

An ongoing erogenous dance had been stumbled on out here in the open. For anyone to see. The conjoined couple was oblivious to anything other than their present pursuit. One dark hand gripped one pale cheek while the other repeatedly slapped the opposing side in rhythm to their pace. A delectably slow and sensuous one.

Facing almost perpendicular to Jake and Cullen, the angle allowed for verification of additional connecting parts as the butts chugged in and out by opposing thrusts. The connector showed itself as one beautifully thick uncut monster of an endowment. Its silhouette glistened intermittently between pushes.

Both astonished voyeurs stood still, mesmerized by the vision. Unable to do anything more than ogle the rutting duo while assessing the finely-toned anatomical specimens. Cullen's eyes were physically bugging out of his head. Jake noted the effect as an errant question flashed through his mind whether his friend would be offended by the ongoing episode. To the contrary, though, the blonde seemed more drawn than repelled. Oh, yeah, those blue balls, he remembered. Interesting…

Panning downward, Jake noted a set of fingers form a cup over the clearly swelling jockstrap. Sweat perfusing the runner had soaked his shorts to semi-transparency. Knit fabric of the Bike brand supporter showed plainly through. Barely supporting anything. Cullen's straight boy crotch was having second thoughts, Jake reflected, as he watched the engorging pipe and sweaty ball sack appear.

In slow-motion, the package stretched the cloth containment past its limits. A pretty helmet head strained its way out the edging in obvious attempt at an 'eye' view of the goings-on from its own level. Jake's head wagged the mess of head-banded curls back and forth in trying to see both the action and crotch growth. It was difficult, but had to be done. Cupping fingers soon switched from only covering to massaging. Jake found the entire thing extremely arousing, feeling his own jock stretch.

For several minutes, Cullen's eyes did not leave the exploit blundered upon. Never once thinking to see what Jake was doing. The roommate's tongue took to licking full lips, lending credence to Jake's observation of an 'other-than-straight' reaction to the queer tryst. His friend was liking it.

Likewise, for Jake. He simply couldn't decide which to watch. Sounds of butt slaps augmented sight of the sexy scenario. Jake identified the twangy banjo theme from that disturbing old thriller, Deliverance, adding flavor. The dark slim top man hummed the tune to the beat of his pumping; laughing and smacking like a bronc-rider.

White boy was enjoying every single inch of acoustic-laden attention. Evidenced by his own very sizeable rigid prick bouncing on and off the log over which he had assumed position. Tight fat balls hugged and bounced right along with a fleshy shaft. Yup, Jake could see, the boy definitely liked what was being done to him.

Jake's hardened piece felt an abrupt tap. Distracting himself from the pump action, he found Cullen staring at him. "Man, you LIKIN' this shit, ain't you? Look at that whompin' hard ass thing standin' right up right there like it was proud," as he tapped the bobbing thing another time. The grin was telling.

"Look who's talking, Cull. Yours looks just like I've seen it when I walked in on your big pussy-boning self. Like you wanted me to. Well, it's sure happy right now. What's up?" Jake wasn't having any of his roommate's BS under the circumstances. Too much lay open and revealed to put it back in the box, he surmised.

Knowing he was busted, bigtime, with nowhere to hide, the blonde leered over at his similarly affected bud, "Well, then, what the hell you waitin' for, man? Do your job!" He laughed as he took Jake's piece in his hand. Jake spit on fingers and followed suit.

Damn, this was hot. The next minutes were spent stroking each other by the emerging light of dawn, seeing the involved jungle fever duo carry on in ignorance of an audience.

With a long down stroke, Jake's arched dick strained upward, head swelling to magnificent size. First a pearlescent bead appeared and then the cyclops popped several big streams of thick creamy juice. The force of it splattered Cullen's thigh and cock. That sizzling delivery set the splattered dick over the peak; it evicted a blossoming load, too.

Through the haze of ecstasy, the two heard and saw the hooked pair twist heads around, finally sensing presence. By the sudden clarity of their unplanned show, the white boy's hard-on spewed its response in jets of answering spurts. Still to the beat of the black mamba inside him.

The tall stud must've been likewise affected, feeling a contracting prostate gland signaling him inside that burning chute. Rumbling emanations of satisfaction came from his throat as his pelvis bumped time and again against the hard butt being poled. No juice was seen from it, impaled as it remained. The black man wasn't there for a show: he was getting that nut. Copiously, by sounds of it.

As the four slowed themselves down in aftereffects of the group gusher, they discovered an additional set of eyes peering from a nearby bush at clearing's edge. A brown-haired boy also stood, pants lowered, feet spread. The self-stroked production of spunk informed the others of his own singular enjoyment.

The connected couple grinned in embarrassment as they pulled apart. The distinct 'splopp' sound announced the biggest member of the circle. All three observed at least nine inches of uncut, big-headed ebony silkiness. Showing itself in its entirety for the first time. Without pumping butt, that is. Utterly beautiful, the huge piece hovered, driveling, between the extremely handsome pair who now showed resolve for retrieving discarded shorts from close by tree branches. Amidst those shit-eating grins.

They took off for the shadows just as the morning sun popped its head from beneath the nighttime horizon. That was a sign. The other youth grabbed shorts back into place, disappearing as well. Leaving only Jake and Cullen in the small clearing. Holding each other's spent and slobbering prongs.

"Damn, Jake. I ain't never gonna ever be this busted again in my whole damn life, man. What did we just do? Abby ain't gonna hear about this… right?" He was worried. Straight men are weird that way.

Of course, had any been present, Jake would have been better able to comment on the oddity…

January, 2006

"Jake, you need to get out more. All you ever do is study, run, or sneak away to that dumpy old theatre on the Drag. It's right next to that loony Scientology church and one of these days, those crazy people are going to kidnap you... I'll wake up some morning and you'll be gone. Boy, think about it. School and that place shouldn't be your whole life." Jake side-angled his closest confidant and fellow med student these past four years. Meeting the very first day, the two had bonded immediately. Abigail got Jake like no one ever had and, likewise, Jake read the girl like a book--- an open-book test, for sure. He knew all her answers.

"Well, Abby, it's top of my list to get through med school and I don't like missing classes--- it wastes money. Maybe if you were paying your own way, you'd be better about showing up, girl... besides I don't have a photographic memory like some people." The mellifluous voice sounded like a Pachelbel melody to Abby. It was what had alerted the girl to the curly-topped kid back at orientation so long before. She cherished its musicality, reminding him more than once he could easily find another profession should need arise. "And, I don't get what you have against the Bijou. It plays all the old classics and hardly anyone goes there. It costs a dollar and I feel like I'm in my own little world."

"Boy, now pay attention to me. Someday soon I am going to drag your ass out to experience some of the world. Pledge week is coming up and Delta Gamma puts on good parties. They network with the Greek men, too. Our big brothers are the Sig Eps. There is a real world, you know, and Jack Nicholson said that 'all work and no play, makes you a dull boy'...or something..." the girly giggle still made Jake smile, even by its memory when she was away. The now twenty-year-old medical student had found his niche here in the heart of Texas, he cogitated, as the two bantered their way down four flights of stairs on the way to the student union.

He missed his benefactors back in Vermont, writing long, old-fashioned, newsy letters regularly. They reciprocated by snail mail, too, keeping him current. But he taught the old couple how to communicate online, as well, contacting them along with his old Spotty dog, back up on Elkin Pond in the Green Mountains of southern Vermont. Chad, Derrick and he shared weekly conversations together. With the new viability of Skype as a mode of visual communiqué, the three rambled on and on from afar. Spotty even seemed to recognize him, yipping comically in compounding the only bouts of homesickness he ever experienced.

The boy's blood family had made contact only once since his departure. On purpose, anyway. There was little love lost, though there was contrition suffered by deserting the family home which his 'real Daddy' had built so many years before in the beautiful forest. With his own two hands. The thought of that loss still brought tears. And with them, perseverance in his little-boy pledge.

Barging through the big doors of the union building, Abby insisted on coffee before parting. The chilly weather was enough to make him agree. He was glad for the ski parka Derrick and Chad had gifted him with for Christmas. The old worn jeans he wore complemented by contrast, though. The threadbare condition of them made his junk shrivel. He loved the pair, holey knees and all, but weather like this demanded more.

Standing in line, awaiting ordered lattes, Abby revisited the subject of Jake's worldliness issue. Insisting he was going to have to break down and join her for at least one mixer common to the spring rush season. She figured by battering Jake with inevitability, he would break. It hadn't worked, to date, but some cracks in the veneer were detectable.

Several of the girl's sorority sisters were forever badgering her to bring him along with her. Having been introduced on occasion to some of them, they had, to a girl, swooned over the boy's beauty. That was the only apt description: handsome didn't cover it, cute was just trite. Beautiful was the adjective even Abby recognized. The wilding of curls topping him framed the whole Cherokee genetics look--- derived from his real Daddy--- in a way that drew people to him. Often to the point of invasive discomfort. So, he hid away, mostly. Coming clean with only Abby, and, recently, his years-long roommate, Cullen.

The two were settling into seats on the side of the big food court to chitchat when a kerfuffle of raised voices and noisy discord filtered down toward them. Someone upstairs shouted a loud comment, "That guy is nuts--- what's in that bag he's got?" In a post 9-11 era, that was all it took for the area to clear. Abby reacted quickly, dragging her boy backwards by the parka into an adjacent women's restroom. Their hot coffees lay abandoned on the table, backpacks alongside them.

From the sanctuary of a big special-needs stall, locked behind them on entry, they sat wondering what the heck was happening. A girl that had rushed in with them seemed to know it all. "There was a huge, tall guy acting crazy out there, rushing all around the walkway, then up and down stairs, pushing people in his way. He was carrying a backpack and acting wacked out. Some people started yelling he was nuts and what'd he have in the pack? That was when all hell broke loose. What if it's a bomb? Or a gun?" She was breathless and nerve-wracked.

The two tried settling her over an ensuing eerie period of a half hour. A person in the next stall madly punched buttons on a phone, apparently contacting everyone in their phone book. Except for the easy number: 911. The person never spoke, only texting, which added to the creepiness.

"Should we get our phone and call 911, do you think, Jake? It's awful quiet out there. We haven't heard any shots. Maybe it would be good to get outdoors." The quiet was affecting them all. Jake reminded that that, in itself, was the best thing they could hear. They stayed hunkered down another stretch of time. Sitting wordlessly. Everything needful had been said. They wanted to know something.

Finally, emerging warily, four hideaways stuck their heads out the door. There was foot traffic. Walkers. And not uniformed. Heartened, Jake and Abby returned to their cool coffees and luckily untouched backpacks. Dumping the drinks, in case of sabotage while they were away, the two searched their packs and made way through normal appearing halls of people to the big main entrance. Scoping out the surrounding plaza, they finally parted, promising follow-up calls to assure each other's safe arrival home.

What was all that weirdness about, Jake ruminated, back in the safety of his room. He wondered who the strange person with such bizarre behavior might have been, informing a sleepy Cullen of the unnerving occurrence.

Crickets provided reply.

"Jake Marshall, so help me, if you go there instead of with me, like you promised, I am going to divorce you, boy!" Abby's mouth pouted as she harangued her closest boyfriend, never mind the one's she dated sporadically. Jake, while not her sexual partner, nevertheless provided a sense of continuity and contentment. While she desired for the both of them to find suitable partners with whom to take on the world, she shared a special bond with the young man that wouldn't ever completely disappear, regardless of love interests.

She deeply wanted the pure-hearted boy to find his soulmate. Knowing his story and the reasoning employed for deciding to enroll at UT Austin, yet not knowing whether such serendipitous metaphysicality or predestination held sway in the real world, she believed he believed in the feeling. So, she held to it with him. And for him. Like a protective mother hen, she conceded that not one suitable candidate had come on the scene in four years since their introduction. Likewise, for herself, she echoed. The difference: she was keeping irons on the fire in anticipation. Jake pursued a veritable hermit's life.

Now, he was threatening to renege on the commitment to join her at the Delta House big brothers' rush mixer. It was always the best one up and down Greek Row, the stately old chapter house providing an excellent venue. The venerable Sigma Phi Epsilon fraternity chapter, one of the few which successfully bridged the social-vs-service chasm, improved the public's perception of the Greek world's worth.

She recognized he was not only fearful to put himself 'out there', he was conspicuously unmotivated to do so. It made no sense, yet he had clung religiously to the anti-social existence. Now, final days of the showing of the classic musical, Funny Girl, at that seedy theater on the Drag looked to be the latest obstacle in Jake's--- and Abby's--- path.

"You gave me your solemn word, Jake, so follow through. It won't hurt you; we'll have fun. Besides, I will give you cover... and protection. No harpies are going to be jumping your bones. Cutie." She drew a smile from him by the tactic. He reluctantly concluded that the Barbra flick could be caught sometime in the coming days before it went off. And relented.

By sundown, the two arrived, arm-in-arm at Sig Ep House. Multiple frat members loitered with sorority girls in the yard and around the grand entryway. All nursed bottles or drinks. Mainly alcoholic. Several Delta sisters met the couple, happy to see them together at a mixer.

Inside, the music hit them first, followed by a sweet odor of pot smoke. Abby navigated them through the cavernous house and winding hallways to the bar. All the while greeting, being greeted, eyeing and being eyed by dozens of college-aged attendees. As agreed, Jake ordered wine. Figuring he could nurse the glass without partying hard.

Jake was fairly overwhelmed by the noise, the smells, the raucousness. The attention. It wasn't his niche. As they awaited the mixologist to deliver the red libations, his eyes were pulled different directions, absorbing a busy room. Everybody seemed exceedingly extroverted. Conversing, joking, dancing, having a good time. Though not as freaked as he'd thought, sensate overload persisted. But not so bad, he decided. This was doable.

He and Abby headed out the back door to the pool and backyard where games with more 'laid back' partying was happening. Less clothing was certainly the norm here, the two noted. Lots of attractive skin wandered. An interesting plus, Jake thought. A blunt passed to Abby and she put it to her lips, quizzically checking Jake's response. She'd never partaken around him and didn't know what to expect. Surprisingly, the boy accepted the smoking ember, inhaling a healthy toke voluntarily. That will make him relax, Abby conceived.

And, it did. Already huge emerald eyes grew larger over the coming minutes. Perusing of the partying people widened; he even sipped the wine. Not bad, the thought was reinforced. As he conversed more easily with a couple of Abby's friendly sisters, they turned to a sudden ruckus breaking out across the pool. Two pretty girls intentionally combined to bump a vocal guy into the deep end. Timbering in lost balance mode, Jake noticed an exceedingly tall black brother, waving arms in helicopter flaps as he hooted his way awkwardly under the water.

The huge splash reached most partiers within twenty feet. Jake and Abby backed up, laughing at the comical antics of the handsome man. Momentary assessment left Jake with an impression of a superbly athletic body. Fully clothed as he entered, it had been difficult to ascertain. But the snap evaluation left the impression of feline agility masked by a clownish affectation meant to entertain.

The clown stayed submerged a minute or so, submarining around the pool, then toward them. Surfacing, he shook, then reversed course, leisurely backstroking in retrograde, continuing the comedy act by spitting pool water in high arcs as he stroked. Bumping the far side, he wrapped arms over the tiled edge for a few moments, surveying the scene.

Hoisting upwards in a single push, another demonstration of athleticism elevated him out and to a standing position in the motion. There, the lean man stood, huge feet planted widely apart. Again, he shook. Boisterously. Looking for the girls who pushed him, he pointed, promising retribution: they were going in, for sure. In the moment of the promise, Jake and Abby watched in surprise as two dozen or so other revelers plunged into the pool. Fully clothed. The man was a trendsetter. The two girls joined them, beating their threatener to the punch.

The next unexpected moves by the sopping wet giant mesmerized Jake. Inhaling another toke passed from Abby, who had taken up conversation with several friends, the curly-headed youth viewed in fascination as the guy began slowly stripping. For effect. Like a pro. The shirt slowly unbuttoned and disappeared, the shoes then the socks were slung away. The undershirt lifted over his head and was flung at someone who didn't seeing it coming.

The revealing act uncovered one of the most ripped bodies Jake had ever seen in real time. It was utterly perfect. Silky dark chocolate skin covered him. Stunningly sculpted pectorals, pointed by luscious-looking erect nipples gave way to an epic set of six rippling abdominal ridges. Not an ounce of body fat covered the honed torso. By the powerful arms--- perfect tricep/bicep groupings--- and the thick, sinewy neck, along with shaved head and attractively apportioned facial features, Jake astutely assessed in anatomically correct detail the breathtaking fineness of the stud.

Dark piercing eyes, broadly flaring nose, strong mouth and square chin chiseled the man's patrician features. He dripped both water droplets and inherent sensuality. Jake had never beheld such a well-put together male. The swarthy complexion only served to intensify the effect. A lone strip of black hair bisected his abdominals. That stripe disappeared under the loose-fitting Bermuda shorts. Exceptionally proportioned thighs, knees and calves narrowed to handsome ankles and the sexiest, wide, two-toned feet Jake had never known existed. He was totally taken by sexy feet. These two immediately topped the list.

Exquisite, the shy med student deduced. He didn't desire to take his eyes away. Apparently, no one else did either. Forcing himself to look around for self-protection purposes--- to avoid obsessing--- he saw every eye in the backyard enclave latched to the slowly disrobing behemoth of a man. 'Magic-Mike-of-color' crossed Jake's mind. He sure knew how to move. Actually, it was more a sultry slink. A black panther couldn't have done it better. And he posed, like a marble statue. The verb coined by Madonna fit: vogue. Mind-blowing in sex appeal, Jake watched him play to the crowd. Totally aware of his own effect.

Jake could feel his junk lurching in inadvertent response, reprising the sex scene on the Town Lake running trail. Damn, he thought. No. Not here. Turning away, he grabbed his girlfriend's arm and pulled her inside with him. The surprised Abby, stoned as she was, followed and listened as Jake described the striptease. As if she'd missed it.

"Do you think I am blind, boii? Everyone watched. I think every woman out there leaked a little during that. And, I'll bet most of the boys had the same reaction as you did. No biggie." This, as she grinned widely at her boy, then glanced purposefully downward at the swollen, zippered shorts. "Oooh, boy... Jake. You liked that! I didn't ever think to see the day anybody could affect you that way. Zing, boy... we found him."

Her stoned state made for giddy effusiveness. She forgot to keep her voice down. Too many other people in like mental states served as cover but Jake nevertheless hustled to untuck his button-down shirt, letting the tails cover his crotch. Couldn't do a thing for his face, though. Abby was totally tickled by the boy's blush response. "Jake is in lust!"

He drew her further into the room with the long bar. Taking the two of them to a far corner allowed time for relief from the inflammation and crotch swell. His wine glass was suddenly empty. Abby continued the ear-to-ear grin as she rehashed the episode. Jake heard next to nothing of her chatter, still mind-bent toward the replaying striptease performance. His hazy mental state gave wide latitude for the indulgence.

In the middle of it, two fresh glasses of something appeared between them: clear fizzy liquid, lemon-rimmed with funky looping straws. They turned to find Abby's friend, Shelley, proffering the highballs. "Ya'll looked thirsty, girl. You shouldn't be letting this handsome man go without, Abby. Drink up." She winked, then pinched Jake's butt, as she disappeared. New redness bloomed. But he was happy. And super light-headed. No more drinks after this one. His internal trigger was signaling.

Abby sidled close, cuddling with him, "You know, Jake, that guy is the big man around Sig Ep House. Name's Cal Something… and he's just back on the scene. Someone said he's just coming out of about a two-year funk after being dumped. By his TWO girlfriends… from France. Doesn't seem like he's suffering much now, does it?"

She made a good point. Jake couldn't picture the supremely confident man ever being jilted, cuckolded, deserted or anything else. He exuded an aura of the-always-in-control person. In any situation. Jake couldn't believe anything else than that truth.

The mind's eye picture couldn't break from repetitive playback of the stud as he stood stripping by the pool. During one freeze-frame second, he looked up and nearly lost it. The man had appeared in the doorway. Cal, did Abby say? Where had he hear that name recently? Cal stood for a long moment, looking inward before strutting toward the bar.

That body was still exposed. But now, the man had lost the obstructing Bermuda's somewhere outside. Present state of reveal left extremely little to anyone's fancy. The handsome lower thighs now curved into superb definition of middle and upper thighs which disappeared under the super brief speedo underwear. A massive mound inside them depicted a sleeping python. Epic proportions of an S-curve lay in fleshy repose. The starkness of the uncut status was unavoidable to the naked eye.

Rising above the upper boundary, fat-free smoothness segued into the 'inny' belly button encompassed by rolling muscle cords. The almost-covered butt curves in back synced with more dark smoothness. Gorgeously proportioned, the tininess of a tight waist broadened to the deeply wide filled-out shoulders and chest--- already evaluated poolside--- of at least a 52-inch circumference.

Upon making a way to the beautifully carved mahogany bar, the man named Cal bounded, cat-like, up on to its surface, assuming the stance of a ship captain surveying a vast sea. All that was lacking was a spyglass. He leaned down to the tapping bartender, accepting a double shot of some dark liquid. Peering over to the DJ in a questioning manner, he ranged upward to full majestic height, tipping back the glass in a fluid one-cock.

Then began an erotic dance of immense coordinative exhibition. It hypnotized the entire room. Doorways were poked full with curious faces, glimpsing the sex appeal appeal rolling off the tall male in waves of erogeneity.

Both sexes present watched the unfolding of the sleeping python as it fed on the attention, burning through the thin nylon/spandex brief briefs. In moments, its burgeoning inside the pocket displayed uncontainable proudness. The stretchy cover served more as an outlining of the thing than a mask. Thankfully, in Jake's perception, everyone was as mesmerized as he. It allowed for full frontal perusal of the virility blasting the room.

Over the next minutes, all melted, at least internally, under the scorching vision. Conversational sounds diminished as overt gawking won out. The sexual lyrics of the hip-hop song accompanied as if written for him. The man clearly basked in the adulation. Shamelessly. Jake was more and more taken by the scene. Glad that he'd decided to come.

Just when that thought gelled, disaster struck. While scanning the crowd, slow deliberation singled out individuals. In a methodical sweep, the man named Cal set those deep dark eyes directly on Jake. They widened as if in recognition. The strength of the gaze left Jake awestruck and he lipped his drink's straw in abrupt mortification. Attempting nonchalance and failing miserably. He blushed like a boiling lobster, the burn rising through even his hair. He couldn't move. Or look away.

The sole cogent thought perfusing the targeted boy's fuzzy mind was that the urbane and sophisticated guy must think him to be the dweeb-out-of-Hell.

Through several minutes, Cal continued the gyrating and fully-sexed onslaught, staying locked on to the big green eyes of the young med student. After an endless period providing painfully self-critical awareness of more and more people following Cal's stare, Jake thought he'd blister to a crisp, leaving only ashes to float out the open window. He felt many eyes turned toward him, but saw only one pair.

The dark eyes never once wavered.

Thankfully, the song finally melded into the next, slower one. Heaving a sigh of relief, Jake thought the worst must be over. He observed the stud nimbly descend from the bar and nearly choked, spewing spiked ginger ale out his nose: still lock-staring, Cal stepped directly toward him, on a collision course.

Multiple hands attempted way-laying him on that path, but to no avail. Within short seconds, the bare-naked male faced Jake up, stopping a solitary inch from nose-to-nose contact. His masculine breath and musky body smell nearly floored Jake.

The drink dropped away from his mouth. Breathing deep of the sweetest male musk imaginable, Jake felt more than saw the man's hand reach over his shoulder, brazenly bracing the wall behind, fingers outstretched against it. A deep armpit halted within a foot of his face. Jake's knees nearly buckled as the whisper into his ear bespoke the totally outlandish pick-up line, "Hey, sexy, come here often?"

With that, the jig was up. Jake, hooked like a one-eyed flounder, frantically flailed for escape, while simultaneously never wanting to leave the man's side. Ever again. The thought broadsided him as he ducked under the arm and toward the far door.

Holding his position, Cal's smile burned Jake's backside in the escape. Abby tucked a folded note into the scant elastic band at his waist on the way after her friend. Flipping it out, he read seven hastily scrawled digits… and a name.

The smile swelled to a toothy grin… Jake's digits.

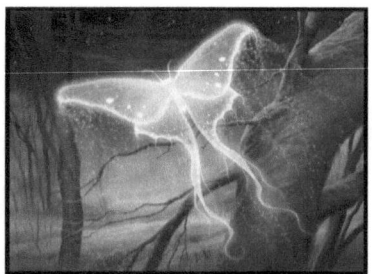

Volume IV: Fallsworth

January, 1991

Rapid-fire staccato bleating battered him back to a reluctant consciousness. Squinting a bleary eye downward, Jeremy took in the vocal band of bearded loudmouths interrupting his reverie. The accompanying goatherd pretended control over the group, yet the helter-skelter progress told a different story. Ensconced in the narrow second-story windowsill overhanging old Odeon Lane, the distraction enabled a wedge of mental distance from ongoing stresses besetting the almost nineteen-year-old high-schooler. Jeremy observed the mini-turmoil play out under his scrutiny in perpetuation of the momentary relief. Silly antics of the Jamaica goats brought a rare smile to the handsome young Maroon. The younger ones attempted scaling every mountable entity and tasting every mouthable organic or inorganic item within reach during their passage below him. Including pedestrians. A couple of the elder caprines espied him, staring directly into Jeremy's smoky grey eyes as if to demand safe transit on the way to their destination. He dutifully suspended desire to pounce on the tribe by the remonstrance, sustaining that faint smile. The boy/man held cumulative effects of school, church, in-laws, love-life and now, impending paternal pressure at bay in this manner. That is, until the sounds of rustling arose from his affianced, Aayla. Awakening from the blessed respite provided by her afternoon nap. Turning away from the window, he bent inward for the purpose of helping her to the water closet. Her nausea, though abated in its alarming intensity of the previous three months, persisted. The effect beleaguered the couple: she in the emetics and he in the hygienic follow-up. The two were nearing exhaustion. Thank goodness, she was experiencing a small bit of reprieve upon entering the third trimester state of things. Coming onset of his upper sixth form level--- the thirteenth grade--- at the esteemed Jamaica College for Boys would require every bit of available attention. Even though Jeremy had exhibited a capable adeptness at acquiring knowledge, it didn't come as easily as was true for some of his classmates. Vital concentration and focus remained paramount. He didn't intend the generosity of his mentor and sponsor to be squandered. Enrollment and underwriting were that man's doing. Making a baby at the untested age of eighteen was Jeremy's doing and it created challenges he had not contemplated. Ones which not many teenage boys ever thought about before enjoying the act. He certainly had not. Heretofore, the idea of a breeding role had been a foreign concept. Living up on Blue Mountain, in Hagley Gap, under tutelage of the farmer/iconic reggae singer, Ambergai Gee IV, his place had been much different than this new reality. The irony which the situation posed was not lost on the boy. While a pleasant alternative method for orgasmic release, it nevertheless created ramifications unplanned prior to and during the process. The impregnability factor with Ambergai, in contrast to his newly assumed station in the sex act, had waylaid any preemptory ambitions. The alien concept of birth control measures could have been helpful should the options ever been understood. His parents would never have considered such an anti-religious intervention nor had sex education been taught in the one-room school on Blue Mountain. Aayla's parents were none too pleased at the prospect of grandparenthood in their mid-thirties. In addition, Father Manley's position at Our Lady of the Angels Roman Catholic Church added burden to the domino event. One of only a handful of married priests on the island of Jamaica, he and Mama Manley felt put upon that their only daughter would take up living sinfully such as she and Jeremy had chosen to do. By getting pregnant they had doubled the sin. Never mind the parents' own sinfulness: breaking a millennium of precedent for celibacy in the priesthood. Jeremy couldn't quite comprehend the level of duplicity expressed by their take on the present situation as he recalled the list of seven deadly sins. Who the hell had ever dreamt up those silly things, anyway? That conundrum in mind, he dutifully aided and abetted by helpful ministrations over succeeding minutes, wistfully absorbing innocent cacophony out the open window as the band of free-spirited ungulates frolicked past. Substantial feelings for the girl in his life--- and currently, his arms--- did not rise to a level of deep love, though the affection he bore her was considerable. Having been born into an atmosphere of indifference by merit of ranking tenth of thirteen in his own careless parents' scheme, he did not mean to enter the pact of parenthood lightly. That which his role had wrought weighed heavily. After all, fathering of a life had occurred here. A promise had been made. In coming hours, Jeremy found plenty of time to think. Nursing and housekeeping processes channeled him deep into the past by the mulling. The Caribbean sun arced significantly through a flood of memories in reliving the serpentine road travelled to present moments. As waning sounds of bleating disappeared, the teenager reminisced on a more languidly innocent period during which he served in the post of goatherd himself. For Ambergai Gee's tribe. The rapscallions had led him on many a wild goose chase over several years spent perfecting the art of thinking himself in charge of the beasts. Memories of levity imparted by the amusing animals entertained him through dinner preparations and after. Aayla was of little help and no conversational good. By things as they stood, he was alone as de facto caretaker. She played the part of mute patient. Graduation from the excellent institution subsidized by Ambergai ranked high on a list of objectives. Studies for the coming weeks and months would need be executed only when she was safely dreaming. Though Jeremy was in position and on timeline for goal achievement, nothing was yet secured. And so, between responsibilities to Aayla, child and future, he rarely found a wrinkle of freedom to travel to that simpler time…

April, 1982

...Trudging the winding mountain trail with procured staples for Madda, Jeremy tripped on an exposed root, unseen due to the bankra sandwiching him front and back. Normally worn by the family jack, he presently assumed it's bulk. The lame pack animal had been left home to heal, wearing a poultice strapped to a swollen hock by him and Shernard earlier that morning. The entire load, from bulla and dukunu to janga and new marinas for Dada all tumbled groundward in a strewn mess. The ten-year-old was cross. And, he had stubbed his toe, to boot.

Sitting in misery for a few seconds, he assessed the rottenness of his lot, rubbing the bent toe in forlorn self-pity. The janga lay thrown from its iced bag, precious seafood delicacies wallowing in the dusty trail... Madda would be mad. Brightly dyed marinas were mussed by smashed dukunu--- spicy cornmeal dumplings--- and a few tears appeared as he contemplated the trouble. After several moments, he heaved on to knees, hurrying tardily to salvage what he was able. The throbbing toe hurt.

While righting the bundles, and repositioning bankra baskets, he perceived a low ululation of muddled words from up ahead, around a bend in the trail. The faint keening set off a prickling of his skin by its soulful lament. Skittering to close-by underbrush at the edge of the trail, he crouched, listening. Maybe it wasn't such a bad thing that the baskets had tumped over, it occurred to him. The double-sided hanging contraption was pulled back off and a silent creep through thick bushes brought him closer to the source.

There, in the middle of the path, squatted a small, dark old man. Bushy black hair curled unevenly around his skeletal head. An emaciated frame and bony limbs were covered by grossly oozing yaws, accentuating the being's strangeness, but what the fellow was doing served to put Jeremy's nerves to jangling.

In the dirt lay a little pile of sticks, feathers and egg shells. As he watched, the man placed a length of twine on top, scrolling it down over the pile in a spiral. The discordant throaty accompaniment undulated in accordance with actions, crescendos and decrescendos weirdly narrative. With a sudden expletive, a hawking and spitting punctuated the 'ceremony'. Viscous yellowish phlegm penetrated the string and pile.

Deliberately, the Obeah Man--- for that was surely what he was, Jeremy surmised--- reached for the pile, gathering the contents into his palm. To a cadence of odd tongue-cluckings, the magic-maker carefully tied the sticky clump in encircling wraps of the twine. Secured and compacted, he stood up straight and cackled. Finished.

Surprising Jeremy further, bushes next to the little ogre rustled in parting and a woman emerged. Jeremy gulped in recognition. The natty dreadlocked female approached the conjurer, proffering a gold coin in an open palm. The two traded possessions as the boy shivered in sudden trepidation. He listened as the diminutive man warned her to disallow any moisture--- even sweat from her body--- from contacting the 'talisman', else the thing's power would dissolve. It should be used by sundown of the third day to avoid its expiration.

With that, each slapped the other's free hand and the two split, heading into deepness of the woods. Opposite directions. Waiting for several minutes to collect frayed wits, Jeremy retraced his trail back to the bankra. Loading up, he fairly raced up a now deserted trail, jumping over the site where the strange scene had just unfolded.

"Kwame, 'twas scareful! Mi din't wanna eben touch any o' da dirt der. Da Devil's a'loose." Jeremy described the scenario in the dirt-floored kitchen of their home. The brothers unpacked bankra baskets as they discussed what he had just witnessed. Identity of the purchaser caused both to trade looks of intense apprehension. All residents of Hagley Gap knew of the buyer's reputation. Her respected husband was another story entirely and added dimension to the brothers' discussion.

To disseminate the news would mean a spike in the community's anxiety level. The brothers weighed their options by that knowledge. In the end, Jeremy's older bredda, Kwame, the Saturday son, decided it best to squelch the information. The two were fearful of reprisals should their awareness be discovered.

"Besides," Kwame added, "dat gorgon grindsman be puttin' da hurt to dat glamity cat--- she be da looka, fo sho. Wit his hortical hood, don' ya know da natty dreads o' da two o' 'em be doin da tanglin' durin dat bumpin an' grindin, huh?" His toothy grin betokened understanding beyond his twelve years in regards to the sex act, yet the allusion impressed his little bredda. Jeremy pictured the longjohn in all the footlong glory that the man's reputation alleged... and felt his baby junk jump at a mental image. Whaddat, he thought?

Madda was only a little mad at the cleaned goods upon her arrival, the washing of the stuffs erasing most of the noticeable damage. She questioned her ten-year-old son closely about the trip, having gotten wind, somehow, of unusual going's on down in Hagley Gap. Before he could squelch it, the picky-headed youth let slip about the odd man he thought might have been an Obeah Man on home trail. Thankfully, the whole story didn't come out and Madda assumed the confessed accident with the bankra must've resulted from startlement.

Fixing her son with a peculiar look, she imparted information which he would remember: it could not have been an Obeah, since those ones only show up in nighttime. If anything, he learned, it must've been a Myalist. The do-gooders. Ahh, thought the boy, that made sense. That must mean the talisman was meant for a positive purpose. It settled the boy's mind and nerves.

After supper, Jeremy slipped out the back door to check on Cudjoe. The lovable jack worried him and he held hope to see a betterment of the swollen joint. The byre door where the ass stayed stood ajar, allowing a low whistle of breeze to overblow the confined space. He found the big-eared beast contentedly munching inside, glad to be off work for a day.

A change of poultice and bandage did indeed reveal lessening in the hotness. Another couple of days should see a return to normal. Relief suffused the silent time spent carefully repacking the first aid materials. After brushing the fuzzy animal, he headed back toward the door for the house but was pulled up short by a soft cry of exclamation harmonizing with the persistent whining wind draft. The sound wafted down from above.

The ladder leading to a hayloft took him to a peeking glimpse over the edge into a padded area holding extra bales. The view unveiled his older brother, Shernard, gripping a pair of round mounds arched before him. Another cry of delight escaped pursed lips of a naked girl backing up to the teenager, pulsing back on the hardened piece of equipment presently impaling her. Noticeably bare and glistening. Jeremy was mesmerized. Having never witnessed sex firsthand, he couldn't look away. Instead, the boy sidled further up to gain better angle of his brother plowing the curving crevice in an excess of enthusiasm.

Plainly enjoying the conjoinment, she pushed robustly back into Shernard with each thrust. On her knees and faced away, the girl couldn't see a new audience poking up over the threshold. But Shernard did. Almost immediately his attention was pulled toward the spiky hair of his little brother. Waving one hand in disgust for the intrusion, he nevertheless continued rhythm, plowing ahead in quest of the desired nut.

The power of the opposing rutters must have been forceful because just as the boy's head began tipping up and back in detection of a peaking eruption, a cracking split of floor boards sounded under them.

Shernard's knee sank through and downward as his rigid prick was yanked prematurely loose from its warm confines. Cries of delight mangled into ones of disrupted frustration upon losing the orgasmic crest. Both writhed in awkward attempts at regaining lost purchase on the disappearing floor holding them. As they sank, plummeting into the jack's stall below, Jeremy noted two things. The freely rollicking rigid shaft began spewing copious globs of spoiled cream, arcs of jism grabbing a freeze-frame moment in virgin eyes. Too, he registered a look of loathing framed in Shernard's features, clearly heaping blame for the climactic misfortune directly on to his little brother's shoulders.

Cudjoe was not pleased to be dropped in on.

July, 1982

Muck sucked his toes deeper into the miasma with each step. Steam, feces and brimstone suffused his nostrils. Xaviera forged fearlessly ahead, her own little feet sinking steadily, heedless of the effect. Intent on a goal.

"Xavi. Wah yuh ah duh? Yuh gwine dweet? Dis could be dangerous gyal." Though youthfully fearless like his older sista, Jeremy did not feel good about this present scenario. Allure of a possible motherload of fecund bat guano in this secluded cave drew the ten-year-old as much as it did his fourteen-year-old compatriot, yet developing impediments were provoking bad vibes by simple instinctive perceptivity.

Just as he reached ahead to pull her arm in physical objection, the mud floor melted beneath bare feet. She grabbed the boy's stretching arm by reaction; both capsized in ungainly surfeit of flailing limbs. Glugging thick stinking mud over the next seconds, thoughts of drowning in the nasty stuff tardily entered two naïve minds.

As realization dawned, sliding began. On a gradual downward slope into the murk of the dank grotto, slipperiness combined with earth's gravity to pull the duo into a headlong, banging rush toward oblivion. Jeremy grasped tightly to his sista's arm--- and she his--- in attempt to hang onto at least one familiar thing.

With forearms locked, both children cascaded in an awkward dance of footless steps for a seemingly endless time, swooshing around rocky corners, bumping past extruding roots and ancient jutting boulders. Harsh in unforgiving severity. The boy reflected belatedly on his sorrow for delving the cleft of the hidden cave, drawn by mystery and odor. Supposed value of the malodorous cache had been just too magnetic.

After countless seconds, sounds of rushing water pervaded plugged ears. Still connected, yet isolated and detached from any cogent reality, a sudden stomach-twirling somersault sent them in arachnidan descent, eight limbs reaching, then kerplunk, into a cold black realm of swirling liquid. The coupled connection persisted, nonetheless. The two refused to be separated, now inexorably swept along in discombobulated incoherence toward further unknown.

Little could the children know of the history of the limestone labyrinth into which they had been sucked. Being but mere specks in the space-time continuum, they held no perspective.

Millions upon millions of years before, subterranean floors of today's Caribbean Sea had been raised by a succession of immense volcanic eruptions, spreading over thousands of square miles. The cataclysm took millions more years to achieve a state of balance. When that was finally reached, a vestigial island protruded above water.

Over ensuing eons, mineral-rich water run-off caused layered coatings of limestone to be laid down. A system of limestone mazes developed as surface water ate into porous limestone which it had birthed, basing the island. Continuing flows delved river beds through valleys of solidified magma, as well as channels deep underground. Millions of years passed. Primordial flora and fauna populated the land, making and using new organic matter, depositing it on and in an adopted limestone home.

Through a period of millennia, tumultuous climate change cycles resulted in warming of the planet. Polar ice caps melted. Water levels around the world rose hundreds of feet, leading to a re-submersion of the island with all its tortuous mazes. Salt water feasted upon a limestone labyrinth, eating out larger and larger swaths of soft stone. Cave networks resulted.

Then, cataclysm struck once again. A new volley of volcanic activity was set into motion deep in the earth's core. Molten magma blew holes through the earth's crust, savaging the area now called the Greater Antilles. Smoke and condensate of unimaginable magnitude blocked the sun, cooling Earth, setting an age of ice into motion. Magma settled and solidified in raised layers.

As polar surface ice built up, ocean levels dropped worldwide. Land emerged again. Large, crescentic rings and semicircles of jagged, solidified magma ranges appeared, interconnected in whorls, shaped by ocean currents. With passage of more time, the atmosphere settled, clearing. Earth warmed; balance returned. Water levels reclaimed some of the land, leaving island systems that presently reside in the Caribbean basin. Jamaica's central land mass remained raised by jagged, solidified magma layers. Basalt. Spine of the Blue Mountains. Rising over seven thousand feet above sea level, the fall off was sheered by prevailing winds and crashing waves, making for the steepest and sharpest rise of any coastal mountain range in the world. And black, basalt-based southern beaches by merit of erosion.

Through all that, flowing water layered more limestone coverage on top of the new volcanic rock. It shaped and reshaped into additional intricate systems of limestone webs. Parts of the waterways traveled the surface but much still drained through underground tunnels. These deposited fresh waters into tarns, lagoons and mountain valley lakes, or emptied into the Caribbean Sea.

Gradual repopulation by decimated species, and new prevailing weather systems allowed for ecosystems to develop. An organic island blossomed into modern tropical environs rife with watery, webbing warrens. It was into one of these marinating cisterns that the youths had stumbled.

Periodically piercing a surface in the growing gush of torrent, Jeremy sputtered to suck breath through the gluey layer of still-clinging muck inside mouth and nostrils. He hoped Xavi could do the same. At least her hand was not gripping any less tenaciously. He took succor in the small boon and allowed traverse--- as if there were another choice--- onward to a presumption of Hades. Where else could the dissociative course take them, he cumulated?

Touching nothing besides one another's limb, immersed in the cooling soup as they were, no sense of space, time or proprioception permitted mindful purchase. He niggled one finger against his sista's skin, receiving a reply in same. All-consuming wet sloshing his mouth had lost the previous warm sulfurous tinge, now sublimely steely against taste buds. Pure. And turning colder, after the surface steam the two had encountered while still mud-bound. The difference gave him pause, making him wonder where in the world they had been transported. Not to mention, where were they headed?

That thought materialized in his disoriented young brain just as another sense of difference hit him. The surround of sound, so alliteratively permeating until then, took on a deeper rumble in not only tenor, but substance, too. Gradually, an impression of proximal borders shaped existentially and he felt as if a chute of cylindrical tangency now enshrouded them in fluidity of motion. Sure enough, his foot scraped lightly against rock-like smoothness. The same must have happened to Xavi: she repeated the fingering niggle in a frantic signal.

Lacking forewarning, but for the rumble, an abrupt tumble over a subterranean waterfall projected the pair into dark air followed by a cold plunge into bottomless black water. Their interlocking nearly failed them then, but Jeremy clung desperately, barely maintaining contact.

Through another insensible passage of time bobbing and floating, the two now noticed other changes. The fluctuation to cold nuanced to gradual warming again, affording assuagement for numb appendages and torsos. Impenetrable blackness seemed a little less dense.

While still completely dark, the thickness diminished. Rumbling undertones abated to nascence; discernible ripples, burbles and whooshes symphonized progressively into a veritable orchestra. The sweeping current slackened and roiling of their conjoined bodies smoothed into more graceful twirls and trundles, pulling in disparate directions. The effect gave plant to a return of proprioceptive focus.

Time reshaped in their barraged brains. Warmth now whelmed them in therapeutic envelopment. They could feel the current slowing, evening out. Returning tactility enabled a drawing together in clasping embrace.

The luxury of bodily support reassured the two. Maybe, they hoped, they would not end up in the bowels of Hell after all.

Xavi's matching grey eyes peered blurrily into her brother's. Her face, though indistinct through refraction by dimly penetrating arcs of light, was indeed hers. It appeared whole and unmarked by damage. She smiled at him and surfaced to gasp another breath. Jeremy followed suit. The sweetness of new air bathed the pair. Movement into tepid waters gained languor.

Embroiled in tumult during the trip through the underground waterway as they had been, liberation proved a balm to their senses. They gleaned new environs. Such was their sense of relief, the siblings did not want to take eyes from one another, but bombardment by sensate stimuli forced the issue.

They first noticed the serene blueness of the girdling water. Its intense clarity depicted bubbles arising out of the deepness. The vacuous things tickled hypersensitive skin, causing a rapturous effect. Both had lost clothing somewhere along the subterranean trip, triggering velvety extravagance in their mutual caress. An azure sky stretched above them, etched by spider webs of intertwining tree branches which wavered in the soft breeze tippling exposed patches of body.

They had survived.

Smell of wood smoke perfumed the air in bucolic scents of blue mahoe, soapwood and juniper. All familiar. Renewed visual acuity rambled in a merry-go-round of awe at the plethora of forest denizens, from hibiscus and breadfruit trees to soapwood covered by clinging epiphytes. Old Man's Beard lichen, climbing bamboo, wild orchids and bromeliads bearing brightly colored complex blooms adorned tall, branching trunks.

Amongst this backdrop, the survivors observed enormous black and gold swallowtail butterflies flutter with birds both larger and smaller than them. Antillean grackles, varied warblers, green by yellow Jamaican todys and robin redbreasts flitted from plant to tree with native cling-clings, ruby-throated solitaires and multi-hued mountain witches. The ground was rife with animal life. A great many frogs and coneys hopped and skittered. Curling up the trunk of a breadfruit tree coiled a six-foot-long reticulated boa, it's throat fattened by recently swallowed prey.

Absorbing the extraordinary scene caused newly cleared airways to suck air by the breadth of so much acute abundance. In a small lagoon-side clearing, Xavi noted the flickering tail of a larger animal. Its legs, body and head remained obscured by thick tree boles behind which it stood. Pointing it to her brother's attention, Jeremy examined the funny appendage. By perusal, he next picked out at least two dozen more, lending smiling stimulus to a scene of flag-waving furriness with wiggly proclivities.

Finally, one body attached to a creamy flagger rustled through the cover of wide trunks, thick with ground growth of wild roses and pink-blooming Hot Lips. It wandered out onto a brilliant green mixture of ground mosses, revealing a svelte bearded Jamaican billy goat.

The silly grazer caught sight of the swimmers, astute as the beasts tended to be, fixing a stare of caprine tenacity upon them. He stood calmly munching tender shoots of fiddlehead in survey. Jeremy and Xaviera were fit to be tied at the humorous antics bespoken by its funny face. They tittered together, treading the crystalline pool into which they had been so inelegantly dumped.

Then, something happened which was to remain stamped in the young Maroon's mind for the entirety of his remaining days.

From around the base of one humongous breadfruit tree, ringed by a thick clump of tree ferns, emerged a tall lithe figure. Obviously just awakening, the individual stretched, panther-like, bending a trim torso back-and-forth atop a gyrating pelvis which balanced upon long, rangy legs. Hairless ebony skin sheened in satiny smoothness over the whole body. Raising sinewy arms up and overhead, the creature slowly waved widely spread fingers in a willowy expression of woodland faun dexterity.

The astoundingly well-put-together man--- for that was indeed what he embodied--- stood, statuesque, in belief of aloneness. Of all the attributes provoking prickles around Jeremy's frame, none stirred him so much as the magnificent garland of onyx coils sprouting from his head. More than two-feet in length, the stuff crowned the maleness in a billow of majesty, bushing outward in a sphere of kinky blackness. Never had either sibling beheld such a head of hair. Shiny lustre of the mass rivaled the greatest mane ever endowed to an African Lion. Truly regal, the whole picture sent goose-pimples ricocheting over the ten-year-old boy in a whole-body shiver.

The Rasta Mon continued an unassuming lassitude of sleep stirrings, oblivious to intruding eyes. In the doing, he visually accounted for his wards: the bearded group. Jeremy found himself in utter thrall. He barely breathed during a measured scrutiny of the noble bearing of the being less than a hundred feet distant.

Mental notes were uploading in pixelating memorization, from the plank-like two-toned big-toed feet, up the long legs from tapered ankles to rounded calves and sculpted thighs, over creamy hemp shorts barely corralling a curving cousin to the tree boa just spotted, thickness of girth plainly outlined. The protuberance wobbled under woven cloth, alive and bobbing of its own accord. An upper edge of low-riding material juxtaposed against ebony sprigs of visible thatch, which then ushered into a set of rock-ribbed abdominal muscles, rippling an upward track to perfectly curved pectorals, topped by areolae of startling pointedness.

Without warning, Xavi volubly giggled her presence. The trill of delight at the sight of amusing goats and this seven-foot Ashanti scion hovered momentarily over the smooth water surface, thence carried around the tree-enshrouded lagoon, boomeranging back to the man's ears more than one time.

It brought immediate attention from the giant who laser-zoomed in precision accuracy to the duo of heads peeking from the middle of the blue pool. Dark, piercing eyes squinted in recognition of fellow humans. He tensed, suddenly wary.

Snapping long finger on thumb, then issuing a series of clipped monosyllabic signals, he ordered the goats. Unlike most wildings that were any breed of goat, these fell in, to almost military formation. Accepting of the man as leader and accustomed to his orders, the tribe was acutely attuned to mood. They all stood now, at alert, facing the direction they saw him looking. And stared. As one. Even the tails were still.

"Wo a de two of yuh an wah mek yuh ah stalking wi?" The sotto voice upbraided the water treaders, not liking the surprise. On the island that was Jamaica, goats were highly prized and valued. Much goat-rustling went on, mainly in lowlands closer to the coast, to be sure, but all goat owners were on guard night and day for underhanded methods employed by kidnappers of the animals. Goats' young were referred to as 'kids', and thievery often occurred during sleep or unguarded moments. Hence the origin of the term: kidnapping. The perceived threat arising from the depths of the lagoon was a sober one. The giant guardian was not a personage with whom to trifle.

The siblings froze. Suddenly, the two saw not the remarkable Koromantyn warrior of a man, but rather a glaring Sasabonsam. An extremely tall, hairy forest monster from lore of the warlike Ashanti. Husband of Srahman. Scary descriptions for straying children portrayed a fiend with feet pointing both ways who ate any travelers he could capture with those feet when they passed under the fearsome freak's preferred Ceiba tree residence... the great silk-cotton tree. Jeremy quickly combed the shore for any sign of the gossamer strands common to that broadleaf species. A shiver of trepidation enveloped him.

Upping their consternation, the towering figure took ten long strides to lagoon edge, brushing past the motionless tribe, then proceeded to... walk... thirty more feet into the water before evidence appeared that his feet were not touching the sandy bottom. The lower penumbra of the billowing headdress sank below the surface, trailing in Medusa-esque fashion, dozens of snaking locks sproiling viper-like as he closed the gap.

At a certain moment, the two youths transformed into what they truly were. The edges of a wide mouth marked by generously full lips curled in mirth at the assessment. Clarity of the water in which the trio were floating allowed for further visual accounting. It served to mesh reality with intimations. These floating bobbers, ornamented only by muddy polyps dangling from hair, earlobes and eyelashes, were simply waifs of happenstance. Not threats. The brilliance of a set of perfect teeth dawned next, bathing the daunted duo in reflection.

"Just wat might be dem yah two likle ones be doing here inna dis deep blue lagoon wid mi?" The melodious flow, in contrast to previous brusqueness, reassured the 'likle' ones of reversion from fearsome

Sasabonsam back to remarkable Koromantyn. They sensed benevolence. Correctly.

Urging them beachward, the man arose from the blueness, tailed by enthralled youths. Rising again to full height, he shook with gusto, then shepherded the two a short way from the lagoon. Through a short walk up a curving forest path the three came to a cozy clearing centered by a rock-ringed fire pit. Smoking embers and coals sent wavering tendrils of heat emanating upwards, slow-cooking four spitted coneys.

The savory smell of the rabbit bombarded brother and sister with an unrecognized famishment. "Mi can tell dat yuh a hungry. Will yuh share wid mi?" The wide smile garnered trust. Over the ensuing half hour, the three chewed and conversed. Succulence of the roasted flesh along with breadfruit, cassava bammy and fresh kallaloo served to restore youthful vigor.

Following belly-filling, the tall goatherd pulled out a horsehair brush and began thoughtfully combing through coiled locks of kinked hair, repairing fullness to the radiating crown. "Fi mi name ah Ambergai Gee. De fourth inna line of fi mi name. Welcum to fi mi fiyah, now, young ones. An, just wo might yuh two be?"

The man's ease of nature in his own skin disarmed the boy and girl; they introduced themselves and described the oddness through which they came to be there. Mr. Ambergai's eyes grew large in the telling, amazed that the two found a way through such an ordeal unscathed. "De mi deem yuh both very lucky to be here sharing, dat being de case…"

The brush went next through the mud-crusted hair of the two, meticulously patient in combing from the tips inward. They permitted the familiarity. As highlanders were prone, all three warmed to one another, age differences notwithstanding. Pulling each to lean on him between long legs, both were coiffed to puffed perfection in similarity with his own drawn-out style. By the end of a lazy afternoon, the three enjoyed camaraderie like old friends. The tribe of bearded goats waggled and grazed in communal proximity, accepting the newcomers now that He had.

Sylvan benignity settled around the engrossed trio. Come evening, wood was gathered for a twilight repast of re-heated leftovers. Invitation to remain for the night around the fire of the Rasta Mon was welcomed. Producing a highland lute led to an evening of serenade by mento, calypso and reggae tunes, the two lyricizing with the avid musician in those ones familiar. After, a reverie was spent in wordless watch of crackling flames beneath the startling luminescence of a mountainous Milky Way. Humans and beasts reposed, intermingling in restful rejuvenation.

The following morning found entwinement of limbs and ease of companionship which cemented a friendship derived under unusual circumstances. Ambergai Gee, the don gorgon, carefully braided his long locks into the plaited dreads normally worn amongst other people, apprising the two of need to be on his way home with wards over whom he watched.

Xavi's girlish crush was on full display throughout morning breakfast fire, yet the suppressed attraction of the youth proved stronger. It was Jeremy who broadened the situation, showing interest toward the trip of goats. A proffer to tutor in arts of goat husbandry ensued, drawing a vocal 'Ick" from Xavi. Attending the man with the goats on a return trip toward the Rastafarian's eyrie at the peak of Blue Mountain took siblings along paths previously untrodden. They wondered how to find their own way home.

"Yuh seh fi yuh home ah above Hagley Gap, eh?" Remembering previous dialogue, instructions for their journey were conveyed, lost as the two were due to manner of entry into the hidden lagoon.

The children only reluctantly took leave of the towering personality at a fork in the trail, fast friends now with the one married to the tall dreadlocked woman known as Starleen. A sharp onset of goosebumps pulsed Jeremy upon verifying the man's reputed relationship to the mysterious woman known all over Blue Mountain as the 'witch oman'. The same one who had traded for a talisman conjured by a buguyaga Myalist on home trail weeks before…

On this new trail home, boy and girl sifted over the definitive prelude in silence, wrapped in private ruminations. Each contemplated the tangled webs weaved on the Trail of Life. The vibe set by Providence imparted import to inklings of destiny.

MAY, 1984

Puking into the rushing water, he scrubbed nappy hair spikes. 'Twas a futile effort to rid the noxious odor, yet there was no alternative. No soapwood root was handy. Jeremy remained totally grossed-out by the event just suffered. Love for the creatures provided the sole reason for not plotting caprine murder as he washed. "De damn tings!"

A dozen goats, various ages of the female sex, surrounded him--- their pseudo-guardian--- waggling chins snickering and sneering in derisive scorn. How dare the pre-teen imposter attempt replacement of the true head of them? Ambergai Gee was not present, they knew, to tell otherwise. Hence, the insult.

As he flushed and scoured beneath the cascade of the brook, the onlookers pretended sympathy--- even empathy--- but the young goatherd knew different. That was the way these beasts were. Two-faced hypocrites.

Ten minutes earlier, Jeremy had sat basking against the trunk of the great ceiba tree. Daydreaming. Always the same one. The dream persevered in his mind's enthralled infatuation, never yielding itself. Perpetuation came regardless of preference. An untenable fantasy, Jeremy Kell was strictly aware that the recurring theme would always remain right where it was: the Neverland of his subconscious.

Possibility of actualization was not only impossible, it was ridiculous… Jamaican culture allowed for no deviance from the set norm. He knew that for a solid fact. No amount of daydreaming would alter that.

Yet the illusion never paled. So, he had leaned, in luxuriant sweat, hard with enjoyment of the regularly relived virtuality. He knew the goats were aware, too. It was the primary reason they detested him. Conveying the fact in every action, every reaction, every nuance, with regard to their relationship.

Lead-up to this scenario had opened in humorous manner. Two bucks and a hopeful buckling had shimmied up the tree after watching a doeling do so. She was tribe acrobat, Jeremy could attest. The common scaling accomplished by the young female since an age of two months was a feat none of the others could hope to achieve. Though, not for lack of trying. Mature males would routinely fail following her up steep trunks and high arched branches. Today had proved an exception.

An especially attractive kid of tri-color calico coat, she had always displayed a will for three-dimensionality. Noticing low-hanging branches while others grazed. From the outset, failure was rarely a result of her goal-oriented climbing. And, over time, the kid's challenges had only increased in difficulty.

This morning, after grazing dutifully like a normal goat, Adelaide--- the name with which Ambergai had 'christened' her at birth--- entered into a search of multiple trees over nearly an hour. Jeremy observed her appraisal with typical interest. Goats' emotions were quite transparent. He watched her sizing up various possibilities, beginning with the impossible: huge smooth boles with no indentions and no branches lower than ten feet above ground; then on to slightly less challenging trickiness; down the line until finally, this day, she surprised no one by choosing the trunk against which Jeremy rested.

The lowest spreading branch erupted only two feet above root flare, an unusually low bar for the gymnast. He had smiled at her overtness. Even Jeremy knew of the doeling's blossoming estrous cycle. The inaugural one.

Males had previously marked tree trunks all around the grazing area by butting and rubbing with their coarse-haired heads. The method by which all bucks motivated 'their' does to submit. Pheromone release from tactile cranial hairs began in early days of 'Spring', spiking in production by vehement stimulation of hair roots.

Spring was a misnomer on all tropical Caribbean islands of the Greater Antilles, as seasons were not marked by that nomenclature. Rather, jet-stream alterations set into motion cycles commonly referred to as seasons by northern standards.

Adelaide had been a late-season kid: her heat cycle had been tardy. Now, she was producing estrogen, and the bucks--- along with everyone else--- knew it. Therefore, ultimate choice of an easily scaled tree had been a given. Even a novice like Jeremy had guessed.

When the soon-to-be-ex-doeling jumped--- no scaling needed--- onto the low horizontal branch, he smiled knowingly. Sure enough, within minutes two horny bucks and one pipe-dreaming buckling had followed. Thinking to trap her on the wide branch and force 'the nasty' right there in the open for all to see. At first, Jeremy found the entire charade hilarious. Viewing 'foreplay', such as it was, the balance beam artists danced the virgin two-step from one end of the broad branch and back. Multiple times.

He rooted for the hormonal males. Always horndogs, their junk dangled provocatively, turgid and bouncing, attempting to impress the female they were chasing. But, with three suitors vying for Adelaide's tail, the drawn-out chess match became boring after a half hour. The twelve-year-old wearied of nuanced antics between competing suitors and drowsed.

Leaning lazily against the trunk, he channeled caprine sexual innuendoes toward that which he preferred, stoking personal misapprehensions. Letting his adolescent brain wander, the nubile organ led the boy toward a caprice for which he had harbored secret aspirations over almost two years. Propped between conscious and subconscious planes, Jeremy descended to that focus permitted only under such circumstances. In a private universe of the mind's eye.

It told a detailed story. The familiarity of which he realized could never ascend to any other level. It would have to suffice. He sank in tranquil carousal as two heads trajected inward to extant sequestration. Where impossibility lay achievable.

During the untimed interlude, soft sunlight dappled bare skin in tinted spangling, meshing the two worlds straddled while conceiving the newest in a mindful tale of many chapters. Heated delusions peppered a wildly nomadic imagination which had already covered miles and miles of psychological turf through evolving attainment of the unattainable. Thwarting obviation.

Indeed, this day, semi-consciousness expanded the sphere of validity to one which not only spanned multiple strata, it intensified the crest by a maturing adolescent hormonal presence. Though Jeremy knew nothing of such intricacies. He felt only the explosion signaling authenticity.

In the tumult of adolescent peaking, demarcations between reality and surreal feat blended: Jeremy experienced an emissive delusion which drenched his head, neck and shoulders. Such bounteous declaration proved the targeted end sought by the investment. The fruits of his illusioned labors.

Throes of repletion gradually dwindled through an elevation to consciousness. Complemented by the real manifestation, of course. As desired. Just never to this degree, he basked. Spasming to eye-opening satiation, Jeremy knew ecstatic success.

Reaching lucidity, initial feelings were of fruition. Second ones were those deducing robust ammoniac malodor. Looking up, he was hit with final squirts from Adelaide on a higher branch. She stood hunched, in her own throes of copulative consummation, punctuated by sympathetic micturitive reflex.

She had pissed him. Copiously…

…So, there he bent, directly under a gush of mountain spring waters, in vain attempt at cleansing the communal share of orgasmic after-affects. As he had already concluded: gross. The upside: his illusion had culminated in simultaneous eruptions for both him and the fantasy partner. He washed his own jismic expression off with the noxious goat piss, allowing a tiny bit of satisfaction at reprising the dream scheme through endorphin suffusion. Again, not an understood mechanism; only a metaphysical bridge.

After harvesting as much restoration as possible by pure water flush, Jeremy finally sat back, basing himself at a different tree following the foul deluge. From there, he watched the goats in their post-coital jig. While the unlucky buck and buckling retreated in resigned disgust, the lucky buck, Billy, who had crashed the proverbial jade gates, descended the tree in rasping fulfilment.

Pretty Adelaide followed, reveling in newfound 'womanhood'. She wandered the meadow in search of just the right spot. Upon its pinpointing, the new doe--- and former doeling--- plopped down, rolling on her back in efforts to mingle uterine and other juices. Then she lolled in the afternoon sun, anticipating conception.

Jeremy observed these efforts, torn between an interesting display and antipathy for targeting him, even if inadvertently, in her fervent release. He couldn't quite abide that it was without intent. He interpreted the female congress around him as some sort of dialogue regarding deflowering. The males scattered over the ensuing hour until time to head home for Ambergai's farm.

The trip there was time enough for the boy to rein in renegade hormones through exertion, at least as much as could be accomplished for any adolescent. A steady state of readiness lay barely under the radar, lacking only a trigger. Gratified to have achieved some level of satiety, he hoped it might hold him in good stead should any other catalyst be encountered.

An hour past sunset, Jeremy settled the goats in barn stalls per routine. Without typical sign from Ambergai, he thought to check in with his employer before departing and knocked on the back door. No lights were visible from outside but the screen door sat unlatched and cracked. Jeremy called inward, thinking best to announce himself. Absence of reply led the boy inside, expectations present for finding the tall Rasta listening to his radio. This time of evening the big man commonly perused weather and farm stations for relevant news.

Static crackle of a weather station did broadcast itself from the forward-placed living room of the mahogany-timbered mountain home. Jeremy tentatively navigated the darkened hallway toward it. Passing the main bedroom door on the way, he heard the sonorous riff of Ambergai's voice. Softly instructive. Partially opened, the gap beckoned. Intent on conveying successful completion and 'change-of-guard' status aimed him toward the amiable 'bass mon'. The door creaked at his push and he entered.

In a flurry of discordant bustle, Jeremy realized his error too late. There before him, he visualized Ambergai in active mounted position… taking pleasure with Starleen. A single dim candle lent shadowy evidence of the two in conjoined concupiscence. His approach hadn't been secretive or clandestine. Nevertheless, footsteps and door noise brought a surprised female face up from prone position of submission. She was not pleased.

Exclamatory epithets deluged four ears. He quickly hunkered, recognizing himself as both cause and recipient of a rising ire. The dreadlocked woman, lissome of form and athletically inclined, angrily shoved a committed Rastafarian aside in haste to disengage. Successful untying was swiftly accomplished. She doubled-down on the intruding youth, vituperative in her castigation.

Ambergai, equally surprised, rolled to the side. The aroused man lay back to watch, dumbfounded, as his common-law wife detached and scrambled up. Grabbing a robe from the nearby bedpost, the attractive woman flashed rage again toward the boy but also at Ambergai. Spreading blame for a blameless incident of innocent miscue.

No matter. The damage had been wrought. There was nothing to be done by either stunned male. Starleen stormed from the room and disappeared down the dark hall toward the water closet, slamming its door in persistent verbal harangue.

Jeremy cowered with fear of the strong female, thinking first of physical reprisal for his intransigence, then hitting on thoughts of occult retribution. The youngster harbored significant anxiety for the woman's mystical proclivities. Even Ambergai seemed respectful on the subject, projecting deference not common from the alpha male.

Presently, the boy debated escape. Measuring distance to the backdoor, he accounted a need to pass the room his antagonist now inhabited. He realized it would be useless; he was already busted. There would be no safe haven. Hesitantly, Jeremy glanced back into the room at Rasta Mon, expecting concomitance of anger from that direction as well. Yet hoping for instruction. Specifically, how to get out with minimal exacerbation of the situation.

A view of the man propped still and prone on the bed brought him up short. No anger emanated from that quarter; only abandonment. He was struck by the crushed image of his boss, interrupted in throes of unrequited passion just a moment before. Stark evidence of the fact rose proudly before him, intensifying the boy's embarrassment.

Not sure what action to take, Jeremy simply froze. In the ensuing minute, not a word passed between them. The only utterances streamed outward from a closed door down the hall. They both stared at one another in listening, Jeremy trying hard to focus on the man's eyes.

Amid an ongoing verbal maelstrom, the water closet door ruptured open, banging a wall in expression of inanimate irritation. Stomping feet sounded in retrograde, stalking to the back door. They listened as another thump reverberated, this time signaling Starleen's departure. In magnificent wrath. Barn doors sounded next. The two males heard the mare, Blackbird, neighing a diminishing whinny as the pair disappeared into dark distance… leaving them gawping back and forth in a candlelit room.

Alone. Wondering what exactly should be done to fix things…

July, 1989

After years of harboring a smoldering odium, the depths of which Jeremy had little inkling, Shernard exacted a terrible revenge. Though the watershed moment had been only happenchance and filled with dripping ironies likely to never be exposed, the result still proved catastrophic. Several cauldrons of bubbling latency came clear by the event's manifestation. Multiple lives were integrally altered in the process.

Jeremy Fallsworth Kell, young Blue Mountain Maroon, mulled the fallout as he trudged down mountain home trail for what was likely a last time. Glancing back over his shoulder ten minutes before had envisioned grim visages of both father and mother, resigned to disgust at their eighteen-year-old son's fall from grace.

Several vindictive conversations had sealed more than one fate the previous night. Ignominious 'evidences' lambasted his psyche, hypocrisy on full display. Truth be damned. Jeremy now grappled with the contradiction of things. Recalling smugness in an older brother's glowering smirk from shadows around the corner, he deduced--- much too late--- facts of the affair. Father had been imperially cold in a stony pronouncement. Disowning his tenth child by paternal decree had cut deep. There could be no defense for such appalling actions of the revolting offspring.

Jamaican culture, hypocritical in boundless ambivalence regarding the subject of homosexuality, looked disdainfully upon easily vilified scum of humanity. The very group into which Jeremy had been cast upon exposure of a predilection covertly practiced by many throughout history and commonly on the island of Jamaica…

…The tall, handsome dreadlocked male bent leisurely over the silky back of the willing bottom so amply endowed with succulent round ripeness. A pace befitting easy union between the duo allowed for blessed prolongation in approach to coupled nirvana. Shared sensations rippled between bodies by the nexus perfected throughout a secret liaison. Serendipity had granted sanctity to the bond so fantasized by one and so unexpected by the other.

Now, during a languid push up the scale of pleasure toward one more notch inexorably linking them, soft Lyaric phrasings narrated the climb. One rigid member slid slippery in familiar custom while the other bounced patiently on and off the taut smooth stomach below which the pretty thing sprang. Such sensuous flatness to that belly engendered common caress by long ebony fingers during progression.

Neither measured the actions enjoyed. Simple reactionary stimulus drove the union. Variety rose by experiment rather than prescribed scheme, ad lib adaptation the basis for the couple's enduring attraction.

Perfusion of velvety stirrings thrilled the long organ into swollen fullness, tumescence proportional to upsurge of eruptive verge. The tunnel of warmth recognized the looming moment. Its swelling powerfully reinforced an untouched bouncer fronting the recipient.

Closed eyes, curled toes, arched backs, purring buzz, tensed musculatures and zooming pheromones all combined to overlook a new presence in the barn doorway.

The irony of the setting for the voyeurism would only later be harkened, in recollection of fractured hayloft floorboards and a disrupted interlude years before. But presently, the older brother absorbed a sensuous scene, verboten as it was, applying perspective in a split second. Shernard's rush of emotions ranged widely in that brief period.

An instinctive response placed him on his knees facing the bouncing appendage before he could judge the act. Brotherly lips engulfed the throbbing corona, swallowing the thick thing without considering. The straight boy enjoyed a deep slide into his throat as well as the simultaneous barrage of thick juice, propelled by the pulsing Rastafarian pumping the younger sibling. In that instant, shared climax imbued a snapshot of the perfection of the couple's carnality.

He swallowed without thinking, ingesting hot spew while picturing, close-up, a hairless pubic patch centering narrowed vision. His hand came up, cupping the spot of paroxysmal link between homunculus and sphincter, enhancing all three participants' cresting. Indeed, Shernard's own untouched junk, promptly hardened by the unexpected scenario, saturated inner drawers covering him.

No one moved over the next minutes, except by spontaneous convulsions. Scaled thresholds disallowed voluntary involvement.

Gradually, spasming ebbed. Hand, balls, phatted shaft and squeezing sphincter all grounded the energy still bolting through the trio. Heat burned the connectivity, digits kneading skin of forbidden zones by virgin experience for Shernard, his tongue and lips perpetuating the little brother's release by suckling the turgid beast never once so familiarly fancied.

Then, a light switch snapped. Eyes widened in realization of the entanglement now shared. Post-coital guilt flooded a twenty-year-old brain as focus on the deed in which he had just partaken came clear. Backing off the oozing organ, releasing his hand from the under site of connection, Shernard flinched as if scalded.

Standing erect, he gagged to one side, tasting his brother's saltiness in a throat just emptied of the suddenly offensive pulser. Pursed lips worked to hawk mingling essences as a dawning face pieced together that which had just played out.

Spitting cream-coated expectorate, he leered toward the still abutted pair, both of whom ogled, stunned at a startling turn of events. Pleasurable glow of simultaneous achievement reflected in their faces; no evidence of contrition. It maddened and horrified the last-second partaker. He felt overriding revulsion at clear enjoyment of their blasphemy.

"Wat inna hell yuh ah two doing? Yuh both gwine burn fah dis!" Then, in a puerile twist, "Mi am guh fi guh tell everyone wat de two of yuh a up to." With that the boy turned tail, beating a self-righteous path to the barn door, and scrammed. A catarrhal cough marked the mood of the telltale retreat… and a brother's impending ruin.

Extreme contrasts between Hagley Gap and Kingston served to dull Jeremy's sentiments of loss. Stimuli from too many varying sources pushed the passage of weeks in acclimating to monumental change. It was a blessing unappreciated primarily because heaviness of the young man's heart lent stifling undertone to that ensuant period. Newness of this world awakened unfathomed genesis.

Basic goodness of heart combined with an agreeable personality opened introductory doors through naïve fluke. Chance exposure to compassionate beings landed him in position for sustenance without the pitfalls common to many inexperienced strangers flooding the capitol city. A job at Half Way Tree General Mercantile as a stocker begat access to an upstairs apartment. The tiny place created security amidst a discordant metropolis. The port in a storm.

Uncertainty blunted forays from that base in the beginning. Absorbing functional pragmatism of the general store afforded grounding. Mr. Rattray, the proprietor, saw potential in the youth, granting time and space for requisite acclimation. After all, mountain life experience left a great deal to the imagination regarding the port city. Introduction to clientele permitted a measured unveiling for Jeremy.

The day a dark compact youth appeared during a sudden tropical squall in search of chicken wire marked a turning point in the mountaineer's lowland education. Using a patois verging on strangely familiar, the bearded young man with short plaited braids twiddled busy fingers as Jeremy measured and cut the ordered fencing. He could feel obsidian eyes boring his backside through the cutting, assigning a first impression of rapscallion to the buyer. Not to be trusted.

First non-business-centric words did little to dispel the notion. "I-Rey and cool runnings, Bammy. Yuh a vexing mi wid de curve of dat batty. Before mi cause ah bangalang, maybe wi shoulda head pon up to Nine Mile an acquaint togeda… up pon de heights weh de Niyabinghi be checking out do battybwoys. Chillaxin' wid de ganja an' chalice, eh?"

Jeremy smiled to himself in deciphering a mixture of compliments and insults. He didn't break off his task, continuing to carefully clip a straight line. This was not the first time to be 'accosted' by a gravilicious horndog. He no longer bothered responding to such good-natured lewdness. No one here in the City knew his history.

He had been made acutely aware of the forwardness of city males when it came to booty calls. Unlike mountain enclaves, such as Hagley Gap, men of the harbor town had quite a problem differentiating batty by gender: both functioned the same way. Complicating matters, one gender boasted an added benefit of impregnability.

Awareness of owning an attractive derriere had been reinforced to Jeremy within earshot more than one time. Delectability factor weighed heavily in the mountain boy's favor, he discovered. Before, only one person had ever commented on that anatomical allure. Buttressing of the knowledge now took on ironic relevance.

Bantering with the swarthy customer, he rolled the length of wire mesh carefully, sacked and priced the sale, then accompanied the shorter guy to the front for checkout. Easy nature of the teaser drew him; curiosity over a peculiar vernacular was branded as lowland Lyaric. Jeremy accorded the man a bit of rare, superficial repartee.

He had been inculcated to Gai's mountain lingo. This dialect pulled on him by its similarities… missing the giant Rasta. No communication between the two could be had what with his hasty departure. Though probably for the best, he reflected, Jeremy still awakened in dark of night, hollowed by loss. This semblance tickled something inside him.

"So, where be dis Nine Mile everybody seems to speak o' all de time, Mon?" Repeated reference to the place did pique his interest.

"Oh, it be called Cave Riva Falls up pon Bull Bay." The smile widened, "Yuh know weh Three Finga Jack Corna be? Rite nex to Zion Hill weh be de Rasta Nest."

Jeremy nodded. The falls were notable all over Jamaica. Ambergai had imparted lore from firsthand familiarity. His Blue Mountain teacher had visited the place many times over years, being the main enclave of Rastafarianism on the island. Bull Bay: Zion Hill. 'De place de Rasta du fi wi ting up dere.' That was what Gai had told him.

It was there where Ambergai Gee IV had run upon a young Nesta Robert Marley washing his dreadlocks. Under the falls. A link was forged. Collaborative musical efforts had been wrought between the duo in effort to bring a talented but inexperienced dreadlocked mulatto into Gai's reggae band. The Mighty Diamonds. Their liaison melded well at first, at least until Bunny Wailer and Peter Tosh had stolen him away in pursuit of a different but parallel destiny.

Yes, Jeremy had heard tales, of course, but was perplexed by the name this man used for the place. Expressing so, the talkative fellow replied, "Ah called Nine Mile cah it be nine miles wey fram Kingston Town." Cracking a big grin at that colloquialism, he added, "An dere a duppy: de don gorgon Nesta Bob Marley Mon haunts de place, tis said fah sure. Tis said dat de don singa washes iz dreads at de sunset. So, Bammy, wi be going up dere to see wat goes dung?"

Friendless during weeks of transition, Jeremy saw a chance for opening up. He introduced himself. In turn, the diminutive male responded, "Fi mi name ah still Kwaku Anansi." Exceeding pride accompanied the pronouncement.

Jeremy remembered folklore of his West African roots at the soubriquet. It was not original. An old Ashanti label, Kwaku--- or Quaco--- the Wednesday-child, had somehow gained notoriety by reproachful inflection. At least in the up-country. Thoughtless teasing by detractors created enjoyment at most namees' discomfiture. The why of it could not be determined, he also recalled. Upon once asking, he had been informed only that the Wednesday Child namesakes commonly chose nicknames to cover embarrassment.

Yet this man seemed completely at ease with the appellation. Jeremy had grown up with Ashanti folklore. Anansi, the trickster spider, was usually referred to as Kwaku Anansi. He was, too quote a Brit translation of Ashanti stories, 'a roguish sort of fellow constantly overreaching himself and guilty of endless sharp practice. But despite it all, he was a likeable chap of a most amusing character'. The young Maroon saw much by comparison to this city man. A careful guard would need be maintained, in spite of liking him.

Emancipation Day dawned bright and clear. The tiny multi-paned window etched rainbows on the pillow and Jeremy's face. Refractions danced back and forth as he blinked awake. The boy jumped up and hastily readied for the coming day.

Mr. Rattray had plans for the long holiday week. The business owner closed his business to partake of the extended festival marked by Emancipation Day at the beginning and Independence Day at the end. He and the family were taking in the carnival atmosphere the first two days, then absconding to their Port Royal seaside home for quietude afterwards.

The family man invited Jeremy, insisting the boy take time away for himself. Jeremy had politely declined, instead accepting the offer from Kwaku to run away to the hills for a few days. Since connecting Nine Mile to the Rastafari refuge, an urge to view the storied site had grown in his mind. He desired to put sight to name where his mentor had spent time.

Hiking and hitching rides through the festival and parade routes, the two made way across a sprawling city, climbing gradually in traverse toward eastern fringes. Routing various neighborhoods over the morning, the new friend chatted busily in describing history and anecdotes behind each. Jeremy hadn't explored to that point, now greedily absorbing the rich background of his adopted home.

He was enamored by a magnificent Georgian palace named Devon House. The beautiful estate dated to the time Britain captured Jamaica from Spain in mid-seventeenth century. It held added significance because that tumultuous period marked the onset of the Maroon Rebellion. As British wrested 'control' of the island then, a slave rebellion was born. Many Spanish sugar plantation slaves escaped thralldom into the Blue Mountains then.

Centuries of subsequent strife between colonial power and self-liberated population set in motion that which made up Jeremy Kell's personal history. His predecessors had spent generations defying would-be masters, never tolerating re-subjugation.

Jeremy was amazed at the opulence of the refurbished mansion and grounds. And even more astounded to find out the place had been expanded and beautified by George Steibel, first black millionaire of the island nation.

Passing King's House and Jamaica House, official residences of governor-general and prime minister, respectively, put more history into perspective. Talkative Kwaku imparted opinionated knowledge of the capitol city, bringing the culture to more focus. The boy's heritage took on added meaning by witty elucidation through the morning. On through Trafalgar Park and Matilda's Corner they came to Bob Marley Museum, tarrying there to see the memorial of the late reggae icon.

Up through Barbican then Barbican Heights, they stopped at the Royal Botanical Gardens. Stunning complexities of the ordered gardens made an impact. Surveying the land drop away on the trek upward allowed three-dimensional overview. All while surrounded by ongoing settings of festivity.

In the ambience of a buoyant atmosphere, their adventure was punctuated by diverse music genres and colorfully costumed partiers. Eccentric characters, handmade crafts, mouth-watering smells all combined to bombard senses. It was overwhelming for a youth accustomed to highland existence. So boundless were the stimuli blitzing him that wide open eyes couldn't quite grasp the array. Kwaku grooved in the renewed novelty playing out through Jeremy's wonder of it all.

Reaching city outskirts, the highway led them through elevated suburbs and burghs displaying even different vibes. All exuding flavors varying with populations. Late afternoon took the two on their winding trail past The University of the West Indies. They turned south along high, sheer mountainous ridges to Harbor View.

Coming into Three Finger Jack Corner allowed purchases for the coming weekend. Kwaku regaled him with Jack Mansong's legend, explaining how the escaped giant servant freed many a slave and terrorized the area in 1780 before being relieved of two fingers by Quashi during a robbery attempt. The same Quashi, Christian slave, who finally vanquished the feared Obeah Man, decapitated him and preserved the head in rum for two decades. How Christian of him, reflected Jeremy. The never-ending font of folklore seized Jeremy's avid imagination. It served to bring cogency to abstract visions heretofore reserved for the mind's eye.

He could imagine Ambergai in many a setting along the way, picturing a seven-foot titan emerging around corners of approaching byways or from vine-arched doorways that fed into the main road they travelled. In front of the wooden palisaded entry to The Ethiopian Africa Black International Congress, painted in horizontal stripes of red, yellow and green, Jeremy envisioned the wise man overlooking brilliant blueness of a Caribbean Sea rolling far below the venerable place. With each vista-filled scene, his Rasta Mon appeared in sentimental surrealism.

An unassuming sign marking Zion Hill came upon them around a broad curve, announcing the center of Rastafarianism on the island. An eclectic enclave called home by hundreds of sect members. The revered religious group had originated centuries before out of a cry from depths of despair. Produced by involuntary servitude forced upon a proud people stolen from a far continent an ocean away. Jeremy contemplated roots and evolution of the patchwork belief system common to his ancestors. The Maroons of Jamaica. The Koromantyn. Scions of the proud Ashanti.

By crisscross exploration of a strangely unconventional Rasta village, the young mountain exile explored the Abrahamic hub mentally conceived through Ambergai's descriptions. The commune basing deification of Haile Selassie and situated above Bull Bay became real.

Descent to Cave River Falls as the sun blazed its sinking farewell under the far west horizon brought the duo alongside cascading shimmers of ephemeral beauty, misty curtains arising from terraced pools, blurring the darkle. The boy was now stirred by a splendorous diorama of budding stars. Brightly hued clouds chased trailing strands of color in the soft glow of dusk.

A Full Red Moon popped over the eastern horizon, imbuing a fading kaleidoscope of puffy clouds with radiance bordering on blood-tinged. Kwaku gathered kindling and wood while Jeremy set a stone fire ring on a huge flat boulder surrounded by rippling rapids, all the while barely capable of yanking his eyes from such magnificence. He wondered at the mystery that this fantastical place was deserted of people. Nobody within eyeshot. The pair had the beauteous spot to themselves. Stripping, they bathed in the clearness of rushing cataracts, laving away a day's salt.

An hour into night found them lounging before an open fire, astounded by the vista and surroundings. Appetites sated by fresh legumes, fruit and purchased dukunu, two bushed youths washed down handmade bulla cakes with fresh falls water. Kwaku pulled out a chalice packed in his bag, then spent minutes contemplating the view while tamping ganja herb procured back in town.

"Well bammy, wi finally be resting here togeda pon Nine Mile de way mi been picturing. Afta gettin an eyeful of fi yuh delicious batty aal de damn day wid it jigglin inna front of mi, now, afta som o dis high grade, mi tinkin to dig into it…" The wide grin accompanying the words made Jeremy laugh. He was as tired as he'd been since moving to Kingston.

The thought of an outlay of exertion on that score wasn't close to happening. Of that he was certain.

Not to mention the fact that a past imbroglio up on Blue Mountain lent itself to little desire for a repeat. The tall mentor left behind would endure as perhaps the only one who might hold the chance of altering that state of mind. Since the man was half-a-hundred miles away, truly little prospect existed for this new friend's idea panning out.

Jeremy was a changed young man. He kindly reflected this without hesitation to the would-be chaser. "Kwaku, mi laik yuh dude but de bly fah dat happenin ah lacka snowball's bly inna Hell, bwoy." He took the chalice pipe from the proffering hand and inhaled slowly, musing on visions past. A smile emoted the good-natured refusal, all the same. "But bwoy, yuh were suh rite bout ou beautiful dis place. Ah ive neva seen notin dis priti. An ole bredren Koromantyn gorgon told mi bout ah aal."

The wistfulness wasn't lost on the shrewd city man. Both dwelt amidst disparate thoughts as zillions of stars washed slowly over them... drowsing 'togeda' in the laziness of fire and weed.

The deep stroke of Shernard's mouth engulfed his stiff piece to the hilt, rotating on the excited thing in a manner not recognized. As the sole head job ever experienced, Jeremy relived the unforeseen ménage à trois which had set the tumult of his life's revolution into motion. That brief servicing provoked a same-moment climaxing. One deep swallow had been the totality of the rapturous experience, by merit of the opposing stimulation exciting his prostate then.

This time, the older sibling was taking his time, investing unctuous detail into a slow ministering job presently in progress. Jeremy was in heaven. No one had ever done this for him. Sprawled and lolling, his hand slowly massaged a bare pectoral, adding to the pleasurable vibe.

Spread legs and bent toes gave measure to an itinerant finger curling its way up into his hole, intent on more. Deliberate strokes caused inadvertent shudders to roll through him and he considered how he had missed out on this up to now. He should've known Shernard would come to his senses...

...From the darkness, he was stricken by the heart-rending yip-yip-yowl of a close by coyote. It brought him out of the trance with a start. Teeth clamped around the base of his shaft in unease at that howl. The sharp grip sent a shot of pain around his body, centered in the sensitive organ being gobbled. As eyes focused, Jeremy was startled to find not Shernard, but Kwaku, consumed by the lustful deed.

"Whoa! Wat be dis ting dat be happenin, mon?" The highlander had clearly been dream-channeling the episode. Shernard simply served as orientative source, hence the role in a dreamed encounter. Jeremy put his hands to the new friend's bushy head, meaning to push him off. Teeth released at the touch, mouth punctuating a smooth slide off by a wet 'splop'.

A silly grin harangued the city boy as busted lips smacked together through an upward glance. "De babi was looking suh forlorn dung here aal puffed up an swelled, so's mi caged de bobb'n ting an tried to soode 'im." As he stated the obvious, 'de bobb'n ting' began spurting ropes of creaminess from the eye, saturating Kwaku's beaming face. Further surprise suffused the smile, which never faded, and the talented lips took to lapping. "Well, at least mi be knowing de why mek bout de bobb'n."

The throes of bliss disallowed anything else except a stoned, sleepy giggle to escape Jeremy's throat. With that, the two knocked down barriers so commonly separating straight males. Had there been any around, it might've proven exculpatory. As it was, the two wriggled together in temporary escape from affectation of a lie. And laughed 'til they cried.

The answering call of the coyote's cohort was drowned by cascading water and fits of delight. Bonding flourished in that moment.

A large, bare toe prodded his cheek. No response provoked a second. Lurching up out of a deep state of sleep, Jeremy next felt the same toe provoke the boner he sprang every morning since onset of puberty. A fuzzed eye blinked to visualize a humongous pale white foot, compadre of the prodding toe, as it scooped underneath the revitalized tumescence. The fondle forced a quick scramble to wobbly feet.

An equally groggy Kwaku Anansi likewise jumped up, jerking his head off Jeremy's belly, cross-eyed and ready for a fight. Fists balled, arms crooked, bushy hair quavering in a disoriented fog. What he and his new best bud saw set off a clamor of reactions ranging from shock to fright to amazement.

Before the aroused sleepers hovered two of the most daunting beings either had ever beheld. One could be the other, they were that much alike.

Hunched shoulders, wide despite ignoble posture, sprouted massive necks from between them, supporting mirror image heads. The pale skin was arresting. Snaking tendrils of matted, spiked, white hair spiraled in patterned whorls around heavy skulls. Excessively thick lips of equal pallor cradled awesomely flared nostrils.

Their eyes alarmed the dreamers, germinating seeds of fear for entrapment within confines of a terrible, inescapable netherworld. Were they even awake? Were these gargantuans real? The whites of those eyes appeared pearled in polyglot hues. The centers: startling crimson. Silvery eyelashes fringed all four. Advancing the disquiet, both bulky men stood dead still, unblinking.

Tracking down their naked torsos, hulking builds manifested similarities as did the faces. Astoundingly heavy limbs, balled in knotted muscle, extruded from those colossal trunks. Tree-bole sized legs positioned in widespread plant before them. Bare feet were hairless, each one as wide as two grown men's big ones. Midsections rested above them, obscured by woven vines. A braided strut rendered support up and over each left shoulder. The weave was loose enough to hint at more than a silhouette of fleshy indwellers. Bulges alluded relevant proportionality.

Crouched and alert by the presences, young campers squinted upward from poses of submission at the two, partially blinded by abrupt appearance of a rising sun. Awkward moments passed before one behemoth shifted away from the other. Resultant wobbling from under the vined loincloths mesmerized both.

Jeremy suddenly hit on the realization that a dawn boner waggled rigidly out from his crotch and by side glance he fathomed similar state of things with Kwaku. The standoff persisted as he next comprehended the twins were equally captivated by the awakened duo. Or, at least parts of the awakened duo. The parts at attention.

He reached to Kwaku's fists, gently but firmly pushing them downward in attempt to defray any aggressive signals. Initial resistance gave way to pressure and the bushy-headed youth dropped from fight stance. As if that bearing impacted the albinos in the slightest. Both sets of red eyes remained fixed on the erect appendages challenging them.

Finally, one set of unpigmented lips parted and a fat tongue flicked outward in expression of an unclear emotion. Bristling white teeth peeked from behind the lips, betraying at least the ability for cannibalism should the goal be germane. The boys wondered if they were about to be boiled, roasted or chomped raw.

A curious middle finger stretched forward, wrapping around Kwaku's arching staff, dirty jagged nail peering upward from the under curl. Juddering of the blooded piece caused it to jump. Kwaku went to full squint, not wanting to see the damage expected momentarily, yet afraid to pull away. The twenty-year-old bit a quivering bottom lip in brace for the worst.

It didn't happen. Jeremy perceived astutely expressive eyes coordinate with that dexterous digit. A new guise of hankering informed him that intent was indeed on the agenda. Just not malicious intent.

Unceasing water torrents surrounding the flat boulder maintained their noisy flow as a blooming sun warmed the smooth slab... enflaming the exertions of identical brothers.

"Mi tink de doondoos be jus' sensitive ta sun. Dey sure were nah shy ta be seen." Kwaku was ebullient. The trek back to Kingston led the two on a different route than before, this time hugging the coastline. He had become infatuated with the prodigious efforts expended by the big twins. Eko and Iko. "Did yuh see de way dem de tings neva wilted? Even wen de don Rastas came dung de falls an saw dem poundin dat bredda batty? Dey neva even slowed dung."

The banter once again caught Jeremy off guard by the duplicitous nature of many Jamaican men. Their obsession with anything sexual overrode machismo scruples such as Jeremy had had to suffer up in Hagley Gap. At least in conversation, and apparently even furtive hook-ups with others, the dichotomy seemed moot to them.

True to form, Kwaku now waxed eloquent about the morning's hijinks, sated as he was. Not to mention his relief at not being lunched on by the fierce looking men. After the two had juggled partners to glutted repletion, then watched as the brothers explored one another in ribald display, they had sat on the rock, legs dangling. For another languid hour, the four quick friends further acquainted with one another.

They learned of the doondoos story: how three-year-old albino twins had been bartered away for food to a travelling circus by a destitute mother deserted by a drugged-out father. Over years, the breddas had depended solely on each other. Finally, nearly twenty years into involuntary servitude, they had become enlightened to the notion of escape. And they did.

Making their way in a round-about way across Jamaica, the breddas had settled close by Zion Hill. The laid-back calm of the safe enclave, one accepting of unusual characters, proved fortuitous. The two flourished. Entering a Rasta School and learning basic trades, they attained stability unknown before. Ever.

The proclivity for sexual didoes came from early exposure to circus mentality. Loose moral codes permitted young prey, such as themselves, to be 'indoctrinated'. Despite the wrongness of the matter, or perhaps because of it, the bonded men throve together. New safety derived, away from danger of re-subjugation, by loose inclusion in the Rasta sect's community. It made them secure.

Coming upon the young holiday campers in their state of repose seemed a natural turn of events to the couple. They simply answered what to them was a natural urge. To completion. In multiples. Even so, Jeremy sensed some substantive omission from the breddas summarization of their life story: something darker; more sublime; that which the two didn't desire be heard. It left the Maroon in puzzlement.

As the sun arced upward, the duo high-tailed for the shadows of their secluded mountain byre, vampire-like. In wait for sunset. Truly, the pallid bodies bore sunbeams to great bane. The boys saw no more of them over the succeeding days spent exploring the falls and the bay area.

Kwaku, deducing no paradox from the episode with Eko and Iko, nor that occurrence the previous night with Jeremy, brushed off any sense of guilt. After several days camping on the big rock, the two headed home. Through a day spent meandering the city back toward Half Way Tree, the friends shared Independence Day celebrations in diverse districts of the expansive metropolis.

Following the jetty-bolstered Manley Boulevard along the harbor edge they saw the fishing village of Springfield with mixtures of citizens both working and recreating through the national holiday. Bournemouth Gardens awed them by the seaside residences there. Passmore Town and Campbell Town were filled with street revelers, raconteurs and general citizenry who entertained the two on up to Sabina Park, which pointed them toward their destination.

The hub for the day's celebrations based at the former site of old Kingston Racetrack, now transformed into a beautifully landscaped botanical center and tribute shrine for Jamaica's national heroes: National Heroes Park. The boys staked out spots to watch festivities and crowds from the steps of Marcus Garvey Memorial.

The national hero, political leader and Father of modern Jamaica rested forever in the handsome sanctuary honoring him. As the two observed, a stage was erected for coming patriotic speeches, concert and fireworks heeding the day's importance. Wandering vendors hawked fresh food, condiments, drinks and even the national ganja smokables.

By late afternoon, fully stuffed and gliding, they listened as minor speakers took to the podium. Time passed and the unfocused, sleepy pair became aware of the prime minister himself taking the stage. Jeremy recognized the esteemed man, marking him as one to accord respect. But it was still politics and he soon again drowsed.

Finally, close on dusk, bands took over and music cranked up. The reason the boys had hung by the site. Kwaku had apprised him of an impressive concert in store with fireworks accompaniment. Perfect, thought the mountain newcomer.

Indeed, the mento, calypso and reggae, mixed with multiple other Caribbean genres totally blew him away. Never had the boy heard such abundance of flavor in so marvelous a venue. Thousands had gathered with them and by the time headliner bands hit the stage, Jeremy and Kwaku had inhaled enough i-shence to be hovering suspended, soaking up the communal aura.

Long after sunset, the master of ceremonies tapped the microphone. Jeremy pulled to alertness by the man's words. "An now, de moment we've aal been waiting fah: please du welcum de cream of de crop an de pride of de Island of Jamdung: De Mighty Diamonds!"

Jeremy was shocked. The Might Diamonds: Ambergai's band! His lost mountain mentor, from whom he had been so suddenly sundered! This couldn't be, he exulted. And, 'the pride of Jamdung'--- Jamaica--- how could that be, too? The boy had listened to the band over years on Blue Mountain, both jamming at Gai's farm and in mountain venues around Hagley Gap. They were familiars to him. How could this ever be?

He stood, tiptoed, straining to see as the band strolled onstage, strumming familiar chords to which he was so attuned. And, there--- not thirty feet away--- right there came Ambergai Gee, IV, himself. In the flesh. His draping mantle of dreadlocks tucked carefully into the oh-so-familiar multi-colored tam. Bulky by its fullness with the magnificent braids. He, Jeremy, had tucked the thing onto his friend's head, yes, into that very tam, more than once. It occurred to him to wonder who may have helped the singer this time? In his exuberance, he stumbled off the flat post, teetering down and on top of Kwaku.

Both tumbled groundward, ending in a heap, the bushy-haired city boy underneath. "Wat de fuck J-bwoy? Yuh losing de grip, or wat? Get up an off mi… mi wanna see dis don band, mon. Dey be de bess band inna de land bwoy… yuh crazy, now!" Kwaku's vexation was evident.

Jumping back up and dragging Kwaku along, Jeremy tried to explain the excitement felt at seeing the man thought lost to him. Kwaku wasn't having any of it. "Yuh be losin de min' mon. De Mighty Diamonds? Cum pon an yuh nuffi pullin pon aal fi mi legs now."

Jeremy re-situated on the wide stone finial post and pulled the disbeliever with him, but backed off nevertheless. The two enjoyed the next hour of musicality, Jeremy beaming ear-to-ear by the utter surprise. Another chalice--- now become a pass-around cutchie--- of Kwaku's ganja lightened them during it. The older boy shared with a couple of concert goers, making invite to squeeze up and join them on the roomy spot. Ideal site, Jeremy basked.

Passing the smoking cutchie, one of the invited girls smiled, having overheard the conversation earlier. "So, did I understand you are friends with the band?" She had taken the side next to the country boy upon Kwaku's offer, now rubbing warmly close. The girl was well-educated, as told by her speech and mannerisms.

He was envious, school-less since leaving home. His mountain patois marked him as a pickny renk sufferer in contrast to this upscale girl. Had he not been quite so high, he would've felt humiliation. As it was, he harbored only covetousness of the education she wore so nonchalantly.

A small thing, she didn't take much room. Long dark curls cascaded in waves around her face and down to her shoulders. A perky nose split two startling brown and green eyes, mixed colors pie-wedging together in unusual patterns. She appeared to be Jeremy's age.

Her obviously Anglo friend, blonde and blue-eyed, had captivated his comrade. Busily chatting together, Jeremy saw that, for once, the loquacious boy had met his match. He cupped the pipe, inhaling a puff and returning the smile. 'Ah de truth doh Kwaku yuh nuffilieve mi… de gorgon singa der lived close to mi fambily pon Blue Mountain. Him taught mi bout goats and coffee… an tings."

He turned back to gaze at his former guru, presently in throes of melodic nirvana. Just his close-by presence provided enough succor. It had to. The boy was aware there would more than likely never be more. That life had ceased the day Shernard burst in on them. For not only was

Jeremy exiled, Ambergai, himself, had suffered loss of face. Starleen had left him in disgust; Hagley Gap had even cooled its respect.

The great and good tall man of exceeding gravitas hired out his farm house, land and herd, taking to a more accepting down-mountain life of musical expression. Full time. All unbeknownst to Jeremy.

No, Jeremy grasped what must be left behind. So, he watched instead. And reminisced. Almost like an old person reciting a eulogy… or a requiem.

The tumult in his groin told his brain a fervently dissimilar story.

APRIL, 1990

"Mr. Kell... Mr. Kell. Ahem. Earth to Mr. Kell. Would you care to share? I am quite certain by the look of marvel besmearing your face that whatever thrives presently between those handsome ears and behind those smoky greys of yours would no doubt provide fascinating fodder for the rest of us...?"

Cynicism was evident in Master Earl Kessler's tone. Jeremy's classmates had broken into twittering after the second intonation of his name; guffaws ensued at the allusion to the handsomeness of those ears. Jeremy snapped back from the momentary lapse in attention, mortified--- once again--- at his own lack of discipline.

Much as he desired to hasten a way to head of the class by merit of academic acumen, for which he had evidenced substantial wherewithal to date, these pie-in-the-sky butterfly-brain antics still mystified everyone. Mostly himself. Why did this happen, he inwardly chastised? Each and every time it occurred he made solemn promise to cure the problem. Then, it occurred again.

There existed a definitive motif to the slip-ups. All centered on one subject. One sole subject. And just when the student thought himself absolved of the weakness, there it arose, blindsiding him once more.

Like now. The simple mention of the term 'bat guano' during a classroom discussion on fertilizers had sent his mind careening down those tunneling water ways through that mountain grotto of yore. The ones which had deposited him and his older sista, Xaviera, into the blue lagoon. Gai's lagoon.

The inaugural vision of the man had pierced his psyche so deeply that at moments such as now, he unintentionally harkened upon the flawless image of the seven-foot-tall giant of a guru--- emerging from the copse of trees amidst which he had napped--- to the exclusion of all else.

Just awakened, the man had shaken to clear his magnificently crowned head, mass of billowing curls luxuriating in lucky proximity to him. The smoothly sinewed ebony nakedness, but for a loin patch covering of the broadly imprinted thickness beneath, stole away with his senses something awful… it was a total and complete obsession of which he was powerless to shake.

It was proving impossible to block mindless wayfaring down so many unrelated avenues of thought, all dead-ending into one of countless savored mental mirages. Very aggravating. And…aggravating. His mind roiled with the undeniable glimpses. Just as did that damnable nether mind. The imbecile-of-a-teenage-piece habitually jolted to attention in mortifying grandiosity, way too proud of itself. He prayed silently for no need to arise from his desk. The devil was oversized and happy to be seen. A bane to his existence. Thank the gods that be for Aayla. His outlet.

In attempt to rectify the faux pas, "Dean Kessler, mi be--- I was--- remembering a grotto up on Blue Mountain which---h-harbors---the largest deposit of renewable bat guano discovered on the island in the past decade, Sir. My sista--- sister--- an mi--- and I--- stumbled upon the… c-cache… while exploring. It is now used on coffee farms there at the peak. Mi be--- I am--- regretful to have been distracted by the memory." He held breath in hopes the fairly succinct explanation sufficed to negate the current bungle.

After a pause, Dean Kessler, mindful of duty regarding his charges, replied, "Why, Mr. Kell. Indeed, I have heard of the stellar development of coffee crops resultant to that discovery. Are you actually telling us that you and your sister were the underlying factors for that breakthrough?" Acknowledging a nod from the rough but bright new student, he pressed forward, "In that case, well done, lad."

"Perhaps you might expound a bit, for the class's benefit, on the history of a nineteenth century Peruvian guano connection…?" It was an attempt to defray the boy's angst, a tactic the veteran instructor deduced as a face-saving pathway for the new pupil. He backed off, signaling silence from the other boys in the class.

This time, Jeremy's thoughts stayed on point, no fleeting intrusions barring his mental acuity. Gathering thoughts, he began. "The Humboldt Current carries cold, nutrient rich Antarctic waters up the Peruvian coast, providing for a rich aquatic ecosystem. Schools of anchoveta, cousins of the anchovy, as well as hovering hordes of night-flying insects, provide food for native seabirds and bats who then deposit droppings where they roost and hunt on the Chincha Islands off the Peruvian coast. The dry climate has preserved millions of tons of feces in an ongoing process over thousands of years."

"The Inca civilization was the first to harvest guano as fertilizer. They placed special importance on the resource, forbidding anyone to hunt seabirds or bats on penalty of death. This way the Inca kept a renewable supply for fertilizer and fed its empire. When Spaniards conquered the Inca, they craved silver and gold. Guano was of little interest to the Conquistadores. They ruined the country and resources in mining both, using local slave labor for centuries."

"After liberation, the new country affected the collection and sale of bird/bat guano to pay off debt. Over thirty years, the Peruvians cornered the market on the worldwide fertilizer industry until the combined effects of dwindling supplies and development of synthetic nitrates, a by-product of the oil industry, ruined their market in the 1870's. The mixture of bat and bird guano remains to the present day as the most efficient, safe and renewable fertilizer in the world."

Jeremy sat back, spent by the regurgitation of facts learned the previous night. The difficult part had been using proper English. The concentration factor was exhausting. But he had done it. Flawlessly.

After class, the first-year student, newly admitted just the previous autumn, hiked toward the church. He was to meet Aayla there and have lunch with her and the disapproving parents. Several students teased him on the way down the steps of the old Musgrave Building but Jeremy took it in stride, teasing in return.

He had found himself more accepted into the boy's school society since joining the football team. Now a proud Griffon, he had established credibility by earning the position of starting goalie a few months before. With that, boys had gravitated toward the drop-dead gorgeous Maroon. A diligence in catch-up school work was paying dividends by merit of a developing scholarship, too. The gap between the one-room multi-grade mountain school and big city high school curricula was narrowing swiftly.

The changes wrought over the previous nine months still staggered him when he reflected on it. He introspected over a twenty-minute hike west toward the Catholic diocese. Since the Independence Day Celebration last August with its doubly momentous events, he had turned corners and scaled walls in his sojourn which could not have been fathomed before they had happened.

Aayla was the major change in his life. The diminutive beauty, only daughter of Father Manley and his wife, had snuggled her way into his world that fateful Independence Day evening. Sitting together on the stone finial watching the concert with her best friend, Emily, and his, Kwaku, the two had acquainted through the music, sharing the ganja pipe. A promise to follow up the next week in free time from work at the general store had established a liaison which would prove providential on several scores. And the future unfolded.

The second event had occurred concurrently. A serendipitous glance by the performing headliner, Ambergai Gee of the Mighty Diamonds, had fallen upon him there on the stone bannister. The drop-jaw look of disbelief almost disrupted the concert.

Jeremy fondly recalled 'the look'. His smile grew in accordance with the reckoning, pulling the series of events up from a treasured memory. The surprised smile of recognition from the music icon had floored Jeremy in that moment.

Before it happened, watching the band perform while conversing with Aayla, he had resigned himself to the fact that what two mountain males had shared was water under the proverbial bridge. Broadness of the tall singer's grin in recognition of the sighting had dispelled that premise. The man had barely removed his huge black eyes from the youth thereafter, either during that song or afterwards. The lead singer was serenading Jeremy from that time forward. Even designing to send a shout

out, naming him between songs, as he sat on the landing with three disbelieving companions.

Kwaku had not credited Jeremy when he had told of the previous friendship between him and the Rastafarian don. The girls, new acquaintances that they were, raised their assessment by the comprehension. Jeremy had gained inestimable street cred in the moment, feeling pride, embarrassment, relief and absolute devotion. The ranging emotions swamped an innocent psyche.

A signal from Gai following the encore performance had brought the two together. For the first time since the traumatic episode on the mountain that severed their relationship the previous year. Subsequent meetings had cemented the tie, changed though it was under new circumstances. In the following weeks, Jeremy had once again been borne along a hectic track. This time, amidst the budding relationship with Aayla and rejuvenated prospects by Ambergai's re-emergence.

So relieved had the dreadlocked man been at finding the youth, he broached an uncommonly forceful route, demanding time, information and attention from the long lost apprentice. As if that were at all necessary. Always a laid-back persona theretofore, the Rastafarian had called in chits and favors in resolute fashion. Redoubtable effort to right perceived wrongs pertaining to his protégé had dumbfounded Jeremy.

First, contact from the esteemed Jamaica College for Boys came during a busy work day at General Mercantile. Mr. Rattray led the well-dressed school emissary to the hardware area, curious at an unexpected interview request. "Jeremy, this gentleman tells me he has business with you, young man." He had double-taken looks of perplexion over a retreating shoulder.

Following a dialogue, the offer for inclusion with the incoming class for that fall semester had stunned the boy. Though having seen the campus on Old Hope Street in passing by The University of the West Indies more than once, he had never entertained any serious idea of attending. Thoughts of that possibility had been discarded without much consideration. Viability of enrollment at such a place was not within his reach... or so he had thought.

The courtesy wrought by Mr. Gee's new standing, established by certified filings which designated official guardianship for the boy, had smoothed an unanticipated path toward acceptance. A contemplative look from Mr. Rattray had shadowed the boy as he climbed stairs to the little cubby that evening.

Then Ambergai, himself, had roiled the calm waters of Half Way Tree General Mercantile with an appearance one Saturday afternoon close to closing. Again, Mr. Rattray had escorted a visitor asking after the young Maroon employee, this time in the person of the celebrity icon. Jeremy had nearly melted at the sight of familiar long dreadlocks swaying behind his employer, knowing to whom they belonged before seeing the face. Sprawled on the floor, unpacking new inventory, the superimposition lent a funny vision to the approach. His beaming smile answered precious few questions for Mr. Rattray's baffled perceptions. Just who might be this young minion in his employ, the good man speculated?

Jeremy had been swept away following his shift, in Sunday-go-to-meeting best, to a local upscale restaurant never affordable until that meal. Over delectable fare, surrounded by romantic lamplit ambience, the unusual couple spent hours catching up. Intrusions came in waves from starry-eyed staff and patrons. The Mighty Diamond accepted every foray and request with munificent aplomb, autographing napkins, menus, marinas and even one small-of-the-back through their extended dinner.

The strikingly attractive eighteen-year-old had next been escorted by the gorgon Rasta through winding ways and wandering lanes of two neighboring burghs, crissing paths never crossed. The adoring youth had eyes for no one but his mentor. Passersby exclaimed in admiration at sight of the exceedingly handsome duo as they traveled. Jeremy registered none of it. He could not have retraced their steps had a life depended on it.

Ultimately emerging onto old Odeon Lane northeast of Half Way Tree, the pair slipped up a tucked side stairway to a second-story unmarked door. Gai produced a skeleton key and handed it to his companion, requesting help with unlocking. Pushing it open, Jeremy visualized a well-appointed apartment of two-bedrooms, a private indoor full bathroom, stocked kitchen with dining nook and an intimate common area furnished in homey collection of understatement. Very cozy, Jeremy surmised. He had wondered where the man might take his leisure and the spot matched expectations. Just the style envisaged.

There, reestablishing a sacred rite, the night had been spent in enthusiastic re-acquaintance. Next morning, Jeremy had been astounded by news that the place could serve as his new abode from then on, should he consent. Jeremy had thought it to be Gai's place. Not. The man had taken the comfortable little dwelling for him in anticipation of the upcoming school term. Enrollment in school and now this? Benevolence stymied the boy.

Sitting on a tiny balcony over coffee and bulla, the two rejoined confidants discussed past and future. "Bwoy, yuh made mi very worried bak up pon de mountain wen yuh left suh suddenly. Granted, wat went dung was suh wrang an unfair, Jeremy, but leavin widout ah wud left mi unable to help wid ya, ma bammy."

While he made a cogent point which Jeremy acknowledged, in the awkward moment and contentious fallout afterwards, an alternative farewell had not occurred to the inexperienced youth. "Ma don dada, yuh affi understand mi had nuh choices inna de matter." Then, pulling up short, the youth straightened his shoulders, "but dat wi deh ya now mi am ah whole person again, an mi ave yuh to tenk fah makin it suh." Tears suddenly spilled; the dark young hand reaching for the big man's wrist effected like response. The two relished their togetherness, acutely aware of a fragile luxury.

They pow-wowed over plans for the coming time, Ambergai making plain his intent to further Jeremy's education, even past the Boy's College. As well, encouragement of his ward's new acquaintance with the pretty girl, Aayla Manley. "Shim ah one uptown gyal fram an upstanding fambily, bwoy, an should ya ave feelings at aal, mi encourage ya to fala dem as de future promises mo fah ya inna dat path ova eni dat wi two might fala. Mi am just sayin, now, cah ours ah ah harda one… as wi ave aredi found out." And, with that, he drew back inside for some proper attention to overdue matters…

Truer words could not have been chosen. Nor truer actions taken, either. The first-string goalie now wallowed in the rumination as he hiked toward lunch…

…The hard backslap rang in his ears. It was that jarring. The rising boner partaking vicariously in the recollection wilted. Jeremy's trip down memory lane on the way to the church was washed away. "J-Mon! Wassup ma battybwoy? Weh yuh been? Mi aint seein yuh at aal o'late. Yuh been visitin' dem de doondoos?" The wittiness overwhelmed the funny man. He lost balance amidst rocking peals of his own laughter. Jeremy gripped his elbow to save a fall.

"Are you messed up, Kwaku?" Jeremy noted the dilated, bloodshot eyes, the sweaty palms, the trembling elbow. His breath wreaked of alcohol. "Whoa, ma bwoy. You definitely are...what's up with you, ma friend?" He pulled the bush man to the fore porch of a fronting house on Suthermere Road, wondering what the guy was doing here and in this state. No bars were within proximity; the residential area was an up-and-coming one with respectable homes everywhere.

Sitting the two of them down on an available front porch swing, he got his friend to lean forward. Guiding Kwaku's head down between his legs, he massaged neck and temples. Trying to piece together what had happened, discernible words became less and less coherent. Through his slurring and slumping, Jeremy quickly escalated to worried. He checked vital signs as learned the previous month in CPR class, finding pale color, progressed dilation to pupils and clamminess of his friend's skin. Feeling inside his shirt, he noted a very fast heart rate. It seemed fluttery. None of this was good, he was sure.

Deciding it best to get him up and to a hospital--- now--- he hoisted the smaller man over his shoulder, backtracking on Hope Street for a long six-block trudge to Andrew's Memorial. Having passed the hospital minutes earlier, he hustled toward it. Kwaku groaned with almost every step and within a few minutes began heaving. Without more warning, he found his school uniform drenched by noxiously bitter chunky pink liquid. Pedestrians cut a wide swath around the two in passing.

Worried about obstruction and choking, he broke into a jog. As he covered a couple more blocks toward the ER entrance, he caught sight of another person in stumbling mode coming toward him from a side street. Frazzled blond hair sprayed down and across florid features. A slim figure was wearing designer jeans, a form fitting button-down white collared shirt and fashionable flats. She was soaked to the skin and only two buttons partially held the shirt front together, braless skin visible beneath. Errant nipples whisked in and out of sight with each ungainly step.

More people passing by on the street stared between two putrid men and stumbling woman. Avoiding all three. Abruptly dawning on Jeremy, he yelled across the street, "Emily? Is that you, girl?" From between strands of matted hair he saw two red-rimmed blue eyes ratchet upwards, picking him out in her dazed stupor. She altered course, stumbling out into the street. Heading directly at them.

Kwaku groaned again, retching more acidy flux down Jeremy's shirt and pants. The girl was all over the place and not in control. Coming faster and closing the gap. Two cars approached from opposite directions and Jeremy estimated collision courses for one or both autos seemingly oblivious to the shambling girl on an intersecting path.

He screamed at her to watch out but she didn't grasp the meaning or was unable to process the danger. He couldn't be certain which. Making a split-second decision, the encumbered student lurched toward her, raising a hand at one oncoming auto. The eastbound car saw him and laid on its horn. Screeching brakes barely avoided him and Kwaku.

One down, Jeremy's mind shrieked, deviating back toward Emily again in effort to alert the westbound vehicle. Through what seemed like hours, the next seconds revealed a desperate Jeremy hastily depositing his friend on the pavement before darting into the path of the still unmindful on-comer. Emily stumbled on in certain-death trajectory, now grinning in recognition of the familiar dark youth hailing her.

Finally, the vehicle registered pedestrians obstructing the major thoroughfare, squealing and veering at the last second before impacting either. Almost. The back bumper swerved past Jeremy, raking his thigh. Something sharp on the chrome appendage cut through khaki school slacks and into muscle. Seen but not felt.

He made it to the still smirking blonde just as her legs torpedoed her body forward and into his outstretched arms. The two plummeted to pavement as two horns sounded in blaring effrontery at the idiots laying tangled and askew on the coarse blacktop.

Smoke spewed, fluids sprayed, lights wavered and blinded, screeching faded. Then, angry voices erupted from opening car doors as freaked drivers viewed what certainly appeared to be a raucous bacchanalia playing out across the busy street. Jeremy lay underneath the collapsed Emily, her mouth within inches of his, wreaking in similarity to Kwaku.

Attempting to speak, copious saliva dripped down, coating his face, adding fuel to Jeremy's chagrin at the vomit already covering his neck, torso and legs. Nothing word-wise came with it. But a sickening leer proved her viability. At least one good thing, Jeremy rationalized in wry silence.

Just then, another horn sounded. Far enough away to measure maybe a block or so, evidently heading their direction by the crescendo. He raised his head and visualized horror. At them charged a Kingston City Bus. The colossus was targeted directly at Kwaku's prone figure, just yards away.

Attempting to rise, Jeremy pushed the dead-weight drunkenness of the splaying girl, managing only to prop an elbow under himself. The bus, apparently not identifying his friend as human, bulldozed forward, bearing down on its course. The driver must be aware of something in front of it, the trapped boy reasoned. The continuous blaring horn bore that out. Even so, he watched in anguish as the veritable tank rolled right over Kwaku's form. Jeremy heard a sickening thump, knowing instantly that some part of his friend's body had contacted the undercarriage or tires.

In Herculean effort, he hove Emily up and aside, onto the curb of the street, praying she would stay put. He then raced to his friend's body. It lay flat, limp and deathly still. He could see blood oozing from a nasty head wound, thick sanguinous fluid coursing in a slow wave to the pavement.

A high-pitched wail keened in bereft despair as he knelt to cradle his friend's head. Why had he deserted him there? The scream tapered into a siren's shrillness as more braking autos screeched somewhere nearby. Jeremy sank beside the lifeless body in senseless gray-to-black oblivion…

July, 1990

"Don Dada… ohhhh…Don Dada, ma… don' be a'playin', now, be doin' ya job… oyeeeeee..." he insisted, as he locked smooth mahogany forearms around raised and spread mahogany calves. Allowing open access to the winking rosebud. Light, fluttery tease of the talented tongue persisted in titillating foil of the demand for more. Ecstasy teemed… the exquisite exasperation created quivering muscle spasms in overlap of the physiological provocation being perpetrated. Jeremy couldn't but barely stand any more of the tantalizing denial.

Eyes remained clamped tightly shut. His neck writhed in agonal throes of looming rapture. Picky sprigs of braided kinks ground into the pillow in rhythm with lingual probes. All lent standing to the rhapsodic lyrics of a begging young Maroon.

Without touching himself, the nine-inch arching anaconda rubbing his bellybutton pulsed globular response to the extreme care deliberately prolonging the sweet frustration. Sinewy legs remained raised, spread in wide extension, two-toned feet rotating to the beat, too, as toes curled in the only possible manner for saluting such anal pleasure.

Opening his eyes, the boy peered down past the self-starter second head pushing cream, over the fleshy shaft and phatted balls, to barely visible curls of that talented tongue's owner, bobbing with the flittering lingual appendage so adroitly puppeteering him.

To the awakening beholder's surprise, the curls raised up, exposing a richly dark heart-shaped face of the pretty girl… Aayla Manley. Pursed lips curved up in impish smirk, smug with satisfaction. "Ohhh, Dada, Don Dada, do ya job, ma Don Dada," she intoned in affected husky vocality, mimicking what she estimated to be maleness. Specifically, though unnamed: Gai.

Jeremy almost flexed those big legs shut and rolled away from the offending interloper availing herself of the sleepy after-effects following wine-induced haze the two had shared earlier in the evening. Now, at zero-dark-thirty, dreamscaping through an Ambergai-induced summoning, euphoric transport had been augmented by the girl's activities… where had that come from, he wondered?

Then, he wondered twice. Instead of the roll away, he matched the sexy maneuvers being employed by the warm fingertips and palms tippling his orgasmic glow, lowering the rangy legs downward in slow, measured stages. This was nice… and a variant on the traditional themes engaged heretofore. Pin-prickles washed over him: he permitted her to proceed.

Tiny fingers brushed lasciviously over the sensitive perineum still pulsing in the fervid release her tongue had just triggered. Petite hands continued up and over the straining hamstrings of her lover, skimming the crescent keloid scar, evidence from a recent accident, curving over the outer aspect. The action protracted involuntary stretches engineered by the calculative skills.

She reached up and over the engorged dick and balls and sensitive groin, scraping fingernails lightly against the smoothness of Jeremy's belly. Upwards, strafing rippling abdominals to curving pecs, to the erect nipples of his sculpted chest, the girl punctuated the ascent in excruciatingly drawn-out pinch of the pair.

Her supple body climbed lightly onto him, settling two small paired melons down over the arcing shaft. The fat thing jumped, slapping lightly against the labile layers hiding a rigid clitoris, embroiling her in acute waves of delight as an orgasmic sonata rocked her teenage world.

Dribbling eye contacted labial folds; fervor struck chords of intense tactility. She deliberately aligned the straining corona with the declivity residing deep to the petals and descended, firmly downward, implanting inch after nine inches of unyielding, spasming shank into the channel entrancing her striated cervix.

The two exhaled as she bottomed on his pubic smoothness, adding heat to new surfaces now linking the lovers. Her fingertips continued the twisting tweaks to Jeremy's nipples and in response, masculine round buttcheeks levitated reflexively off the sheet, prodding conjoinment to a maximum.

Aayla felt the swell of the slippery piece's head inside her and rotated on it, stimulating a resurgence to fullness common for her repetitive teen amour. Twice and thrice were notable terms for the regularity with which the two consummated their usually traditional interludes. Now, with this added zigzag to their norm, the two writhed, gyrating into third and fourth races to shared peaks. His fingers completed the whisking climb up her own taut belly to perky areolar tips, effecting elliptical completion of their loop.

Profuse secretions of unbroken convulsive waves persisted throughout for the sensual girl, happy to tote her lover along in undulatory pursuit, male-bound as he was. That he shot in multiples served to accentuate their connectivity. Happenchance on the shareable anilingual ripeness gave gravity to sexual connotations between the two.

Patterning her rotative swirls to his pulsing punches, the two rose another time to the edge... then toppled together, cascading downward on that climactic slide, oozing all the way... into and onto one another. Leaking juices lubricated the ride. She bent down, chasing his extended tongue to the full lips labeling the mouth she loved to bump. The grind between the pair extended the eruption below, her flair for mutual extenuation ample, indeed.

Spent, they lay sublimely enmeshed amidst the slipperiness validating expended exertions. Mouths maintained Catalan embrace.

Across the room, from around a corner, sets of curious eyes, one blue and one onyx, reveled in their share of the couple's guilelessness. Not quite out of sight, had the satiated couple thought to look, crouched contrasting skins of ebony hirsuteness covering creamy whiteness. Plugged together in their own union, long stiffness throbbed its seed inside velvety darkness of the chosen impregnable channel the pair preferred.

Plump balls slapped subtly on, then off, the set of perfect white assglobes offered up in cross-racial détente, testing their own limits while savoring unattainable fantasies residing atop the bed. Kwaku kept a swarthy set of fingers in place over pink lips. Emily might have given evidence to presence had he not. Smothered mewlings had been stifled, holding their confidence.

Emily had deduced the desire residing inside the bush man's brain regarding the boy. Plainly, Kwaku's bulls-eye attention toward his friend craved proxy involvement over none at all. She leveraged it for selfish purposes. Indeed, the blonde held aspirations of her own toward the enchantress with whom the young Maroon had just coupled...

By mutual consent, the incongruent pair enjoyed the two in the next room by vicarious succor where it had been found. Shared paroxysms invoked that denied them in the only manner available… as they privately confirmed.

"Did you sleep well, ma friend?" Jeremy labored at French-pressing rich beans local to the island, fortunate for propinquity to the best the world had to offer. The girls shared the bath in their own little sphere while the counterparts compared notes. Riffs of giggling fits and splashing filtered through a closed door; the boys wondered at the cause, perplexed by it.
"Well, hell to da yes… wat ya expek wid dat creamy batty a'pokin aal up inna dis face o'mine bwoy? Sleepin… afta aal o dat nastiness da gyal ad to ave… der been ah bit o'dat a'goin pon, ayah." Eyes blinked fast, casting multiple meanings in the telling, Jeremy privately wagered. "An, wat bout yuh an da likle bit o dat gyal? Ah dere eni babies a'stewin up inna de prime booty dis mawnin?"
"Kwaku, bwoy, bite your big ole' red dog tongue and swallow that thing. We are not--even--planning any of that, now. Way not ready," said as he plopped down a steaming cup of Blue Mountain's freshest for him on the way to the balcony.
The worldly city boy 'a-stewed' over that declaration, having been privy to carelessly bare techniques employed firsthand. While sizzling to watch, unintended consequences might not adhere to the vehement reply's directive… flippantly blown-off warning be damned.
Following the boy, Kwaku decided it best to back off the subject, not desiring belabor of the point. Unready to admit his and Emily's remote presence through the previous night's episode. His junk was still attuned to the memory, limber and daring.
Since the bus fiasco that had played out on Hope Street weeks ago, the friends had strengthened in their bond. Near-death experiences have that effect, he reflected. As the entire imbroglio was probably forever lost to him by the mental state he and Emily had experienced, second-hand accounts filled gaps.
Awakening in a hospital bed, point of perception totally lacking and head throbbing like a mo-fo, Kwaku had been informed by a sympathetic nurse of the basic timeline. Not all attending him were of like mind, he

recalled. Scathing condescension had mired the boy in feelings of inadequacy through two days of intensive care.

Only during a follow-up police detective deposition was he granted explanation and, ultimately, exoneration. It seemed that in the bar where Emily and he had met, the pair suffered targeting by a drug dealer with a vendetta. Unbeknownst to him, Kwaku had witnessed a deal gone sour the previous week on the way home from a night on the town. He and two other witnesses were marked by their knowledge. The following day, upon meeting the young blond girlfriend of Aayla's for a drink, both had had their cocktails spiked by an emissary of the dealer with instructions to bring Kwaku and the coincidental companion in for 'a talk'.

By a fluke, the inept envoy split a dosage of Rohypnol between the two instead of using a full hit. The result had left the two in sad state but not knocked out as intended. Staggering out of the bar, they had become too ensnarled with public crowds for direct intervention. In the commotion, they were separated from not only one another but abductor-to-be as well. Dumb luck had brought them both within Jeremy's route that midday. A different dangerous situation had supervened.

Close on the heels of the bus mishap, authorities had entered the scene by multiple reports of a disturbance. Delivery to the ER Jeremy had been headed for resulted after all, but with Emily and Jeremy as additional admissions along with Kwaku. Though lacerated and concussed, the bloody head wound hadn't proven more serious. By blood testing and shrewd detective work, the plan-gone-awry had been pieced together. Jeremy's sliced thigh required sutures but would leave little more than bragging rights in its wake.

The resulting bust of several notorious dealers in an adjacent parish had put blame to right. Now a witness for the upcoming trial, Kwaku Anansi had achieved notoriety and a modicum of respect as unwitting player in the police case. Under loose watch for protective purposes, both Emily and he had taken refuge in the cozy new abode with Jeremy who was just moving his and Aayla's relationship to the nesting phase.

Jeremy had struck up the liaison with Aayla soon after that chance meeting on Independence Day. The two had been dating under her parents' radar. Before that chance meeting on the street, Kwaku and Emily were relegated to sidebars in the fast-moving circumstances regarding himself and Aayla. Jeremy's dramatic heroism instilled a warmness to which the friends had clung. All four fused more closely by the messy affair than might have otherwise occurred.

It was the boy's restoration with the Rastafarian guru, however, which paved a commonality for all paths. The Odeon Lane flat and out-of-the-blue enrollment at Jamaica Boy's College propelled Jeremy toward constancy and educational achievement. Little presumed at the time, the haven would take on added import by rote of the happy-dancing the naïve young pair practiced… or didn't.

April, 1991

"Baron Blood… de badass vampire of de world. Ya sure dat yuh haven't heard of dat immortal mon?" Ambergai was mystified. By the fact of his own ignorance of Jeremy's middle name--- Fallsworth--- for one thing, but also by the protégé's obliviousness to dark undertones associated with the awesome bloodsucker. The English peer had taken refuge in Jamaica at more than one point during the fabled life lived a century before. There were some who said he still did… live, that is. The Rasta was gripped by the subject and could not grasp Jeremy's having missed the possible correlation before.

"Gai, no one but ma folks might know that name… not even ma breddas and sistas. I didn't even know it was attached to me until tapping ma birth certificate from ma dada's desk when I left the mountain." His English sank back a bit into highland patois when in the company of fellows, particularly this man. "But no, the name is foreign to me. Care to enlighten a bitty babi in his uninformed plight, ma don Dada Mon?" He smiled at the tall gorgon amidst stirrings always close to the surface in the presence of his teacher. Now proving no exception. The lurching junk pitched to thigh side under the table the two shared.

Rarity of an impromptu get-together provided welcome access for both men. Having taken to the streets two hours before, the soon-to-graduate Maroon youth had escaped the discombobulation at home as his new mother-in-law unloaded a fearsome mix of maternity and reproval upon the apartment.

His new wife had been prostrated almost the entire first two semesters of a surprise pregnancy. In the last trimester, now, the mama-to-be was less so, but still, the pregnancy had been a difficult one. Under the gun to provide 24/7 care for his bedridden bride, the too-young-to-be-a-daddy gave way readily upon being informed of a plethora of mistakes raining suffering onto the beloved daughter of Father and Mama Manley.

Coincidence had crossed paths of the long-time friends when Jeremy turned the corner directly into the warm armpit of the musky giant so dear to him. Arm raised in adjusting dreadlocks so iconically identifiable around Kingston, Jeremy's nose plunged deep into the axillary cleft ripe with memories of past proximities. The shock had left him further confused, senses on high alert and sanguine leg snake prowling inner confines of his pants by implicit call-to-arms.

Two hours into the dinner at their shared bistro found the pair chuckling inside a comfortable verve peculiar to just them. The subject of Jeremy's middle name had been raised by the roving inanities guiding the conversation over too much sangria.

"Ya, bwoy, de name deh pone wid whole heap of historical weight, now. De dread vampire be ah true pea of de realm o' Ole England an da fambily one wid whom to be reckoned. Might ya ave blood ties to dem du yuh tink? Or ah it just dat dey named ya afta de endearin' bedpan changa?" The tease caused the boy to grin. The dry wit evinced had molded his own personality through the past decade under the man's tutelage. Loss of that input made the humorous comment more poignant.

"Well, Gai, I cannot say for sure what may have been on ma parents' minds when they were coming up with a tenth babi's true name… I imagine there were either very profound or very fatuous methods used for the purpose. What think you?" The source of the nomenclature had made him wonder a time or two since discovery, having no basis for conjecture. "Think you that it may have to do with the vampirism rampant in the bestial lord you have just now described for me? If so, I do believe I may prefer to choose the second possibility."

"Pon de deepa subject mi a'go du ah likle research wid somebody mi know wo may be aware o som particulars pon de matta." The preponderant look made Jeremy think he would do just that.

"Are you able to tell me of the tie that interests you, don Dada? You do seem quite riveted on the subject, like maybe you have some personal connection…?" History and philosophical subjects always increased the student's level of interest; deep-thinking, enlightened theory drew the youth.

With that, the wise Rasta delved into the context of the English Falsworth family's bloodline, imparting details of a family tree entwined with centuries of English, Scottish and Welsh olden times. Seemingly, the nearness of the titled peerage to the crown had welded generations of Falsworths to intrigues and schemes rumored to have dogged royal lines since William seized power in the eleventh century conquering.

Should the Kells derive lineage of any sort from that, Ambergai desired to know of it. The boy was integrally important to him. In the context of the man's connections to Jamaica's hierarchy, Gai felt the subject merited more than just simple curiosity. Maroon bloodlines had been tangled into both Spanish as well as British ancestries by clandestine linkage over hundreds of years. Importance may be germane for more than just banal reasons.

He described the legacied transition to vampiredom resultant to an overzealous younger son's search for a raison d'etre. Changeling status came after exposure to Count Dracula during a sojourn dating to the tumult of the Great War period, aka: World War I. Subsequent underpinnings to dastardly doings by inveiglement into British politics had solidified the Falsworth name into murkier annals of antiquity commonly swept under history's rugs.

When the era of exile was recounted, pertinence skirted the personal. In the time of the First World War, John Falsworth had been immortalized and brainwashed by the legendary Count who then sent the young aristocrat to wreak havoc in Britain. After achieving truly evil status while working with German Intelligence around the English Isles, he had been identified and defeated in combat by the Union Jack. The vanquished noble barely escaped, somehow exiling himself to obscurity on the Jamaican Island, primarily around Port Royal, before an earthquake obliterated the old capitol city.

Rastafarianism and Santeria--- La Regla Lucumi--- had burgeoned in power and scope during that age. Santeria's ties with occultism reputedly attracted a weakened predator who revived his strength and confidence honing the dark arts learnt then. Rumor held that acolytes and sycophants had been secured during the refinement. By collective allusions in dialogue with Rasta elders, Ambergai had apparently gleaned a link of some sort with the Zion Hill commune.

Jeremy was entranced. He followed the serpentine tale while relaxing amid the unforeseen intimacy with his idol, mesmerized by it all. He learned that during the Nazi takeover in Germany, and the onset of the Second World War, Lord Falsworth's revitalized and immortal younger brother had returned to Europe. Colluding again with German Intelligence and, additionally, the monstrous Dr. Mengele, the malevolent aristocrat targeted important Allied personages and military leaders. The Union Jack again became involved upon taking notice of the signs, this time succeeding with wood-staking the heart of the ageless bloodsucker, thereby thwarting diabolical intentions of Dr. Mengele.

After the fall of the fascist regime, the blood-loving younger brother's demon body had been resurrected during a nocturnal visit from the Romanian Count himself. The spectre of the refashioned fiend surreptitiously retired to the countryside of England, seeking rejuvenation near the family estate, Falsworth Manor. There, he had murdered his old family doctor--- the person who had revived him through the wiles of the Count--- and fed on the fated man's daughter, assuming their house and identity.

Only upon being outed by the older brother's grandson, the next Lord Falsworth of the family lineage, were the ongoing serial murder conspiracies of Baron Blood--- as the cursed John Falsworth became known--- ended. For safety, his decapitated body had been secured in none other than The Tower of London this time, using a potion of Santeria extraction known as the Montesi Formula in order to sustain the vampire's deathly demise.

There existed lore which claimed that 'death' had been pronounced prematurely, even then. Gai related how, through a surfeit of stealthy moves, the again restored vampire had absconded himself to a 'far away land'. Unnamed. Jeremy's mentor seemed to believe it was, once more, the land of Jamdung... Jamaica.

Shivers assailed Jeremy in taking the meaning of his guru's interest to heart. Should the truth of matters deem relationship to the Falsworth bloodline a valid factor, it could convey a dark plot involving the handsome young Maroon. He disliked the prospect. An endearing bedpan changer suddenly appeared the better namesake option. The boy desired verification forthwith.

Would that he could.

"As much as I would like to, Gai, my responsibility lay with tending Aayla, even should Mama Manley prefer my absence. I have been away overlong already." Jeremy stood at the tucked side stair on Odeon Lane, wishing to throw care to the wind. Yet, he responded in the only manner that he knew could happen.

Ambergai nodded in sage acquiescence, "Mi understand, fi mi young fada-to-be, an ah gud one yuh will nuh doubt prove yourself as mi know aredi." Long fingers caressed the shoulder of his dear one, cognizant as the wise man was that profound changes were about to coalesce for the youth. Both lives were set on paths of change once more. Ambergai would need be satisfied with provisions he had set into motion and stand aside.

The embrace between them meant many things then. Just as the two pulled apart, shuffling sounds of booted steps sounded from above, on the upper landing. They peered into gloom as descending legs appeared, covered by a long rustling dress. An old woman materialized next, taking shape and gaining context. The midwife. Jeremy recognized the woman of perpetual frown over succeeding steps downward toward them. Concern filled him upon the apperception: she only came when Aayla had problems. He knew, because he had been the one to summon her thrice before, using Ambergai's recommendation.

"Ah gud eve to yuh, Missus Bledsoa. Ah aal to rights wid de likle moda an de wee one to cum, Madda?" Gai intoned the concern Jeremy felt. The younger man's consternation at her surprise appearance muted the boy's speech, Gai noted wryly. He stood, staring and agape, as the last three steps were trundled streetward. Jeremy's gulp was plainly audible.

"Well, mi see dat true to form, de fada an de bredren du show demselves afta aal be said an don. Yuh two may relieve yourselves by de knowledge dat dere be dree bonnie lasses a'cooing an a'milking togeda up dem yah stairs inna de babi's criss home…" her rare cackling laugh faded in a new daddy's ears upon the hearing, racing upward as he was.

Gai tarried to speak with the woman a few moments more, passing her a wad of notes in recompense for aid provision. Brimming eyes and mile-wide smile combined to placate what misgivings the revered midwife harbored, no doubt accustomed to such antics by erstwhile males of her species under these circumstances. Besides, she thought, this labor and delivery was unexpected and early. The men could not have known. He bowed respectfully to the medicine woman, then took leave, following Jeremy's triple-step trail upwards to the new baby bower.

He loved watching her sleep. Blissful innocence reflected in the miniature replica of Aayla never failed to halt his heartbeat for a few. This time was no exception. Jeremy cooed softly, whispering puffs of Dada breath over her babiness, laying there in her bassinet, angelic in repose.

At the lingering trace of the love wafts, whether by recognizance of the flavor infusing her nose or the tickles tantalizing cherubic cheeks, a wispy upturn of ruby red lips hinted at a subconscious instinct telling only one tale: I, Elle Worth Kell, am unconditionally loved.

Never could the attractive young man ever have dreamt of an iota of the feeling his big heart felt every time he thought of this tiny munchkin. Which was every moment, always. The strength of the feeling saturated every cell in his body. It was like a drug-induced state of euphoria that peaked in a continuum of infinity. No one had warned him.

The first night of her upstage to this world, Jeremy had bounded into the room and on to the scene in expectation of… well, he didn't have any idea. But whatever 'It' was turned out to be the most mind-boggling event of his short life. Indescribable.

Now, observing the teeny twitches responding to his breaths, the embodiment of perfection wrapped up in this elfin being--- sprung from his loins--- granted satisfaction to everything else. Her caramel skin, the peach fuzz head, the lacy eyelids hiding the smoky grey full-moon eyes within. The picture could neither fade nor lessen.

Then, the sun came out. Those almost silvery smoke-colored eyes peeked from inside the laciness. Envisioning the mirror image of them in the hovering face, babi Elle smiled brighter than any sunrise could hope to match.

Jeremy decided, once again. He would keep her.

October, 1992

The faint shimmer of the gauzy curtains, pushed by a light breeze off the street below, danced accompaniment to teensy high-pitched mews. Arising from inside the room, the tinkling nattered, reverberative and ethereal. The maker's lily-white throat trilled to the flitter of cunnilingual apprize. Spread-leg position--- locked and loaded--- V-shaped the sunbeams surrounding them. Her petite hands held thighs securely in place to preclude interruption of such heavenly sensations.

Traffic noises from the street, a mix of motorized, human and animal dissonance, complemented the surreal act of which the blonde had almost given up on ever experiencing. Vicarious enjoyment, she had thought, would just have to suffice. Until this day. This very afternoon.

Let it never stop, she mewed.

In the next room, a softly rhythmic mento melody intoned ambience to the interlude. Long overdue, she thought. When rational thought could be conjured. Impossible in the present spot. Lyrics were not discernible from the distance, yet the augmentative beat nevertheless obscured that which should not have been.

A falling lock latch didn't reach the girl's eardrums, taxed as she was. Without vision in functional mode, the swinging open of the flat door was concealed, too, and the light gasp of astonishment only barely registered. But, by then, it was too late.

The shriek pierced the mood like a sharp knife across a pig's throat. "Aayla! Girl! What in Hades is this going on here? Has the Devil invaded you?" Mama Manley's shocked derision could not have been more incisive.

Aayla's sex-smeared face popped up over bared lady-parts betokening Emily, whose legs withered in abject failure of muscled ability to respond in any fashion other than wrapping around her lady-friend's neck. A worse move could not have been devised had the two meant to do so. They had not.

Continued shower of pelting invectives alien to any good Catholic priest's wife's mouth issued in machine-gun volleys. Words Aayla had not ever heard out loud, let alone from her mother's mouth. The vituperation wreaked of blasphemy and hellfire. And spelled out just that in retributive description of what the dear daughter could expect. From Heavenly Inquisition, if not Earthly. Alighieri Dante had envisioned no level in Hell for which to place the mother of Mama Manley's granddaughter. None could suffice to permit atonement even should torture be meted out over an eternity, she declared.

Under her glower, the two bumfuzzled lovers disentangled their pretty bodies in mortified disgrace, rushing into the bedroom to clothe themselves, tardy as the action would prove. Neither desired returning to the maelstrom named Mama. Luckily… maybe… they were saved that further embarrassment by a sudden appearance of little Elle and her doting Dada.

Coming upon Mrs. Manley at the height of her righteous anger, the woman missed their entrance. Her expletive-laden sermon, certain to have been broadcast across the length and breadth of Half Way Tree, incited a ringing squeal of terror from six-month-old Elle.

Compounding the amalgam, the surprised father and his mother-in-law entered into their own contrastingly overlapping tête-à-tête. 'Have you any idea what your despicable wife has done?>> Why, no, Mama Manley, I am sure I don't…>> Well, she's already feeling the fires from Hell burning her worm-eaten soul as I speak these words!>> May we just settle down a bit and talk this over in a civil tone? Elle doesn't understand any of this and she's scared>> Better that she is forewarned of the iniquitous shame of this Jezebel than suffer the scorching Hellfire damnation of her touch!"

All the sentences were punctuated by the dissimilarity of her volume and his calmly deliberate responses. The tirade picked back up, ratcheting to even higher volume and epithetical harshness.

Seeing no alternative, he struck. "Mama Manley! Shush your filthy mouth… this instant. That is totally enough. If you are not able to control yourself in front of my child, you must leave."

Not a pause to be heard.

"All right then… I demand that you do so. NOW!" The take-charge voice cut into the harridan's harangue, smothering her into immediacy.

The silence deafened. The baby stopped. Even street sounds were blunted. Never in his life had Jeremy reacted in such fashion. Like a papa lion, he rose to his little girl's rescue by simple instinct. When the flabbergasted Catholic woman opened her mouth to finally respond, he shushed her again. With steely resolve. "Too late," he ordered, hand up. "You may take your leave. If, and when, you believe that you have yourself under control, you may call--- not show up--- and we shall discuss it. Give me your key."

The calm demeanor and resolute words upheld the term: decisive. A shocked woman minded. Handing her key to him, she stalked haughtily out and away. The baby and he listened to the retreat of her footsteps through a clomp down the stairs.

Stillness reigned.

April, 1993

Kitten kicks jostled Jeremy to wakefulness. Opening his eyes, he first, as always, focused on the little kit, Elle, her teeny feet reflexively kneading Dada's ripped belly. Silvery grey eyes wide shut, dreaming. Arms wrapped around his neck, darkly curled head nestled serenely into the safe muskiness of a muscled pit. Connecting them, languidly crossing both the elven two-year-old and her husband's smooth pec, palm cupping an erect nipple, lay Aayla's arm. The mirror-image mama reposed, sleepily ensconced as bookend to baby daddy's protective cocoon.

Perfectly proportioned little legs persisted in their prodding dream-channeled sprint, engendering a fatherly smile of bottomless affection by the innocent picture. He felt an ooze of dopamine-induced rush glimmer through his body. The charge grounded itself in a long arching stretch of the morning boner. The happy thing poked enquiringly from beneath the knit coverlet.

Lifting morning eyes to the adjacent doorway, he visualized an enthralled set of fixed onyx ones. The familiar sight caused another spasm from the inquisitive piece. Gai's caring paternalism bathed him in encompassing wholeness. How could every being important to his existence be so omnipresent in this moment, Jeremy mused? He lay, awash with contentment.

Smell of percolating coffee complemented a faraway rumble of low rolling thunder from far out over the incessant sea waves crashing distant rocks, making reminder of the situation here in the Zion Hill home where the three now interred. Discretely sequestered. Away from the tempest.

Extending rangy legs in slow creep so as to but gently jounce his feminine sleepers, twenty-one-year-old college Dada basked within the warmth of this guru's largesse, utterly sanguine in the vulnerable state.

The move pushed the quilt lower, exposing his body for further scrutiny by a cleverly disguised lead singer of the renowned reggae group, emblem of Jamaican essence as he was.

Now, Jeremy allowed--- no, he invited--- the man's dependably loving observation of himself with his woman and the lovechild between them. In all their natural glory. The man's display of fatherly intimacy imbued virtue. What enhancement could ever be added to such a moment, the lucky young Maroon reflected?

Retreat to their benefactor's home in Zion Hill the week before had smoothed the cutting edge of helplessness from the nasty scenario depicted by Aayla's formerly devoted parents. The gravity of animosity descending upon the little family by the combined wrath defining the beloved daughter's fall from grace was breathtaking.

That the son-in-law had refused to join the moralistic duplicity condemning the unforgiveable act only verified the Catholic priest and his wife in their righteous indignation: Jeremy, too, must be corrupt and godless. All beneficence previously bestowed by the orthodox Catholic couple had been misplaced. Disownment was demanded by their jealous, loving god. Sentence meted out like a Grecian thunderbolt.

Here, in the haven overlooking Bull Bay, balance had been reestablished. Jeremy made plain his distaste for the parents' estrangement, unaffected as he was by the 'sinful' act in which his wife had been caught. It mattered little to the new papa that Aayla had found a moment--- or even more--- of pleasure outside the privacy of their own relationship.

The intent for cuckolding bore absolutely no weight in his unjealous mind. Orgasm did not equal love… nor did it describe betrayal. It supposed pleasure. He simply could not wrap his head around the matrimonial promise demanding monogamy, seeing hypocrisy in such a slighted premise.

By his reckoning, love was not a marketable or contractible commodity. It was a willing state of mind, given freely in openness and faith. And sex was just that: sex. Nothing more. Finally, he had deduced, if these religious people walked truly along their righteous path, whatever had become of Jesus' code of forgiveness? Apparently, the turning of cheeks held a different meaning for some.

Settling the little elf into her mother's arms, he arose, padding unselfconsciously to the adjoining kitchen for a seat there and a cup of coffee with the man who understood. The two quietly communed about things: the coming day; the coming time.

"Suh fi mi young buck, shall wi mek fi wi way to de falls an de market… an de lady's lair… as wi planned fah tideh before mi guh pon de tour inna America as mi told yuh aredi?" The idyllic week was marking its end. At the question, Jeremy was momentarily butted by niggling concern. Yet due to agreement by previous capitulation, less so than he would have been. It was only that the time was now upon them that the misgivings fleeted through him. They were smothered in a trusting flash.

"I am looking forward to the day with you, ma don Gai. It will be a good way to spend the time in saying g'bye to you, ma dearest friend." He stood, cup in hand, and made way to the back door where he stepped down, pointing a fat shaft at the pot outside, off the stoop. Letting loose a stream, he peered back over a shoulder, grinning at the tall gorgon, expressing one more weak effort at voicing concern, "Do you still feel we must carry through on the meeting with your ex-wife? You do recall the continuing rift, and its cause, between us?"

The knowing grin illuminated the answer without a word, yet he said, "Indeed, de past history ah well known wid yuh two. Mi rememba de lass day yuh bot interacted. An mi included. Inna fact, mi seem to rememba som strifeful taak. An de afta-effects bring bak som clear memories, doh dem de a ah mite bit mo pleasant. Suh believe mi wen mi seh de meeting needs to be, ma bwoy. Dee be one afta-effect left dat needs to happen."

"Now, before mi let fi yuh present state of baring de stuff rite inna front o mi, wah mek nah put de clodes pon an wi mi can get pon wid it, instead o makin mi be doin someting here dat mi fint outta, wat wid fi yuh fambily inna de nex room, huh?" The respectable man nodded sagely toward Jeremy's nakedness as the tactful words emerged. The slap to the rounded glute lent gist to the good-natured smirk. A true Jamaican diplomat…

…The men climbed a faint trail on its winding pathway through thick underbrush. Lush copses exuded verdant viability; busy wildlife ignored their passage. Emergent underground rivulets trickled in burbling transection of their route on the trip to the hidden hideaway housing Starleen. The very rivulets marking the beginnings of the Cave River Falls by which the pair had passed earlier. Where they had tarried to enjoy the beauty awhile.

The stop by the market on the way gathered together a goods pack of suitable worth. Meant to secure a welcome. Little dialogue passed between them, each introverting to thoughts and impressions bent on private ideas either already or not yet spoken.

Several miles distant from Zion Hill, the mood shifted to a foreboding stillness. Through the upward trend, undertone echoes off the sea and wildlife chatter both diminished, setting an air of apprehension. The change effected rising trepidation. In following his mentor's footsteps, he felt each step fall heavier than the one before.

The atmosphere thickened instead of lightening as typical of higher altitudes. The grown boy's reticence to go forward took more and more effort to overcome. Only by the sangfroid of the trusted male's lead was he made capable. He did not look with ease on the coming encounter. Rather, he focused on the measuredly composed father figure before him, musing how he maintained it.

Even so, as the hikers climbed, Jeremy detected a faint hitch invade the supremely confident man's gait. Approach to the priestess' bower, so far above the center of Rastafarian influence, conveyed a taint of Santeria-based quintessence. It hung on the edge of consciousness.

Just the contemplation of the formidable woman's name sent small shivers about his body. Starleen. Her abrupt departure from Ambergai's life years before had ushered in unforeseen alterations to the relationship with the don gorgon, changing both men's lives forever. Unquestioningly a betterment, it came with a heavy premium.

While 'that incident' afforded impetus for an exit, her scarcity did not settle a much-younger Jeremy's qualms. Or, more relevant, this older, more educated Jeremy's qualms. The truth regarding her left a festering seed of dread. Her nebula, a dark silhouette against other luminous matter, hovered just outside Jeremy's sentience, injecting a sense of impending fate. Lacking distinction between good or bad, the ominous unknown created a nodus of anxiety. One which would need be dealt with at some point.

It seemed the day had arrived… Starleen. How had this strong man with so many valued traits, the man so many people respected, ever become involved with such a woman? And to the point of matrimony? It was a true puzzle, the concept of which eluded him.

Starleen: fourth wife and mystic, fearsome priestess of that called Santeria. She, the one versed in the occultist ways of that sacrifice-based, blood-obsessed cult practiced in the dark of night far off the more common orbits of religion.

She, the one in purported league with a strange Sasabonsam who held hegemony over a crew of fabled toadies. Minions of bleak thralldom who carried out his sinister aims and on whom it was whispered he fed periodically. Of their flesh. And blood.

Individually untenable wiles joined in congruence of method, if not purpose, for achievement of their exploitive ends. The two--- priestess and Sasabonsam--- were rumored to wield power over a bizarre stable of chimera by blending their nefarious practices. Simpleton beings of variable size and shape, mimicking the roots from which they sprang. Exhibiting vampiric, animalistic and hominid characteristics ranging from immortality to heightened senses to manic sexuality. Occultism personified.

It was alleged that the profane feedings left indolent ulcers and indurated lesions over bodies and necks which Starleen supposedly nursed with milk-infused mandragora poultices. Leaves of redoubtable renown. From the very plant, which, curiously, held repute as the clones' conceptive font. By conjure from the strange humanoid-shaped root of it.

Mandragora officinarum, the species. Mandrake. The same one alleged to register complaint by shrill screams of distress and moans of agony at being yanked from its preferred soil-nestled, deep-rooted state.

The ironic substantiation of the foul rot forged by this collaborative fusion betwixt moral fringes--- for no one doubted Starleen's virtuous Myalistic attributes, nor the nefarious Sasabonsam's devilish ones--- lay in the altruistic virtues of the ancient plant's properties.

Used medicinally for millennia, the root functioned as anodyne and soporific. Even as anesthetic in surgical procedures undertaken by advanced civilizations from the Far East to Persia to Egypt, Greece, then Rome; all the way through Henry VIII's and Elizabeth I's reigns in English history.

As an amulet, it was once placed on mantelpieces to avert misfortune and to bring prosperity with happiness to the house; longevity and storge to linked inhabitants. A strong talisman, indeed.

All this, Jeremy had studied, somehow needing to school himself in that which was perceived as threatening, at least on some levels. He pondered the range of subjects Starleen reckoned within her purview as the two closed in on the priestess' lair. Under no illusions that he but scratched the surface of her plethoric abilities and pursuits, the need to be forewarned nonetheless beckoned. Hence, the study. And resultant trepidation.

Coming over a wooded rise, spatter of water tinkled over rocks somewhere nearby. The two men slowed, then halted. Before them, a larger copse of non-native hemlock trees ringed a small rounded hilltop. Shadowed, yet visible within, there appeared a stone cottage.

Swathed in deep green bryony vine, a chimney poked defiantly through the dense cover, like a bayonet. The thing came to masonry point at its apex. Curling tendrils of smoke rose out of it, strangely spectral, dispersing in the fanning highland breeze. Toward the Caribbean.

A shimmer reflected from the thick covering, almost velvety from their vantage point. Varying sized orange and yellow pepos dotted the growth. The attractive house lay swaddled by beds of wood betony, spiking flowering heads of crimson and violet hues. Though a quite pleasing picture, an omnipresence of something otherworldly dampened the place. It struck Jeremy that all the flora on the hilltop were of non-indigenous origin. The effect whelmed them to silence.

Ambergai's hand reached to Jeremy's shoulder, in signal to remain quiet. A look between them reinforced wariness of the scenario. Whispering into his ear, piffling outflow of words tickled the grown boy. The mentor intoned a warning, "Du nah mek known fi yuh middle name while here, Jeremy. Mi feelin' dat could be ah mistake, suh hole dat close an leave it between just wi, huh? An carefully fala fi mi lead inna aal tings." After another moment, he added an extra cautionary, "Yuh nuffi eating or drinking notin while here." The admonition spiked a spineward chill.

Almost as punctuation, the heavy door to the nestled cottage creaked slowly inward, revealing an unsettling sight. Filling the doorway stood a smiling Starleen. The emanation of unexpected charm sent alarm bells jangling the boy's frame. He'd expected lightning bolts.

Cascading dreadlocks of almost body length captured a bell-curve shape in overview. The tall woman exuded motherliness in calculated effort to disarm. Handsome features of an alluring face showed no signs of aging since Jeremy's last interaction with her some eight years before. A willowy body filled a clinging robe of diaphanous fabric, leaving little of the woman's anatomy to be imagined. Nothing else covered that beneath. Ebony curves and buxom fullness made a voluptuous statement of sensuality, as also clearly intended. Between the discordant maternal and sultry vibes, Jeremy wondered at the undercurrents being driven.

The breeze above dipped in downdraft over the place where the two men stood, directing smoke from the discharging chimney. Odors of wood smoke imbued with cinnamon and apple, and something mawkish, saturated their olfactory senses. It relaxed the men in seconds. Again, as meant. How long had the woman been awaiting their arrival? For plainly it had been anticipated.

Ambergai's hand stayed on Jeremy's shoulder, instructive by its inaction. Starleen finally broke the silence, "Ahh, ah sight fah sore eyes… de ranking don dada Rasta from de uptown be paying mi ah visit wid iz sambo. An dey luk to toting ah cache of goods--- fi mi? Well, just be coming inside an wi will seh som tings." Jeremy could see by his companion's wide eyes she was not just 'saying some things'. There was a bit of 'showing some things' going on, as well. Ambergai was noticing.

The reference to himself as Sambo left him bemused, speculating whether it was a simple allusion to his lighter skin, his state of maturation or his relationship to her ex. Not even certain the woman recognized him as the boy from that night long ago, he wordlessly trailed Ambergai toward the door, hoisting the pack down from his shoulder.

Passing the threshold, he was astounded by the transformation. No way the spanning extent could be this, said Jeremy's brain. His eyes registered otherwise. The interior appeared four to five times larger in area than the outside. Whereas the cottage had appeared diminutive and enshrouded, upon entering, the abode reconciled the senses to an open, airy atmosphere of much larger girth than augured. Arching timbers accentuated high ceilings; unshaded upper windows permitted and dispersed bright stippled sunlight. The effect established a feeling of expanse.

One huge room lay sectioned into distinct quarters, delineating various functional parts.

A utilitarian kitchen populated by pot belly stove and large copper sink, with small icebox and cupboarded shelves, anchored one side. Draping an adjacent space, there hung artful quilts shielding an apparent private cove and sleeping space. The middle lay anchored by the base of a large fireplace, open on opposing sides. Its chimney rose to the ceiling, clad in rounded river rocks. The circumference diminished as it stretched upwards, giving credence to the exterior appearance of a spiked flue.

A far wall displayed multitudes of ongoing projects, undertakings and craftwork. A complex glass distillation apparatus sat assembled, colored liquids gurgling through elaborate tubing. Miniature doll-like figures, intricate knitting devices, a loom, suspended herbs, drying plants, curing spices and desiccating roots occupied the long wooden work bench hugging half its length. The other half was lined by a bracketed trestle table, itself covered by bottles, canisters, boxes and containers. Ranging sizes, they lay in stages of open spillage to closed clasped lids.

Competing aromas of roasting meats and sautéing vegetables assailed their nostrils from a wide array of cookery on the stove but the cloying odor noticed earlier from the fuming chimney undergirded all by its stewing pall, pervading close confines.

Ushering the men inside, Starleen pointed out overstuffed easy chairs, "Mek som cumfat to de handsome two o y'selves while mi get yuh som food an drink, eh?" She relieved Jeremy of the proffered pack, clucking enquiringly in picking over its contents.

"Very hospitable of yuh, Starleen, an wi a dankful to be invited into fi yuh home like dis widout notice, mi am sure. But we do not be here for social reasons an mi am fairly sure yuh know it." Ambergai's fulsome smile projected precognition. By it and the words, the consummate diplomat informed his ex-confidant and wife of the status of things. "As yuh a awah, mi lady, mi nah partial to cajolery an doh mi am feeling de vibe yuh be putting into fi mi face--- ah mighty powerfully alluring one mi might add--- wi deh ya fi de discussion of one subject wish mi am guessin yuh aredi know of, too…?"

The short speech deflated the room. And the woman. Her flowing gown wavered around her as she fairly 'hrumphed' a wordless response. Gliding seductress and beguiling smile dropped in similar suddenness to a hooked fish hitting the landing deck. Her dreadlocks fell forward as she dipped her head, masking her face. She became unreadable. Ambergai sat chill still, chin on hand, elbow propped. An enigmatic smile remained frozen on his face as his black eyes bore into her.

Seconds stretched to a pregnant pause. Jeremy was taken aback, thinking something dreadful must be imminent. He tensed, ready for a catapult to the door in attempt at escape. Why had Gai just done so blatantly rude a thing as to affront the chatelaine immediately upon their entry, he thought?

The older two held immobile in tacit battle of wills, energy flowing back and forth which, though palpable, was invisible. Jeremy sensed it, however, feeling both embroiled and left out by the exchange. What was he missing? These people were engaged with one another on a plane that he could not comprehend. It was discombobulating.

Then, in a flash, the atmosphere cleared. The woman raised her head, dreads receding from her face, and a grin of almost self-deprecating resignation replaced the substance that had just darkened the entire space. "Well, ah gyal mus du wat shi can ah it nah suh, fi mi dear resolute mon? Yuh mus allow mi at least dat, eh?"

She cast a glance in Jeremy's direction. "Suh, Sambo, mi understand dat yuh ave aspirations fah school an fi yuh fambily but a inna ah bit of ah tight spot. It seems to be de repeating theme fah yuh, now doesn't it young mon?" As she had never had meaningful conversation before with him, he remained quiet. Looking between the dreadlocked pair, 'Sambo' felt both perplexed and quite juvenile under the circumstances. The nappy-haired pikny of years before re-emerged, withholding any reply. How could the woman be aware of any of this, he pondered?

"Yuh a sure to be able to speak inna adult manna wid dis lady ef yuh first open fi yuh mout now, Jeremy," Ambergai chortled at the speechless chagrin gripping his ward, mindful of history between the two as he was.

Gathering wits, as he had learned to do at Boy's College these previous years, and on multiple occasions at his current school, University of the West Indies, the mountain boy hastily tackled the bafflement confounding him. He glanced toward his mentor, then barged ahead.

"Yes, madam, all that you say is correct, though I admit surprise at your knowledge of it. Mr. Gee and I have discussed the matter of my future and have concluded it would be helpful if you might see your way to adding counsel. I am here to seek it. My benefactor has been instrumental in paving a way for improving myself, something never dreamed possible. Without him, it could not have been." Casting another sidelong glance of warm affection that direction, Jeremy continued.

"The path you have already traveled is one of which I might also benefit. Along with the expertise you have in... certain areas... I would be very beholden should you find your way to enlightening me. Please." The mentally practiced speech, planned weeks before, tumbled out. He had thought to never actually make it, feeling such a plan could and would never come to fruition. He exhaled and sat back in relief, having confronted a childhood demon. And survived. Once again.

The ensuing hour saw three heads come together, addressing methods and stratagems for dealing with dilemmas now plaguing, as well as challenging, his life. Starleen proved particularly forthcoming proposing ways for addressing issues he and Ambergai had stumbled over in ignorance of a system foreign to them both.

While the reggae singer and former farmer had achieved celebrity and status by navigating paths amidst the hierarchy of Jamaican society, the man's natural ingenuity did not allow for challenges posed by academia and the educational system. His enablement for Jeremy's inclusion in Boy's College was resultant to favors drawn on. The stellar student's acceptance into university had been hard won by personal study ethic and diligence of purpose which gained him acceptance on merit. Both found themselves out of their league regarding an American system of higher learning.

A system with which Starleen was integrally familiar. It had startled the student to learn of the woman's academic achievements. More so, to converse with her in Queen's English. He learned that her reversion to highland patois reflected a calculated tactic for return to her roots; enabling fulfillment of vows for cultural enrichment of her country.

Jeremy now absorbed that the face put out publicly was just that. A cleverly designed front. The meme functioned to advance multiple goals in pursuit of an elusive one. One which would apparently remain unstated. Allusions by both men to that mystery were deftly deflected. After devising a plan of action the trio finally sat back, now at ease enough to converse personally.

"So, Jeremy, will you be including Hagley Gap family in your plans?" Starleen was clearly curious as to his situation on Blue Mountain, having left Hagley Gap, like him, years before.

"No, Madam, I won't. They have repeatedly rebuffed any attempt at ending our estrangement. My parents and siblings prefer that I not be part of their life, and frankly, my reconcilement to that has been achieved. I won't be a part of anything so negative as that which they profess. All has been left behind. I am quite surprised to find your openness in the matter, now. It was not what I would have expected. As you remember, our last encounter was one which left quite a bit up in the air between us. Child that I was."

His wryness was not lost on Starleen. "Yes, 'tis true, youngster, we did part on uncertain terms, did we not? By look of things, my ex here has left you in the dark on some things, now that I see you together. However," and she addressed Gai when she continued, "you were not left entirely without options, you know. After all, you knew of my desire to avoid an encumbering predicament which would no doubt have occurred had I remained."

"The substitution," here, a nod back at Jeremy, "provided a viable option… of which I note you embraced quite readily. And, in hindsight, pretty much on the spot. Probably best that I departed in the manner already hashed over, I believe. You made do rather well, Sir Rasta don gorgon…" she snickered through the last comment, unabashed in addressing the remaining elephant in the room. "And, now, what with the young man's dabbling in the art of conception, it would seem we may have traveled full circle. Or might I be mistaken?" The arched brow said everything that remained to be.

"Indeed, now, de battybwoy would appear aal grown up an pon iz way to making ah way fi de bess, m'lady, but mi du nah forsee miself ah burning bridges such as de way of wish yuh seem very adept edah, huh?" The handsome man smirked good-naturedly, continuing, "Suh wah mek dont wi just be tinkin bout partaking of som dat delectable smellin food before mi decide mi ah needin to partake o som o de batty here inna dis room, of wish mi am intimately familiar wid yuh both, as wi aal know…?"

The kneading grope to his full crotch evoked a snort of disdain from Starleen. Jeremy's incredulous look brought laughter from them, close on the heels. "Oh, an mi almost forgot bout dat warning regarding nuh food or drink here inna de witch's domain. It sure did mek fi de gud furderance of de mystique of de place, nuh?" It was now Jeremy's turn to smirk.

The trip of retrace back to Zion Hill was remarkably lighter. Bellies filled several hours before and herbal chalice shared between the three afterwards had sufficed to send the men on their way home much satisfied. Ambergai pocketed the amulet and potion concocted by the wise priestess of the hemlock-ringed cottage, taking care to follow instructions for preservation of the dual aids. They bantered contentedly on the trail.

"Suh, fi mi bwoy, an new dada, du yuh feel relieved at aal, afta fi wi meeting up pon de fearsome hill wid fi mi ex-lady de witch oman?" Still high on sinsemilla from Starleen's private stock, he was fairly floating in good humor. Renewal with his protégé this day had ushered in a sense of satisfaction to their dynamic. One notably lacking over previous months. What with the singer's international concert tour set to begin and Jeremy's sequestration with the small circle encompassing his wife and baby, the men had been unable to share in ways so previously comfortable between them.

"Yes, Gai, I am so. Though I am puzzled by the manner the entire affair was carried out. Was all of the mysterious intrigue really necessary, ma don dada?" Jeremy remained somewhat confused even with the successful excursion. His present mental state of contentment matched his guru's, yet he wanted to know.

"Be yuh telling mi dat yuh a nah glad of fi wi results an gud plan wrought tideh?"

"Not at all, Gai. I am exultant. Nothing could have been figured better, the way the two of you have intervened for me and my family. I will be forever in your debt... ma gravilicious-hooded gorgon". Whatever engendered that allusion at that moment stumped him, but response was immediate.

"Now, ma delectable battybwoy. Be ah prodding de billy goat inna de manna o dat at fi yuh own peril. Yuh mussi aware of fi mi lack of parting de gates of pleasure of late, wat wid de way tings a, huh?" The faraway look and inadvertent rustling of the poorly hidden mound jostling between the tall man's thighs brought Jeremy up short.

"Are you truly telling me that the don dada of us all is coming up without necessary help taking care of the grindsman dweller there?" He pointed, close as he was, directly at the homunculus with whom he had been tethered for so long in his training days. A massive lurch of two stoned crotch shafts nearly made noise, such was their vehemence. No other words were spoken.

Jeremy, rarely the leader in past escapades, grasped the behemoth in both hands, pulling the seven-foot-tall stud of a man into brush cover beside the pathway. Close to dusk as it was, shadows shielded them from sight, should any passersby happen. They pushed deeper into the woods. A tall ceiba tree stood amidst groundcover of both cottony cloaking from the huge tree and emerald moss beneath, making an inches thick cushion.

An excess of exuberance triggered long latent horndoggery, engulfing them in rut of passion. Whipping the ever-present hemp belt from hemp trousers, the handsome Maroon yanked both from their perch over familiar muskiness that was the engorging groin. The hood arose in beckoning plaint, needing the long-lost batty so long dominated in preceding innocent years.

Now, the giant thing bounced up in surprise at the unexpected appeal for its attendance. The haste with which Jeremy made to descend caused colliding anatomies to smack together, contact points sizzling in abrupt apposition. His talented tongue, unused of late, slathered and slid in exploring the begging protuberance. Insistent on attention, the arching shaft butted and batted all around the ready mouth intent on placation.

Half a dozen sliding trips up, down and around fatly neglected balls and sproinging prong proved all that was necessary for the thing to howl ejaculative crest. Heaving an exhalative sigh, no words came with the noisy release, overlong in its absence. Long ebony fingers caressingly encouraged the head executing a prerogative once taken for granted. Copious emissions drenched a welcoming set of tonsils, starved as they were for the nectar upon which they had been nurtured.

Without hesitation, the eye still dribbling murmurs of creamy assent, an unmasked demon that was the huge spongy corona aimed and pushed back throatward. Not about to permit an ending so premature, Gai prodded deep, knowing of the recipient chute's ability for making it disappear. Heat nearly melded two well-fitting pieces into one, so eagerly did the duality unite.

Gagless acceptance marked Jeremy's compliance. Chin-hugging ballsmack bottomed the plugging. Cessation of voluntary motion cemented the deal. The contract between the engagers called for, and received, mollification by instinctive deepthroat seating. For moment on top of honeyed moment.

Epiglottal glugging marked the sole enhancing motion of that acquainting swallow. Nascence of rotative stimulations then evolved into ongoing play that marked the men's enjoinment. In apprehension of additional need, the boy's hands slid to trim ankles. Massaging deliberately, fingers made incorporation of adjunct ministrations a role-playing reprise in an opus of tactility, moving from wide feet upwards to as high as they could reach, swirling and rubbing in their progress over the honed body.

Gai leaned back, already sapped yet not even begun, against smooth bark of the heritage silk-cotton tree shielding the pair. Wispy projectiles of cottony strands floated down over them as the interlude developed, dressing them in gossamer downiness. It tickled.

His torso rested next to the wide bole over minutes of careful measures long idle in the chore so lovingly joined. Never, ever enough for either's appetite, actions defined mutuality of effort toward repletion peculiar to them.

Each reveled in the motifs dancing their continuum of a fugue fiddling poetic personification. Past, present and would-be future... both were aware of fragile permanence. Time held no relevance; absence thereof, likewise. The latter afforded only whetting.

Following a third zenith, the couple ebbed momentarily, lazing downward as one. Presaging coupling, anilingual empathy then bade purring promulgation by missionary clasp. Both ends, heads and tails, merged for a homestretch abuttal of inclusive rapparee, plundering one another in encompassing rapture.

The long final slide of eleven inches to a resting place of oozing tincture, deeply embedded together, brought wrestling tongues to writhing entanglement. Jarring the senses, two as one rang halcyon bells known only unto themselves.

Satiety teemed two souls in indivisible fulfilment. They slept.

Perhaps it was minutes, perchance hours. Unmeasured, they lay sealed together through sleep and rejuvenative sequelae of concupiscent repetition. Need forced the proceeding union, unabated. By natural affinity, the two remained one during it all.

Only upon awakening together during the nocturnum did the pair register a cocoon of feathery down enmeshing their linked state. Naked as they were, the stuff offered warmth where skins did not touch. Eye to eye, black eyes surveilling grey, a delusion of hooked perpetuity plastered their psyches. Would that they could remain forever bound such as they were.

The tie persisted until predawn. Only lightening of the branches overhead awakened consideration to things apart from their linking. Reluctant separation and ridding of the feathery dusting brought the two upright once more. Brushing away interlacing cotton strands proved regretful by its inference, sundering that to which it had been bound through the night.

Washing together in a brook nearby, the Maroon boy harkened on a presence not perceived before. Into peripheral vision came nuance of movement. Pulling away from his lover's look, he visualized not one but two manifestations. There, not thirty feet distant, stood the twins. Eko and Iko. The albino brothers from the Cave River Falls camping trip with Kwaku. Red eyes studied the two bathers, seeing every move; every inch of bare skin.

"Gai, don't look too quickly, but we are being observed, ma don dada." He was not fearful of the two, not since the episode on the big rock at the falls. The two had been harmless. Insatiable, yet harmless.

Seconds passed, then Ambergai altered his wash pattern on Jeremy, turning both around in the motion so that the dreadlocked man was facing the onlookers. His face turned stony upon visualization. "Ma young bredrin, dere be ah pair of astral beings. Du yuh see de faint sparkle to fi dem skin? De like of wish ave been ah conjured fram anoda domain. Dem ah familiar to mi fram de telling by oders."

Though they did not transmit menacing behavior, the tall man was noticeably disturbed by the appearance of the breddas. "Ma understanding of dem ah dat dem ah dralls… an it be de masta dat be de dreat. Dependin pon dat being's intent be de danga, ef ah one to be had."

Jeremy was perplexed. "But Gai. I know them. They spent time with me that first summer I came down the mountain. They were friendly---overly friendly. Not dangerous." He placed warm palms on the giant man's smooth chest, seeking explanation.

Stony look went narrow, pupils to slit-like. "Yuh be tellin mi da doondoos dere... yuh be knowin dem? Ou close did yuh get to dem? Did yuh speak wid dem, ma bwoy?" Alarm bells were sounding in the sage man's skull at these tidings. "Tink hawd now. Ou close to dem did yuh get?"

"Gai. My don dada. We were very close. Spent time together. They showed up at the falls when Kwaku and I camped there over Emancipation Day holiday. They... didn't hurt us, Gai... although, at first we feared them. But when they got high with us, they became... more friendly."

The spectral visions continued rapt. Attention, as with the previous encounter, fixed on the appendages so recently over-used. Intentions plain. No other overt movement occurred. Even eyelids were still, as before. But the sparkle Gai had pointed out was perceptible. A faint limning on their edges. It was a difference, Jeremy registered. It hadn't been there the first time. He would've seen it... or felt it. So, no, it was new. He told this to the Rastafarian, too.

"Suh, yuh be tellin mi dat yuh an Kwaku shared de chalice? A cutchie?" The trepidation factor zoomed upward.

"Yes, Gai, I am saying that. But we also... shared more than that. They gave each of us some primo head... several times each. Then, they had sex together. Mad rough love, right in front of us. And several Rastas who happened on us during it. It was a communal thing, Gai. Is that bad?"

Slitted eyes went dead, boring into him at the description. The sotto voice went to whisper, "Yuh had sex wid de pair of dem yon doondoos? Yuh bein certain it was dem? Nuh oders?" He introspected. Cogs were turning, on full display now. Jeremy was flummoxed. He turned, peering over his shoulder, watching the breddas in fascination, trying to understand.

As he did, the pair began fondling one another. Each touch sparked tiny spews of light fizzles, arcing off points of contact. In different directions, some projecting geometric designs in the air. As if gravity had no effect.

Finally, Gai came back. He focused first on the boy--- his boy, of enigmatic name; then the twins. "Just wen did yuh seh dis happened? Emancipation Day? Wat--- inna August den, wen yuh disappeared bak inna de year 1989, yuh seh, Jeremy? An did yuh seh dere were de sparkles going pon... or not?" He was interrogating now.

Jeremy was getting hard, despite himself, watching elevating megadongs across the clearing. "That was it, Gai. Yes, I remember, because we left the city on the first, got to the falls at sunset that evening. It was beautiful. We climbed down the falls as dusk came on. The clouds were amazing--- different colors. So was the moon. It came up as the sun went down. Truly dazzling, Gai. And blood red. They awakened us the next dawn. Does that help?" He reached for Gai's languid piece.

"Yes, bwoy it does. Suh, de Full Red Moon of August. An, nuh sparkles? Even wen yuh touched dem, or wen de doondoos shot fi dem wads?" Though he grinned saying it, he was intent on a reply. The head shake in response answered another part of the conundrum.

Explaining to his grown ward, he told how the images now were only that... images. Projections from another dimension or place. Not real. However, on that day in 1989, during the blood moon, the two were actually present in the flesh. An ongoing and repetitive phenomenon. When cast into this dimension, the brothers loosely tied themselves to the Zion Hill community, having appeared the first time several generations before. The incidents portended times when their controller might travel to, or take refuge on, the island. As he spoke, Gai pieced together the truth. Long a mystery, it now gelled in the man's mind.

He explained how the duo's master, a doom Bakra of inveterate evil--- Obeah-esque, but much worse--- must have secured a narrow window of opportunity to reappear where a portal might only periodically be forced open. Highly treacherous, he sent the doondoos or other acolytes ahead first to test it. Only then might he make use of an aperture. Maybe.

Sometimes the overlord must have only observed. Depending on nefarious aims at each occasion. Gai induced that on the blood moon date, Eko and Iko became distracted by Jeremy and Kwaku. Their notably overactive libidos had kicked in. Had the doom Bakra watched the goings-on that time, Ambergai apprehensively considered?

By staying too long, they must have inadvertently been locked into the locale for a time afterwards, staying in their byer close to Zion Hill until another portal re-opened. Apparently, one had done so sometime after the blood moon in 1989, or the two would be present in the flesh now. Gai and Jeremy watched the two spectres from the safety of the brook. Though a portal was not open for passage, the astral window must allow for periodic visuals with other places. The doondoos apparently liked this site... or maybe its inhabitants.

At the moment, they seemed preoccupied by one another, going at it in effusive evidence of goal-oriented work, on full display for Jeremy and Gai. The pair desired an audience, without doubt.

Jeremy, still squeezing the tool next to him while voyeuring, thought of something, "Gai, does anyone know the identity of the master who controls them and comes here?"

"Oh, fah sure, dat. Dere beinna de ogre's main opposition, but also iz ah sometime partna an colleague. Starleen." The look of dismay brought Gai's quick reassurance. She provided the major bulwark against his attempted hegemony over the island nation and was not the overlord's true partner. The priestess nursed sick and wounded acolytes when needed, thereby securing partial allegiance. Unbeknownst, and surely frustrating, for the traveling evil doer.

"Gai, who is he?" The name hadn't been spoken. He wanted to know why.

"Well Jeremy, mi had hoped to kip dat fram yuh fah fi yuh own safety an fi yuh fambily. But now, mi feel yuh mus need to know. Mi only be willing to seh dis now knowing of fi yuh imminent plans fah relocation far fram dis place. De name of de being be Baron Blood... de dread Lawd Falsworth.

June, 1996

The annals of Rome--- in particular: 'Lives of the Twelve Gods' as narrated by Suetonius--- were causing him blurred vision. Jeremy sat back from the tome, rubbing weary eyes with balled fists. Although enraptured by historians and philosophers of old, presently he was only barely regaining his concentration and catching up. There were still times he found it hard to focus.

What with his and Aayla's separation, marked by her abrupt departure, he had experienced difficulty on practically every living level. The graduate student gazed distractedly out an adjacent window, thinking back on the debacle. Only recently resolved, he still suffered stressful periods such as now. Looking down on the starlit lane below, Pease Street exhibited scant activity at this hour. Three AM had jarred his brain by gonging of the mantle clock. The one picked up at the thrift shop off Guadalupe Street when Aayla and he had first settled in central Texas more than three years before.

Hasty departure from Kingston back then was facilitated by his friend and mentor, Ambergai Gee, who had worked together with Starleen, the Santeria priestess. She who was well-versed with the machinations of emigration, having done so herself upon deciding to seek further education in the United States. At the University of Texas in Austin.

The flagship institution with Tier One status had fit the bill nicely for the young Maroon from Jamaica, seeking respite from vindictive in-laws and an unforgiving Catholic Church bent on destruction of his sinful wife. And by extension, himself. Little Elle was just collateral damage.

Austin had provided refuge in the form of a liberal arts bastion populated by highly-educated citizenry and striving student body. It had proven to be a niche for which Jeremy Kell was particularly suited. His pursuit of a PhD in Philosophy had rocketed toward a successful advent in an America of which the boy had been only circumspectly aware. Hagley Gap on Blue Mountain, and even Kingston, were worlds apart from the cosmopolitan Hill Country metropolis.

Having melded easily into the higher education venue, winning a full academic scholarship in the first year of attendance, he had thought his life could not get any better. Between Aayla and Elle, the little light of his life, the island boy had thrown himself headlong into achieving goals set back at the Jamaica Boy's College years before. That he could concentrate on studies without working full time to support his budding family had been a boon of great worth.

Unfortunately, Aayla had not agreed. While at first the couple had done well in the new city, the baby growing and thriving, the changes had ultimately unhinged his Jamaican wife. Aayla misunderstood American culture. Societal aberrations from that which she had known, along with the loss of status enjoyed amongst Kingston society, elevated the girl's anxiety level way past the point of boiling over.

In the angst of her discontent, she had somewhere along the line boomeranged from a highpoint of dawn-in-America, into the depths of depression, then back upwards in opposing trajectories. Jeremy had not been invited along.

Without warning or explanation, she had taken up with a worldly law student of parent-supported means. A lifestyle of highfalutin consumerism had stolen the girl from him before he had even been aware transition was in the works. One moment worried for her sanity; the next, wondering what had just happened.

A certain evening two previous autumns, soon after fall term began, he had come home to a note on the kitchen counter and a vacated closet. The worst part, though, had been rushing into the empty bedroom of his little jewel, Elle. Aayla had moved the two, lock, stock and barrel, into a palatial home of the law student just beginning life as a litigator in his father's firm.

Jeremy was devastated. He came within a hair's breadth of dropping school and leaving the city. After all, he reasoned, what was there here for him? His raison d'être had been taken from him: baby Elle was gone.

Regrouping in solitude for a time, he discarded chaff and focused: what was important to him as a man and a father? He then came out swinging. Mounting a herculean effort, he procured legal aid. Determined to gain rights in the matter. Left with no alternatives, Jeremy had been forced to file a bigamy charge as a battering ram against his doubly married bride. The distasteful tactic rescued his own sanity. Over the succeeding year, the dedicated dada finally wrested back his rights. In the guise of his little elf. Judgment for shared status had been granted.

Now, as he thought back, all had been worthwhile in the endeavour. He was on fast track toward the coveted degree. PhD. Jeremy Fallsworth Kell was on the verge of a title, professional that it be. He could not be more proud for himself. And, Elle Worth Kell was along for the ride.

Aayla Who?

"Daddy, why do you always keep your head shaved? Are you bald?" The precocious sprite was constantly pushing limits. Inquisitive nature mixed with quickness of mind had been challenging the loving Daddy since that most cherished of words had first been uttered. He smiled benevolently now in contemplating this newest puzzle.

"Why, no, young lady, quite the contrary. Your Daddy is quite capable of covering his entire head with nappy plugs at any old time he might desire. But, he left the fashion of that look far behind him in his home country of--- do you know where?"

"Jamaica land. Jam-Down. The island of Rastariverimee! Where Uncle Gai lives," came the excited reply. Then the imp went on, "Daddy, don't you think that you would get more looks from egg-lible girls if you had more of it up there?" The question begged several itself.

Jeremy chortled at the presumption, and the off-base conclusion, in all its youthful temerity. "The word is 'Rasta-far-i-an-ism'. What, exactly, makes you think your extremely handsome and debonair Daddy would need yukky old hair just to land a yukky old girl, little missy? Where did that idea come from, anyway?" He continued perusing cereal aisle shelves, unable to locate the non-sugar saturated variety he preferred for the hyperactive girl helping him. American grocery stores were overwhelming by their breadth of abundance.

She climbed the front of the grocery cart in spelling out the very obvious answer, "Beverly Beasley says that men without hair are crybabies and weaklings. She says that Dorilee shaved Samson's head on purpose just so she could beat him down."

"Well, first, I believe you are referring to Delilah, temptress from the Book of Judges... but did Beverly Beasley also tell you that Samson pulled the pillars down on everyone even without his hair? And did she tell you that he grew it back when he wanted to, but not until Head-and-Shoulders came out with apple-scented shampoo that didn't burn his eyes and make him cry? All that is 'da truf' too, so what do you think, now?"

"Oh, Daddy, Daddy, and Daddy," Elle huffed, "you know good and well that they didn't have Head-and-Shoulders way back in Bible Times. You are just pulling my toes again."

He couldn't help laughing at her as they passed the matronly lady who overheard and was frowning at this tête-à-tête. Seemingly, it was inappropriate on some scale. The grad student was aware at this point in his acclimation to Texas culture that there existed a seriously close-minded portion of the population bent on a different agenda. That he had plainly strayed into blasphemous waters was deduced from the glare.

The two continued their round-up of staple items on the grocery list, then headed for a checkout line. Using coupons and cash, Jeremy was able to stay within budget for another few days and still have enough to visit the bookstore the pair loved to frequent. He could get the 'Asbjornsen and Moe's Folktale Collection' book espied the last time they'd been in. Having just now saved the half-price amount needed to add it to their home library. Elle would love 'East of the Sun West of the Moon' and 'The Three Billy Goats Gruff', he assured himself.

The dance down the sidewalk--- for the little girl never went anywhere doing less--- brought them to the lovably tattered old two-story edifice housing Half Price Books over the next thirty minutes. A cornucopia of colorful factoids and gossip spilled over Daddy's ears throughout the hike. The sunshiny day augured good things in Jeremy's eyes. He was content.

Graduation was approaching. He had procured a position at UT as an assistant professor of philosophy by merit of scholastic achievement. Though his placement would not open until he finished the degree, which was not set yet, it was a done deal. He'd been assured in writing. The pantry cupboards were full for the next two weeks. With his best girl by his side, he was bubbling over with optimism for the future. Nothing else was necessary.

He suppressed the fact that two scant months were all that separated them from fall school semester's onset which would necessitate Elle's departure to Aayla's home in Houston. She was enrolled in a private catholic school, St. Pious. That horizon was far away, he had already consoled himself.

Then, out of the blue, a heartstring pulled on him as the two passed a tall dreadlocked bredda in transit. Loss of contact with Ambergai had hit hard these last years. He reminisced amidst the chatter of the mighty mite escorting him, missing the dear guru who had led him safely through adolescence and early adulthood, paving ways for him otherwise unattainable.

A two-year-long European and Asian tour by the Mighty Diamonds currently hampered their communication, yet Jeremy's happiness over the good man's musical success would have to suffice, he reflected. Rarely now did the two talk. Though scarcely a day went by when something didn't happen to pull Gai front and center into his consciousness. Like now.

Glancing back over his shoulder, the pangs of deprivation grew proportionally. Seeing the rocking dreads disappear around a corner, he felt the effect acutely, in transference of the pining.

Drawn back by a sharp remonstrance from Elle, he was reminded of his duty to pay close attention…didn't he get that, she demanded? As he turned away, there registered a quick flash on the person supplanting the dreadlocked doppelganger. The fleeting impression of an extraordinary youth filled the space.

The boy was strikingly beautiful, yet his mien bore a burden. Shoulder length auburn curls bounded in bouncing accompaniment around the youth's tanned face, giving framed flash of huge brown eyes. The well-proportioned form supporting that beauty added credence to an exceedingly in-shape male. Clearly an athlete.

Having no outside interaction with other people at this point in life, Jeremy felt a sudden lack of camaraderie. As fortunate as he was in the presence of the tiny imp called Elle, lonesomeness for a significant peer hit him. The brief snapshot of the male uploaded in his head for future recall… things that make you go Hmmm.

Perhaps the time would arrive when a person of quality, maybe like that boy, might happen across his path. Grabbed and pulled by two tiny caramel hands into the bookstore bearing a book of fables, Jeremy well knew the chances were slim. … as if someone might just fall into his arms. He smiled and followed his baby girl.

Life was good. He would keep dreaming.

* * *

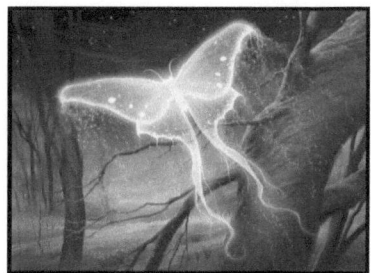

Thank you for reading my book. If you enjoyed it, won't you please take a moment to leave me a review at your favorite retailer?

Or contact me directly:
Follow me on Twitter: http://twitter.com/@ZackJack69
Friend me on Facebook: http://facebook.com/ZachariahJack
Subscribe to my blog: http://zachariahjack.com
Website: http://zachariahjack.com

Favorite me at Smashwords:
http://www.smashwords.com/ profile/view/zackjack

Look for other Zachariah Jack publications
A High Country Tale Series
The River's Bluff

Afterward
A High Country Tale...

Luke Cevennes, M.D. He liked the way it sounded even after a decade and a half of wearing the mantle. Jeremy Kell, PhD. That rolled over Luke's tongue with more flavor than any name in his world. The sexy Jamaican immigrant literally swept him off his feet nearly two decades before. The two fit each other. Luke and Jeremy's best friends, Jake Marshall and Calumet Broadhearst, likewise professional and accomplished, lag in years by a decade but the bond between the four was as deep as the Mariana Trench. Traversing the 21st century as a new age American family, the two interracial couples complement each other in ways the majority of people could only look upon in wishing. Hi-jinks, ribaldry, a touch of activism plus candor and humor, all souffled with a smattering of profundity, gel into a roving epic, from America to Europe to the Caribbean, on the shores of WWII Normandy, to Blue Mountain in Jamaica, up the wuthering heights of the Rockies, and down the alluvial plains of the American deep south as these self-deprecating, refined yet lusty menfolk wend their way, together, while luring the flotsam, jetsam and A-listers of Humanity along, on the sojourn that is the Tree of Life.
      The Sagas commence.
 Meet four men of alternative lifestyle. Sexy, secure, seductive, selective, urbane, provocative. Existential, extant, erudite, educated...ecdemolagniac. The jungle fever couples thrust themselves on to the new American scene, ready to project and proclaim themselves.
            Whether bidden or not.

Biography

I am a professional with a history in veterinary medicine, zoology and marine biology, but a fledgling in the realm of talespinning, just now launching a new stage of life. The existence of a contentedly settled home life with my man, our dogs and cat makes me whole. I finally took to heart the sage advice from the esteemed author and activist, Sir Armistead Maupin, who advised his audience over two decades ago to 'Proclaim Yourself!'. As a member of that audience, it was never forgotten. The remonstrance was belatedly acted upon in a mountain wedding two months following the SCOTUS concession of yet one more of our 'certainly reserved rights'. In accordance with the much overlooked ninth and tenth amendments to the United States Constitution. See for yourself. Think on it. Check my publications out at your favorite retailer. And, please, review my work. Thanks, ZJ.

www.ingramcontent.com/pod-product-compliance
Lightning Source LLC
Chambersburg PA
CBHW020607300426
44113CB00007B/538